The Translation of Relig

Linguistic Insights

Studies in Language and Communication

Edited by Maurizio Gotti,
University of Bergamo

Volume 69

PETER LANG

Bern · Berlin · Bruxelles · Frankfurt am Main · New York · Oxford · Wien

Domenico Pezzini

The Translation of Religious Texts
in the Middle Ages

● ● ● ● ● ● ● ● ● ● ● ● ● ● ● ● ● ●

Tracts and Rules, Hymns and Saints' Lives

PETER LANG

Bern · Berlin · Bruxelles · Frankfurt am Main · New York · Oxford · Wien

Bibliographic information published by Die Deutsche Bibliothek
Die Deutsche Bibliothek lists this publication in the Deutsche National-
bibliografie; detailed bibliographic data is available on the Internet at
‹http://dnb.ddb.de›.

British Library Cataloguing-in-Publication Data: A catalogue record for this
book is available from *The British Library,* Great Britain

Library of Congress Cataloging-in-Publication Data

Pezzini, D.
The translation of religious texts in the Middle Ages : tracts and rules, hymns
and Saints' lives / Domenico Pezzini.
p. cm. – (Linguistic insights, ISSN 1424-8689 ; v. 69)
Includes bibliographical references and index.
ISBN 978-3-03911-600-3 (alk. paper)
1. Christian literature–Translating. 2. Translating and interpreting.
3. Christian literature, Latin (Medieval and modern)–History and criticism.
I. Title.
BR117.P49 2008
274'.05–dc22

                        2008011849

Published with a grant from the Department of LINGUISTICA, LETTERATURA E
SCIENZE DELLA COMUNICAZIONE of the University of Verona

ISSN 1424-8689
ISBN 978-3-03911-600-3

© Peter Lang AG, International Academic Publishers, Bern 2008
Hochfeldstrasse 32, Postfach 746, CH-3000 Bern 9, Switzerland
info@peterlang.com, www.peterlang.com, www.peterlang.net

Printed in Germany

Contents

Part II – Hymns

Part III – Saints' Lives

Appendices

Introduction[1]

The translation of religious texts in medieval Europe is a vast field of which only some boundaries and a few general features can be traced in this short presentation. The difficulty lies in the fact that, both in secular as well as in religious literature, research only began to develop and acquired new breadth and depth in the later eighties.[2] Until then, the approach to and the analysis of literature as translation were practically absent, although scholars acknowledged the fact that research in this area would be fruitful. When, as is the case in England at least, the majority of medieval religious texts are translations of some sort, it is not easy to illustrate briefly the rich articulation of translational practices which coincided with the production of most of what we call literature.

The two main facts underlying these translations are an ever increasing new readership far beyond the Latinate clerics, mostly nuns and pious lay people, especially women, and the simultaneous growing in self-confidence of the various vernaculars, of which these renderings were at the same time the sign and the precipitating factor. Taking the need for diffusion as the first reason for a translation, Latin is crucial in a double sense: 1. on the one hand it is necessary to translate *from* Latin in order to reach a wider audience within a single country and its speech community; 2. on the other, works originally conceived and composed in the vernacular must be translated *into* Latin to ensure a wider diffusion beyond the limits of a nation. To

---

1   This introduction was first produced as a contribution to Delisle/Woodsworth (1995), where it appears in a very compressed form on pp. 170-171. A version of this study in its integrity has been published in *Koiné* V-VI, 1995-1996: 185-195 under the title *The Translation of Hymns and Other Religious Texts in the Middle Ages*. Given its character of general presentation of the subject I chose to rearrange its parts to match the order of the sections in the present volume.

2   Introducing the first volume of papers read at the Conference "The Medieval Translator" held in 1987, Roger Ellis could write: "We are still [...] very much at the question-asking stage" (1989: 1).

give just two examples, this is the case with St Catherine's *Dialogo della divina provvidenza*, dictated in Italian, translated into Latin, to become the English *Orcherd of Syon*; it is also the case with St Birgitta's *Revelations*, dictated in Swedish, translated and organized in Latin, and from this base text translated, at various times and in different styles, into the main European languages. Latin is crucial also because of the prestige this language enjoyed both for its history and for being the language of the Bible and of liturgy, a fact which gave to texts in Latin an authoritative stamp: some vernacular translations were revised according to their real or supposed Latin originals. Within the field of religious writings this constant movement of texts from one language to another had far reaching consequences and can provide an interesting case for the study of the history of translation. We know of works originally written in Latin, then translated into English, and then into Latin again from the English version (Barratt 1984: 418), or translated three times and by different hands in the same century, as is the case with the *Imitation of Christ* (Sargent 1984: 157), or retranslated into the same language, English in this case, two centuries after the first version (Sargent 1984: 159).

To assess the role of the medieval translator of religious texts it is necessary to make a few distinctions on three levels at least, and consider:

1. the *genre* of the literary work;
2. the new *audience*;
3. the possible new *use* of the original work.

The genre can be subdivided in three types of works:

1. texts for religious instruction.
2. liturgical hymns and religious poetry in general;
3. narrative texts (Lives of Christ and of the saints);

These are very broad distinctions, and the genres may at times overlap. The transfer of audience is mainly from a religious to a lay context, or from contemplative to active or 'mixed' life. The transfer of use may be, for instance, from liturgy to sermon, from a rule for

10

monks to spiritual reading for everybody, from a text provided for personal meditation to a tract, or a legend, envisaged for oral delivery.

1. Works of religious instruction

The main feature which characterizes the translational style in this group of writings is *adaptation*. This is already evident in the Anglo-Saxon translation of the Benedictine Rule made by Æthelwold, where a combination of different versions of the Latin original is used as a source, and comments and glosses are inserted (Gretsch 1973). This is also the case with Aelred of Rievaulx's *De Institutione Inclusarum* of which two ME translations exist, both adapted to a new readership. The novelty could be a female instead of a male audience, or even people living in the world instead of recluses, as is the case with some adaptations of the *Ancrene Wisse*. In fact the difference between a rule and a spiritual tract is not so great as one would expect, given that these medieval rules were intended to direct the spiritual life, rather than to regulate daily activities or liturgical offices. Nevertheless, when the text is more evidently a tract of spiritual guidance, we have a wider variety of translational techniques: these affect the version proper (that is, language in terms of lexis, syntax, style and tone), the possible compilation of different parts of the same or of different source texts, the organization of the material in new units. The translation may be literal, at times with many cuts and omissions, which suggest perhaps a 'draft' more than an accomplished translation, while at the other end of the spectrum a clever use may be made of various rhetorical devices such as different figures of inversion or parallelism, ultimately based on Latin rhetoric, but not actually found in the Latin original text. The story of the reception in England and Italy of St Birgitta's *Revelations* is a good case in point – see chapters 1, 2, 6, 7 and 13. Similar adaptations are testified in other European countries – see, for example, Hogg (1990 and 1993).

To give just an example of the probable oral destination of these translations see what happens in a short passage taken from a fourteenth-century Italian translation of William of St Thierry's *Golden Epistle*:

Ille sibi *invenit* in *eis* domum quietis et securitatis; *illa* nidum sibi ubi reponat pullos suos (187).

La passera truova in *essi tabernacoli* casa da riposo e di sicurtà; *la tortora vi truova* il nido, nel quale ella ripone i suoi figliuoli. (De Luca 1954: 669).

(*The sparrow finds in these tabernacles* a home of rest and security, *the dove finds there* a nest where to lay her children).

The substitution of concrete nouns for pronouns, and the repetition of the verb to better balance the two clauses is a device quite often found also in English translations of the late Middle Ages. I suggest that these choices have to do with the oral delivery of these texts, normally in the sense of a loud reading to a religious community or a household. On a larger scale the tone also of the work can be ostensibly altered, as is the case with the Italian rendering by Bono Giamboni (thirteenth century) of Innocent III's widely circulated *De miseria condicionis humane*: an intensely pessimistic analysis of human life becomes a moral treatise which rectifies the original tone according to a more serene and realistic mood (Segre/Marti 1959: 228).

The main point underlying all these translational practices, including compilation and reorganization, was the conviction that what was produced in the field of religious literature was a common heritage, a quarry from which to excavate what was needed for the spiritual profit of the faithful. So an originally mystical work like Edmund of Abingdon's *Speculum Ecclesie*, composed in Latin, translated into Anglo-Norman, then into Latin again, and subsequently in various Middle English versions, could be turned into a catechetical treatise to answer the demand for instruction set out in the Lambeth Constitutions of 1281 (Barratt 1984: 418-419). In addition to the content, the particular structure of these works often allowed them to be exploited in the sense here described: in fact "the ease with which such works are excerpted, abridged, expanded, and rearranged shows that they are intrinsically 'modular' in construction" (Barratt 1984: 427).

2. Liturgical hymns

Latin hymns were translated in late medieval England essentially for three purposes: to be quoted in sermons, to be used as private prayer and meditation, to be sung to their original tunes. These new destinations appear respectively in the three main collections of these translations: William Herebert's, the so called *English Hymnal* and James Ryman's (Gneuss 1968: 207-236) – see chapter 9 here. To these we may add a few renderings by John Lydgate which may also be interpreted as experiments in liturgical writing in the vernacular (Pearsall 1977: 234). Apart from the third group, where the need to maintain the same number of syllables of the Latin is particularly constraining, the other two sets exemplify some characteristic choices apparently demanded by the new intended audience. The preacher tends to emphasize the iconic and emotional elements of the text by stressing or introducing concrete nouns and visual adjectives, to clarify elusive words by explaining their meaning, to simplify the syntax by the regular use of parataxis. Here is just one example taken from Herebert's version of the hymn *Conditor alme siderum* (Reimer 1987: 123):

Conditor alme siderum,	Holy wrouhte of sterres *brryht*,
Aeterna lux credentium,	Of *ryht* byleue ay-lastyng lyht,
Christe, redemptor omnium,	Crist, þat bouhtest mon *wyth fyht*,
Exaudi preces supplicum.	Her þe bone of *moeke* wyht.

The words in italics do not exist in the source text: they seem to be carefully chosen, and reveal a typical preacher's stance in their stressing of a visual detail (the brightness of the stars), doctrinal orthodoxy (the rightness of belief), spiritual attitudes (the humility requested in prayer), and Christ's painful-heroic suffering ('with fight') which was the price of the redemption, Translations meant to provide meditative texts adopt largely the *paraphrase*, favoured by the choice of longer prosodic units (the royal stanza instead of the Latin quatrain). The term 'paraphrase' should be read not as a simple expansion, but in terms of a skilful use of the large referentiality embedded in any Christian text: the translation in a sense incorporates the gloss – see chapter 11 here. Similar procedures are to be found in other European countries, as for example in the translations of the Monk of Salzburg (Spechtler 1972). The sense of belonging to a tradition, thought of as a living transmission of truths together with the consequent spiritual attitudes, is also apparent in these translations, where new images can be introduced, or some suggestions can be either expanded or omitted according to a mutated theological or spiritual climate. It is to be expected that the medieval 'affective piety' makes itself felt in the translation of hymns composed in the different theological background of the early Christian centuries. On the other hand it is precisely the sense of belonging to a tradition that prompts the translation of old texts instead of, or together with the composition of new ones. To give just another example I quote Herebert's translation of a hymn by Theodulf of Orléans written c. 820, whose first part was sung as a Processional for Palm Sunday (Reimer 1987: 113):

> Gloria, laus et honor tibi sit, Rex Christe, redemptor,
> cui puerile decus prompsit Hosanna pium.

> Wele, heriȝyng, and worshype boe to Crist, þat doere ous bouhte,
> To wham gradden "Osanna!" chyldren clene of þoute.

The English translation can be sung to the original Gregorian melody, but within the limitation he has chosen the Franciscan preacher manages to remind us of his time and his profession: he replaces the royal Christ with the suffering man of the cross who rescued us at a high price ('doere'), and turns the grace and beauty of the applauding children into a 'purity of heart' which he probably thought more proper to a religious context.

Where the translation can be more clearly studied as a trans-cultural operation is in the versions of Latin sequences and other poems more or less contemporary with their Englishings. Some conclusions have been drawn, mainly stressing the fact that the English vocabulary is poorer and less connotated than the Latin, although it seems that its emotional quality is stronger, or perhaps more strongly felt due to the everyday context of its use (Wenzel 1986: 21-60).

14

3. Narrative texts:
Exempla, Lives of Christ and of the Saints

The main work to be considered here is Jacobus de Varagine's *Legenda Aurea*. The first printed English translation is by William Caxton in 1483. An analysis of the technique he used, following what he declares in his preface, sheds some light on his idea of translation: in fact he produced his 'new' version by keeping an eye simultaneously on the original Latin, the French translation made by Jean de Vignay, and an anonymous English translation commonly known as *Gilte Legende* (1438) (Kurvinen 1959; Blake 1969: 117-120; Hamer 1978: 24-26). In this group we can also include the vast literature of *exempla*, which were often used to enliven a sermon or to bring home more forcefully a moral truth to the audience, as can be seen in *The Northern Homily Cycle*. The study of the circulation of these *exempla* could well illustrate the way micro tales of say ten Latin lines would grow into stories which could run from fifty lines to three times as much. Oral delivery together with the natural instinct of the storyteller are largely responsible for the ever growing elaboration of narrative features and dramatic details introduced to attract the listener's attention. The narrative genre, though, is only one element which explains a number of changes visible in the continuous process of translation. We must not forget that these texts, as the abundant literature of the *exempla* shows perfectly well, were primarily used for their spiritual potentialities, sharing thus the characteristics of sermons and edifying treatises on vices and virtues. The translator may either enhance the homiletic qualities of the stories, or reduce them to strengthen the dramatic pace of the original. Adaptations to different audiences explain for the most these changes: to give just an example one can go through the three extant Middle English translations of the *Tractatus de Purgatorio Sancti Patricii* to see how an originally ascetic work produced in and for a Cistercian milieu is translated to suit a lay audience, for which the *tractatus* is re-told as "a pious adventure story aimed at inducing penance", and in two other versions is so dressed as to be more easily appreciated by the reader of romances (Easting 1991). In this group, the leading exemplar is the 'genre' *Life of Christ*, of which so many versions exist (Salter 1974: 55-118) and where the different possible roles of the translator as compiler, commentator and preacher at the same time can intermingle in significant ways (Johnson 1989), and must be taken into account to evaluate the translator's typical procedures.

4. General overview

To summarize the results of this very brief survey, we can divide the territory in three parts, and consider: 1. various attitudes to the source text; 2. various attitudes to the idea of translation; and, consequently, 3. various ideas of the role of the translator.

4.1. Attitudes to the source text

The source text tends to be thought of as a mine. It can be translated in full or in part (see Aelred's *De Institutione Inclusarum*, a work in two parts of which only the second is translated in one ME version – see chapter 3). It can be used to extract a quotation, a single chapter, or parts of different chapters which are differently organized to compile a new work (see the *Vita Beate Marie* in MS Rawlinson C. 41: chapter 13 here). Compilations are obviously created also by uniting different materials from different works: this is the way new books are written from old ones, a procedure which is typical of every kind of medieval literature, but which finds a more favourable ground in the religious field.

4.2. Attitudes to the idea of translation

The idea of translation largely depends on the audience the translator has in mind, and the possible use of his new text. So he can oscillate between a more or less literal rendering (more likely to occur in a

16

quotation) and an elaborate translation making skilful use of rhetorical devices (more probable when the excerpt is dealt with as a self-contained new unit). Oral delivery explains a number of choices. The audience is another important conditioning factor: the elimination of homiletic passages in favour of narrative ones clearly suggests a less sophisticated lay audience. Slight differences of tone may be relevant, as when the stressing or the introduction of romantic elements undoubtedly hints at a more aristocratic public.

4.3. The role of the translator

It is now a commonplace that the medieval writer can be at the same time author, scribe, translator, compiler, interpreter and glossator. At times these different roles are set off by the translator, who clearly indicates in the manuscript where he adds a remark or a comment of his own to the original text. The translator may also consciously define the general style of his work, as when Henry Watson, translating a French adaptation of an Italian sermon by Bernardino da Siena, states that the adapters "added and dymynysshed that the whiche they sawe serve unto the matter" (quoted in Gray 1985: 440). More often the gloss is hidden in the new text, even at the minimum level of the clause or the sentence, as in this example taken from Domenico Cavalca's translation of Gregory the Great's *Life of Saint Benedict*: "cor gerens senile" becomes "*costume* di vecchio e cuore *maturo*" (having the manners of an old man and a mature heart), "in eis", referred to the literary studies, is rendered by "nelli studi della *vana* scienza" (in the study of the vain science), "sanctae conversationis habitum quaesivit" is translated by "prese abito di *penitenza* e di santa conversazione" (he wore a dress of penitence and holy conversation) (De Luca 1954: 539): the first addition is explanatory, the second inserts an evaluation of the translator reflecting his homiletic intent, the third may mean either some religious custom typical of Cavalca's fourteenth century, or more probably, the word 'penitence' is here used as synonymous with monastic life, creating thus a doublet with 'holy conversation'.

4.4. Concluding remarks

The history of translation in the Middle Ages is becoming a fashionable subject of research. It is to be hoped that this will result in different attitudes to the editing and analysis of texts. This study will certainly be greatly encouraged when the practice is established to edit hitherto unpublished texts together with, when it is the case, the text/s on which the translation was based. Consequently, the editor cannot limit himself to indicating the source text/s: this information ought to be supplemented by a study of the translator's choices not only in terms of language but also in their relations and relevance to the new genre, audience and use to which the texts are transferred.

The investigations presented in this volume rely on this theoretical and methodological approach. I would like to express my gratitude to Roger Ellis for encouraging my research in this field, and to Maurizio Gotti and Marina Dossena for their generous help in the preparation of this work.

Part I

Tracts and Rules

CHAPTER 1

Birgittine Tracts of Spiritual Guidance in Fifteenth-Century England[1]

In a study on "The English Cult of St Birgitta of Sweden" F. R. Johnston comes to the conclusion that this "widespread" cult was "mainly a literary one based on her writings" (1985: 93). Probably Birgitta herself would have welcomed this development, given the remarkable editorial care and firm theological control with which the *Liber Revelationum Celestium* was produced. We cannot wonder at the success of a book which Alphonse of Pecha, formerly bishop of Jaén, an enthusiastic disciple of the Saint and the final organizer of her writings, presented as a "librum gloriosum, scriptum in corde predicte domine digito Dei vivi".[2] The wide reception of the *Liber* in many European countries shows that this conviction came to be shared by a growing number of people.

When the *Revelations* arrived in England, probably no earlier than the 1380s, they aroused the interest of Oxford theologians such as the Carmelite Richard Lavynham and the Dominican Thomas Stubbes, but in the course of the fifteenth century they became favourite reading for a steadily increasing audience, religious as well as secular, looking for books of meditation and spiritual instruction. Margery Kempe was by no means alone in choosing "seynt Brydys boke" to foster her spiritual life. Cecily of York, mother of Edward IV and Richard III, had the book read to her during dinner time (Pantin 1955:

---

1 An earlier version of this study was first published in Ellis (1991: 175-207).
2 In his *Epistola Solitarii ad Reges* 1,6 (Aili 2002: 48). Latin quotations of the work by book (Roman numbers) and chapter (Arabic numbers) are taken from the modern critical edition of *Sancta Birgitta, Revelaciones* (see References). On Alphonse of Pecha see further Colledge (1956).

254), and wills from the end of the century show that the *Revelations* were among the belongings of other pious lay women.[3]

To a modern eye the popularity of the *Liber* appears as surprising as the work itself seems disappointing. It is not a work with a clear structure: it has no centre, it seems to sprawl everywhere, and is best described as a huge storehouse where spiritual food can be picked up according to one's own personal needs. Despite considerable attempts by the first editors to organize the collection, the *Revelations* retain, in order and content, the occasional character of their delivery over thirty years of Birgitta's life, and the book offers side by side meditations on the life of Christ and the Virgin, prophecies mixed with pastoral advice, miniature treatises of spiritual guidance, and even letters and debates in the form of questions and answers. Still, if the overall appearance is discouragingly uneven, the smaller units offer a solid sense of order. This is particularly evident in those chapters which contain teaching on the spiritual life: here the subjects are nicely developed around a numerical organizing principle, with the theme divided and subdivided into different parts, and the final result is a tightly structured network of ideas. This was extremely useful, especially in the case of spiritual instructions orally delivered and needing to be memorized.

The wide circulation of the *Revelations* is proved by a remarkable number of English versions different in kind and quality. This is clear evidence of the varied and continuous interest in the book itself. And, since they are independent of one another, they present us with a rare opportunity of studying different techniques of translation applied to the same Latin text. This will be particularly rewarding in the case of the Birgittine writings, since little has been edited so far, and even less study has been done on them.

The leading authority in this field was, until quite recently, W. P. Cumming, who published *The Revelations of Saint Birgitta* in 1929. This is the edition of Princeton University Library MS Garrett 145

---

3   See Johnston (1985: 86). The author of a treatise on the Passion which opens the compilation of spiritual tracts in BL MS Arundel 286, where a translation of *Rev.* VII,5 appears as the second item, says that he was asked to write his treatise by "a worschipful lady hauynge a symple spirit ful of heuenly desires", so that she "in hir honourable age of elde myȝt haue som comfort in contemplacion of þat blessed and profitable passion þat is þe welle of lyf (f. 1r).

(previously 1397), and in his introduction Cumming gives the first detailed description of seven manuscripts which form the corpus of Birgittine translations in fifteenth century England. This corpus reflects a remarkable variety of attitudes towards Birgitta's works and illustrates different ways of using it. Three manuscripts translate the *Revelations* either in full (London, BL MS Cotton Julius F.II and Cotton Claudius B.I) or in part (Book IV and beginning of Book V in BL MS Harley 4800). One manuscript (Garrett) contains a selections of chapters translated in their integrity and organized not according to the original order, but in a sort of 'thematic units' (Cumming 1929: xxii). Two manuscripts (Oxford, Bodleian MS Rawlinson C.41, and London, Lambeth Palace Library MS 432) contain texts in which excerpts from different books and chapters are amalgamated to form new 'compilations'. Finally, in London, BL MS Arundel 197 we have either a single chapter (VI,65) or part of a chapter (II,16) which were extracted from Birgitta's work and circulated as independent tracts.

P. S. Jolliffe (1974) drew the attention of the scholars to these last,[4] while F. R. Johnston (1985) ignores them. Only Roger Ellis, to whom we owe the best and most informative study to appear so far on the circulation of Birgittine writings in England, mentions them and comments briefly about the process of adaptation in the translation of VII,5 (1982a: 175-176 and fn. 31). I edited this chapter (Pezzini 1986) from the two manuscripts in which it is extant, and was favourably impressed by the originality and the high quality of the translation. I have formed the same impression of the other two chapters, II,16 and VI,65, which I also edited.[5] What emerges from the detailed study of these translations in the following pages of this chapter obliges us to

---

4   From Jolliffe (1974) we learn that the translation of VI,65 appears in three
    other manuscripts (Oxford Bodley 423, C.U.L. Ii.vi.40, and Magdalene Coll.,
    Cambridge, Pepys 2125); the same is true of II,16 (BL Additional 37790,
    Oxford Bodley 131, and Taunton Horae); and finally there is also a translation
    of VII,5 extant in two manuscripts (BL Arundel 286 and Harley 6615). For
    full reference to these manuscripts see Jolliffe (1974), respectively: Item I.13
    for II,16; Item H.13 and O.23 for VI,65; Item D.10 for VII,5. Jolliffe prints
    VII,65 instead of VI,65, and VII,7 instead of VII,5.

5   All the versions of II,16 from the four manuscripts in which they are extant,
    together with the translation of the whole chapter from BL Cotton Julius F.II
    have been edited (see Pezzini 1988), as well as the translation of VI,65 (see
    Pezzini 1994b).

revise the rather harsh opinion expressed by Cumming (1929: xx) about the Birgittine translations:

> The Garrett MS. has passages of excellent prose and gives evidence of care in the selection of the *Revelations*; the other manuscripts vary from businesslike translations to mere rough jottings which show the general content of the work [...]. The translators of most of the manuscripts, when they follow the Latin at all, hold as nearly as possible to the Latin order in the sentence, and frequently use the Latin word in translation.

None of these statements is applicable to the texts of the third group, which for practical reasons I shall call 'independent tracts'. As for the "passages of excellent prose" in the Garrett manuscript, this hardly seems adequate. Comparison with the Bodley translation of VI,65 does not work in Garrett's favour. Cumming is more convincing, in fact, when he writes that "The translation (in the Garrett MS) follows the Latin closely. Occasional passages which are awkward and unidiomatic are so because of the strict adherence to the Latin order. The sentences are sometimes long and involved" (Cumming 1929: xxii). Literalness seems to be the most regular feature of these Birgittine translations. Literal is Garrett, and so is Harley 4800, which shares also with the two Cotton manuscripts "a tendency [...] to abbreviate by the excision of words and phrases", a method more pronounced in Claudius B.I. Cumming's remarks fail to consider Arundel 197 and Lambeth 432 as translations.

Cumming's opinions went into S. K. Workman's much quoted and highly influential book, *Fifteenth-Century Translation as an Influence on English Prose*. Workman (1940: 84) analyses some passages in Lambeth 432 and in Garrett, where two scribes were at work, and concludes:

> All three translators have worked in a similar way. They did not try to "augment"; and they rephrased only enough to Anglicize the language. The inevitable consequence was that the structural characteristics of their English prose, down to considerable detail, were derived from the foreign original.[6]

---

6   See also Pezzini (1993a) for an edition of the Birgittine portion of MS Lambeth 432 with an analysis of the translational style, particularly of the conflation techniques, here used.

Workman's words, though true as far as they go, do not apply to the texts I am going to analyse, which adopt a technique of translation based on a highly original rephrasing and restructuring of the Latin. At the end of his general survey Workman says that the prevailing method in the fifteenth century was "to keep as close as the syntax and grammar of English permitted [...] to the sentence structure of the composition under translation", but adds that "there were [...] several interesting exceptions" (1940: 84). The 'independent tracts' are just such interesting exceptions in the panorama of Birgittine writings in English.

1. The 'independent tracts'

1.1. Rev. VI,65

Rev. VI,65 is a treatise on contemplative and active life likened to Mary and Martha. It was probably the most popular of these independent tracts, since it is now extant in four manuscripts as such; this same chapter was chosen by the compiler of the Garrett manuscript, and is present, of course, in the full text translation of Cotton Julius F.II: surprisingly it does not appear in the other full text translation in Cotton Claudius B.I. The reason for this success is probably due to the subject itself and to its traditional link with the two sisters of Lazarus.[7] To this we should add the skill and vivacity with which the *Revelations* develop the images of hospitality as metaphors of different important attitudes in the spiritual life: the result is a compendium where nothing essential is lacking. The three versions are sufficiently different to enable us to compare their techniques of translation: one (Julius MS, hereafter J) is a sort of skilful summary,

---

7   So, for example, in the *Epistle on Mixed Life*, "a deuout boke compyled by mayster Walter Hylton to a deuout man in temporal estate", where the two lives are linked with Mary and Martha in the second chapter: "þat þe lyf of Marie and Martha menged to-gedere is acordyng to hem þat are in hiȝ degre" (Horstmann 1895: I/264-292).

literal but with many omissions; another (Garrett MS, hereafter G) is also literal and strictly faithful to the Latin; the third, the independent tract, is also faithful, with a few omissions and additions mostly due to the adaptation to a new audience, but surpasses the others in its clever use of rhetorical devices. If we also note that one of the four manuscripts, Arundel 197, has been heavily corrected by a later hand, we may say that we have also a fourth 'revised' version of this chapter, one worth an analysis of its own. I shall take my examples from the Bodley 423 version of the tract and compare them with the other translations to show the difference in technique and response to the Latin text.[8] The quality and originality of the former can be shown not only in wording, but above all in the large use of parallelism and inversion, and in the restructuring of the periods in harmonic units: these figures, although ultimately derived from Latin, are not found at the corresponding points of the Latin text of the *Revelations*.

The most striking feature of the Bodley translation is probably the constant love for musical parallelism which the author often obtains by slightly modifying the Latin: the idea remains the same, the addition or omission of a word in English creates a different and more visible balance. For example we have cases where an adjective is added or repeated:

> Non debet gaudere de mundi honore et eius prosperitate
> He [...] shal not ioye of no worldly worship ne bodily prosperite
> (G: not to Ioye of the wyrship of the werlde ne of the prosperyte þer-of).

Repetition can be used to form a perfect antithetical *isocolon*:

> Maria non debet esse ociosa sicut nec Martha
> As Martha was euere besy / so shal Mary neuer be ydel
> (G: Marie oweth not to be idelle no more then Martha)

> Quando opera bona reputantur multa, et mala sunt in obliuione
> Whan he holdith moche by his good werkes
> and foryetith lightly alle his euel dedes.

---

8   The translation of VI,65 in Bodley is on ff. 150r-156v; Cotton Julius F.II, ff. 216r-217v; Garrett MS, ff. 14r-21r (text in Cumming 1929: 25-36). Pezzini (1994b) provides fuller discussion of the Bodley translation. On later editions of this chapter see Gilroy 2000.

Here the sequence verb-adverb-adjective-noun is exactly repeated so that the two clauses maintain the same rhythm and cadence, and the result is quite different from Garrett's: "when goode dedes ar counted money, and evyll few and foryett".

A similar technique can be found in another case, where a noun is added to keep the balance between two clauses derived from the resolution of a hypotactic order:

> ut tolerando opprobria temporalia fugiam sempiterna
> þat I mowe haue grace to suffre temporal blame /
> þe raþer to escape euerlastyng peyne
> (G: that by suffraunce of temporall repreues I may escape euerlastyng).

In other cases the parallelism is obtained at the expense of the Latin by ruling out one or more words to have a better balanced series of clauses; greater precision and clarity results:

> tunc excitat eum ad facilitatem magne ire, aut ad dissolucionem vane leticie, aut ad verba dissoluta et iocosa
> he wil þan lightly excite him to be wrothe / or elles to veyn glory / or elles to dissolute wordes.

I am not contending that the English text is here superior to the Latin: some words giving a more refined articulation to the sentence in the original have disappeared, like *magne, dissolucionem*, and *iocosa*, and one might ask whether "veyn glory" is the exact correspondent of *vane leticie*. The English translator has worked very freely on his text: the noun *facilitatem* becomes the adverb "lightly", *ire* is turned into "to be wrothe", *dissolucionem* is eliminated as a quality repeated, and faithfully translated, in the following *dissoluta*; as a result, the stress falls rightly on the two nouns at the end of each clause, "glory" and "wordes", with their negative qualifications. What is lost by the excision is outweighed by the clarity and precision that results.

Other examples confirm the impression that our translator is fond of figures of parallelism. In a three-sentence period, where the Latin has only two verbs, the English text restores the balance by the addition of a third one:

> cohibere linguam ..., et manum ..., et animum debet continere
> to wiþholde þe tonge ...

27

and wiþdrawe his hondes ...
and refreyne his hert
(G: kepe his tonge ... and his honde ... and hys herte).

The expansion can be considerable, as in the case of a metaphor developed into a perfectly balanced comparison:

et sicut mater diligebat universos
and as a good moder loueth alle hir children
so loueth she alle men and wymmen
(G: and loved all as a moder).

In some cases, to be sure, the parallelism may seem exaggerated and even pedantic, as in a connecting passage between the two parts of the chapter:

Ideo dicam tibi nunc quomodo Martha institui debet. Ipsa quippe debet habere sicut et Maria eciam quinque bona.
I saide before that V thinges be nedful to eche man and woman that wil folewe Mary. And in the same manere V thinges be nedful to eche man and woman that wil folewe Martha.

This is the fullest possible realisation of the implications of the Latin *sicut*. The first sentence has almost no correspondence in the Latin, but this distinctive resolution is much favoured in the Bodley tract and in the following text, the translation of VII,5, and is obviously a useful mnemonic to the reader and listener alike.[9]

A well-known figure of repetition is the doublet, on which much has already been said. Our translator has, not surprisingly, a good many examples of this very widespread practice, like *vocat* rendered by "clepith him and drawith him", or more complex forms like *que conturbant cor eius* translated as "they whiche trouble his hert, and brynge hym out of rest". At times the doubling of an adjective is further elaborated on by the use of *hyperbaton*, a figure which occurs when a noun is put between two adjectives:

---

9   The manuscript Arundel 286, which contains the translation of VII,5 examined here, appears to have been used for public reading: from f. 82 to f. 99 there are catch-words written by a later hand on every recto folio, a device absolutely unnecessary for the binder, but very useful for the reader.

omnis infirmus	eche febil man or sike
eos letificare verbis bonis	to say gode wordes and holy to comforte
damnabile est	a foule thing it is and a dampnable

But the trend is not always one way:

immo laudabilis et beneplacens deo	but muche to goddis plesynge
ab omni inhonesta et illicita operacione	from dedes þat ben vnleful

And this is a further indication of the freedom of our translator.

The other figure often used in this translation is inversion in its various forms. Frequently a sentence begins with an adverb or an adjective: "strongly he must arise", "bisely he must take hede", etc. Perhaps the best example of this procedure, where we have parallelism and inversion combined to a fine effect, is:

recurrat statim ad mentem suam cogitando quomodo ...
spedful it is to haue in mynde / and ofte theron thenke / how...
(G: renne he then anon to hys mynde, thinkyng how ...)

The front-shifting of an infinitive or a participle is also frequent (arise she most, born he was of a mayde, blesse he shal his enemys), and so is the inversion object/verb (clothes he must haue, greuous gestes he resceiueth, his owne wille vtterly to forsake), or even the combination of two inversions (litel hede wil I tak).[10]

A more complex case, where the object is inserted between the auxiliary and the infinitive, and the verb between its two objects (*hyperbaton*) can be seen in:

quibus proximo et sibi ipsi prodesse posset
by þe whiche he might himself profite, and oþer of his neighbours

---

10   These patterns of inversion, and the more complex splitting of auxiliary and infinitive by dependent object, are also found, for example, in Chaucer's *Melibee* and Usk's *Testament of Love*: see Ellis (1986: 109-111). They reveal, as in the more famous writers, a translator consciously aiming at a 'high style', a feature we do not find in the other Birgittine translations, except, of course, the versions of VII,5 and II,16 here examined.

Nothing of the kind is found in Garrett.[11]

Our text has very few examples of chiasmus. The best instance is probably:

> cuius bonitate anima creata est, et sanguine benedicto redempta
> by whos godenes he is made, and bought wiþ his blode

The elimination of *benedicto* creates a better balance in the English clauses and results in a distich with the stresses on the essential words: godenes-made / bought-blode. Another example where the chiasmus is combined with *paronomasia* is this:

> ne [...] oraciones et predicaciones diminuat, seu alia bona ex hoc omittat
> wherby his praiers or other gostly workes shul be amenused
> or ellis þat he leue oþir gode werkes

This independent translation of *Rev.* VI,65, then, is highly original, especially where the structure of the period is concerned, and far from literalism on the one hand, and paraphrase on the other. The author knows very well how to use other rhetorical devices too. One of these is *prolepsis*; for example:

> Sic erit e contra de illis qui ambiunt honores et prelaciones
> The contrary mede shal thoo prelates haue, whiche taken prelacies and gret
> worldly worshipes;

---

11   We may notice in the last case given that the sequence *proximo/sibi* of the Latin has simply been inverted in the translation. This is not a single case, but would seem rather a habit of our translator, a sort of stylistic idiosyncrasy. I have collected eight other instances, for a total of nine, of this curious procedure:

- dicunt et cogitant: thenke or say;
- tacuit/locutus est: preched and taughte/helde his pees;
- leuioribus verbis/seuerioribus: harde wordes/light;
- vincuntur/tolerantur: suffre/ouercome;
- potentibus/parentibus: kinnesmen/grete or riche;
- exemplis/verbis: wordes/ensamples;
- Maria/Martha: Martha/Mary;
- honores et prelaciones: prelacies and gret worldly worshipes.

The frequency of this choice might indicate a very distinctive personal style.

30

> cogitando quomodo ego deus contemptus et despectus pacienter tolerabam
> he shal also thenke hou stille he stode, þat good lorde, while he was demed

The change of subject in the second example is due to the fact that, while in the original Christ is imagined as speaking directly to Birgitta, in the translation his words become general spiritual doctrine addressed to any Christian soul.

This rhetorical ability is seen at its best in the reworking of longer sentences:

et apponet omnem diligenciam	he shal also besy hym with ful wille
ut opera pietatis	to fulfille alle dedes of mercy
et oraciones deuote augeantur	and gladlye occupye him wiþ deuout praiers
quibus	for where they be vsed
spiritus sanctus delectatur	þe holygost wil bliþely abyde

The three Latin clauses have become five in English, and many modifications occur: *apponet [...] diligenciam* has been translated by two equivalent verbs (besy / occupye), which, together with the elimination of *augeantur*, create a new parallelism; *omnem* is interpreted as "with ful wille" and "gladlye", and the result is again a parallelism absent in the Latin; the sequence verb / adverbial phrase (besy hym with ful wille) is repeated but in inverted order (gladlye occupye); *augeantur*, which in the Latin refers both to *opera pietatis* and *oraciones deuote*, goes only with the first of these two things, and, rendered by "fulfille", creates a sort of internal rhyme with "ful wille"; the relative clause is turned into an explicative one plus a dependent relative clause which introduces the new image of the indwelling of the Holy Ghost, while the Latin main verb, *delectatur*, is turned into the adverb "bliþely".

The originality of the translator can also be seen in smaller units, such as the individual words:

sapienter respondere
yeue a wyse aunswer
(G: aunswer wysely)

ascendere ad gradus Marie
come to the hye degre of contemplatif lyf
(G: ascende up to the degre of Marie)

ex nullis se in cogitacione preferat
he shal not holde hymself moor worthy than other in thoughte ne in dede
(G: that he ne prefer notte ne exalte him-selfe in his owen conceyte).

We must consider now additions to the text of the original, and omissions from it. Some of these, as has already been shown, are used to readjust a sentence. In other cases the result is a modification of the Latin text, where perhaps the translator attempts to make his original more specific:

castitatem sine vlla delectacione praua
chastite of body wiþoute al maner shrewde delit of flesshe

A more substantial addition with a clarifying intent appears in:

sic Maria debet distribuere spiritualia sua
so must he parte aboute his gostly godes in praieng and in techyng

Again:

Si Maria non valet predicare
If it so be þat [...] he is lette þat he may not, or elles it longith not to his degre
(to teche and preche)

Elsewhere amplification produces a stronger emphasis:

nec consentire viciis, nec in eis delectari
neither to assente to her false suggestions, ne haue delyte ne likyng in her wicked sterynges

The possessive adjective "her" (= their) refers to the "wicked thoughtes" which in the preceding sentence have been compared to mischievous guests who cannot be kept out when they come to the house of the soul, "as an hostiler suffrith bothe good and badde come in", but must be strongly opposed once they are in; *viciis* has not been translated because the word had occurred in the preceding sentence, and was translated there. A particular and noteworthy kind of expansion occurs when the translator repeats what has already been said or adds a short summary as a sort of *aide-mémoire* – e.g.,

32

Sic Maria faciat
In the same manere he that wil be in charite must haue compassion of al other men

This addition glosses the Latin *faciat* by resuming the whole content of the preceding paragraph. This feature occurs seven times in all in the tract, and shows a translator clearly conscious of what he is doing, and revealing a purpose and a deliberate choice. There is also a short summary at the end of the two parts of the treatise, and one, already noted, which serves as a link between the two.

This translation, contrary to its usual choices, has two considerable expansions towards the end: one is a tirade against bad prelates, the other is a warning and an invitation to widows "to take gode hede and folewe Martha in liuyng".

As part of a long *exemplum* of a ship led to the port where she was bound notwithstanding storms and strong winds, we find a comparison of prelates to helmsmen: the good ones will receive a double reward, the bad a double punishment. While, following the Latin closely, the translator deals quickly with the reward, he describes the punishment at much greater length:

Sic erit contra de illis qui ambiunt honores et prelaciones: erunt quippe participes omnium penarum et peccatorum eorum quos susceperunt regere, secundo quod confusio eorum erit sine fine.

The contrary mede shal thoo prelates haue, whiche taken prelacies and gret worldly worshipes noþing for helpe and comfort of oþer mennes soules, but for foule couetise and pompe of þe worlde. Alle suche prelates shul parte wiþ her peynes, and also wiþ her synnes, whos soules they shuld haue kepte, and presheden for mysgouernaunce, or for defaute of teching, and for her owne pride, and oþer wicked vyces, þey shul haue by goddis rightwesnesse confusion wiþouten ende.

Such an expansion is unique in the text, but the negative attitude revealed towards authority is confirmed by a consideration of other changes to the original. The invitation to Mary to intercede for her ill treated neighbour *eciam apud potentes seculi* has not been translated, neither has what follows: *si vero Maria talis est quod non exauditur apud principes nec proficit egressus eius de cella* [...]. This same dismissive attitude is found again at the beginning of the second long addition, which serves as an introduction to the second part of the treatise, where instruction is being offered on active life:

> Therfor, hou euere it be of soueraynes, and prelates, whiche shuld haue contemplatyf lyf and actif, as in outwarde besynes of preching and techinge openly, I counceyle netheles wyues and widowes, maydens, and other peple to folewe Martha, as muche as they may, in wille, and in dede, and namely widowes ...

It seems clear that our translator had a feminine audience, probably secular, in mind. Other additions and omissions reinforce this conclusion. For instance, the author has not translated the exhortation to fast reasonably in order to keep strong *ad puniendos rebelles et ad subijciendos iugo fidei infideles*; he thus appears to have excluded clergy from his readership: the addition concerning the impossibility of preaching already quoted (see above) follows the same line, since preaching "longith not to his degre". Professed religious also are probably not included by our translator, who omits the phrase *consilia euangelice veritatis*, the well-known monastic expression for the religious vows, and leaves only the practice of the commandments; moreover, he translates *opus dei* probably a reference to the monastic choral office, by "praiers and deuocioun".[12] It seems safe to say that a lay audience, if not specifically intended, is certainly allowed for as users of the tract.

Other omissions are not so easy to explain. Our author, for example, seems not to like metaphors: he eliminates the nice image of a fox examining the ground in order to find a good resting place, used to say that, if Mary cannot preach, although she wants to and knows how, she should explore the hearts of the people she meets, and when she finds someone more capable of receiving the word of God, there she should stay and rest, and give her spiritual advice and exhortations. The translator also cuts the long *exemplum* of the ship led astray by storms and contrary winds, and steered to the port to which she was

---

12   Whereas Garrett renders *opus dei* by "the seruyce of god", and Julius "the werke of god", the translator of Bodley 423 catches more clearly the specific reference of *opus dei* to prayer. It is thus the more significant that by translating it by "praiers and deuocioun" he does not confine the meaning of the expression to the liturgical office, but includes also the private devotions, which were the daily practice of ordinary people.

directed by a good mariner faithful to his lord's orders. Even the biblical reference to Paul's flight from Damascus down the city walls has been cut. Other sentences have been omitted for no apparent reason, like *et de aliis sicut de seipsa curabat. Ideo semper cogitabat caritatem meam et passionem meam.* This last omission is particularly surprising if we consider that in much devotional literature any slight hint at the Passion was regularly emphasized. But even when he omits part of a sentence, our translator is always careful and attentive to make sense of what he keeps.

So far the comparison has been between Bodley and Garrett. A quick look at the Julius manuscript will show that, although this translation is literal with substantial cuttings, it is not insensitive to the demands of style and structure. In the following passage, for example, the clauses are nicely constructed and finely organized:

> Tercio Maria non debet esse ociosa sicut nec Martha, sed peracto somno suo necessario, surgat et regracietur deo ex cordis attencione, quia omnia ex bonitate sua creauit, et ex caritate sua assumendo carnem omnia recreauit, ostendens per passionem et mortem suam dileccionem suam ad hominem qua maior esse non posset.

> Also Mary shuld nat be ydil no more þan Martha, but aftir his nessessary slepp shuld arise and thanke god with intent of herte, for þat he has creat all thingis of his goodness, and he has takyn mankende of his cherite shewing his loue to man be his passion and his deth.

Only two elements have disappeared: the "recreation" of mankind, and the excellence of God's love shown in Christ's passion and death. This is a very good example of literal translation.

Julius is not always so respectful of the text. For a single example:

> Maria quoque sit discreta in oracione et laudibus dei ordinata. Nam si habet necessaria vite sine sollicitudine debet facere oraciones prolixiores. Si vero in orando attediatur et accrescunt temptaciones, potest quidem laborare manibus aliquid honestum opus et vtile, vel ad vtilitatem propriam si indiget, aut ad commodum aliorum. Si vero attediatur in utroque, scilicet in oracione et labore, tunc quidem potest habere aliquam occupacionem honestam vel verba audire edificatoria cum omni grauitate, omni scurrilitate remota, donec corpus et anima habiliora ad opus dei efficiantur.

Yf he haue nessessary thingis to leve, he shuld make lenger prayoris. Yf he be yrke of prayours, than to werke sum honest and profitable werke to put awey temptacions. And yf he be wery of bothe, þan he may haue sum honest occupacioun, til þe body and þe soule be moore abill to the werke of god.

1.2. Rev. VII,5

Rev. VII,5 appears in the Latin text as a spiritual instruction delivered in the form of a letter addressed to a young man, Elziarius, son of the countess of Ariano, in answer to his request for prayers; the revelation was given to St Birgitta by our Lady when she was in Naples. The translation of this chapter as an independent tract exists in two manuscripts: BL Arundel 286 (ff. 15v-19v), and BL Harley 6615 (ff. 104r-109v). My earlier edition of the text included a detailed analysis of the translation. I would like to supplement that discussion by consideration of sentence-structure, following the same lines of analysis as in the preceding section: in both tracts the translators' choices in respect of sentence-structure are strikingly similar.[13]

The subject of *Rev.* VII,5 belongs to the well-known genre of 'remedies against temptations',[14] and is developed in an elaborate allegory of a mighty king (God): this king has built a house (the body), and put in it his daughter (the soul), and assigned her a keeper (reason) as a defence against a host of menacing enemies (temptations). The author of our translation has given a title to the tract taking what is strictly essential for his purpose from the short Latin summary at the head of the chapter: "How resoun schal be keper of þe soule to putt out and to wiþstande temptaciouns, þat þei entre not into þe soule", and omitting its references to where and why Birgitta wrote to Elziarius.[15] This is a normal procedure with these independent tracts,

---

13 For the English and the Latin text of this chapter I refer to my edition of the tract: see Pezzini (1986). For the analysis I use the Arundel text, unless otherwise noted.

14 In Harley 6615 our tract is inserted between *The Chastising of God's Children* and two versions of William Flete's *De Remediis contra Temptaciones*.

15 Compare the Latin heading: "Domina Birgitta habuit istam reuelacionem in Neapoli ad requisicionem domini Elziarii filii comitisse de Ariano, qui iuuenis tunc et scolaris bone indolis erat. Et tunc ipse rogauit dominam Birgittam, quod oraret Deum pro eo. Ipsa vero in oracione existente apparuit virgo Maria

which suppress any historical or other context the original might have so as to generalize its message as widely as possible. But in this case our translator was unable for long to keep the Saint and her disciple out of his text, and was soon obliged to insert a gloss to tell his reader about the "ȝonge scoler [...] to whom þis holy lady seynt Bride wrote in a pistel þese wordes before, and þis informacioun þat folewiþ". In fact some knowledge of these biographical circumstances, of a man who was *iuuenis tunc et scolaris bone indolis*, is necessary to understand the kind of temptations he underwent.[16]

The translation itself immediately reveals an impressive fondness for parallelism. At the very beginning we have a real triumph of *isocolon*. Reason, the keeper of the house, is instructed about the dangers he must beware of:

> Primum est, quod nullus fundamentum domus suffodiat;
> secundum est, quod nullus murorum altitudinem transcendat;
> tercium est, quod parietes domus nemo frangat;
> quartum est, quod nullus inimicorum per portas introeat.

The parallelism, already present in the Latin, is strongly emphasized in the English translation.

> þe firste is þat noon enemy vndermyne þat hous;
> þe seconde is þat noon enemy clymbe ouer þe heyȝ walles wiþout;
> þe þridde is þat noon enemy breke þe foure wowes wiþinne;
> þe ferþe is þat noon enemy entre by þe gates of þat hous.

The effect is brilliant, the stress appropriately on the two crucial terms of the problem: the enemy, repeated four times using the same phrase (compare the Latin *nullus, nemo, nullus inimicorum*), and the house, which must be watched over and kept safe by reason, the keeper. In fact, the four last words of the coda are "hous / wiþout / wiþinne / hous" and one is left with the impression that the walls are the point where the battle between the soul and the temptations is fought, and

---

ei, que dedit ei istam reuelacionem, per quam informat eum de modis tenendis in vita sua, valde pulchre dicens, quod racio debet esse hostiarius et custos anime ad expellendum omnes temptaciones et resistendum eis viriliter, ne intrent domum interiorem hominis."

16 Ellis (1982a: 175-176) had already noted this adaptation.

they receive the proper emphasis in the English text, replacing in an original way the emphasis of the Latin on the four verbs meaning danger and destruction. By this subtle solution the rules of a different syntax are obeyed, but the force of the original text is retained, although translated into a new image.

To obtain perfect parallel phrases our translator uses the same techniques as noted in the previous section. He may repeat a word which is not in the Latin:

> Prima est via auditus, secunda visus.
> þe firste weye is heerynge, þe secunde weye is siȝt.

Or he may modify the Latin:

> corpore et bonis totisque tuis viribus
> wiþ al his body and wiþ alle hise wittes

He maintains this choice even when using the doublet:

> omnes proximos tuos   alle myn euencristen and alle my neiȝbores[17]

The text of this translation is almost identical in Arundel and Harley, but it is interesting to note that some of the few differences are due to the attempts of the Arundel scribe to restore a clearer parallelism. For instance, in the first example above "weye" is not repeated in Harley, which has "þe firste weye is herynge, þe secunde is syȝt". In the second case, too, Harley has a different word-order: "wiþ alle hys body and alle with hise wittys". The same may be said of two more complex examples. Where Harley has "lerne þan lyberal scyence [...] and be preyer and be ȝiftys procure to þe", Arundel puts the two verbs at the beginning of the clause, and writes "lerne þan liberal sciencis [...] and procure to þee by prayer and by ȝiftes". The second example occurs in a passage where the Latin itself is nicely balanced:

---

17   The changes from 2 p.sg. to 1 or 3 p.sg. in these as in other examples of this section are due to the new destination of the text: originally a letter addressed to a specific person, it has been transformed into a tract meant for the general reader.

humilitatem [...] quam Spiritus Sanctus inspirat
superbiam [...] quam malignus spiritus cordibus infundit

Harley's translation runs:

mekenesse, whiche is inspiryd to mennys hertys be þe Holy Goste
pryde of þe worlde, wiche þe wickyd spiriȝt puttiþ into mennys hertys

By choosing a passive and an active construction Harley destroys the
original parallelism. Arundel restores the balance by resolving the two
active verbs as passives, and reinforces the effect of radical opposition
within a pattern of similarity by the repetition of the verb "inspire":

mekenesse, which is inspired to mennes hertes by þe Holy Gost
pride of þe worlde, which is inspired to mennes hertes by his venimous
stirynge

"His" refers to the devil, the subject of the first clause of the period.[18]

This pattern of repetition is maintained even in longer and more
articulated periods. In the following example, the translator links three
Latin coda employing a mixture of passive and active constructions:
he makes the first verb active and so generates a formal similarity
between the three clauses:

fures vel tinea non timentur	I schal not drede þefes ne moþþes
Deum non offendam	I schal not deseure me in no wise
nec [...] me separabo	I schal not wilfully offende my god[19]

---

18   As I have shown in my edition and analysis of this tract (Pezzini 1986: 267),
      the Arundel scribe has a much stronger sense of 'regularity' than Harley. My
      view is that Ar works on the translation found in H, or in a copy from which H
      has been derived, trying to 'tidy it up', while keeping at the same time an eye
      on the Latin original. This is certain at least in one instance: *delectaciones
      internas*, translated "gostely meditacions" in H, is rendered in Ar by "inwarde
      delectaciouns". This may be supposed in another case: *quandoque eciam
      turbari et letari* appears in H "and somtyme be glad, and somtyme be sory,
      and somtyme be trobelyd"; Ar restores the double opposition, and writes "and
      somtyme be glad, and somtyme be sory and troublide", using a sort of half-
      way solution in that he keeps the doublet for *turbari*, but eliminates the third
      "somtyme".
19   For this tendency to invert the order in a sequence, which can also be
      observed in fn. 18 (*turbari / letari*), see also fn. 11 above.

39

Elsewhere, too, the sequence of the elements of the Latin text is re-arranged in order to create a perfect parallelism:

> Sicut in sumpcione cibi et potus cauendum est / ne inimicus per superfluitatem introeat / que corpus ad seruiendum Deo accidiosum reddit // ita eciam cauendum est ne per abstinencie nimietatem / que corpus ad omnia facienda defectuosum reddit / hostis ingressum habeat.

> Riȝt as it is nedeful to be war in takynge of mete and drinke / þat þe enemy haue noon entre by excesse and superfluite / whiche liȝtly wole make þe body slowe and heuy to þe seruyse of god // in þe same maner it is nedeful to be war / þat þe enemy haue noon entre by to mych abstinence / which liȝtly may feble þe body þat he mowe not do his dewte.

The Latin sequence 1-2-3 // 1-3-2 has been regularized and turned into a perfect parallel 1-2-3 // 1-2-3, with the central clauses (2) verbally identical, except for the contrast "excesse / abstinence".

Another feature of the figure of repetition appears at times as the use of a sort of verbal echo:

> per quem altitudinem murorum intelligo caritatem,
> que omnibus virtutibus est sublimior
> by þe whiche heiȝte I vnderstande þe vertue of charite,
> which in heiȝte passeþ alle vertues

Here the brilliant idea is to translate *sublimior est* by "in heiȝte passeþ", which, together with the repetition of "vertue", builds up a parallel totally absent from the Latin.

An even better example of this technique is the figure of *ana-diplosis*, or *gradatio*, skilfully used by our translator:

> Per fundamentum (intelligo) bonam et firmam seu stabilem voluntatem; super ipsam namque omnia bona opera construenda sunt, quibus anima optime defenditur.

> By þe fundament is vnderstonde a good and a stable wille; vp þis stable wille alle goode werkes schul be sett, and wiþ siche werkes þe soule schal be strengþed and defended from enemyes.

40

We find in this tract all the types of inversion already seen in the translation of VI,65. Chiasmus is also intelligently employed, as can be seen in the following instance:

vt soli Deo possis totaliter complacere, ipsumque in omnibus honorare
so þat fully I mowe plese only god / and hym worschipe in alle þinges

Here a perfect inversion can be observed, and the new order is: 1 *fully*, 2 *plese*, 3 *god* / 3 *hym*, 2 *worschipe*, 1 *in alle þinges*. The same tripartite inversion occurs in another case:

(diuicias) que numquam illi, qui eas adeptus fuerit, auferuntur
who so may ones gete hem / þei schul neuer be take awey fro hym.

Again we have 1 *who so*, 2 *gete*, 3 *hem*, reversed into 3 *þei*, 2 *be take awey*, 1 *hym*, with the opposition stressed by the contrast "ones (once) / neuer". The Latin has none of these choices, and the originality of our translator is once again confirmed.

In this text, as in the previous one, the attention of the translator to his reader/listener is shown in the addition of explicative passages resuming what has just been said. So *sic* becomes "þus, wiþ siche answeres", *predictos parietes* is turned into "þese foure wowes of heuenly delyte", and *si forte tibi aliquis talia persuaserit* is expanded into "whan eny siche enemyes comeþ wiþ queynte and flaterynge wordes to vndermyne þi good wille and torne þi holy purpos", where anyone can see how generic words like *aliquis* and *talia* have become definite expressions, and the action suggested by the verb *persuaserit* has been, so to speak, visualized. The same attention to the reader appears in the addition of two short summaries in the middle and at the end of the tract, where the reader is reminded that "þus schal resoun be keper of þe soule, and putt out enemyes, and wiþstande temptaciouns of þe deuel, of þe world, and of þe flesch, wiþ clepynge of god and askyng of grace".

Occasional alliterations are found in this text, like "delectaciouns of *s*eculere *s*onges or of oþere *s*wete *s*ownynge instrumentes", "*m*any *d*isches or *m*esses of *d*iuerse *d*eynte *m*etes for *w*orldly *w*orschipe and fauour of *m*en", and finally "*sl*ugrye of *sl*eep or of *sl*umbre". These are a further, final sign of our translator's interest in matters of style, and a fair indicator of his achievement.

1.3. Rev. II,16

Little needs to be said about the translation of the third independent tract taken from *Rev*. II,16. Its popularity was widespread, since we have it in three different versions in four manuscripts: the writer of the chapter heading called it "optimum documentum", which proved to be a good advertisement.[20]

I shall mainly consider the first of these three versions (Jolliffe's 1974a Item I.13a) which is found in two British Library manuscripts: Additional 37790 (f. 236v), and Arundel 197 (ff. 46v-47v), the other two being very literal. For various reasons this tract is less interesting than the two previously examined, and its study adds almost nothing to what previous analysis has shown. First it is too small a sample. Only the second half of an already short chapter has been translated; the first part, giving the occasion of a teaching on humility and an exemplum explaining God's behaviour towards Birgitta, has been left out in all three versions. This, as earlier noted, is a rule with these tracts, directed as they are to the general reader. Secondly, the text in Add. 37790 is further reduced by one third, since 13 lines out of a total of 40 have disappeared with the excision of the last folio of the manuscript. Thirdly, and most important for our purpose, the Latin text itself did not allow any significant reworking except for the expansion by means of the doublet. Apart from the opening period, which in the Latin original serves as a bridge between the two parts of the chapter, we have twelve short sentences, linked by three in four groups, and reduced to bare essentials: the verb and its object, and sometimes the object only. The subject is God, who gives

---

20   For the texts, full description of the manuscripts, and a detailed analysis of the translations, the reader may refer to Pezzini (1988), where I have also published the version of the chapter from Cotton Julius F.II. For comparison with Cotton Claudius B.I the reader may refer to the edition of this manuscript by Ellis (1987).

this series of three positive and three negative orders, three conces-
sions and three counsels.

The basic choice of the translator is then amplification. See
what becomes of a very simple Latin sentence in Add. 37790:

> Dilige omnes eciam qui te odire videntur et tibi detrahere.
> Luf alle in me / and them that hate the / and detracte the / and scorne the / or
> any iuel do to the / luf them for the luf of me.

This is a good and balanced use of rhetorical devices such as
anaphora, epistrophe, and *epanalepsis*, which gracefully encloses the
whole passage in two repeated parallel clauses. One may argue if this
can still be called a translation, since it goes a long way from the
original. But this is not the end of the road. The second scribe of MS
Arundel 197, who corrects the original version by erasing, rewriting
and adding words and phrases over the line and on the margins,
expands even more:

> Love al maner of pepul for mi sake / and þem þat þou knowiste dothe hate /
> and wille bacbyte þe / and speke eville of þe / sclaunder or scorne þe / or any
> oþer wronge or harme do vnto þe / yet love þem for þe loue of me.

Other expansions are more reasonable. We have the doublet, like
fugere rendered by "fle and forsake"; explanatory additions, such as
superbiam et arroganciam which Ar. translates "alle maner of pride
and hiȝ berynge, boþe in herte and in countenance"; or a combination
of the two, as with *carnis luxuriam* which becomes in Add. "the vices
of thy flesch, þat is to vndyrstonde the syn of lechery". In this
translation, then, and given the peculiar character of the Latin, the
translator treats the original like a naked pattern on which he
embroiders freely without ever losing the main thread of his argument.

The other two independent versions of II,16 do not show any
particular reworking of the Latin text, and have no close link with the
previous version. They both omit the opening sentence containing the
teaching on humility, and concentrate on the "twelf poyntes", as
Bodley 131 calls this summary of Christian practice, revealing once
again how fascinating was the numerical organizing principle in
medieval times. The versions in MS Taunton Horae (f. i r-v) covers
the first folio of a Book of Hours and is written in a different hand,

43

most probably from the second half of the fifteenth century; the bottom of the first folio has been partly torn off so that now the text of the translation is incomplete. The translation itself is literal, except in two cases, where an explanatory sentence is added. The difficulty of making much of a text so reduced to essentials can be further demonstrated by brief consideration of the two full-text translations, in the Julius and Claudius MSS. Generally the two texts cut the Latin in a substantial way; they are not so free here, although, as soon as they can, they eliminate a rare Latin doublet, or conflate two similar sentences into one. Claudius is more ruthless than Julius: he substitutes all the cardinal numbers of the sequence with a colourless "also", for example. But when he rules out an entire sentence, *hec cogitacio excitat caritatem ad deum*, which refers to the meditation on the Passion, the result is a positive blunder, since the thought of the Passion becomes one with the meditation on Doomsday, and "þese two sall engendir drede and fere in þi herte". This is wrong and one-sided: the delicate balance between love and fear, which is the fruit of the double meditation, and a corner-stone of a sound Christian life, is thus destroyed.

2. Conclusion

A few closing remarks are in order.

1)   These tracts show further evidence of a widespread practice of taking smaller parts out of longer works, which were translated for and adapted to what we may call the general reader,[21]

---

21   In this process of generalization the tract may at times lose its link with the work from which it has been taken. This happens with the translation of VI,65 which appears as an anonymous treatise in MS Pepys 2125, while in C.U.L. Ii.vi.40 it has not got even a title, coming immediately after the *Fervor Amoris* so that it was taken, until quite recently, as the last two chapters of this work. Also in Bodley 423 and Arundel 197 this tract comes after the *Fervor Amoris*, whose author seems quite familiar with the *Revelations* (see Ellis 1982: 175),

meaning by this a growing literate audience increasingly composed of lay people, mostly women.

2) The style of these translations, rich in figures of parallelism and inversion, points towards the use of these tracts for private meditation and spiritual instruction. I agree with Smedick that "Parallelism has a special suitability for meditative texts [...]. Memory is aided, attention focussed, and the effect of incantation produced through the reiterative style" (1979: 405). But the same suitability can be found in the figures of inversion, which stimulate the mind with the effect of surprise induced by the frustrated expectation of parallelism. This is to say that the rhetorical devices were not primarily used for their own sake, but as a help to meditation.[22] The same principle applies to the use of these tracts as spiritual instructions orally delivered, for which parallel sentences, explanatory additions and summary passages were particularly useful. The technique of reducing or expanding the Latin for the sake of better precision and clarification follows the same line.

3) Given the remarkable similarity of certain stylistic habits, it is tempting to suggest that the translations examined here as 'independent tracts' are the work of the same hand. But this is only a supposition at present. The evidence of the manuscripts, although not decisive, does not particularly favour a common origin: the tracts appear singly, except in Arundel 197, which contains VI,65 and II,16 in sequence. Moreover, the study of late medieval devotional prose in English is still in its infancy, and a good deal of analysis, like the one I offer here, is needed in order to draw a clear and articulate pattern of translational

---

but in these two manuscripts the short title of the tract says that it is "drawe oute of the Reuelacion of seint Bride".

22 Salter has rightly suggested that "An account of the development of highly-wrought English devotional prose might well [...] lay great stress upon the development of certain kinds of religious sensibility, and the varied needs of a teaching Church, interpreted in varied literary ways: the 'rhetorical tradition' is established and corroborated by religious demand and only secondarily determined by literary taste" (1974: 212-213).

techniques[23] and, more generally, define the map of medieval prose in England as a tradition comprising both continuity and variation.[24] Only against such a background could the value and meaning of single texts be assessed.

---

23   The need for "a much larger study of intertextuality in Middle English devotional writing" is aptly stressed by Nolan (1984: 90): "Such a study would necessarily include medieval Latin as well as English texts; and it would involve discussion not only on themes, imagery, and meditative structures, but also of rhetorical techniques adapted from Latin into English and then transformed to become part of the native literary idiom." This is exactly what we may observe in our three Birgittine tracts. Also relevant in this respect is the chapter by Barratt (1984), particularly the remarks and suggestions made on p. 427.

24   A first draft of this map is Blake (1974). The criterion adopted by Blake is "the purpose for which a particular text was written, since the purpose will often determine the form and approach, as its most important feature" (p. 349). To this may be added Jolliffe (1974a), which, although more limited in scope, is far more articulate in its sections. I would also like to indicate Stone (1970) as a good example of detailed analysis, although not applied to a translation. The merit of this book is that the texts are really analysed in full detail, and not just superficially skimmed through and described with random inconclusive impressions.

CHAPTER 2

Book IV of St Birgitta's *Revelations* in an Italian (MS Laurenziano 27.10) and an English Translation (MS Harley 4800) of the Fifteenth Century[1]

When W. P. Cumming edited *The Revelations of Saint Birgitta* for EETS in 1929,[2] a work which, despite its title, was only an anthology of chapters taken from the *Liber Celestis* as extant in the Garrett MS, he listed seven other manuscripts containing English translations of Birgittine materials – see ch. 1. His description of the manuscripts, although incomplete and inaccurate in places, is good, but the value judgements he gave of the type and quality of the translations are, to say the least, ungenerous and hasty, and they should be mercifully forgotten. In any case Cumming's merit was to draw attention to these texts and to 'where' they could be found: his map was only slightly enlarged by further discoveries recorded by P. S. Jolliffe in his *Check-List of Middle English Prose Writings of Spiritual Guidance* (1974) – see ch. 1, fn. 4. In a well-documented and wide-ranging article, Ellis (1982a) showed how the *Revelations* were used in fifteenth-century England, both in the original Latin and in some English versions. Ellis described 'what' was selected and copied or translated, grouping the material around three main headings: prophecies, meditations on the life of Christ and Mary, instructions for the spiritual life.

---

1   An earlier version of this chapter appeared in *Aevum*, LXX/3, 1996, 487-506. This essay is a revised and expanded version of a paper I read at the Conference on the Life, Writings and Order of St Birgitta of Sweden (Buckfast Abbey, Devon, July 18-21, 1994). I wish to express my thanks to the Trustees of the British Library and to the Direzione della Biblioteca Medicea Laurenziana for allowing me to quote from their manuscripts.

2   Quotations of the Garrett MS are from the edition by Cumming (1929).

Starting from these two publications I began in 1986 to edit and study various Birgittine tracts and meditations, and at the same time to analyse their techniques of translation and compilation. Given the 'where' and the 'what', established by Cumming and Ellis respectively, I tried to see the 'how', and to suggest the reason for and the possible readership of these translations. After editing the translations of *Rev.* II,16, VI,65, VII,5 (which I call 'independent tracts'), the meditation on the Passion in MS Lambeth 432, and the spiritual treatise in MS Rawlinson C.41, and after studying the *Vita Beate Marie*, a Birgittine compilation extant in this same manuscript, I think that I can now draw a new list based on the type of text produced, and identify the style and the quality of the translation provided. Needless to say, I do not intend to establish any necessary link between the type of the text produced and the type of translation used, and what follows is no more than a description of the actual state of things. However, my conclusions after editing and analysing many of these texts lead to a complete re-assessment of Cumming's comments on the matter.

We may classify the English Birgittine translations in five types, given here in order of length. We have:

1. quotations and short passages, found on the flyleaf of a Book of Hours, within a sermon or a spiritual treatise: here the translation tends to be literal, except for occasional doublets, and the text is rather summarily dealt with;[3]
2. single chapters treated as self-contained units providing spiritual teachings or meditations on the life of Christ: normally the Latin is creatively reworked and use is made of rhetorical niceties: my opinion is that some technical features of these versions suggest the possible use of these texts for spiritual reading in a context of oral delivery;[4]
3. large compilations drawing their material from different books and chapters, like the *Vita Beate Marie* or the fragment of a

---

3   See some translations of *Rev.* II,16 in Pezzini (1988). See also the quotations from different books inserted into a sermon for the Feast of the Assumption of Our Lady edited from C.U.L. MS Hh.i.11 by O'Mara (1994).
4   See Pezzini (1986, 1988 and 1994b). In the introductory pages of these articles I study the style of these translations. For a more general and comparative survey of these versions see chapter 1.

long spiritual treatise extant in MS Rawlinson C.41: here too the translation appears to be very careful and considerable freedom is taken with the source text;[5]

4. an anthology of several chapters: the difference from the preceding type is that this is only a selection of single chapters, rearranged in their order, but remaining in their integrity, and not used to compile new texts: given the fact that we have only one English example of this type (but see an Italian analogue described and analysed in ch. 7), the already mentioned Garrett MS edited by Cumming, no relevant conclusion can be drawn as to the characteristics of the translation within this category: in the case in point we may say that it tends to follow the original pretty closely;

5. two translations of the full text, apparently intended to make the work available for study or for reading: in this case the translation is very near to what is normally described as 'literal': apart from the obviously different linguistic structures, the text is rendered in a highly economic way, expansions are avoided, instead many omissions are found which at times reduce the text to a kind of summary, more similar to a draft, or a working copy: this is particularly true of the translation in MS Cotton Claudius B.I, less so of the one in MS Cotton Julius F.II, although this must not be taken as a rule, the opposite choice being found as well.[6]

In this last group we may include the translation of Book IV and Chs. 1-2 of Book V found in MS BL Harley 4800: it is not a rendering of the full text of the *Revelations*, but it is very much like it, since it is the text of a whole book, plus the beginning of another, which is entirely translated following the order of the original. The state of the

---

5   Two treatises are edited in Pezzini (1992 and 1993a). *The Vita Beate Mariae* is analysed in ch. 13.

6   MS Cotton Claudius B.II has been edited by Ellis (1987): the quotations are from this edition indicated as 'Ellis'. Besides the parts of Cotton Julius F.II Ellis used to supply the missing leaves in Claudius B.II, only small portions of this manuscript have been published so far: the translations of II,16 (ff. 69r-70) in Pezzini (1988) and ff. 246v-254r in Voaden (1993): my quotations are from the Cotton Julius manuscript indicated as 'Ju'.

manuscript does not allow us to say whether this is only part of a more ambitious enterprise which remained by some accident incomplete or uncopied, although I feel inclined to think that this is the case. The richly decorated initial of Book IV, Ch. 1, clearly marks the beginning of a work, especially if we compare it with the very ordinary initial of Book V which follows. There is also a curious mistake which would confirm this hypothesis: in the upper margin of each folio there is a running title 'Liber quartus', but up to f. 28 *quartus* has been written after cancelling a previous *primus*. It means that the scribe had taken his book as the 'first', and this can be explained imagining a translation in two volumes, the first containing Books I-III, and the second, that is our manuscript, Books IV-VII: Book IV could thus be taken as Book I of the second part of the *Revelations*.

Differences in style become evident if we compare the same chapter, II,16 for example, used in two or three of the above categories. It seems that stylistic awareness is at its highest in the texts selected and treated independently and in the compilations (types 2, 3, and 4). I would suggest that the very fact of selecting reveals an aggressive attitude towards the base text which may result in a more careful way of rendering it. On the other hand the longer translations, probably also because of the dreadful effort they demanded, given the huge dimensions of Birgitta's work, produce a text where cuttings are numerous and amplification as a stylistic device is very rarely used. This is not to say that these versions are "businesslike" (Cumming 1929: xx) and devoid of any interest for the scholar, neither does it mean that this was the only possible method of dealing with a very long text: the Italian translation of Book IV, which I will consider, proves exactly the contrary, since I can anticipate that the various forms of expansion and reorganization of the original, which in England are more peculiar to the short texts, are in this case used throughout the 130 chapters of an entire book.

While to edit and analyse comparatively short texts can be exciting and rewarding, I have tended to delay the study of Harley 4800 for various reasons. One was the length of the text, another was probably Cumming's judgement, who considered this translation "a poor one" (Cumming 1929: xx). But since Cumming's opinions about the literary value of the Birgittine translations have proved highly debatable, if not utterly wrong, I thought that the time had come to analyse this manuscript. This choice was stimulated by the casual discovery of a late 14th-/early 15th-century Italian translation of the same Book IV, which undoubtedly offered an interesting occasion for comparison in language, style, and translational techniques. I am aware that the risk of making undue generalisations is very high. But, keeping within the very limited purpose of a chapter, I think it is nevertheless worthwhile to draw the attention of the readers to two still unexplored manuscripts, and above all I believe that something may be learnt through the analysis of some passages, which can start further investigation into the still largely unknown land of the translation of religious texts in the late Middle Ages.

I shall divide my chapter in three parts. The first is a kind of introduction containing a short description of the two manuscripts; then I will proceed to study the Italian and the English translations, first by considering some general problems on how to analyse a translation through the study of a few selected samples; second by concentrating on one single chapter in more detail, to see how different rules of evaluation can be applied. In doing this I shall compare the Italian translation mainly with the one in Harley 4800, but also with the other two longer translations, those in Cotton Claudius B.I and Cotton Julius F.II, since they belong to the same type, and share a similar style, which I would roughly define as 'economic' in the sense given above.

1. The two manuscripts

1.1. *L: Firenze, Biblioteca Medicea-Laurenziana, 27.10*

The Italian MS is a paper codex of the Biblioteca Medicea Laurenziana in Florence under the shelf-mark Laur. 27.10. It consists of 158 folios, measuring 210 x 140 mm <ca. 160 x 98>. Each page contains from 29 to 34 lines. It is written in a fifteenth-century hand called *corsiva mercantesca*. The manuscript collates in tens, and the gatherings can be identified by regular catchwords on the verso of f.

10, f. 20, etc. The numbers of the pages are given in black ink in the upper right-hand corner of each recto, but in many pages no number is marked (those given are: 1-2, 4-15, 28-30, 36-46, 48-50, 69-80, 123, 126-127, 129-130, 139-142, 145-158); in the lower right-hand corner there is a regular modern numbering in pencil. The first capital letter of the first chapter is painted blue with light red decorations; every first letter of all the other chapters is painted red, except in one case on f. 61r, while within the text capital letters are evidenced in yellow. The book has a 16th-century binding, bearing on the front and the back cover the Medici arms on small copper plates, which were most probably applied when the private Medici library, to which it belonged, was donated to the public library of Florence, now the Biblioteca Medicea Laurenziana, on 16 June 1571. There are two clasps, and a chain is still attached to the book.[7]

The translation, dated by Bandini to the end of the fourteenth century, is anonymous. We do not know whether it is part of a full text translation: as it is, it appears to be a self-contained work. Since the translation is very careful, with practically no omission from the Latin, it is possible to trace it back to the source text, at least in the sense that we can safely indicate to which manuscript tradition the original Latin text belongs. Checking the translation against the variant readings provided by Aili in his critical edition (1992),[8] it seems quite sure that this is the tradition attested in the group called VPY, which originated in Italian scriptoria and whose redaction is very near the tradition established by Alphonse of Pecha. A few examples will show the connection: the first number indicates the chapter and the second the paragraph in Aili's edition. The version of MS Harley 4800 (H) is given against L to show the different manuscript tradition attested in the English version.

---

7   See a very concise description of the manuscript in Bandini (1778: 184). According to the register of the Library the manuscript has been inspected by seven people since 1891, but to my knowledge it has never been described or made use of for any printed edition. I wish here to thank the staff of the Manuscript Room of the Biblioteca Medicea Laurenziana for the information and the help they gave me while inspecting the manuscript.

8   This is the edition I have used for the Latin text: the first number in the quotations indicates the chapter, the second refers to the paragraph.

4.26: quendam captiuum positum in *turri*] *carcerem* P
L uno il quale era in *pregione* constretto (f. 14v)
H a persone put yn a *towre* (f. 6v)

7.63: dei presenciam et eius visionem beatam] deum PVY
L dio (f. 21v)
H the syght of god (f. 11 r)

13.7: dispendia animarum VY, anime other MSS
L il danno dell'anime (f. 28v)
H for harme of the soule (f. 16v)

17.16: viuificabit VY, iudicabit P etc.
L uiuificherà (f. 36r)
H deeme (f. 22r)

17.21: quid vero est carnis nisi cibus vermium? *om* PVY
L *om* (f. 36r)
H what ys oure flessche but wormes meete (f. 22r)

Beg. of ch. 70: a long introduction only in V, translated in L, not extant in H

80.32: letania] letaniis V Gh
L colle letanie (f. 108r)
H with the letany (f. 61v)

The examples given do not lead to any clear-cut conclusion, except the fact that L works broadly in the tradition attested by VPY. If we want to be more specific we find contradictory evidence, as is shown in the examples given above, where in some cases L goes with P against VY, in others with VY against P. But there are also cases in which L does not follow V: for example in 7, 28 *in te* omitted by V is translated in L; in 7, 26 V has an addition not present in L; in 7, 46 V has *Lodouicum et Iohannem*, which corresponds to H 'Lodouyk and John', while L has *Lodouico e Giovanna* according to the reading of the critical edition. The translation of 32, 3 *nec de cupiditate eius et voluptate carnis*: *né della cupidità né della uoluntà della carne* (f. 48v) shows that L follows the reading *voluntate* of PV (H has 'lust': ne to the lust of þe flesshe, f. 32v), while in 32, 5 L follows P's reading *bona sillaba* (*la buona silaba*: f. 48v), against all the other MSS where *una* is found (H: oon sylable). Again, L follows P in 46, 2a where the phrase *indignatus rex vineam* is omitted, and does not appear in the Italian translation (*Ma pero che non piacque al posseditore d'essa uigna di uenderla, tolseglela e osurpò per ingiustitia uiolenta*: f. 59v). It seems, then, that within the tradition of VPY, the translation appears nearer to P, although in some cases it follows V against P. This further confirms what Aili says about the characteristic of VPY, a tradition which appears to show mixed and irregular evidence in the ties linking the three manuscripts.[9]

Although the translator of L is very faithful to his original, he has in one case rearranged the work, by inserting after ch. 2, which contains an allegorical vision, the explanation of the same vision, which is actually ch. 129 of the work. To do this he repeats the number, providing thus two ch. 3, then he follows the normal numbering until ch. 126, omits no. 127, so that his chs. 128-129 correspond actually to chs. 127-128 of the Latin, the gap left by the anticipation of ch. 129 is filled, and the book closes regularly with ch. 130. Omissions are very rare, and so are mistranslations: a funny case occurs right at the beginning, where *saucium* has been read as *sanctum*, a blunder not uncommon, given the similarity of the letters <u/n> and <i/t> in the manuscripts, and accordingly translated by *santo*.

1.2. *H: London, British Library MS Harley 4800*

MS Harley 4800 has been described by W. P. Cumming (1929: xvii-xviii), although with some approximation. It contains Book IV and chs.1-2 (incomplete) of Book V. It is paper, and it consists of 109 folios measuring 295 x 210 mm; the written area measures 227 x 150/160 mm, with 26-33 lines to a page. The MS is written in a clear fifteenth-century bastard secretary hand; the first capital letter of the first chapter is decorated, all the other initials are simply in red ink. The manuscript is not in perfect condition. A leaf is missing between

---

9   See Aili (1992: 34-36). After saying that the manuscripts PVY "have des-
     cended from a common exemplar", Aili continues: "the textual tradition of
     this group [...] is not quite so straightforward as this statement would imply,
     since there is ample evidence of separate ties between PY against V, of VY
     against P and of VY2 against PY" (1992: 34).

f. 8 and f. 9, creating a gap between ch. 6, 7a and ch. 7, 17b; two gatherings (e-f) are also missing after f. 38, so that a considerable section of about thirty chapters, from ch. 40, 7b (*et minuit peccatum...*) to ch. 67, 4 (*...diuine caritatis*), not ch. 70, as Cumming says, is wanting; one leaf is also missing after f. 67 with the greater part of ch. 89, from 4b (*...reduxisti me ad viam rectam*) to 19a (*...quidue omittendum*); two leaves (f. 1 and f. 105) are partially torn at the bottom, but the damage here is not really serious. The numbering of the folios belongs to a later age, when the manuscript was already in the present condition. The manuscript collates in tens, as it can be guessed from the old original numbering on the lower right-hand part of the leaves, where small letters followed by numbers mark the original thirteen gatherings ([a]-n), of which only eleven remain. A number <v>, presumably preceded by a lost <a>, on f. 4r, indicates that this was originally f. 5, which implies that the original f. 1 is missing. This is also confirmed by the fact that the first catchword is found on f. 18v, instead on f. 20v where one would expect it: this means that the original f. 10 is in fact the leaf lost between the actual f. 8 (originally f. 9) and f. 9 (originally f. 11). After f. 18v catchwords are found regularly every ten folios, from 28v to 58v; f. 68v is missing, which explains why in the following gatherings the catchword appears on 77v-107v. As already said, in the upper margin of each folio there is a running title 'Liber quartus' (with *Liber* on the verso folio, and *quartus* on the recto) up to f. 106, then 'Liber quintus' on ff. 107-109; on ff. 1-28 *primus* was previously written, and afterwards cancelled by a stroke to be replaced by *quartus*.

On the first folio there is the name 'Edward South', possibly a seventeenth-century owner of the manuscript (Wright 1972: 309). On f. 53v is written in the lower margin: 'Luke vnto Mr Syr James Parson of no churche and vycare of the same', and on f. 54r the same seventeenth-century hand has written a short poem: 'I lent my mony vnto my frend/ as many men dothe in land / I axed my mony of my frend / by cause yt was so longe. / I loste my mony and my frend / me thought it was great wrong. J. Bray'. Is this an indication of a seventeenth-century reader of the manuscript? It may be so, since these lines could be taken as a sad consideration prompted by the title of chapter 76, which is given at the end of f. 53v: 'Whych ar goode freendes and fewe of them ar clerkes'. In fact the scribe visibly connects his writing to this short title, of which it becomes a gloss, and we are led to suppose that J. Bray is the deceived money-lender, and that James Parson is one of the many 'clerkes' who are not 'goode frendes'. The phrase is actually a mistranslation (the Latin has *amici Dei*), and we can also suppose that the reader's attention has only been caught by the few words pointed out in the title, to which what follows does not correspond, since by a curious misplacing the title of ch. 76 is followed by the text of ch. 77, while ch. 76 is found under the title of ch. 77.

A manuscript described as badly mutilated, containing a translation labelled as 'poor', does not normally invite the curiosity of the scholar. This may be the reason why Harley 4800 has been totally neglected so far. The 'poverty' of Harley 4800 is set by Cumming (1929: xx) against the 'passages of excellent prose' which he finds in the Garrett MS. The first comparison I made was in fact between Harley and Garrett, since some chapters appear in the two versions. Much to my surprise I discovered that when Cumming valued the translation in the Garrett MS as 'excellent' and the one in Harley 4800 as 'poor', he in fact shot himself in his foot. The two versions show indeed such a strong similarity as to coincide, at times, almost verbatim. To give just one example, see a passage from chapter 9 as it appears translated in Garrett (G) and Harley (H):

> 9.9 Post ista apparuit quidam quasi homo modestus valde in visu, cuius vestes erant albe et fulgide quasi alba sacerdotalis, cinctus zona linea et stola rubea ad collum et subtus brachia eius. 10 Qui inchoabat verba sua isto modo...
>
> G After this appered one as it wer a man right sobre in syght, whos clothes wer white & shynyng as a prestes albe; he was gyrde with a lynnen gyrdele & a rede stole abowte his necke & vnder hys armes; & he began his wordes on this wyse: (Cumming 1929: 51)
>
> H Aftyr thys appered oon lyke a sobre man yn syght yn whyte clothynge shynynge as a preestys avbe, and gyrd wyth a lynnen gyrdel and a rede stole aboute hys nekke and vndyr hys armes, that began hys wordys yn thys manere. (f. 12v)

So, what does 'poor' mean? Is it a poverty of lexis, or syntax, or style? Cumming seems to conceive excellence in terms of fidelity and integrity, since almost all his remarks concern the tendency to excise words or phrases from the text, which he finds in Harley 4800 and Julius F.II, although not "as pronounced as that of Claudius B.I" (Cumming 1929: xx). Apart from the fact that in the parts I have checked Harley is much more faithful to his source than Julius, to abbreviate does not necessarily produce a poor translation: one should judge whether the new text succeeds in rendering the main ideas of the original in a clear prose: there are also good summaries, not less good for their being summaries. But anyway, this is not the case with Harley 4800. As the examples I give will show, it is true that Harley's rendering is normally more economic than its Italian counterpart, but the product is simply a different type of translation.

Starting from the very beginning, the point is that the deeper we go into the study of a translation, and the more possibilities we have to compare different versions of the same text, the more difficult it becomes to establish a coherent evaluative pattern, to the extent that only positive blunders can elicit a common agreement. In fact neither fidelity nor integrity can be taken as absolute rules, nor is hypotaxis necessarily more refined than parataxis. Let us consider, for example, a short passage at the end of ch. 87:

> 87.12 Sicut in fenice colligere poteris, que senectute grauata colligit ligna in monte altissimo et illis ex calore solis succensis proiicit se in ignem et sic ex illo igne mortua reuiuiscit.

> L Si come tu puoi comprendere nella fenice, la quale essendo uecchia, raccoglie le legne nel monte altissimo, e per lo caldo del sole accendendosi, gittasi nel fuoco e ardesi, e così morta in quel fuoco riuiue. (f. 115r)

> H As thou myght vnderstonde by a byrd called Fenyx, the whych at a gret age gadryth stykkes vnto an hyghe hylle, and whan the stykkes brenne by the heete of þe sonne, he fleeth yn to þe fyre, / and whan he ys dede and brent, he quykkeneth agayn and lyueth.(ff. 66v-67r)

The Italian translator seems to follow the all too natural temptation to rival his Latin source, and produces a very compact text, but he does this at his peril, since he cannot avoid the ambiguity of *accendendosi*, in the original referred to the sticks, but in his version attributable to the only subject he has kept, that is the phoenix. The English version is not so tight, and runs more smoothly in parallel clauses, showing a good architectural design: the overall effect is of great clarity.

It is obviously not possible to take into account a whole book of the *Revelations* to compare different translations. Having to be selective, I thought first to use a few samples taken from different parts of Book IV to investigate some general problems of translation such as variety and repetition, amplification and cutting; second to analyse a single chapter, which I found particularly interesting and promising, to see how general rules of evaluation can be applied to the close reading of a text.

2. How to evaluate a translation

2.1. Variety versus repetition

A good test to verify to what extent vocabulary is rich and richly exploited by a writer and/or a translator is to see what choices he makes when the same things recur frequently in a given section in a more or less synonymic variety. Ch. 4 is devoted to a debate between a good and an evil spirit, who are variously named using some nouns I have marked in italics in the key sentence which starts the chapter:

> 4.1 A duobus *spiritibus* suggeruntur et infunduntur *cogitaciones* et *infusiones* in cordibus hominum, a bono spiritu scilicet et a malo.

The words used in the chapter to indicate the spirit, apart from the first sentence, are: *spiritus* (7 occ.), *infusio* (4), *inspiracio* (1), *cogitacio* (1). For these words L has: *spirito* (7), *infusione* (4), *pensiero* (2). H has 'spyryt' (12), 'sterynge' (1) and 'ynspyracion' (1), but we may remark that these last two words are not used in isolation, but coupled with 'spyryt' in a doublet which ensures their understanding (There is a doublet also in L: *la buona infusione e il buono pensiero* for *bona infusio*). We may conclude that the English translator was less confident than his Italian counterpart about the possibility of understanding any word different from 'spirit', which he uses in all the twelve occurrences. For the adjectives the situation is more varied in comparison with the Latin, and more balanced between the two

MSS: while the Latin has only two adjectives to mark the contrast, *bonus* and *malus*, we have in L *buono* (8) on the one hand, and *cattivo* (4) and *malo* (3) on the other, whereas in H we find 'goode' (7), beside 'wykked' (5), and 'euyl' (2): if we add 'ylle' found in Julius, we have here a solution which goes against a common assumption, in that the vernacular shows a greater lexical variety than the Latin.

Every possibility of variety is ruled out from Claudius (hereafter Cl), where all through the chapter we meet only a 'gude spirit' and an 'euell spirit', and from Julius (hereafter Ju), where the contrast is between a 'good spirit' and an 'ylle spirit'. Repetition in a prose passage is not always easy to assess: it may be a token of verbal poverty, or a conscious choice either to form a parallelism or to help memory. Here are a few examples selected at random:

(1)   67.6 dulces arbores portant dulcia et econtra que amara sunt.

L pero che i dolci albori fanno i dolci frutti, e per lo contrario gl'amari fanno i frutti amari (f. 79r)

H for sweete trees beren sweete fruyte, and soure trees soure fruyte (f. 39r)

(2)   70.2 Tunc autem ad terram ita trahitur et impulsiue prosternitur *crudeliter*, ut concusso capite dentes colliderentur, et ad collum et maxillam *percutitur* ita *fortiter*, ut sonus percussionis ad aures meas perueniret.

L Allora tanto *crudelmente* fu menato e con pugnia cacciato in terra, e *percosso* nel capo si *spiacevolmente* che y denti si *percossono* insieme e riceuettero lisione, e fu nel collo e nelle mascelle si *spiacevolmente percosso* che io udii il suono della *percossa*. (f. 81v)

H Than he was throwen *so soore* a-yenst the grounde that alle the teethe yn hys hede wer hurte and shoken, and they smote hym *so soore* yn the nekke and on the chekes þat the sovnde came to myne eerys. (f. 41r)

(3)   40.6 Ergo scito, quod ille moritur contemptibiliter et male qui dissolute viuens moritur in voluntate peccandi...

L Adunque sappia che colui muore di morte vituperosa e male, il quale uiuendo disolutamente, muore nella uolunta del peccato. (f. 56v)
H Therfor wete thou that he wykkedly and *synfully* and dampnably deyeth that *synfully* lyueth and deyeth yn wylle for to *synne*... (f. 38v)

Parallelism and clarity seem to be aimed at in the first example in both translations. The Passion passage in the second example shows that L chooses both variety in the adverbs and repetition in the obsessive use of *percuotere* and *percosse*, so that the reader may, with Mary, hear the strokes of the soldiers; H is lexically poorer, but besides simplifying his text, he too uses repetition, and the reappearing of 'so soore' may be an intended refrain, and does not necessarily imply that English had then fewer words than Italian. The third passage, with the triple recurring in H of 'sin / sinfully' against the one *peccandi* in the Latin, would suggest that here the emphasis is intentional. Notice also, in the same passage, how the English version clearly prefers parataxis against the solution adopted by the Italian one.

An opposite case is where we find a greater lexical variety in the translation against repetition in the base text. Ch. 7 reports a vision in which the devil appears under the likeness of *quidam Ethiops, terribilis in aspectu* (7, 4). L renders it first by *uno hetiopo nero, il cui aspetto era terribile*. We may note, incidentally, that L transforms a Latin adjectival apposition into a dependent clause, and the choice to complicate syntax instead of simplifying it is quite usual in this Italian version, contrary to what we find in the English longer versions, where the procedure is rather the opposite. Against the Latin, where *Ethiops* is the only word we find, L has *hetiopo nero* twice, *il nero* once, and *glezzo* twice.[10] This last item, together with other rare words like for example *leppole* for 'eyelids' and *transchiattare* for 'to die', can point to the regional origin of the translation. The English translations vary: Cl has normally 'the Ethiope', except in a case where he becomes 'a blake Ethiope'; Ju starts by calling him 'a blac thinge', and then, not waiting until the final discovery of his very nature, calls him regularly 'the fende': all these three versions share the setting off of blackness as a peculiar mark of the devilish being. Unfortunately it is not possible to check this variety against the Harley translation, since the part of ch. 7 where the word more frequently recurs (nos. 1-17a) is missing, but there is one instance at the end of the chapter (no 48) and here H, with a touch of exotic flavour, calls the *Ethiops* 'The man of Ynde'.

---

10   On the meaning of this word as 'black' see ch. 6, fn. 16.

This last case reminds us that unusual names may create problems of interpretation, and in this case different solutions may reveal different levels of knowledge or different attitudes in the mind of the translator. This is clearly illustrated by three different versions of *eunuchus ille* (21, 9): while for L he is simply *quello heunuco*, for H he becomes 'that man that was cleped Eunuchus' (f. 26v), a choice similar to the one adopted in 'a byrd called Fenyx' for *fenice* in ch. 87,12, while Cl chooses to gloss the name by inserting an apposition of Acts 8:27 (*potens Candacis reginae qui erat super omnes gazas eius*) from where the reference is taken, and writes: "he, þe tresorere of þe qwen Candace" (Ellis 1987: 278). One would conclude that the Italian translator thought his readers would immediately understand, H feels obliged to explain that this Eunuch is a man, as much as he did with the Phoenix specifying that it is a bird, probably taking the common for a proper name: he is not perhaps a good biblical scholar, unlike Cl, who seems to suppose a good familiarity with the Bible in his intended audience.

There are other cases where the choice of different words reveals an unmistakable national colour, as can be seen in two examples from ch. 80, which contains practical instructions addressed to a cleric, taking him through the daily round of devotions and occupations. Both examples concern liturgical practices. The first is about the naming of the Office of the Dead, which sounds infallibly English:

80.29 omni die pro mortuis vigilias legas cum tribus leccionibus ante cenas.

L ogni di per gli morti leggi le uigilie con tre lectioni nanzi cena (f. 108r)

H sey euery day for the dede placebo and dyryge afor souper (f. 61v)

The same naming occurs in the other two English versions: Cl has 'Than say þi Placebo and Dirige' (Ellis 1987: 328), Ju has 'dirigy with iij lessonnys for þe ded be fore soper' (f. 138v). The second example is the rendering of *legantur benedicciones mense* (80,22), which in L is *leggasi la beneditione della mensa* (f. 107v) while H has 'loke graces be seyde' (f. 61r), Cl 'þe grace is seide' (Ellis 1987: 328), and Ju 'gracis shal be red or seide' (f. 138r).

In these examples the three English translations show a remarkable uniformity: this may be due to the fact that such words as 'placebo and dyrygy' (*Placebo* and *Dirige* are the first words of the Evening and the Morning Office of the Dead respectively), and the phrase 'say graces' all belong to the liturgical vocabulary, where a certain fixity can be expected. In other cases a similarly idiomatic solution is more rarely found, as can be seen in the following example concerning food:

> 80.34 omnes quartas ferias ad unam comestionem in caseo et ouis et piscibus
>
> L Ogni mercoledì digiuna, e puoi mangiare cacio e huoua e pescie (f. 108v)
>
> H And euery wennesday oon meele: whyte meete and fysshe (f. 61v)
>
> Ju euery wednysday to oon mele, in chese, eggys and fish (f. 138v)

The idiomatic choice is here found only in H (Cl omits the sentence), where *in caseo et ouis* is rendered by 'whyte meete'. The OED defines 'white meat' as 'food prepared from milk, dairy produce (occas. including eggs)'. The phrase is now obsolete. It comes from OE 'hwit mete', corresponding to the Latin *lacticinium*, and goes back to a time when 'meat' had still the more general meaning of 'food'. The last occurrence of this meaning is recorded in the OED for 1886.

2.2. Reduction versus integrity and/or amplification

To reduce, or to simplify, was perceived by Cumming as the main cause which produced a bad translation: 'cuttings' were the obsessively repeated faults of the Birgittine translations he listed in his introduction. But we need not think so. To eliminate variety and to maintain the same noun and the same qualification throughout a chapter may help cohesion, and sustain memory in a reader or a listener. To excise some phrases in order to build a different structure may favour clarity. Here is an example taken from Claudius's version in ch. 4 (Ellis 1987: 254):

> 4.11 Scio duo esse eterna, celum scilicet et infernum. Omnis enim, qui Deum diligit super omnia, non intrabit in infernum. 12 Qui vero non diligit Deum non habebit celum [...] Quam gloriosa sunt celestia, quam amara dyabolica malicia et quam vana sunt terrena!

> Cl Two thynges ar euirlastynge: heuen and hell.
> And þa þat loues noʒt God ouer alle thynges sall noʒt haue heuen.
> And he þat loues God ouer all thynges sall noʒt haue hell.
> Heuen is full of ioy and blysse, and helle is full of sorow and malice.

No one will deny that the translator, although not exactly faithful to his base text, has caught the main sense of it, and above all he shows a remarkable sense of structure by stressing the suggestions for parallelisms already present in the original. And here is Harley's solution:

> H Y know hevyn and helle to dure euyr:
> he that loueth god aboue al thynge schal not entre helle;
> who so loue not god schal not haue hevyn. [...]
> O, how gloryous ben heuenly thynges,
> ful byttyr ys the deuylles malyce,
> and erthely thynges ben ful veyn. (f. 6r)

The translator does not abbreviate, but follows the Latin text very carefully, although he too works originally, at least in the way he arranges the final triple Latin clause, where he manages to create echo effects by repeating and crossing similar phrases: 'heuenly thynges / erthely thynges', 'full byttyr / ful veyn'. To compare, here is the Italian translation:

> L quanto sono gloriose le cose celestiali,
> e quanto e amara la diabolica nequitia;
> o quanto sono buone le cose etterne,
> e quanto sono uane le cose terrene. (f. 13v)

Another solution has been chosen: while Cl reduces the three clauses to two, L amplifies them to four, translating more closely to the Latin, but reworking the text all the same, to establish a pattern of two contrasting pairs.

Cuttings and abbreviations of the text have been recognized as a common practice with the English longer translations. This method is at its highest in Cl, and at the lowest in Harley. Problems arise with cuttings when these concern very large sections. It is obviously not easy to discover the possible reasons for these omissions, if there are any. But we may speculate. Let us consider, for example, a long passage taken from ch. 7, which is part of a confession of faith on the part of the devils. I have marked in italics the parts which were selected by H to build up a much shorter text.

> 7.18 Tu fuisti in te ab inicio, nichil habens diminutum in te nec transmutabile sicut decet Deum. Extra te nichil est et nichil extra te, quod gaudium habeat. 19 Ideo *caritas tua fecit angelos ex nulla alia materia nisi a deitatis tue potencia; et fecisti sicut misericordia dictabat.* 20 Set postquam nos intus accensi fuimus superbia, inuidia et cupiditate, tua caritas diligens iusticiam eiecit nos de celo cum igne malicie nostre in abissum incomprehensibilem et tenebrosam, que vocatur nunc infernus. 21 Sic fecit caritas tua tunc, que nec separabitur adhuc de iusticie tue iudicio, siue fiat secundum misericordiam siue secundum equitatem. 22 Plus dicimus: *si* res illa quam pre omnibus diligis, que est *virgo que te genuit* et que nunquam peccauit, si, inquam, illa *peccasset mortaliter et sine contricione diuina mortua fuisset,* 23 *sic diligis iusticiam, quod anima eius* numquam obtineret celum set *esset nobiscum in inferno.*

> H Thou made aungelles of non othyr mater but of the myght of thy godhed lyk as thy mercy wolde. And thou art so ful of ryghtwysnes that, and the mayden that bare the had synned dedly, and had deyed wyth oute contricion of god, thou louyst ryghtwysnes so moche that sche had gon to helle with vs. (f. 9r)

What can we deduce from such heavy omissions? Cl selects in the same way, adding only the fall of the angels into hell (see Ellis 1987: 258); Ju ruthlessly cuts the whole section, from 17b to 23a, and concentrates all in a short paragraph:

> Ju We knowe god in iij personys, and was withoute beginnyng and without end, ne ther is no god but þou. Þerfore þou juge, whi demys nat to us þis soule þat we may ponish it after his dedis? (f. 102v)

Apparently the English translators are not much interested in theological discussions such as the difficult combination of *iusticia* and *caritas* in God. What they select are the bare fact of the creation of the angels, and the dreadful hypothesis of the Virgin Mary being damned to hell. Purely theological statements as those in nos. 18 and 21 are entirely avoided, but the translation is by no means careless, since both H and Cl anticipate the *sic diligis iusticiam* of no. 23 in order to better organize their sentence. Actually, one should resist the temptation to infer from these heavy cuttings either that medieval English was an inept tool to write theology,[11] or that the translators' choices show the celebrated supposed preference for practicality as a basic English attitude of mind. In fact the whole passage appears neatly translated in the Garrett MS, and the lucky possibility to compare different translations of the same passage confirms what Ellis (1991: xiv) rightly remarks: in evaluating a medieval translation "every instance of practice that we may be tempted to erect into a principle has its answering opposite, sometimes in the same work".

The Italian translator follows the Latin closely, although it seems that he had some difficulty in understanding the exact meaning of some sentences, as in his rendering of no. 18:

> L Tu fusti dal principio in te non auendo d'alcuna cosa necessita ne scemata e in te non transmutabile si come a dio si confà (f. 18v)

As it stands this sentence is not immediately understandable. Even Garrett is not crystal clear in the same passage: "þu was in thy-selfe from with-oute begynnynge, hauynge ryght nott lassede ne to lytell in the ne changeble" (Cumming 1929: 44-45).

3. An analysis of ch. 70: a vision of the Passion

Turning away from sophisticated theological language, we now move to the other end of the spectrum, and will consider ch. 70, a vision in which our Lady recounts to Birgitta how she participated in the passion of Christ, to which is appended, in total contrast, a description of the physical beauty of Jesus when he was twenty years of age. The prose of the chapter is an intensely emotional narrative, according to

---

11   See Baugh/Cable (1978: 184), where they quote an anonymous writer who complains that it is not easy to translate from Latin into English, for "there ys many wordes in Latyn that we have no propre Englysh accordynge therto" (*The Myroure of Oure Ladye*, EETS ES, 19, p. 7). See also Blake (1992: 507-508), where reference is made to "the assumption that the literary language in the Middle English period was relatively unsophisticated and that its vocabulary had few connotations".

the well-known methods of meditation typical of medieval affective piety. These two aspects of the text, narrative and emotion, are likely to elicit different responses, both in pace and in tone. The rhythm of the story may be speeded up or loosened, by favouring hypotaxis or parataxis; the tone may be either enhanced or deflected, by a skilful treatment of adjectives and adverbs.

A short example shows how by the repetition of an adverb, their union in a chiastic structure at the centre of the sentence, and the doubling of a clause, the Italian translator tends to give a stronger emotional tone to the text, even if he omits the detail of the thorns:

70.13 Et tunc corona spinea capiti eius artissime imposita fuit.

L Allora gli fu posta la corona in capo tanto strettissimamente, e si fortemente gliela calcarono in testa. (f. 82v)

H And than a crowne of thornes was most streytly put on his hede. (f. 41v)

Another good example of emphasis obtained by the addition of an adjective and an adverb, plus the naming of the cross which in the Latin is only implied and the insertion of a short clause, is the following, in which the additions have been italicised:

70.12 et euigilans Filium meum confixum video.

L E poi tornando in me *e leuando gli occhi*, uidi il mio *diletto* figluolo, *duramente* chiouato *in quella croce*. (f. 82v)

H And whan I was awaked y saw my sone on þe crosse. (f. 41v)

Cl and when I woke agayne, þan saw I my son hangyng on hye
(Ellis 1987: 314)

Ju and whan I wakenyd I saw my sone nayled (f. 128v)

So short a sentence can have four different solutions. The vast literature on the Passion, in poetry and in prose, may have influenced the translator in his very wording, like in the case of 'hangyng on hye', used by Cl, which has no correspondent in the Latin, or the 'stremes of bloode' used by H in the following sentence:

70.7 qui tunc vultum suum sanguine manantem tunica detersit.

66

H and than my sone with hys koote wyped the stremes of bloode that ran from hym (f. 41r)

L Egli stesso colla sua propria gonnella si forbì il suo glorioso uiso, il quale per le crudeli battiture e percosse tutto era sanguinoso (f. 82r)

We see again the Italian translator at work to emphasise his text, both by the insertion of adjectives (*glorioso, crudeli*), and by the addition of a sentence, itself containing a doublet (*battiture e percosse*), which is not in the Latin, but comes quite fittingly in the context, and may be a good reminder for the reader or the listener of the text. Such procedures, although very rare in the three longer versions of the *Revelations*, are common in the English translations and compilations of Birgittine materials I have edited. It is not without interest to find them in a contemporary Italian translation. Going back to the sentence quoted, I should like to remark that the incredible repetition of possessive adjectives after the reflexive pronoun at the beginning (*egli stesso, sua propria, suo*) hints clearly at the utter solitude in which Jesus was immersed in his passion. On the other hand H gives an original solution of *sanguine manantem*, which is neither literal nor poor.

Amplification is often felt as a factor which slows down the pace of a text. The passage quoted above shows that our Italian translator knows how to use it to offer emotional details useful for contemplation. At other times he succeeds in speeding up the pace of his base text, as in the following example, where he adopts an anaphoric rhythm which is probably meant to convey an emotional response in the reader:

70.13 plurimis riuis sanguinis ex aculeis infixis decurrentibus per faciem eius et crines et oculos et barbam replentibus, ut quasi nichil nisi sanguis totum videretur.

L intanto che molti riuoli di sangue, per le punture delle spine, discendeuano per gli capelli, per la faccia, per gli occhi, e per la barba sua, intanto che quasi non si uedeua altro che sangue. (f. 82v)

H and of the prykkes many stremes of blode ran downe by hys face and alle be-bledde hys yghen and hys berde þat thyr was no thyng seyn but bloode (f. 41v)

Cl Þan þe blode ran downe by hys visage and filled his eres, his eene þen and his berde, þat þer was not almoste sene on hym bot blode (Ellis 1987: 314)

Ju The blood ran downe in his eyin, his mouthe, his chekis and on the here of his hed (f. 129r)

The same choice is visible in another passage, where the hypotactic structure of the Latin is disentangled and resolved in a paratactic sequence of short sentences, by which the dramatic tone of the text is intensified:

70.14 Me igitur discipulo suo commendata per eum,
vocem ex ymo pectoris erecto capite,
oculis in celum directis et lacrimantibus,
emisit dicens: 'Deus, Deus meus, ut quid me dereliquisti?'

L Raccomandato che m'ebbe al suo diletto discepolo,
rizzò un poco il capo
e alzò gli occhi lacrimosi al cielo,
e mandando fuori una voce disse:
'Idio mio, Idio mio, perché m'ai tu abbandonato?' (f. 83r)

H He betoke me to John hys dyssyple
by þe voyce of þe lowest part of hys brest,
and he reysed vp hys hede and hys yghen dyrected towarde hevyn,
and wepyng seyde: 'my god, my god, why hast þou forsake me?' (f. 41v)

Cl And þan he comendid me to hys discipill Jon,
wyth a voice þat was fer owte of hys breste.
þan lyft he vp hys heued, and hys eyn full of blode and teres,
and saide, 'God, my God, why has þou forsakyn me?' (Ellis 1987: 314)

Ju He comendid me to his discipyl,
he spak fro þe lowest part of his brest
letting vp his hed and his eyin to heuen
seyinge: 'myn god, myn god, whi has þou forsaken me?' (f. 129r)

The Italian translator has completely subverted the Latin clauses, save the first, which he keeps as dependent; besides he adds two words meant to enhance the affective tone of the passage, that is *diletto* and *un poco* but he cuts the phrase *ex ymo pectoris*. This phrase, on the other hand, undoubtedly because of the distance between *vocem* and *emisit*, created some problems to H and Cl, who misinterpreted it attributing the voice coming from the depth of the heart to what Jesus said to Mary, and not, as it is, to his Father. Ju has the driest rendering: he even eliminates Jesus' weeping, which is instead emphasised by Cl, who adds blood to the tears (again a memory of the 'blody teres' of so many Passion lyrics?): this is to say that Ju is not necessarily superior to Cl, as it would appear in other cases.

The visible preference for paratactic structures, both in the Italian and the English translations, does not mean that this is the necessary choice, even in a text which is mainly narrative. Here is, for example, a case where L and H make totally different choices:

70.17b Tunc ego exinanita corrui in terram

L E io uedendo questo, mancandomi tutti y sentimenti, tramortita caddi in terra. (f. 83r)

H and y was brought to nought and felle to þe erthe (f. 42r)

Cl þan fell I for fantnes downe to þe erthe (Ellis 1987: 314)

Ju Than I half ded fil to the ground (f. 129r)

Mary's swooning, foregrounded by Cl, resolved by H in two paratactic clauses, is emphatically set by L at the end of the sentence, as a consequence of what is said in the three preceding dependent clauses, of which two are a development of *exinanita*, the third, *E io uedendo questo*, reminds the reader that Mary is contemplating her dying son, and is probably meant to invite him to do the same.

Another example of the sophisticated sense of structure testified to by the Italian translator is seen in a descriptive passage:

70.19 et corpus iam mortuum demissum pendebat,
genibus autem in partem unam inclinatis,
pedes ad partem alteram super clauos quasi cardines declinabant.

L Il corpo, già morto, pendeva in giù e agrauaua.
Le ginocchia s'inchinarono da una parte,
e i piedi dall'altra parte s'inchinarono in su chioui
per la grauezza del corpo. (f. 83r)

H And hys body hyng than deede, and lefte and forsaken,
and hys knees boweng to the too syde,
and hys feete to the tothyr vppon þe harde nayles. (f. 42r)

L produces a remarkable rhythm by the use of mirroring structures – see what he does with *inclinatis*, and *declinabant*, both translated with the same word, in the same finite mood, and set in a chiastic position; and changes the Latin (he does not translate *quasi cardines*) to repeat at the end the detail of the heaviness of the dead body, which creates a sort of *inclusio*, further visualized by the repetition of *corpo*. H too works originally: he prefers an anaphoric pattern, and inserts a higher emotional tone by interpreting *demissum* as 'left and forsaken', and by adding 'harde' to the nails.

Another example shows how, while L favours echoes and rhythm, H seems to prefer simplicity and clarity, and perhaps this is the reason why in the following sentence he changes the subject, foregrounding 'the son of Mary' instead of 'his pain':

70.20 O, Domina, iam pena filii tui ad eternam suam gloriam soluta est.

L O Maria, già è passata la pena del tuo figluolo, egli già è alla sua etterna gloria (f. 83r)

H O thou lady, now ys thy sone vnbounde of hys peyne to joye (f. 42r)

Cl Lady, now ys þe payne of þi sone at an end, to his grete blis
(Ellis 1987: 314)

Ju O lady, þe payne of thy sone is now turnyd to his joye (f. 129r)

Small details may catch the attention of the reader. One wonders, for example, why L emphasised *iam* so greatly, or why the English versions mark 'joy' instead of 'glory'. I suggest that, although apparently very different, both responses share the same emotional attitude, that is the sense of relief following the end of hard suffering. The English solution may also have been suggested by the easier and more common pain/joy contrast compared with pain/glory.

To conclude this section on ch. 70, I would like to quote an example from the final part of the chapter, where the Virgin gives a detailed description of the physical beauty of Jesus. The whole passage is literally 'massacred' in the poor summary given by Ju, receives diligent consideration in Cl and H, while it is the occasion for L to deploy his usual ability to invent new architectural patterns:

70

70.25 Iusti vero spirituali consolatione consolabantur,
sed et mali a tristicia seculi tanto tempore, quo eum videbant, releuabantur.
Vnde et dolentes dicere consueverunt:
'Eamus et filium Marie videamus, ut saltem tanto tempore releuemur'.

L I giusti uedendolo erano consolati di spirituale allegrezza:
i cattivi e i rei erano consolati d'ogni mondana trestitia,
tanto quanto il uedeano.
Onde coloro ch'erano malinconiosi e afflicti usavano di dire:
'Andiamo e uedremo il figluolo di Maria,
però che mentre che noi il uedremo,
saremo rallegrati e rileuati da nostri dolori e malinconie'. (f. 83v)

H The ryghtful wer comforted wyth goostly comforte,
and the wykked from wordly heuynes and releued for that tyme;
wherfor þe sorovful seyde:
'Go we and see we the sone of Mary
that we may be releued of oure hevynes'. (f. 42v)

The Italian version is remarkable for the nice net of parallelisms
created by lexical repetition, not to speak of the perfect mirroring,
even at the rhythmic level of the first two lines. The translator marks
his independence from the Latin original while keeping some
suggestions derived from the base text. For example, while he eliminates the Latin echo *consolatione consolabantur*, he creates one of his
own by translating two different Latin verbs, *consolabantur* and
releuabantur by an identical *erano consolati*, while the word
allegrezza used for *consolatione* is echoed by *rallegrati* inserted in the
last clause. The same happens with *dolentes* expanded into a clause
coloro ch'erano malinconiosi e afflicti and repeated at the end in the
echoing doublet *da nostri dolori e malinconie*. The incredible
expansion of *ut saltem tanto tempore releuemur* at the end of the
sentence is a fine example of the practice of repetitions and
explicitations frequently found in the English spiritual tracts derived
from the *Revelations*, a practice which suggests, as I have remarked in
my editions of these tracts, the probable oral use of these translations.[12] H is less sensitive to structure, and prefers to follow the Latin

---

12   See ch. 1: 45, ch. 13: 335, and the introductory remarks accompanying my edi-
      tions of Birgittine translations (Pezzini 1986, 1988, 1992, 1993a, and 1994b).

closely, except for the addition of 'oure hevynes' at the end. Cl translates rather originally:

> Cl And þe gude men had, ouer þat, gostly likynge.
> And þai þat were bad, for þe tyme þat þai saw hym,
> were þai neuer so hevy,
> þai were cumforthed,
> insomykyll þat þai were wont for to say,
> 'Go we and se Mary sone, þat we may be so longe esyd'.

(Ellis 1987: 314-315)

At the end of this examination of the two translations of Book IV of the *Liber celestis* I would like to propose a tentative evaluation. In terms of completeness, verbal and structural variety, and use of rhetorical skills, the Italian version soars above the English one. But one should remember that the same qualities that have been evidenced in the Italian translation of an entire book are also to be found, as I have just remarked, in some English translations of shorter pieces or in the compilations. And above all this does not mean that the rendering in Harley 4800 should be dismissed as 'poor' or thought of as lacking any interest: the examples given have shown, I hope, that the translation is correct, and if it favours parataxis and lexical simplicity, this is not to the detriment of the text, which emerges as readable and enjoyable. The difference is simply in style.

To show how the Harley translator is far from being a 'poor soul', and to rescue this manuscript from W.P. Cumming's merciless judgement, I shall end by quoting two very short sentences. The first shows the clever solution of an adjective into a prepositional phrase:

> 13.2 eciam infidelem Cesarem eleuauit ad alciorem gradum.

> L lo infedele imperadore leuò a più alto grado (f. 29v)

> H he reysed þe Emperour oute of hys mysbeleeue to an hygher degree (f. 17r)

The other triggers a spark of rustic vivacity:

> 23.1 Ille est, qui dicit se me diligere set vertit ad me posteriora, quando seruit michi.

> L Colui dice che ama me, ma uolgemi le spalle quando mi serue. (f. 47r)

H Yender man ys he that that seyth he loueth me, but he turneth to me hys bak
and hys ars whan he serueth me. (f. 31r)

The speaker is our Lady. Perhaps the soul of W. P. Cumming, now in
the glory of heavenly life, would have appreciated, at least for this
case, a 'cutting' more than an amplification.

Such a difference between what Cumming thought of the
English translations of Birgittine texts and the opinions I have
expressed in this chapter, can be accounted for on the basis of two
points. One is that he did not minutely analyse the texts he was
speaking about; the other is that as times have changed, so have our
ideas about translation. I would like to stress that there is a necessary
circularity between these two reasons, and that the more we edit and
study medieval translations, the more properly we can theorise about
translational techniques in the Middle Ages. This is the point where I
stand, agreeing with Gianfranco Folena (1991) that an adequate
historical investigation of translational practices is needed to
counterbalance the inundation of theoretical studies on translation
which we have had since the 40s.[13] To use a geographical metaphor,
this is to say that the discovery of new lands and the refining of the
maps go hand in hand with the invention of more sophisticated
instruments to analyse and understand the territory.

---

13   See Folena (1991: viii): "Da quando negli anni Quaranta gli studi teorici sulla
     traduzione hanno ricevuto un forte impulso dalle ricerche applicate alla tradu-
     zione automatica e la scienza della traduzione è caduta prevalentemente sotto
     il dominio della linguistica, c'è stata in questo campo un'alluvione teorica, al-
     la quale non hanno corrisposto adeguati approfondimenti storici: scarsi e
     sporadici restano gli studi sulla storia della traduzione e delle idee relative."

CHAPTER 3

Two ME Translations of Aelred of Rievaulx's *De Institutione Inclusarum*: The Varieties of Medieval Translational Practices[1]

Although it is well known that many medieval texts, at least in England, are translations of some sort, the study of medieval literature as translation has gradually come into focus only in the last two decades. This makes it a very promising field of research, as confirmed by the growing number of conferences and publications devoted to the matter. A milestone in this direction was Roger Ellis's initiative in organising in 1987 the first of what was to become a successful series of conferences entitled "The medieval translator: the theory and practice of translation in the Middle Ages" (Ellis: 1989 and 1991). The second and explicative part of the title is there to proclaim that no serious theory can be elaborated unless we first, and continually analyse the texts in detail. In this respect a virtuous circularity can be established, in which, as in any process of research, conclusions reached at a certain point become the premises of further developments.

Accordingly, I shall divide my study into two parts: the first will be devoted to presenting some generalizations on how to consider and evaluate a medieval translation; in the second I shall apply some of these interpretative criteria to a few selected passages taken from two late medieval translations of a Latin work written at the middle of the twelfth century, Aelred of Rievaulx's *De Institutione Inclusarum*. Although what I am going to say could in many cases be applied to any medieval translation, the scope of my contribution is limited to religious texts, as this is the field on which this volume concentrates.

---

1   An earlier and shorter version of this chapter was first published in Iamartino (1998: 81-95).

1. Some general considerations on medieval translations

If we look at many modern editions of medieval texts which are translations, the first, and quite often the only thing which is considered in the footnotes is to show whether there are omissions or expansions of the original text. This approach suggests that what lurks behind such mental attitude is the conviction that omissions are the product of ignorance or lack of real interest in the text on the part of the translator, and expansions are read as various forms of paraphrase, by which it is understood that they could easily be reduced to a more sober form, or omitted altogether, without any loss of whatever kind. This may seem a very harsh judgement, but I can support my statement by simply quoting what the editors of the text I am going to analyse, Ayto/Barratt, say of the two ME versions they publish:

> The Vernon translation is as long as or longer than its original, owing largely to the translator's diffuse and expansive style; the Bodley version, however, is a far more drastic and thorough-going redaction of the Latin – abbreviation, conflation and omission are extensive. (Ayto/Barratt 1984: xiii)

This is all they have to say in an Introduction of 55 pages. It is true that in the numerous footnotes they indicate and at times try to explain what differs from the Latin, but here too it becomes clear that their attitude to the text as translation is rather unsatisfactory. Just to give an example, in note 200 (p. 110), they write:

> wyckede and vnclene: L. merely *inutiles*

A closer look at the Latin, and a comparison with the Vernon translation, invites another conclusion (p. 30, 199-200):

> Nihil enim magis cogitationes excludit inutiles, uel compescit lascivas [...]
> [...] for ther is noþyng þat so put awey wyckede and vnclene þouȝtes

The translator has in fact discarded the idea of useless (*inutiles*) thoughts, and chosen to emphasize by a doublet the unclean (*lascivas*) ones. Besides the misinterpretation, which may be due to a hasty annotation, the example shows that while it is rather risky to analyse a translation simply in terms of words ignoring the larger unit, it is above all important to inquire why some choices are made. In the case given, for example, I would suggest that, while Aelred was considering two deadly sins, sloth (*inutiles*) and lechery (*lascivas*), the translator is only interested in the second, which he chooses to select and emphasize by a doublet. Incidentally, a quick look at the quotation chosen calls seriously into question the judgement pronounced by the editors, who label the Vernon translator's style as "diffuse and expansive".[2]

The remark is also a warning and a reminder of how difficult it is to evaluate the type and the quality of a translation, and how risky it may be to express sweeping generalizations. The case examined suggests that random annotations can easily be misleading, false, or meaningless, especially when they are hastily made on single words. But even the consideration of larger units, which is certainly more correct, does not always allow general conclusions to be inferred. A better method would be to keep an eye on the entire text, and list for example all omissions and expansions in order to see of what type they are, and where there is any consistency it may be possible to induce by whom, for whom and to what purpose the translation was made. Any conclusion of this kind should obviously be supplemented by and checked with any information we can gather about the people who ordered, purchased, owned and bequeathed the texts. But here too, especially when we are in the presence of huge and miscellaneous manuscripts, as the ones in which the two translations under scrutiny are contained, it is practically impossible to reach any conclusive assessment.[3]

---

2   In fact the same editors affirm elsewhere that "The Vernon version is in general a very close, almost verbatim translation" (Ayto/Barratt 1984: xxxiii). On a certain carelessness and other flaws of this edition see the severe criticism expressed by Hendrix (1989): he concludes that "cette introduction ne satisfait guère". For a more favourable review see the brief notice of Dahood (1987).

3   On the Vernon MS, and its companion, the Simeon MS, A. I. Doyle says that "It is likely that such important religious as well as seculars had an active share in the compilation as they must have been called upon for assistance in

When the text is short, as in the case of Latin liturgical hymns, the list of the changes in the original is easily drawn, and a careful reading of these alterations allows many interesting observations, for example about the new use of the hymns as quotations in a sermon and the extent to which this change of context operates in many of the translator's choices (see ch. 9). For works of larger scale it is a bit harder to reach clear and homogeneous conclusions, but it is possible, for example, to infer that the presence of a considerable number of didactic expansions implies a less sophisticated audience than that envisaged by the original text.

Here I am not going to analyse in full detail the two translations of Aelred's treatise, since this would be largely beyond the scope of this chapter. My more modest aim is to show different possibilities of interpretation, which may be taken either as a series of caveats, or as indications of the various ways by which it is possible to evaluate a translation. To look at the text in itself is clearly not enough: the textual analysis is only the third and final stage of a process which is preceded by two other series of considerations. To illustrate this process I shall gather my remarks under three sub-headings: the first concerns the mental background of the medieval translator; the second shows how the text 'travels' and what is implied in its movements; the third points to the text itself in terms of words and structures.

1.1. The medieval translator's mental background

In what can only be a concise summary[4] I would characterize the figure of the medieval translator by focussing on three points: (a) his attitudes to the source text; (b) his idea of translation; and, consequently, (c) of his role as a translator.

---

the provision of texts. The persons for whom all this was done must have been of rank as well as devotion, and indeed wealth, to sustain the cost of these books [...]. They would have suited convents as well as individuals, and wherever they went they must have been prominent pieces of furniture and means of both communal and private occupation" (Doyle 1951: II, 171-172).

4   For a more detailed presentation with suitable examples of Parts 1.1. and 1.2. see the Introduction to this volume.

a. The source text tends to be thought of as a quarry. It may be translated only in part, or parts of it may be used to compile new works. The frequent modular quality of medieval texts favours this attitude and its practicability. The sense of belonging to a common spiritual and literary tradition also assists in the various operations by which old books are re-worked to create new ones. Connected with and derived from this mental attitude is the widely practised habit of expanding and glossing texts both with other texts or by the use of reference to the common core of ideas, beliefs, images, and so on. While in some texts, especially those of 'scientific quality' (Scripture, canon law, philosophy, etc.), the gloss is written separately, and kept graphically distinct, in others of more popular and practical grain, expansions obtained by a large use of referentiality are silently incorporated in the text itself (see ch. 11).

b. The type of translation to be chosen depends largely on the audience the translator has in mind, and on the possible use of his new text, as we shall see in the second series of remarks. While a literal rendering is more likely to occur in a short quotation, expansions are to be expected when the text is prepared for reading aloud: oral delivery is paramount to explain quite a number of the translator's choices (Pezzini 1992, 1994b) and ch. 1. Omissions are predictably more likely to occur in longer works for various reasons, including the sheer fatigue of the work. The means chosen has also some bearing on the translation: the choice to cast the Latin quatrain of a hymn into an English quatrain or into a royal stanza has very different consequences on the type of the text which is produced.

c. As everybody knows the status of the medieval writer is shifting and not well defined: he can be at the same time author, scribe, translator, compiler, interpreter and glossator. In this light, and in the light of the other two points, modern ideas of 'faithfulness' to or 'respect' of the source text, when applied to medieval translation are largely meaningless, and should not impinge on the evaluation of texts produced in that time.

1.2. How a text travels and changes

The very word 'trans-lation' reminds us that the text 'moves', or better is trans-ferred to something which is new.[5] What is new is obviously not only the language into which a text is translated. To draw an imaginary map in order to define the various itineraries and travels of medieval works of literature three areas at least should be considered: the genre, the audience, the use.

As far as religious texts are concerned, the genre can be further and broadly subdivided in four types:

a. liturgical hymns and religious poetry in general;
b. narrative texts such as lives of Christ or of the saints, and the vast literature of *exempla*;
c. sermons;
d. treatises of spiritual instruction.

These genres may at times overlap, or coexist in the same work, since an *exemplum* can, and normally does occur within a sermon or in a spiritual tract. On the other hand, it is not always easy to clearly distinguish in a Life of Christ the meditation from the narration: in fact passages may be selected from a book of revelations to compile both a *Life of Our Lady* (see chapter 13) and a tract of pious instructions (Pezzini 1992, Hogg 1993). The difference in genre, however, must be considered, since every genre has its rhetoric, and to transfer a text from one genre to another implies changes which may be substantial.

The other two factors can also be of some importance as regards the influence they may have upon a translator's choices. As for the

---

5   See what Ellis (1989: 3) remarks commenting on the ME word *ouyr-berynge* for 'translation': "It is a literal resolution of the Latin (trans = over, across; latio = carrying, bearing). Early occurrences of the word in English, in the Wycliffite Bible, refer to the removal of an object from one place to another (a tent, a neighbour's boundary marker, the life of the wicked man) or to the destruction of a physical or a moral state (the overthrow of an empire, the forgiveness of sin). Translation, that is, changes an existing boundary, turns one thing into another, refashions an original as totally as God's forgiveness annihilates sin."

audience, the transfer can be mainly from a monastic chapter house to the hall of a lay household, from an aristocratic to a popular milieu. The transfer of use may be from the choir to the pulpit, from a rule written for monks living a community life to a manual conceived as spiritual reading for everybody, from a text provided for personal meditation to a tract, or a legend, envisaged for oral delivery.

1.3. Textual analysis

With these two series of premises well established in our mind, we can then approach the third and final stage of analysis, that is the text itself in its very matter of words and structures. I would like to start this section by frankly avowing that the more I edit and analyse medieval translations, the less confident I become of the tools I use. Or, to put it in more favourable terms, I increasingly feel the need to refine the same tools while the growing variety of texts and of the translational choices found in them suggests more articulate, especially more positive, criteria of evaluation. This is the reason why at the beginning of this chapter I said that theory and practice must go hand in hand if we want to do justice to the old texts we study.

I do not want to enter into much detail here. What I want to say is that the refinement of interpretation is greatly helped when there is the possibility of comparing two or more different translations of the same text, whether in the same or in different languages (see chapter 2). Contrast, as is well known, has always been an excellent method for advancing knowledge.

Just to give a couple of examples, I would like to question, if necessary, two of the most common assumptions when judging a translation: the idea that abbreviations involve only a loss, or that expansions are superfluous additions of material not strictly necessary. Omissions may be casual or conscious, clever or stupid, caused by fatigue or carelessness, or decided to better emphasize the essential points of a sentence or of an entire paragraph. On the other hand, expansions may be used both at lexical and structural level to explain a difficult word, to clarify a point, to parallel a sentence or a clause.

An identical need can produce two contrasting effects. Take, for example, the semantic weakness or indeterminacy of ME vocabulary:

on the one hand, this drawback can be repaired by amplification through a generous use of doublets in order to convey the meaning more surely; on the other, it may require a lexical reduction obtained by the repetition of the same word while the original Latin has a greater variety. To say that ME vocabulary was poorer than the Latin, although historically true, is not always a viable explanation for the choice of a reduced range of words: in fact at times, as I will show in an example taken from the two translations under scrutiny, the opposite is what happens. This also means that 'variety' and 'simplicity' should not be read in terms of a more or less clever choice, or used to determine the quality of a translation.

Before ending this first part, I should like to mention a factor which cannot be critically evaluated, and consequently is regularly forgotten or discarded: I mean the human element. To copy, and/or to translate in the Middle Ages was a terrible fatigue, a work which in the monasteries was often imposed as a penance. We can hardly realise how painful it was to work in a medieval scriptorium, a pain which is indirectly testified in the immense sense of relief which is visible, for example, in the following colophon to a copy of the second part of St Thomas Aquinas's *Summa Theologica* found in an Oxford MS of the fourteenth century:

> Explicit secunda pars summe fratris thome de aquino ord. fratr. predic. longissima, prolixissima et tediosissima scribenti; Deo gratias, Deo gratias, et iterum Deo gratias.

The need for relief could take strange ways though, as in the request expressed by the scribe at the end of a penitential treatise, who wrote not exactly in a penitential mood: "Pro pena scribentis detur pulchra puella."

The hardness of translating and copying explains errors of various kind, and may at times be the reason why longer works tend to be drastically reduced to a summary. Length and fatigue are certainly very prosaic factors, but one wonders whether a composer chooses to put the *Agnus Dei* of a Mass to the same music of *Kyrie eleison* because he wants to bring the work back to its beginning so as to draw a sort of celestial circle, or simply because he is fed up with his work. In the same vein the painful work of translation could have various

82

results which can be differently explained. In some cases it produced what has been called 'poetry by mistake'. More generally, this factor should be taken into account by the modern reader to help him not to be precipitate in judging whether a shortening is due to a deliberate choice or to the dullness of the brain. It is only kind, however, not to forget this double possibility, and to be ready to forgive when the error is evident.

2. Aelred of Rievaulx's *De Institutione Inclusarum* in two ME translations

Aelred of Rievaulx's *De Institutione Inclusarum* (Instructions for the Recluses) enjoyed a great popularity in the Middle Ages, being often copied and translated; in England, in particular, it influenced the author of the *Ancrene Riwle* to a considerable extent. The work, written in 1163-1164, is a short treatise in form of a Letter addressed by Aelred to his sister, who was a recluse. It is usually divided in three parts, following a distinction prompted by the author himself:

1. the external rule of the anchoress's life: her relations with the outside world, her clothes and diet, the division and occupation of her time;
2. the spiritual life, or interior rule, mostly concerned with chastity, humility, and charity;
3. theory and practice of meditation on God's benefits past, present and to come: this section, particularly the highly emotional meditations on the gospel, is the most original and had wide and far-reaching influences on the Christian meditative practice of the Middle Ages and Renaissance.[6]

There are two ME translations of this work: one extant in the Vernon MS (V), belonging to the end of the fourteenth century; another in the

---

6   For a fine analysis of the main themes of the work, see O'Connell (1988, esp. 58-69).

MS Oxford Bodley 423 (B), datable to a period between 1430 and 1480. While the Bodley version is clearly connected with religious life, and the manuscript in which it is extant has been described as a "Carthusian collection", the Vernon version is, according to its editors, "clearly written primarily to be read aloud, possibly to a court or community; it might have belonged to a community of nuns, or, given the 'opulent' quality of the manuscript, to a lay person, either a devout and aristocratic lay woman, or else a highly-placed secular ecclesiastic" (Ayto/Barratt 1984: xviii).

The first thing to be noticed is that the Vernon version lacks the first part of the work. I think that the most convincing reason for this omission is the new audience for which the translation is provided: was it a community of nuns or some pious lady living a kind of religious life in her house, they were probably not interested in the external rules of a recluse, but only in the spiritual instructions of the treatise.

To provide sufficient variety, I have selected four examples from the first part to present some choices of the Bodley translator, two from the second part and two from the third: in these cases Vernon and Bodley are cross-compared.[7] With this choice I mean also to analyse passages written in different kinds of prose together with the different type of response we can find in the translation.

(1)   Iam pluribus annis exigis a me, soror, ut secundum modum vivendi quem arripuisti pro Christo, certam tibi formulam tradam, ad quam et mores tuos dirigere et necessaria religioni possis exercitia ordinare. Utinam a sapientiore id peteres, et impetrares, qui non coniectura qualibet sed experientia didicisset, quod alios doceret. Ego certe qui tibi et carne et spiritu frater sum, quoniam non possum negare quicquid iniungis, faciam quod hortaris, et ex diversis patrum institutis, aliqua quae tibi necessaria videntur excerpens, ad componendum exterioris hominis statum, certam tibi regulam tradere curabo, pro loco et tempore quaedam adiciens, et spiritualia corporalibus, ubi utile visum fuerit, interserens. (1, 1-16)

B: Suster, thou hast ofte axed of me a forme of lyuyng accordyng to thyn estat, inasmuche as thou art enclosed. That wolde Iesu thou haddist axid it of suche oon as coude haue fulfilled thyn desire. Natheles after that simple

---

7   Latin quotations, by paragraph and line numbers, are from the critical edition published by Talbot (Hoste/Talbot 1971); ME quotations, by page and line numbers, are taken from Ayto/Barratt (1984).

felynge that God hath youen me, I shal write to the a forme gadert out of holy
fadirs tradiciouns afore-tymes (p. 1, 5-9)

The example, taken from the very beginning of the treatise, shows
immediately how starkly the Latin text is reduced. The author
translates the title *De Institutione Inclusarum* as "a rule and a forme of
lyuynge perteynyng to a recluse": this clearly indicates that the
audience is not changed and we may suppose that the translator wants
to keep the same intention as his source text. The style instead is
remarkably different. It is as if the translator had decided to select
only what is really substantial, and he succeeds in maintaining the
three main points of the introductory paragraph: the request, the
confession of humility, and the intention of writing a rule gathered out
of the traditions of the holy fathers; the mention of Aelred's family
link with his sister has been simply cut off as irrelevant, although the
term "suster" is maintained, given its known spiritual meaning in a
Christian context. It is true that there are large omissions, but this does
not mean that the content of the source text is blurred: the result can
be called a 'summary translation' where all that matters remains intact.

(2)   Primum igitur oportet te scire qua causa, quave ratione huiusmodi vita ab
        antiquis vel instituta sit vel usurpata. Sunt quidam, quibus inter multos vivere
        perniciosum est. Sunt et alii quibus et si non perniciosum, est tamen
        dispendiosum. Sunt et nonnulli quibus nihil horum timendum est, sed
        secretius habitare magis aestimant fructuosum. (2, 1-6)

        B: First the behoueth to knowe why that suche a solitary lyf was ordeyned.
        Somme ther wern to whom it was ful perilous to lyue among many. Ther were
        also somme [to whom], although it were not perilous to lyue amonge many,
        natheles it was ful greuous. And many ther wern whiche dradden noon of the
        too but chosen this lyf as a lyf moost fruytful to helthe of soule. (p. 1,10-15)

This passage, which follows immediately the first quotation, shows
that the translator can adopt a completely opposite choice when
abbreviations are not practicable, for example in a compact list where
each item is important as is the case here. I should like to make two
other remarks. One concerns the sense of structure and of its hidden
virtuality which is revealed by the translator: the Latin sequence
quidam... alii... nonnulli... is reworked and appears in English as
"somme... somme... many...", with the resulting effect of putting a

85

dramatic stress on the third group of people choosing a solitary life to which belongs the addressee of the treatise. The second remark is about the nice solution of a dense Latin expression:

> secretius habitare magis aestimant fructuosum
> chosen this lyf as a lyf moost fruytful to helthe of soule

The English text is certainly more simple and clear than the Latin and this is a good example of the way medieval translators often used to provide an easier text to their less aristocratic readers.

(3)   Sic cum discedere ab invicem hora compulerit, inclusa voluptatibus, anus cibariis onerata recedit. (2, 32-34)

> B: so that atte last the recluse is fulfilled with lust and likynge, bakbitynge, sclaundre and hatrede, and the tother with mete and drinke. (p. 1, 34-36)

Example (3) in a sense confirms and amplifies what I have just remarked. The Bodley translator is not only able to abbreviate the text, he can also expand it in order to make explicit what in the source is so concise as to escape attention. In this sense "lust and likynge, bakbitynge, sclaundre and hatrede" for *voluptatibus* and "with mete and drinke" for *cibariis*, are not redundant amplifications, but more forceful and pictorial expressions of what was to be kept in the mind of the reader or listener. Incidentally, the first list is not invented by the translator, but it is only a summary and a reminder of what the text says in the previous lines.

(4)   Cella vertitur in postribulum, et dilatato qualibet arte foramine, aut illa egreditur, aut adulter ingreditur. Infelicitas haec, ut saepe probatum est, pluribus tam viris quam feminis in hoc nostro saeculo communis est. (2, 44-47)

> B: This wrecchidnes hath often be seen of hem that han ben enclosed, by the whiche the wyndowe hath be maad moor, that euereyther might come in or out to other, soo that atte last of a recluse or of an ancresse selle is maad a bordel hous. (p. 2, 43-46)

Example (4) is given to prove that the Bodley translator is not only able in abbreviating or expanding his text, but he can also skilfully master the organization of different elements in a structure. In this passage he reduces the many clauses of the Latin into four segments, and follows an order of its own, so that the Latin sequence in which (1) the cell becomes a brothel through (2) the enlarging of the recluse's window and (3) the consequent possibility of going in and out, with a final consideration on (4) the wretchedness of this situation, appears in a reversed order in the English version, with the effect of emphasizing the sad transformation of a monastic cell into a brothel. The omission of any mention to men (*adulter* and *viris* are not translated) may point to a female readership envisaged by the translator.

(5)   Vnde non parum pudet quorundam impudentiae, qui cum in sordibus senuerint, nec sic suspectarum personarum volunt carere consortio. Cum quibus quod dictu nefas est eodem lectulo cubantes, inter amplexus et oscula de sua castitate se dicunt esse securos, quod frigescente corpore ad scelus perficiendum tepescentia membra deficiant. Infelices isti et prae cunctis mortalibus miseri, quibus cum desiit sceleris perpetrandi facultas, adhuc manet in ipsa foeditate voluntas, nec quiescit tempore desiderium, quamvis ei frigiditas neget effectum. (19, 589-598)

V: þerfore hit is gret schame of manye mannes woodschype, why[c]e þat whanne þey haue lyued al here lyf in sty[n]kynde fulþe, ȝit in here oolde age þey nulleþ not wit-drawe hem fro þe companye of suspekt persones, bote seyn þat þey ben siker ynow of hem-self, for þat þey veleþ here body sumdel akeled; ant þerfore þey spare not to taken hem nyȝt and day to occasiones of sunne. Bote among alle resonable creatures þise beþ foles and acursed wrecches, in þe whyche, alþouȝ þat myȝt lacke, ȝit wyl and lust dureþ in hem of stench of synne; and so fowl desir ne resteþ not in hem, þey feblenesse of age denye power of dede, as þey seyn. (p. 30, 178-187)

B: what shulden we say of hem that holden hem so seker that, though they hadden oportunyte, leyser, tyme or space, thei witen wet thei shold not falle? Certeyn I dar wel seie, thay ben deceyued, for though the hete be quenched in somme, the wille and the desire is not so. (p. 12, 460-464)

With (5) we come to a part of the work which is common to both translations. A cursory look at the text given shows immediately the different style of Vernon and Bodley. Vernon's expansions create an overall effect of a solemn pace and are normally used to inflate the text emotionally. So *sordibus* becomes "stynkynde fulthe", *foeditate* is explained as "stench of synne", *infelices* is rendered as "foles and acursed wrecches", and *desiderium* is turned into a "so fowl desir". It must be said that the tendency to make explicit what remains implicit in the source text, and to emphasize feelings and actions, especially when they are bad, is common stuff in this literature of spiritual instruction. On the other hand, this moralistic language floats so to speak in an abstract atmosphere, since one cannot fail to notice that some very concrete and visual details of Aelred's text, which describe people lying sinfully together in bed, kissing and embracing each other (*eodem lectulo cubantes, inter amplexus et oscula...*) are delicately omitted and watered down into a much weaker "occasiones of sunne". We have what would seem a contradictory procedure, by which the source text is inflated in one respect, and deflated in another.

The Bodley version is in this case extremely concise. The translator has decided to select the main point only, a warning against presumption. Of the original he translates the best, that is the powerful four-clause sentence:

> quibus cum desit sceleris perpetrandi facultas,
> adhuc manet in ipsa foeditate voluntas,
> nec quiescit tempore desiderium,
> quamvis ei frigiditas neget effectum.

> though the hete be quenched in somme,
> the wille and the desire is not so.

One would say that the force of this statement is its brevity: one verb, "quenched", against four in the Latin, whose meaning is emphasized by its relation to the image evoked by "heat", in which we find a shrewd combination of the *facultas* and, through an oblique choice, the *frigiditas* of the original.

(6)   Nihil enim magis cogitationes excludit inutiles, vel compescit lascivas quam meditatio verbi Dei, cui sic animum suum virgo debet assuescere, ut aliud volens, non possit aliud meditari. Cogitanti de Scripturis somnus obrepat, evigilanti primum aliquid de Scripturis occurrat, dormientis somnia haerens memoriae aliqua de Scripturis sententia condiat. (20, 609-615)

V: For þer is noþyng þat so put awey wyckede and vnclene þouȝtes as dooþ good ocupacioun in holy scripture, to þe whyche a good womman, and specially a mayde, schulde so vse al here herte and wit þat, þeiȝ sche wolde, sche mowe not þenke bote on Godes lawe. Let slep fynden here þenkynde on holi scripture; whan sche awakeþ of here slep, let renne to here mende sum clause of holy techyngge; and whil þe slep is on here, let cleue to here ribbes sum sentence of holy wrytyngges, þat mowe moor surliche kepe here menbrys, and also boþe body and soule in here slep. (pp. 30-31, 199-208)

B: for ther is no thinge that ouercometh so sone the fende as doth redynge of deuoute thinge and prayer and meditacyon of Cristes passyon. A mayde shuld so be occupied vpon oon of these thre, prayer, meditacion, or redynge, that though she were stured to do vnlauful thinges, she shuld not be suffred for remors of conscience. Vse wel this remedye, that whether thou slepe or wake, thy mynde be euere vpon som sentence of holy writ or vpon som seyntes lyf, for it is a souerayne remedy ayenst temptacyon. (p. 12, 468-475)

This passage has some interesting features, both at the historical and lexical level. Aelred's text focusses on the meditation of the word of God (*meditatio verbi Dei*) as a powerful resource in order to withstand bad thoughts and temptations. He gives force and strength to his argument by repeating three times the word *Scriptura*, by which he clearly means the Holy Bible, and that alone. The Vernon version makes an opposite choice, using "holy scripture, holy techyngge, and holy wryttyngges" respectively. This is a case where a richer English vocabulary is used against one Latin word. But are the three English words to be taken as synonyms? One would say so, especially if we consider that the three words are identically qualified by the repetition of "holy".

The Bodley version points to another direction. Here the *meditatio verbi Dei* has become "redynge of deuoute thinge and prayer and meditacyon of Cristys passyon". Does it mean, as the editors comment, that in the fifteenth century the reading of the Bible in the vernacular is suspect and certainly not encouraged by the ecclesiastical leaders (Ayto/Barratt 1984: 82, note to 469-470)? Not necessarily so, since at the end of the passage the translator suggests to keep the mind "vpon som sentence of holy writ". What is more probably true is that this version is a witness to a few shifts in spirituality which occurred between the twelfth century, when in the monastic milieu the Bible was the central reading, and the fifteenth century, when an emerging female and lay readership was educated to read preferably other pious matters such as tracts and lives of the saints, while the narrative of the Passion had become the favourite subject of biblical meditation and the very heart of Christian devotion.

We may notice in passing that by a repetition not in the original the Bodley versions 'includes' more clearly the whole passage in the literature of the "remedies against temptations", which are mentioned at the beginning and at the end of the paragraph. The final addition of the Vernon version follows the same line.

(7)   Sed iam mane facto traditur ad Pilatum. Ibi accusatur et tacet, quondam tamquam ouis ad occisionem ducitur, et sicut agnus coram tondente se, non aperuit os suum. Vide, attende quomodo stat ante praesidem, inclinato capite, demissis oculis, uultu placido, sermone raro, paratus ad opprobria et ad uerbera promptus.

Scio non potes ulterius sustinere, nec dulcissimum dorsum eius flagellis atteri, nec facies alapis caedi, nec tremedum illud caput spinis coronari, nec dexteram quae caelum fecit et terram arundine dehonestari, tuis oculis aspicere poteris.

Ecce educitur flagellatus, portans spineam coronam et purpureum vestimentum. Et dicit Pilatus: Ecce homo. Vere homo est. Quis dubitet? Testes sunt plagae virgarum, livor ulcerum, foeditas sputorum. Iam nunc agnosce, Zabule, quia homo est. (31, 1129-1143)

V: *Bote now, suster, forþermore* on þe morwe *þi spouse Crist* is itake *treterously* to Pilat. þer he is accused, and he halt his pees, and as a schep þat is ilad to his deþ, or as a lomb þat is on scheryngge, riȝt so he ne openede not his mouþ. *Avyse þe inwardly* and tak tent how *bonerly* he stant be-fore þe iugge, wit his hed inclined, wit his eȝen icast adoun, wit good chiere and fiewe wurdes, al redy *for þi sake* to dispysingge, *al redy* to *harde* betyngge.

I am siker, *suster*, þu miȝt not longe suffre þis, *þu miȝt not suffer* his comely ryg be *so* to-torn wit schurges, his *gracious* face to be bouyd wit bofattes, his wurschipful hed to be corouned wit *scharpe* thornes *to þe brayn*, his riȝt hand, þat made heuen and irþe, be dishonest[ed] wit a ryed; *I wot wel þu miȝt not longe dure* to see þis wit þyn eȝen.

Bote ȝit napeles behald, after al þis he is ibrout out *al forbled* and beten, beryngge a coroune of þornes *on his heed*, and a purpre garnement *on his body*: and þanne seyt Pilat *to þe Iewes*: Ecce homo – 'Lo, hir is þe man.' Iwis, *wrecche*, a man he is: who douteþ hit? þe *harde* betyngge of ȝouȝre *scharpe* ȝerdes, þe wannesse of þe woundes, þe felþe of ȝouȝre *stynnkynde* spatelynge witnesseþ wel þat he is a man. (p. 47, 874-891)

B: Beholde now and se hou he stondeth as a meke lombe before the iuge, bowynge down his heed and his eyen, spekynge fewe [wordes], redy to suffer repreues and betynge. Se than hou his face is buffeted, his heed is crowned with thornes *and his hondes despitously bounden with bondes*. I woot wel thou mayst not suffer this, *natheles yit loke vp*, with thyn *wepynge* eyen

(p. 21, 838-843)

To choose a passage from the meditation on the Passion looks particularly promising, in view of the dramatic potentialities of the subject. Aelred's pace is speedy, playing on short and essential sentences; the drama is suggested in the presence around Christ of Pilate, the devil, and the unnamed crowd of the Jews. Vernon's translation intensifies everything, as a cursory look at the additions marked in italics can show: emotional adjectives and adverbs abound, repetitions ("all ready" twice for one *paratus*, and "you may not suffer" or "endure" repeated three times for one *sustinere*) are used to enhance the affective participation of the reader, consistently addressed as "suster", who is reminded that Christ is her "spouse", against which her response looks the more ungrateful. What is more interesting is that, in the dramatized scene of Pilate's showing of the tortured body of Christ, the mention of the devil (*Zabule*) disappears, substituted by the Jews who, besides being specifically named, seem to take his place as incapable of recognising Jesus as the Son of God, and are directly addressed through the repeated "your" prefixed to the mention of the scourges and the spittling. Any Christian reader cannot fail to recognise himself as the actual addressee of this reproach.

In the Bodley starkly reduced version we find, surprisingly one would say, a kind of restraint, and while Vernon displays the meditative quality of the text by ample elaboration rich in figurative and affective details, he adopts the opposite procedure, giving a mere list of parts of Jesus' suffering body on which the imagination of the reader is supposed to expand. Both methods are well-known in the Christian tradition: the second is, for instance, the one used by Ignatius of Loyola in his *Spiritual Exercises*. But a further and closer consideration shows that this 'restraint' is partial and only apparent. In fact, while on the one hand this translator, as already seen, tends to reduce the original text, in other cases he too may expand, as here, where he adds to the Latin the mention of "his hondes despitously bounden with bondes", and encourages the reader to overcome his reluctance before the Passion scene by inviting him to look it up with "weeping" eyes.

(8)　　Sedet pro tribunali iudex, prolata est sententia, iam propriam portans crucem ducitur ad mortem. O spectaculum! Videsne? *Ecce principatus super humerum eius* (Is 9:6). Haec est enim *virga aequitatis, virga regni eius* (Ps 44:7). (31, 1149-1153)

V: *Now, naþeles, þe false* iugge *Pilat* is *sollennely* in þe jugge-sege, *Ihesu stant pouerly to-fore hym*, and þe sentence *of deþ is ȝyue aȝens hym*; and so berynge *pitously his owne* galewes, he is ilad to þe deþ. A *wundurful* spectacle! Sykst þu not? *By-hold, suster, wat a signe of princehood and wurschipe þyn husbounde Crist berþ vp his schuldre – as þe book seyt*: 'Ecce principatus super humerum eius'. And certeyn, þat was þe ȝerd off *þy* riȝtwisnesse and þe sceptre of his kyngdom, *as holy scripture spekeþ of*: 'Virga equitatis, virga regni tui'. (p. 47-48, 898-906)

B: (I woot wel thou mayst not suffer this, *natheles yit loke vp*, with thyn *wepynge* eyen and) beholde hou he berith his cros to his passyon with a clothe of purpure arrayed, *cleuynge ful sore to his forbeten woundes.* (p. 21, 843-845)

What is interesting to remark in this passage, beside the predictable impressive amplification of Vernon, is the way Scriptural quotations, from Is. 9:6 and Ps. 44:7, are treated in this vers ion. While in Aelred they are not really quotations, but integral part of the text, to the point that the original *tui* of Psalm 44:7 is converted into *eius* to keep the text running, the Vernon translator feels obliged to distinguish and explain. Whereas in Aelred the Bible is a 'vocabulary' which for him it is only natural to use, in Vernon the Scripture is a 'sacred text' whose authority, well marked by the formula "as the book says" and probably also signalled by the keeping of the Latin original and the use of red ink, serves to evince and sustain the 'theological meaning' of the man who is climbing the Calvary hill carrying his cross. In translating the scriptural quotation Vernon renders the Latin *tui*, which Aelred had correctly changed to *eius*, first by "thy righteousness", obviously a nonsense, since it is Christ's justice and not the reader's which is mentioned here, and then more properly by "his kingdom".

What to say about the extreme conciseness of Bodley? The summary is so dense that to make the sentence understandable it has been necessary to repeat part of the previous quotation, since this translator compacts under the same invitation to behold Jesus with weeping eyes both the details of the tortured body and his going to the Calvary on the *via dolorosa*. He chooses to place here the detail of the "clothe of purpure" (*purpureum vestimentum*) extracted from the passage previously quoted, and even goes to add something which is not in Aelred's text, that is the pain caused by the adhering of the cloth to Christ's wounded skin. This detail was becoming very common after the *Meditationes Vitae Christi*, a work widely read in the late Middle Ages, and well-known in England especially through Nicholas Love's version entitled *The Mirrour of the Blessed Lyf of Jesu Christ*.[8] The addition is anyway an example of the way a translator feels free to use a larger frame of reference beyond the letter of his source text.

3. Concluding remarks

After this selection of examples can there be any conclusion? I do not think so. The purpose of this chapter was not to present a coherent, and least of all a definitive model of how to evaluate a medieval translation of religious texts: my aim was rather to raise problems, and to question easy and sweeping generalizations. As Ellis rightly recalls: "every instance of practice that we may be tempted to erect into a principle has its answering opposite, sometimes in the same work" (Ellis 1991: xiv).

If a lesson can be derived from what I have expounded, this concerns first of all the idea of translation, which in the Middle Ages was so various and far-reaching that it not only included what we would call adaptation, but it could stretch so far as to mean a real re-writing of the text in a rather creative mood. This has a consequence on our ways of evaluating medieval translations. We should resist the temptation to elaborate clear-cut theories and be more sensitive and sympathetic to single texts and authors, whether known or, as is often the case, anonymous. The examples considered show that the modern reader needs to have many antennae if he wants to understand and possibly explain the choices of the medieval translator. History and linguistics, spirituality and church life, authorship and readership,

---

8   "And so is he now þe þridde tyme spoilede & standeþ nakede in siht of alle þat peple, & so bene nowe þe þridde tyme renvede þe brisours of þe wondes in his scourgyng by þe cleuyng of þe cloþes to his flesh" (Sargent 2005: 174). The *Meditationes* have had an uninterrupted influence on Christian preaching and meditation: some of us have probably heard in their childhood the same detail mentioned and emphasised in the sermon delivered on the night of Good Friday.

manuscript production and their circulation, and probably some other factors must be taken into account. But this is precisely what makes the analysis of a medieval translation so exciting and, at times, rewarding.

CHAPTER 4

David of Augsburg's *Formula Novitiorum* in Three English Translations[1]

The work which is the subject of this chapter is a long treatise in three books, written around 1240 by the Franciscan David of Augsburg, entitled *De exterioris et interioris hominis compositione*, but more often known by the shorter title of *Formula novitiorum*, that is "a short instruction of novices", which corresponds more or less to the content of the first of the three books.[2] The work was widely read, copied and translated in the late Middle Ages, as is shown by the fact that about 400 MSS of the Latin text are still extant, spread over a territory which practically coincides with the map of Western Christendom. These include Spain and England, Italy, Switzerland and France, Belgium and the Low Countries, Germany and Poland, although the majority belong to the area covered by Bavaria, Austria, Slovakia and the Czech Republic, of which Augsburg, the birthplace of its author, is in a sense the centre, and from which the fame of David and his book radiated.[3] It has been suggested by Rayez (1957: 44) that the main reason for its popularity was the attribution of the work to St Bernard and St Bonaventure, but the argument can be reversed, since one reason for this attribution was certainly the intrinsic value of the work itself. J. de Guibert does not hesitate to write that, together with William of St Thierry's *Golden Epistle*, and

---

1   An earlier version of this chapter appeared in Ellis/Tixier/Weitemeier (1998: 321-347).

2   The only modern edition of the work is Fr. David ab Augusta, *De exterioris et interioris hominis compositione* (Quaracchi 1899), hereafter Quaracchi. On David and his work see the corresponding item in the *ADB* (1968: 782-784) and Rayez (1957). For other studies see Hecker (1905); Stöckerl (1914); Heerinckx (1931); Clark (1949); Ruh (1956, 1993); Bernarello (1961); Steer (1987); Rüegg (1989); and Bohl (2000).

3   See Quaracchi, pp. xiii-xxxiv, where a list of 370 MSS is given. More have been found, as can be seen in Ahldén (1952).

probably even more so, "David's treatise was over many centuries the classical manual of monastic asceticism" (*DSp* I/980).[4]

David was born in Augsburg between 1200 and 1210. After joining the Franciscans, probably around 1235, he became Master of Novices in Regensburg, dividing most of his time thereafter between Regensburg and his birthplace, where he died on November 12th or 19th, 1272. He was a successful preacher, and a prolific writer, producing about thirty works, partly in Latin and partly in German, but his fame is mainly due to the *De...compositione*. In a letter he wrote to another famous Bavarian preacher, Berthold of Regenbursg, formerly his disciple and later a companion (*socius*) in his ministry,[5] we learn that the work originated from the allocutions (*collationes*) he used to address to his novices and other friars, which he had intended to collect both for them and for his own personal use. The eminently practical function of the work is stressed by the author himself, when he says that the reason for dividing the *Formula* into many parts and several chapters was to enable him to find quickly what he needed. In the Prologue to the second Book he gives a third reason for producing the book, that is, the personal profit he gained from reading and writing about spiritual things, which he did as an exercise in meditation, although he laments that he was not able to write all that he wanted, because he rarely had the necessary tranquillity to do that, having to travel quite often due to the numerous tasks he was charged with.[6]

The declared oral origin of the work explains some of the repetitions and the generally colloquial tone of David's prose. His Latin is simple, as his intention is mostly practical, and the sentences are often short, and linked in clear paratactic syntax. At times one has the distinct impression that some chapters, especially in the first Book, are a draft of an allocution for which each sentence in a list, which may be very long, looks like a theme, or a topic to be expanded upon while talking. The content and the structure of the *De exterioris et interioris hominis compositione*, as indicated in the title, is inward and upward

---

4   David's dependence on William of St Thierry has been studied by Heerinckx (1933) and Matanić (1991).
5   The text of this letter is printed in Quaracchi, pp. 59-62, as a preface to Book II.
6   "Non potui in otio et quiete ista colligere, sed vagando per diversas terras, vix perraro propter multas occupationes habui opportunitatem scribendi modicum" (Prologue, in Quaracchi, p. 64).

moving; from the corporal discipline and rules of exterior behaviour (Book I) to the spiritual ascent of the soul through seven different degrees of proficiency (Book III), via the reformation of the three faculties: *memoria, intellectus* and *voluntas* (Book II). The general tone can be inferred from the key-word in the title: *formula*, or *compositio*, which suggest a 'harmony' to be achieved through maintaining a strong union and a delicate balance between different parts which are always in danger of being destructively split. In the light of this emphasis, we need not be surprised that other words, such as "order", "discretion" and "measure" are of paramount importance and form the undercurrent of the treatise. In a sense David popularizes the great mystical doctrine of Gregory the Great, Bernard of Clairvaux, and particularly William of St Thierry, and hands it on in that simplified way which was to foster the great movement of spirituality which flourished at the end of the Middle Ages, whose best known expression is the *Devotio Moderna*. This is the opinion of the modern editors of the *De compositione*, who write that, although there were other thirteenth-century writers of greater and deeper spiritual doctrine, no one was like David "in the adaptation of doctrine to the practicalities of life, in the smooth and wise translation of the great principles of spiritual life, and in the moderate, devout and efficient tone which he gave to his exposition" (Quaracchi, p. xvi).

The widespread influence of the *Formula* was undoubtedly favoured by several translations of the work into German and Dutch. But this very fact is also a clear token of a growing demand for books of spiritual guidance from a new public who could not read Latin. In this respect the English translations of the work are in themselves the sign both of a considerable new readership of spiritual literature, and of the readability of the work for this new audience. A cursory look at the text reveals that David's work possesses the best qualities of the prose of religious instruction: didactic clarity clothed in simple syntax normally based on parataxis and easy parallelism.

1. English translations of the *Formula*

We have three English translations of David's *Formula*: two of the whole work, and one of Book I only, and they are extant in the following MSS:[7]

- Cambridge Queens' College MS 31 (Books I-III): siglum Q
- CUL MS Dd.ii.33 (Books I-III): siglum U
- London, BL MS Arundel 197, fols 48r-64r (parts of Book I): siglum A

Both Q and A belong to the end of the fifteenth century, while U was written in the early sixteenth century. Happily for us, their difference exemplifies three possible ways of treating a base text: since Q is qualified as "literal", and U is "more expanded and decorated",[8] while A is, in the very words of the translator or copyist, an "abstract". Another feature of these translations is that they were produced for, or at least presented as open to audiences different from that originally intended by David. One is avowedly for a convent of nuns; another, while preserving the original destination, points towards a very large public, that is, the new cultivated laity in search of a spiritual food which could be palatable in both language and content; the third is clearly for a mixed readership, in that it regularly turns the Latin "fratres" into "brothers and sisters". The intrinsic quality of the *Formula*, both in content and style, was certainly the basis for its adoption for different purposes, even before it was translated into the various vernaculars: T. Ahldén has published from an Uppsala MS a Latin version of the work adapted to a convent of Birgittine nuns.[9]

---

7   These translations are listed in Jolliffe (1974a), under the item *Formula noviciorum*, in O.4. A short extract from Book I, ch. 40, is extant in CUL MS Mm.v.37, f. 135r, and in Oxford Bodleian Library MS Ashmole 41 f. 135v (Item O.6); a passage derived from Book II, chs 7-10, can be found in MS Bodley Ashmole 41 f. 135r-v (Item O.10).

8   For these comments, see Sargent (1984: 167).

9   This adaptation is extant in the MS C 802 of Uppsala University, edited by Ahldén (1952).

Since I will analyse only part I of Book I of the work, I think it useful to give an idea of the subjects dealt with in this part, which in its practical outlook reminds one of the secular genre of courtesy-books, as will be apparent from the following summary of its subject-matter (chapter division is as given in Q: see Appendix 2). After a beginning which points to God as the only reason for choosing a religious community, and to obedience as the very foundation-stone of religious life, the author proceeds to describe such topics as the peaceful relationship to be had with one's superior (3), rising early from sleep (4), behaviour in the choir (5) and in the chapter-house (6), how to take corrections (7), behaviour at table (8) and in the dormitory (9), community chores (10), service at mass (11), confession (12), activity in the cell (13), reading (14), preaching and hearing confessions (15), discipline everywhere (16), behaviour with brothers (17), modesty (18), how to walk (19), sit (20) laugh (21) and talk (22), how to avoid detraction (23), boasting (24), gossiping (25), excessive talk (26), idle words (27), contentions and quarrels (28), how to speak cheerfully (29), how to avoid idleness (30), how to follow the example of Christ (31), how to avoid vainglory especially in singing (32), how to behave when going out (33), how to keep watch on sight (34), how to travel with the brothers (35), on prayers to be said while travelling (36), on the good example to be given (37), on fleeing the company of women (38), on liberty of heart (39), and, lastly, a summary of what has been said in the form of short directions (40).

In recent times the English versions have been studied by P.S. Jolliffe and Michael Sargent. In an article published in 1974, Jolliffe was the first to draw attention to a treatise which is "one of the longest of its kind extant in Middle English", and whose translation is relevant in that it testifies to the "importance which was attached to placing this teaching in the hands of those who could read English but not Latin" (Jolliffe 1974b: 273).[10] Jolliffe mainly describes the content of the work, and comments on the versions, affirming for instance that the two containing the full treatise "may be considered different translations of the Latin" (p. 263). Later on in the article he adds that the third version, the one in Arundel 197 (A) containing only Book I of David's work, "represents essentially the same translation" as the

10   Other references are given in brackets in the text.

one in Cambridge Queens' College MS 31 (p. 271). He uses the Q version, which is the older of the two renderings of the whole text, to analyse how the translator works, starting from the conviction that there is "a remarkably close agreement" between this English version and the Latin text edited by Quaracchi in 1899 (p. 265). Having said that, he finds some 'minor' differences between the two texts, which he indicates in some omissions and in the reorganization of the material, such as different chapter divisions and titles, and concludes by saying that "the translation sometimes alters the meaning of the Latin" (p. 267). On this last point, the only example he gives actually shows a difference from the Latin of the Quaracchi edition, but it perfectly corresponds to the recension of the same text in the English MSS of the Latin text. The question, which Jolliffe seems not to have considered, is *which* Latin text forms the basis for the English versions. Apparently, we cannot assume that it is the Quaracchi text.

Michael Sargent touched on the *Formula*'s circulation in England in a long essay entitled "Bonaventura English: A Survey of the Middle English Prose Translations of Early Franciscan Literature" (1984b).[11] Unlike Jolliffe, he finds that the two long versions "represent two recensions of the same translation, of which the second is expanded" (p. 166), but it remains an open question whether this statement will be borne out by a close analysis of the two texts. Sargent is more aware than Jolliffe of the problems with the Latin base text: he affirms that "Jolliffe also demonstrated that the ME versions do not derive from the recension of *De compositione* represented by the Quaracchi edition" (p. 168), but I wonder where he found this statement, since, as I have just quoted, Jolliffe's opinion is exactly the opposite. Sargent reports Jolliffe's findings concerning the differences between the English versions and the Quaracchi edition, noting, unlike his predecessor, that these differences can be explained by looking at the English MSS, to whose text they correspond. Not all these remarks are convincing. For example, to say that the English versions and the insular Latin MSS lack the *Epistola auctoris* proves almost nothing, since the Quaracchi editors say that this prefatory letter does *not* properly belong to the first printed edition of the work

---

11 Sargent's work is hereafter cited by page number alone, in the body of the text (David is dealt with on pp. 164-172).

(Brescia 1495), although it is found in many MSS and in the second edition published in Augsburg in 1596 – see Quaracchi, p. i. More pertinently, Sargent provides four examples of single paragraphs lacking in the English versions, which are lacking in the English Latin MSS as well. This is certainly a good indicator, but the testimony is too weak, and does not allow a clear conclusion to be drawn. Moreover, it could suggest that the difference consists mainly, or solely, in the omission of a few sentences or paragraphs, as can be deduced from the examples given,[12] or in the fact that "the English text employs different chapter divisions and titles" (Jolliffe 1974b: 267). A detailed comparison on the whole text of Book I will show that the differences are much more pervasive, and concern the very wording.

Before introducing some examples, let us first describe the family of MSS of David's work which are now in England. From the list given in the Quaracchi edition, which is all but exhaustive, it appears that they amount to a total of twelve, of which only four contain the entire work. The fact that David's treatise appears more often only partially copied is not surprising; indeed, it is normal for a work essentially modular in character, like David's, which is formally divided into three books, but actually consists of five parts (Book I and II are each subdivided into two parts), so that any of them could be used and/or translated as a self-contained unit. For our purposes, given the fact that two English versions translate the full text, and a third, partial one is related to one of these, it seems reasonable to refer only to the four complete MSS, which are:

- Cambridge St John's College MS D.9 (14th c.): J1
- Cambridge St John's College MS G.2 (14th-15th c.): J2
- Cambridge Corpus Christi College MS 256 (15th c.): CC
- Durham Cathedral Chapter Library MS B.iv.42: D

I have collated the four English MSS of the Latin text of Book I, part I (chapters I-XXVI of the Quaracchi edition), and from this it clearly emerges that the four English MSS which contain the whole Latin text show a remarkable uniformity, and represent a common recension

---

12   See the examples given and analysed by Sargent (1984b: 168-169) and Pezzini (1997).

which is different from the one printed by the Quaracchi editors. They are not, however, a copy of the same exemplar, and a more precise division into two groups can be made, connecting J1 and D against CC and J2, as can be shown by the following examples (throughout this chapter I follow the numbering of chapters in CC: see Appendix 2):

ch. 1: igitur: J1, D   enim: CC, J2
        disponit: J1, D   disposuit: CC, J2
ch. 3: preuenias cor tuum ad aliquam deuocionem excitare: J1, D
        preuenire studeas vt cor ad aliquam deuocionem excites: CC, J2
ch. 5: a marginal note "quare sumus tepidi in officio diuino" appears in CC and J2, but not in J1 and D
ch. 6: tunc vero: *so* J1, D; CC, J2 *add* humiliter
ch. 8: inopiam generat spiritualem: *so* J1, D; CC, J2 *om.* spiritualem
ch. 9: inquietetur: *so* J1, D; CC, J2 *add* aliquo modo
ch. 14: [in intellectu] scripturarum et illumineris ad fidei intellectum: *so* CC, J2; J1, D *om.* due to homoeoteleuton on "intellectu", which proves that these two MSS share a common exemplar.

All copies contain individual readings which are most probably scribal errors, but which might be significant both for the establishment of their common ancestor and still more for the establishing of links with the ME translations. For example, in ch. 2 J1 reads *ideo commisisti*, against *ideo commisit* in CC, D and J2; in ch. 7, *flexis genibus* in J1 does not correspond to *flexis genibus humiliter* in the other three MSS. Other examples are *complectere* (ch. 8) in J1 against *amplectere* in D, CC and J2, or in ch. 9 *mensura* in D, against *medium* in the others. Moreover, D lacks the whole short chapter 10, "De obsequiis". CC has *pacienter* (ch. 6) against the correct reading *procaciter* in the other three (Q translation: "obstinately"), or *alienacionis* (ch. 12) against *alleuiacionis* in the others.

A detailed analysis conducted on the first part of David's book shows that the best basis for the two linked translations (Q-A) is the tradition represented by the group CC-J2, while the third (U) is closer to the J1-D recension. This is the reason why I chose CC as the base text for the Latin, collating it with D and J1 when necessary, since the English version Q can sometimes be explained only by reference to the group J1-D, and sometimes has no correspondence to any of the English MSS of the Latin, but coincides with the Quaracchi text. For example, the phrase in ch. 14 quoted above, existing in CC and J2, but missing in J1 and D, does not appear in the Q translation. Other examples are: CC *diligere*, J1 *dirigere*, Q "to drawe" (ch. 36); CC *votari*, J1 *notari*, Q "be noted" (ch. 37); CC *aspectio*, J1 *affeccio*, Q "affection" (ch. 38). This leads to the conclusion that none of the extant Latin copies was the one actually used by the English translators, and rare variant readings should be supposed in a lost Latin source text. So, for example, when we have in the Q version, col. 70, a *benigne* corresponding to a "benigne" in the Quaracchi edition, J1 and D have *libenter*, and CC has nothing; or, on the same page, the phrase "made knowen to hyr" presupposes a *notum* in the immediate source and present in Quaracchi, but lacking in all the English MSS. By contrast with the literal translation preserved in Q-A, it is not easy to find a textual tradition for the Latin original of U, because of the latter's generous amplifications; yet the U version seems to share some readings with the J1-D group. For example, in ch. 18 ("De verecundia") there is one case where an authority quoted as *Augustinus* in J1 and D, appears as *Gregorius* in CC and in the Quaracchi edition: this is "saynt Austen" in the U version, and "saynt Gregory" in the Q and A versions. This small example clearly challenges Sargent's hypothesis of a single English version behind the surviving copies. Incidentally, no one will be surprised to hear that the quotation actually comes neither from Augustine nor from Gregory, but seems to be broadly derived from a sermon of Bernard.[13]

Since my purpose is to decide what Latin text should be taken as a basis for the study of the English versions, let me illustrate the situation with a few examples. I cite, in order, the Quaracchi printed text, the Latin text of MS Corpus Christi College Cambridge 256 (CC), and the English translation found in MS Queens' College Cambridge 31 (Q), which, precisely because it is "over-literal", can be a great help in establishing the Latin source, which this English translator follows very faithfully.

---

13   The Quaracchi editors refer to Bernard's sermon 86.1 of the *Sermones super Cantica Canticorum* (p. 20, n. 2). In fact the passage cannot be properly called a quotation, although many of its ideas and some phrases can be found in the text suggested.

(from ch. 11, on confession)

> Quaracchi (p. 16): Ista enim omnia potes Deo in oratione quotidie confiteri et defectus tuos ei exponere, quos sentis in singulis virtutibus, et [multum expedit super his ab eo remedium postulare miserationis. Parum etiam valet confessio, nisi proponas de cetero cavere] ab his, quae confiteris et studeas te emendare.

> CC (ch. 12, f. 4r): Ista enim poteris cotidie in tua oracione confiteri et defectus tuos exponere, quos sentis in singulis virtutibus, et ab eis que confiteris studeas te emendare.

> Q (col. 31): And also thowe mayste make euery daye such a maner of confession in thy prayer, and shewe forthe thy defautes that thou haste done, ayens any vertue; and tho defautes that thou knowlecheste, study to amende.[14]

(from ch. 2, on obedience)

> Quaracchi (p. 5): Idcirco talem te exhibeas ei, ut libere iubeat, te facere vel omittere quidquid videtur ei expedire, si ipse timet te, iam servus maior est domino suo, et discipulum super magistrum.

> CC (f. 3r): Et iam seruus non est maior domino suo. Talem te ei exhibe ut libere te iubeat facere vel dimittere quicquid videbitur ei expedire.

> Q (col. 9): And now the seruaunde ys nott more then hys lorde. Therfore shewe the suche to hym that he may frely commaunde the what hym semeth expediente.

While the first example shows that David's original text has been shortened by the omission (or, alternatively, lengthened by the addition) of the material in square brackets, the second reveals that the text has been rephrased and the word order altered. Although my comparison refers only to the first part of the first book of David's treatise, the point I wish to make is clear, and here a double conclusion can be drawn: first that the Latin text represented by the English MSS is remarkably different from the text printed by Quaracchi; and second, that the English versions derive from this

---

14   When I quote one of the English versions I cite normally only by folio or column. The number of the chapter, when not given, can easily be found by checking the list of chapters in Appendix 2. When the reference may not be entirely clear, however, I also indicate the chapter number of the English versions.

English recension to such an extent that no analysis of them can be serious unless we first establish the Latin text of these four MSS. For practical reasons I shall hereafter call this MS evidence 'The English recension' of David's work, which I shall use for comparison, while I reserve the phrase 'The English versions' to indicate the translations which are the object of this study. It should be noted that the label 'English recension' does not mean anything characteristic or exclusive, since, given the huge number of MSS of David's work, the English group must have some links with one or another continental family. Such links cannot, however, be decisively established in the present state of research.[15]

Let us now pay closer attention to the three English translations of the *Formula*. Both Q and A belong to the end of the fifteenth century, and they share a common ancestry, although some variant readings show that neither is a copy of the other. Besides, the comparison is heavily marred by the fact that the Arundel MS has been extensively rewritten, or corrected in such a skilful way that at times it is very difficult to distinguish the original writing from the corrected one.[16] This means that all I say about the readings of this MS should be checked in detail to see whether readings are original or they belong to a revised version.

The Q version is signed by the scribe "W. Paterson" on the last page of the MS. As I have already said, this version seems to follow the text very literally, and one is tempted to say that its greatest advantage is that it helps to establish the Latin source with unusual security. But owing to the fact that in the other full-text version, made for Syon, several folios are missing from the MS, and some chapters have been excised because of the adaptation of the work to a different audience, this is the only really complete English version of the *Formula*.

The U translation was written by Thomas Prestins (or Prestius, or Prescius), a Birgittine brother present at the convent of Syon, according to records, in 1539, and it is specifically addressed to the

---

15   For example, the wording of the Latin passage quoted above in the second example coincides with the reading of MS Mainz 187 quoted by Ahldén (1952: 27).

16   On this MS see ch. 8 here and my editions of the two Birgittine tracts it contains: Pezzini (1988: 292-298) and (1994b: 381, fn.7, and 391-395).

nuns of the abbey. In this case, unlike what happens with the Q translator, the new audience has a far-reaching impact on the version and necessitates a number of changes to the text. The most obvious have already been noted by Sargent: these include the "alteration of masculine pronouns and references to a male religious community, to feminine pronouns and references to a female community"(1984b: 167),[17] the excision of the chapters dealing with serving at mass (Quaracchi ch. 10, CC ch. 11)[18] and with preaching and hearing confessions (Quaracchi ch. 13, CC ch. 15), the changed title and the adaptation of the material in the chapter originally entitled "De feminis fugiendis", which becomes in U "Of eschewyng of mens company" (Quaracchi ch. 24, CC ch. 36; cf. Quaracchi ch. 15, CC ch. 17, where "inter fraters" becomes in U "among thy sustrys"); there are also interesting additions pointing to a female readership, such as in the chapter devoted to the activity in one's cell (Quaracchi ch. 12, CC ch. 13), a long passage on sewing. But much remains to be said, especially concerning the style of this version, which may also be explained, as we shall see, by the idea(s) the author had of his hearers. In this respect the study of a translation illustrates not only the personality of the translator, but also that of the implicit reader.

The third version, A, is a large selection of chapters from Book I, and is qualified in the MS as an "abstract", which suggests that some chapters of the said book have been omitted. The version was made for a mixed community, as testified by the constant use of "brothers and sisters" for the Latin *fratres*, and in such alterations as that to the summary at the end of the first part, where *In omnibus fuge mulieres* becomes "In al thingis fle eville wymmen, and wemen oweth to fle eville men" (f. 57r); for this Q has "In al thynges fle women" (col. 75), and U "Fle mens company, except where a grete cause requyrith the contrary, and then be not with them aloon" (f. 21r). This little example sheds a clear light on the different readers addressed by

---

17   Other monastic rules originally written for men, for example those of Sts Augustine and Benedict, were similarly adapted for female religious: see comment in Ellis (1996: 79, fn. 26).

18   Since the numbering of chapters in the English MSS does not coincide (CC even lacks any numbering at all), here I follow the Quaracchi numbering side by side with that established by the collation of CC with J2. For a complete comparison, see Appendix 2.

106

the translators. The chapters of Book I/1 which do not appear in this "abstract" are, according to the numbering of CC/J2, chs 3 ("De pace cum prelatis"), 15 ("De predicacione et confessionis audicione"), the final part of ch. 22 ("De verbis"), and chs 29 ("De exemplo Christi"), 31 ("De egrediendo foras"), 33 ("Quomodo te habeas cum socio in via), 34 ("De oracione in via"), 36 ("De feminis fugiendis"), and 37 ("De libertate cordis"). Taken together these omissions would seem to indicate a non-clerical mixed community, for whom travelling abroad or going out of the religious house was not allowed, or not interesting, or not usual. But other excisions remain which are not easy to account for, such as the chapter on the imitation of Christ, or the one describing the good relationship to be had with the superior in the community. Besides the *Formula,* the MS contains a couple of texts on prayer (a meditation on the *Veni Creator* and one on *Te Deum laudamus*), a version of *Fervor amoris,* and two tracts drawn from St Birgitta's *Revelations* II,16 and VI,65 which appear in other MSS.[19] I wonder whether all this does not suggest a Birgittine community, if not Syon itself, as the place where and for which this MS was produced.

Any study of a translation should, if possible, answer a number of questions. Besides the most obvious ones, such as faithfulness, correctness, style and tone, we cannot avoid asking why, by whom and for whom a translation was made, since this may explain some choices on the part of the translator and help us to evaluate whether and to what extent the enterprise was successful. In our case, in addition to remarks already made, we can take further advantage of what is said in the two prefaces which accompany the two full-text translations.

The point to start from is the Preface to the version in Queens' College Cambridge MS 31 (Q), which appears also, but with some significant modifications, in the CUL MS Dd.ii.33 (U), which, for the sake of brevity, I shall call the 'Syon version'.

---

19   The *Fervor Amoris* and the translation of St Birgitta's *Revelations* VI,65 are also extant in Oxford Bodleian Library MS Bodley 423 and CUL MS Ii.vi.40. On the relationship between these two MSS and London British Library MS Arundel 197 see Ayto/Barratt (1984: xxvi-xxix) and Pezzini (1994b: 381-383).

The preface begins with the exposition of a topic, which shows too well, in its wayward movement, that the author/translator is at a loss with syntax and structure when he lacks the clear track of a Latin text from which to work. The theme is the devil's envy of the most virtuous men (incidentally, this theme has been evidenced by the phrase "envy of Satan against good men most of all" written in the upper margin by a later hand). Satan is particularly shrewd at tempting people living in a religious community in that their way of life, according to their rule, is "a compendiouse path to the verrey felicite". The author mentions the fact that many books were written to help people withstand temptations, among which "ther ys a lytell booke called *Formula nouiciorum*, whoys auctours name ys unknowen as wele to many of my betters as to me". But, notwithstanding this anonymity, he goes on to call the "maker" of that work "a speciall organe or instrument of the holy gooste", which clearly proclaims the very high esteem in which the *Formula* was held. The information he did not have was supplied later by the hand of a sixteenth-century reader, who wrote on the right margin, near the line where it is said that the "auctours name ys vnkonwen": "The auctors name is david, a frere minor, as we fynde in the boke that is called *De scriptoribus ecclesiaticis*, Johannis Tritemii." This is Johannes von Heidelberg, a German benedictine, known as Tritemius after the name of Trittenheim, the place where he was born in 1462 (he died in Würzburg in 1516, where he is buried at the Neumünster). The work mentioned in the note was published in Mainz in 1494, and re-edited in 1508-13 with the addition of 1155 new items. Another hand, later than the previous one, wrote at the bottom of the page: "David, ordinis Minorum (Germanus, inquit Gesnerus) scripsit Formulam novitiorum bipartitam, scilicet De Exteriore hominis compositione, ac de interioris hominis et mentis reformatione"; on the bottom right corner it is written "vide Possevini Apparatum et Gesneri Catalogum".[20]

---

20   The works referred to are Konrad von Gesner, *Bibliotheca Universalis* (1545), in which about 15,000 Latin, Greek and Hebrew works are listed and described, and Antonio Possevino, *Apparatus sacer ad scriptores V. ac N. Testamenti...*, a work in three volumes (Venezia, 1603-1606), where David is briefly described in vol. I, p. 386 (13 lines) and p. 680 (2 lines): his only work recorded is exactly the *Formula Novitiorum*. It may be interesting to remark

More important is where the author gives his reasons for the translation:

> And for as moche as the langage of latyn ys vnknowen to many religiouse, and namely to wommen, therfore I haue purposed by the grace of god our lorde to translate the seyd booke in-to englysche to the edificacion of the symple people in religion and of all other that desireth to be seruantes of god.

If "simple" here means "ignorant of Latin", and refers to people in religious orders, it is clear from the phrase that follows that the intended readership extends well beyond the walls of a convent, as is more explicitly stated a little further on:

> And though (MS thought) yt so be that thys booke, aftyr hys name and aftyr the matiers that he entretyth of, towche principally the religious persons, neuer the later euery seculer man or womman that desyreth to be the seruand of god may fynde here-in sufficient instruccion and direccions to the performynge of hys seyd entente.

The preface to the Syon version is clearly based on this one, as it follows its very wording. This makes the more significant the omissions and additions of the Syon translator. For example there is no place either for the author or for the praise of his skill: the "lytyl boke" is simply judged as "moch necessary to al religiouse persons". Nothing is said about the reason for the translation or its utility for the general reader. Being addressed to the Syon nuns, the preface expands on the description of the content of the treatise, and concludes by calling attention to the detailed tables the scribe has put at the beginning of each Book, adding that this was done so that the reader "may the sooner turne to that that lykyth you". Since this translation was made in the early sixteenth century, the remark seems to point to the use of the book for private reading, or in any case to the idea of the work as a collection of loosely organized chapters to be selected for reading according to one own's "lykyng", or according to what is deemed useful and/or necessary.

When an intention is stated, it does not necessarily follow that the translator operates accordingly. In this particular case we have two

---

that these annotations on the MS show that the English translation of David's work was still being read at least until the early seventeenth century.

different responses. The Queens' translator does not alter his text in any significant way: although he addresses himself to the general reader, he maintains all the monastic and conventual elements of the treatise. We may surmise that his declared intention is no more than a gentle suggestion stressing the high religious value of his text, leaving it to his reader to make the necessary adaptations. On the other hand, the Syon version, which was made for a convent of nuns, although this purpose is not expressed in the preface, introduces significant changes which apply more properly to the new audience. The adaptation is deep and consistent, in that the translator not only changes the personal pronouns, but rules out such priestly duties as preaching and hearing confessions on the one hand, while on the other he inserts a long section on the vanity which can be derived from such typical female occupation as needlework.[21]

The third version, as has been said, is suited to a mixed public, comprising "brothers and sisters". This causes no alteration in the text, except for those introduced by the later "corrector", but these do not belong to the original version, and should be analysed in themselves for what they might indicate as a new response to the text.

What follows is meant to illustrate essentially three points: 1. the dependence of the three versions on the English recension of the work where it differs from the Quaracchi edition; 2. the relationship, if any, between the three versions; 3. some general remarks on the qualities of these translations, mostly in terms of lexical sensitivity, structural elaboration, and strategies of cohesion. These three aspects obviously may, and quite often do, overlap. In fact the first point has already been made, and it will be simply confirmed by the constant use of the Latin text of the English recension. As for the second, since I have already said that Q and A are interconnected, I may also anticipate the discussion by noting that in my opinion U is independent of the other two. As for the third point, whose full study would require much more detail than this chapter can provide, I must specify that for obvious reasons I have limited my analysis to the first part of the first book, which can be taken as a sufficient sample from which some well-founded generalizations can legitimately be drawn.

---

21   On similar adaptations of Syon's own legislation for the monks, the nuns and the laybrothers, see Ellis (1984: 124-143).

2. Analysis

We may start our analysis of the three versions by considering what has already been stated by Jolliffe and Sargent: that Q is literal, that A shares a common ancestry with Q, that U is either a different version (Jolliffe), with which I agree, or an elaboration of the previous one (Sargent), with which I do not.

We all know that 'literal' is a slippery adjective, in that the border between literalness and freedom, or creativity, is not so clear, nor given once and for ever. In a sense no translation can be literal, and what we may establish as a standard consists in fact of a greater or lesser degree of fidelity to the base text, be this fidelity lexical and/or structural, but in any case within the limits allowed by the new language in which the text is being cast.

The tendency to literalness in Q can be observed even in that small unit, the single word. Here are some examples which are particularly interesting in that the words include images with a metaphorical meaning.

One case is *tepescere* (ch. 1), which is "to waxe lowke" in Q, "to wexe wery" in A, and "to wax slacke or slowthful" in U. The word reappears elsewhere, for example in ch. 9, where the cognate *tepedior* is variously rendered as "the more dull" in Q, "the lener" in A, and "the more ondevowt" in U; in the same chapter the phrase *ex tepeditate cordis* is "throwgh leukenes of the herte" in Q ("weth lewkenis of þe herte" in A), and "by ouermoch favoryng of ourselfe" in U. The same contrasting choices appear in the rendering of *incalefiat spiritus tuus* (ch. 4), which is "that thy spiryte waxe hoote" in Q and A, while U, according to what seems his normal way of doing, cuts out the image of "heat" and prefers to concentrate on the following *deuocior* writing "þat þy spirit may wax the more devowt". Since in this case expansion is out of the question, indeed the contrary, we may deduce that U is more sensitive in choosing words which convey the spiritual meaning of the text with more immediacy. This is confirmed by other examples, such as *discordie scintillas* (ch. 35 in CC, "De bono exemplo dando"), which in Q is "sparkell of wrathe or discorde" (col. 67), while in U it becomes "al hasty wordes and contencions or stryvys" (f. 19v). This should obviously not be taken as a rule, since, for example, in ch. 34 ("De oracione in via"), the image of cold is retained by U in the phrase *infrigidatus a fervore devocionis*, which is "ouer colde [...] for feruoure of deuocion" (col. 65) in Q, and "if þu suffer thy devocion so to slake and wax colde" (f. 19r) in U, who feels in any case the need to add "slake" as a means of being more specific. I must add that the same translator is not totally insensitive to the language of images, provided this is clearly expressed as a comparison, for example in ch. 24 ("De rumoribus"), where *quasi vas sine operculo* is literally translated in U by "lyke to a bottell that hath no stoppel" (f. 14v), as it is in Q by "lyke a vessell that hath no couerynge" (col. 45). But, again, in ch. 9 ("De dormicione") the word *sarcina*, used as a metaphor for the hardness to which the body should not be too excessively submitted, is rendered by "burdone" (col. 26) in Q, while in U it is "labores" (f. 11r). The reluctance of the Syon translator to render figurative language literally shows not only in nouns, but also in verbs, as when *dilabimur* (ch. 26, "De multiloquio") is rendered by "we fall" (ch. 24 in U, f. 15v) against the more literal and more vivid "we slide" (ch. 27, col. 48) of Q; *abscinde a te* (ch. 39, "De feminis fugiendis") becomes "putt from the vtterly" in U (ch. 36, f. 20r) against 'kytte a-way' (ch. 38, col. 71) of Q; similarly *demulceret* (ch. 30, "De vana gloria") is rather softened into "plese" in U (ch. 30. f. 17v), where Q has "delite" (ch. 32, col. 58); the same happens with *indignetur* (ch. 36), rendered by "haue indignacion" in Q (ch. 38, col. 70), and "be displesid" in U (ch. 36. f. 20r).

Literalness can be marred by a factor which I would call the emotional aspect of words, where interesting different choices can be found. For example, in a dense catechetical passage in ch. 1 where it is said that God takes care of man *sicut mater parvuli sui*, Q has "as a womman hath of hys lytell chylde", A writes "as a woman of her tendur beloved childe", and U "as the tender mother hath toward her child".[22] In this example it seems that Q deflates the emotional quality of the text, but the opposite can happen, as in ch. 3, where, evoking the story of the drunken Noah, the phrase *verenda patris* becomes in

---

22   The translation in U follows the reading *mater* given by Quaracchi, while all the English MSS have *mulier*.

Q "the hyndrer and the fowler party of hys faders body", while U has simply "pryvy partes". In the same vein, in a quotation from Leviticus 19:23 in ch. 15, Q translates *prepucia* as "the fore party" (col. 34), when "prepuce", and variants, were available (*MED* s.v.), and would have been more appropriate, and certainly more "literal" (this chapter lacks both in A and in U, so that no comparison is possible).

Touching single phrases it is certainly not without significance the fact that the Syon version, written for a community whose name was "The Order of the Most Holy Saviour", tends to translate *Dominus noster Iesus Christus* by "oure saviour Criste" (ch. 32), or even to reduce "the sone of god oure lorde Iesu Cryste" of the Q version (ch. 31, col. 50) to "oure saviour Criste Iesu" (ch. 29). The example can also serve to demonstrate that, contrary to what one might think, the Syon translator may be insensitive to images, but he is not indifferent to emotions: at times he can even inflate them, as in the following case, where David gives rein to his disapproval of various forms of coquetry and flirting between men and women:

CC: O quam vere sunt truphe, et bonus homo non debet ea aliqualiter admittere, nec cor suum cum talibus occupare (ch. 36, "De feminis fugiendis")

Q: O, how verry tryfels are all they, the whyche a goode man owght not to admitte, nor occupy hys herte wyth suche thynges. (ch. 38, col. 70)

U: *O good lord*, what trifulles ben these, *alas*, that euer a religiouse person shuld occupy her mynde with such *vanytees*. (ch. 36, f. 20r)

Literalness as against creativity can be seen not only in single words or phrases, but in larger units such as paragraphs, where the verbal net formed by a 'company of words' can be either maintained, or destroyed, or creatively reworked. Take, for example, this passage, where I have marked in italics the words forming a net of reference.

CC: Priusquam incipiatur officium, prevenire studeas vt cor ad aliquam *devocionem excites*. Ideo enim tam *desides et tepidi* sumus in divino officio quia ante non sumus *devocione excitati*, et ita eximus sicut intravimus, *frigidi et dissoluti*. (ch. 5)

Q: And afore the office be bygonnen, study to *stire* thy herte to sum *deuocion*. Therfore we ar so *slowe* and so *vnlusty* (A '*weke*') in goddes seruice for we ar nott *stired* vnto *deuocion* afore, and therfore soo as we entre, so we goo oute *colde and dissolute*. (col. 14)

U: Cum to the quere before the begynnyng and prepare thy hert to god before þu begyn, and that shal *kindle* in the som *devocion*. For surely the cause why we be so *dull* and *ondewout* in the service of god is for that we *prepare not* our hertes before to god with som *devocion*, and so we depart from the service as *cold* and *drye* from *devocion* as we cam thether. (f. 8v).

We see again how far Q is literal, the only exception being "vnlusty" for "tepidi", with a stress on the evidently intended spiritual meaning of the word; the same may be said of the A version, which is clearly connected with Q. On the other hand, U underlines by a repetition the "preparation of the heart" which is needed before entering into prayer, and creates a better cohesion in the two pairs of adjectives, the first moving in the area of spiritual vocabulary (dull and undevout), the second in a metaphorical field (cold and dry). The paragraph has been rewritten with originality, and looking at this passage we may wonder how this translation could have been seen by Sargent as derived from the other.

There are other cases where the reworking of the paragraph looks so nice that one is obliged to ask whether Q could really be said to be a "literal" translation, as in the example which follows, in which this translator, while translating literally the contrast *apud se / longe a se*, creates a new more evident one in "decrece / encrece", where he uses the prefixes de- and en- instead of the Latin *plus / minus*:

CC: magis te vellet esse minus perfectum apud se, ut sepe posset tui copiam habere, quam longe a se [J1 *adds* plus] perfectum (CC ch. 36, J1 ch. 32)

Q: she wolde haue the ofte tymes wyth hyre, wyth decrece of thy perfeccion, rather then farre from hyr, wyth decrece therof (ch 38, col. 71).

U: he wold haue the often tymys in hys company, with the hynderance of thy profet, rather than þu shuldyst be absent from hym, to the grete increase of the same (ch. 36, f. 20r)

Given that U normally amplifies the text, we may consider what kind of amplification is used. The first, evident way of enlarging a text is by a generous use of various form of doublets, on which so much has been said by other writers that I need not linger over it. Rather, I would indicate other kinds of amplification, such as the pedantic underlining of a detail, or the specification of a scriptural reference which may also be expanded. Here are some exemples.

CC: Verba psalmodie distincte et integre pronuncia (ch. 5)

Q: The wordes of psalmody pronounce distinctely and holy. (col. 14)

U: Pronunce the psalmody distinctly, *so that euery word and sillable may be perceuyd and herd.* (f. 8v)

CC: ita ut eciam non consideres que coram te sint foris, nisi quando *necessitas vie* vel utilitas alia requirat (ch. 32)

Q: that thou considere nott what thynge ys byfore the oute-warde, butt as muche as *nede of thy wey* or other profyte woll require (ch. 34, col. 61)

U: consyder not what is before the outwardly but as *necessitee shal requyre the to loke to thy fete for stumblyng* or as som other profett shal move the
(ch. 32, f. 18v)

CC: sicut Adam, qui refudit culpam in deum et mulierem, dicens: "mulier quam dedisti michi decepit me" (ch. 6)

Q: as dyde Adam, that putt all hys owne defaute vpon God and vppon Eve, sayeng in thys wyse: "the womman that thow yavest me decyued me"
(col. 16)

U: as Adam dyd, which dyd putt *the defawt that he made in brekyng of goddes commandement* vpon god and hys wyfe, seyyng: "The woman that þu gavyst to me deceyved me, *and made me to eete of the appul", where-as I wold not ye se what com of hym for this excuse* (f. 9r)

Quite often in U Prestius is keen to amplify biblical references, as if he suspected that his reader did not necessarily know the story very well, or thought it useful to remind them of its details. Hence, for example, he elaborates on a very brief Bible reference in the Latin, in a context in which the religious person is invited not to speak evil of his superiors by remembering what happened to Cham for scorning his father (see Genesis 9:21-25):

CC: ut in cham patet, qui verenda patris sui nudata fratribus nunciauit, et sibi maledictionem in hoc irremediabilem adquisiuit (ch. 3)

Q: as yt apperyth in cayme, noye-ys son, the whych shewed hys brethren the hyndrer and the fowler party of hys faders body, that tyme beyng bare, and so purchased hym a cursyng irremediable (cols 9-10)

U: as it apperith in cam, the son of noe, which fyndyng hys father lyyng in slepe, and hys pryvy partes bare and oncoveryd, scornyd hym, and not so contentyd, he showyd it to hys brether, sem and jafeth, and there-fore he and hys chylder were cursyd of god and also of his father noe, and was subdewyd to perpetual (euerlastyng *overwritten*) servitude and bondage (f. 7v)

In other cases U's additions are due to Prestius' fine attention to his female audience, as when, in a chapter devoted to the custody of the eyes when going outside the convent (CC ch. 32, Quaracchi ch. 22 "De visu"), he counterbalances the mention of David's adultery with a reference to the Egyptian wife of Potiphar who tempted Joseph:

CC: Dauid cecidit in culpam adulterii ex incauto aspectu mulieris.

Q: Kynge Dauid fell into avowtry throwgh the inwardly[23] byholdynge of a woman. (ch. 34, cols 61-2)

U: Kyng David, thorough the ondiscreitt beholdyng of a woman fel to advoultry, and the lady beholdyng Ioseph the patriarke onwysely desyryd hys company synfully. (ch. 32, f. 18v)[24]

As is customary with Prestius, we find the two biblical references marked in the margin: "2° regum 11°" for the first *exemplum*, and "geneseos 39°" for the second (f. 18v). Prestius is particularly careful to indicate his biblical sources, and even tends to expand on them, or even double some quotations, as in ch. 29, where, to a sentence from Lk 22:27 ("I am among you as a minister or servant": f. 16v), he adds

---

23 Both Q and A have "inwardly" for "incauto", which, if not a blunder, is at least a very inaccurate translation. But this is clearly a proof of the inter-dependence of these two versions, either from each other, or – more probably – a common copy.

24 A similar change occurs in ch. 29 where, commenting on Jesus' tendency to avoid familiarity with women "for oure example that we men shuld not be to moch familiar with women, be they neuer so holy", Prestius adds "and of the contrary that women shuld not be to familiar with men". (f. 16v)

116

another of a similar tenor taken from Mt 20:28 or Mk 10:45 ("I cume to mynyster and serue and not to be servyd": f. 17r) which is not in the original, although, curiously enough, here we do not find the reference noted in the margin. But, again, no absolute rule can be established, since there are cases where he ignores biblical references, as when the text mentions Eliu Buzites (CC ch. 24, from Job 32:18), or else drastically cuts them, as in CC ch. 9, where a quotation from Ecclus 42:14 is omitted, along with the commentary which follows.

In a version which normally expands on the base text, omissions should not be overlooked. I suspect that in the first case the reference might have been ignored because no text is quoted. In the second it may be that, the text being very negative towards women (*melius est iniquitas viri quam mulier benefaciens*: in Q, col. 24, "better ys the wickednes of a man, then a womman wele doynge"), the author thought it better to omit it out of consideration for his audience.

2.1. A specific case

In addition to single words or phrases, and short sentences or para-graphs thus far analysed, I should like to examine now a larger unit, where the translators' different response to the text can be better appreciated. I have chosen the passage from ch. 33 in CC entitled "De egrediendo foras", which becomes in Q "Off goynge owte" (ch. 33), and in U "Of goyng forth" (ch. 31). The text is rather typical of David's style, combining a long string of simple sentences arranged in anaphoric order with the skilful analysis of an allegorical image.

CC: Quicquid in domo deuocionis colligis, hoc foras egrediens spargis pocius quam augeas vel conserues. Unde sepe experti sumus, tam in nobis quam in aliis, quod frequens exitus, et conuersacio cum seculo, et occupacio nimia exteriorum, deuocionem mentis extinguit, feruorem spiritus tepefacit, fortem propositum virtutis emollit, cor dissoluit, studium proficiendi debilitat, delicias docet amare, tempus sine fructu expendere, verba ociosa multiplicare, iocis et trufis intendere, oraciones negligere, horas canonicas desidiose et in cursu dicere. Tandem subintrant aque temptacionum (J1 "subintrat aqua temptacionis") in nauem cordis per rimas dissolucionis, ex deuocionis ariditate, et cum non exhauriantur per discussionem proprii status et puram confessionem, nec fortiter obstruuntur rime per diligentem custodiam, paulatim augentur donec submergunt hominem in peccatum et confusionem. (f. 8r)

117

Q: What so euer thow gadre to-gyder in the howse of god, all that thow disparplest when thow goyste owte, rather then thow encreaste ytt and kepyste yt. Wherof we haue experience, as well in oure self as in other, that ofte goyng owte, and conuersacion wyth the world, and owtewarde occupacion quenchyth the deuocion of the sowle, maketh hoote the feruence of the spiryte and maketh softe the myghty purpose of vertu, dissolueth the herte, maketh feble the study of goostly profitynge and encressyng, ytt techeth to love delyces, to spende tyme wyth-owte fruyte, to multiply ydell wordes, to take hyede to playes and to tryfuls, to take noone heyde of prayer, to sey theyr houres and theyr seruice sluggedly and in a rennynge ower. Atte laste they rennen in waters of temptacion into the shyppe of the harte throwgh the chynes of dissolucion for drynesse of deuocion. And when the waters be nott take owte by discussion, nor the chynes be not stoppede by diligence kepynge, a litell they growe more and more tyll they drowne the man in to synne and confusion. (cols 60-61)

U: Surely, if þu vse to go forth what-so-euer devocion or sweittnes þu haist gatheryd or goten at home, in goyng moch forth þu shalt rather disperkle and lese it than encreas or kepe it. We haue moche experience of thys, as wele in oure-selfe as in other, that oft goyng forth to wordly company and medlyng with worldly matteres quenchith the devocion of the soule, slakyth the fervour of the spiritt, hyndryth the gostly purpose of vertu, makyth the hert to waver and be onstable, and abatyth the gostly desyr of profettyng in grace. *Worldly persons* techyth also to loue worldly delyghtes and vayn plesures, to dispend the tyme onfrutefully, to multyply ydyl wordes and vayn communicacion, to vse vayn disportes and tryfulles, to sett lytyl by prayer, to sey goddes service hastyly and without devocion. And at the last, *if þu vse moch theyre company*, the wateres of temptacion shal so enter in-to the shipp of thy soule by the chynnys of dissolucion and lyghtnes, that if they be not shortly stoppyd by good discussion and consideracion of thyne own helth, and cast out by confession and thyne outward sensys diligently kept from al 'vayn' delectacion, by lytyl and lytyl *the seyd wateres of temptacion* shal so grow and encreas, that they shal drown the in syn to thy grete confusion and shame. *Loo, here maist þu see what profett þu shalt wyn by worldly company.*

(ff. 17v-18r)

Two remarks are in order here. The Syon translator seems again rather insensitive to the language of images: he misses, or better he neglects the highly figurative value and potential of such suggestive words as *tepefecit, emollit* contrasted with *fortem* (he has instead something which "hinders" what is "ghostly"), and *dissolvit*, for which he prefers an explicative clause: "to waver and be onstable", following the same tendency which appears in the rendering of *studium proficiendi debilitate* by "abatyth the gostly desyr of profettyng in grace".

Similarly, he seems not to be moved by the realistic touch of David's text, where the cracks in the ship are attributed to *ariditas*, literally referring to the dryness which makes the wood shrink: instead he translates what in Q was *drynesse of deuocion* by "lightness", which is certainly faulty behaviour, but not really what David had intended, and certainly not coherent with the allegory of the ship. In the allegory David uses *two* images to indicate how to avoid being drowned: first, one should "pour out" the waters of temptation by a pure confession; second, one should "stop" the cracks through a diligent custody of oneself. The Syon translator, while keeping the two verbs ("stoppyd" and "cast out"), merges the two images into one, that of the invading waters of temptation.

The second remark concerns the way this translator gives cohesion to his text. I have marked in italics four passages which are not in the original: they are neither decorative amplifications nor doublets. The first three function as crucial rings in a chain, and serve to remind the reader of some key subjects which risk being forgotten in such a long paragraph;[25] the fourth added paragraph is a useful summary of what has just been said. Having found the same practices in other versions of Birgittine texts in late medieval England, I wonder if this was a procedure common to a school of translators, be it Sheen or Syon. We may also note that Prestius locates temptation in the outside world, whose "company" presents the enclosed Birgittine nun with a different sort of temptation to that envisaged by David of Augsburg for his Franciscan novices. Other Birgittine texts similarly point to the challenge posed for the convent by the presence of seculars.

---

25   See the same in the rendering of *que scis non omnia effundas* (ch. 24, "De rumoribus") on gossiping: "if it fortune the in maner ageynst thy wyl to here one such, report them not to other of thy sustres" (f. 14v), against the rendering in Q: "putt not [out] all that thow knoweste" (col. 45), and "clatur not oute al þat þou knowiste" in A (f. 54v).

3. Concluding remarks

I would like to summarize my conclusions in three points which answer the three questions posed before:

1. I hope to have proved beyond question that the Latin text which was translated is the one we find in the 'English recension' of David's work.
2. While the translations in A and Q may be said to be the same, the one in U is too different to be simply considered an elaboration of the other.
3. As for the style, I have particularly drawn attention to two problems, concerning the way we should understand *literalness* and *amplification*. It should be clear that we cannot simply proclaim that a translation is "literal" or not. Even at the word level, we should investigate what it means. In our case, apart from instances where the emotional content of a word is involved, I have shown that the U translator seems not to like figurative language. In what we may take as his pedagogical and didactic attitude, instead of relying on the force of the image, he seems to trust more confidently in the overall, penetrating effect of a company of words which formed a comprehensive 'religious' vocabulary, which was probably clearer for its being more familiar, and could be thus more readily apprehended.

On the other hand amplification may mean different things. We have seen two of these. One has to do with clarity, the other with cohesion. I would suggest that this procedure points towards the oral delivery of the text, as was customary with spiritual reading in a religious community of that time.

CHAPTER 5

Three Versions of a *Rule for Hermits* in Late Medieval England

Contrary to what happens today, when his dialogue on *Spiritual Friendship* is the most popular of his works, being often translated and widely read, Aelred of Rievaulx's *De Institutione Inclusarum* written at the request of his sister, who was a recluse, was immensely popular in the Middle Ages.[1] In England it was translated at least twice,[2] and it was often quoted, or silently exploited, or referred to as an 'authority' in such important works as *Ancrene Riwle* and *Speculum Inclusorum*. The reasons for this popularity are to be found in at least two aspects of the work. One is the subject itself, the other is the lively and variegated treatment of the same.

Solitary life was a rather widespread religious choice in the Middle Ages, when, particularly in the form of reclusion, both for males and females, it enjoyed a comparatively extraordinary success especially in Italy and England.[3] Called 'hermits' if they were free to move around, and 'anchorites', or 'recluses', if they were enclosed, solitaries were figures widely known and appreciated in medieval society. Their position in the Church, with no specific authority to obey to, allowed them a great freedom, but this was exactly what engendered at the same time no little risk in the pursuit of personal sanctity. This situation demanded and fostered the production, particularly abundant in England,[4] of 'Rules' to direct their spiritual

---

1   Latin text in Hoste/Talbot (1971: 635-682).
2   The two translations have been edited by Ayto/Barratt (1984).
3   See Warren (1985). For a summary description see also Pezzini (2003: 9-26).
4   Four out of the nine Rules described by Rouillard in *Dizionario degli Istituti di Perfezione*, VII, 1533-1536, are English. In a list provided by Livarius Oliger of Rules for recluses written between the 9th and the 13th century, one is from France (Grimlaic), three are from Germany, and five from England:

life and to specify daily duties both about prayer and work. The three English rules I am going to illustrate, written between the end of the fifteenth and the beginning of the sixteenth century, are proof of the success of this eremitic literature. They come at the end of a long and substantial production of texts for anchorites which we may call 'rules', as they were frequently labelled, although this must not be confined to the idea of totally external norms and dispositions.

1. Rules as a 'genre'

To understand what a rule may be like, I shall briefly describe three major works of this literary tradition. Aelred's *De Institutione Inclusarum* is not the first rule for anchoritic life. In the Western Church the foundation stone of this literature for recluses was laid by the *Regula solitariorum* written at the end of the ninth century by a priest of the diocese of Metz called Grimlaic. It is a rather long text, divided in 69 chapters stretching over about 90 columns of the *Patrologia Latina*.[5] A summary description of its contents throws some light on what is to be intended as a 'rule'. The variety of the materials can be gathered under a few headings, such as: the meaning of reclusion, exhortations to the practice of virtues, canonical and legislative norms concerning the enclosure (who to admit and how to prove the vocation of the applicant), rules for the organization of the liturgical office and more generally on how to regulate the use of time (work, reading, rest and sleep), norms about clothing, food and meals, and in between all this, commentaries on scriptural passages, interspersed with quotations from the classical Christian authors, stories drawn from the *Vitae Patrum*, and frequent complaints against the widespread corruption of the age, especially manifest in various sorts of reproachable behaviour among the recluses themselves to

---

Regula Reclusorum Angliae et Quaestiones Tres de Vita Solitaria, in *Antonianum* 9 (1934), 37-84, here 47-49.

5   A rather detailed presentation of Grimlaic's *Rule for solitaries* as well as of Peter the Venerable's *Letter to Gislebert* can be found in Pezzini (2003: 27-58).

whom the *Regula* is addressed. Spiritual and biblical, narrative and legislative, hortatory and complaint passages all mingle in this complex literary genre, which can be simplified and reduced to two substantial parts which will later be distinguished as *outer* and *inner* rule, integrated with passages, whether of either biblical or patristic content, meant to be read as *meditations*.

These three aspects correspond to the threefold plan that we actually find in Aelred of Rievaulx's *Rule of Life for a Recluse* (*De Institutione Inclusarum*), written towards the end of his life, between 1160 and 1162. This plan is presented by the author himself, who writes as a conclusion to his work speaking to his sister:

> You have now what you asked for: rules for bodily observances by which a recluse may govern the behaviour of the outward man; directions for cleansing the inner man from vices and adorning him with virtues; a threefold meditation to enable you to stir up the love of God in yourself, feed it and keep it burning. (Aelred of Rievaulx 1971/[β]1995: 102)

I shall only mention a third and admirably written text, the *Letter to Gislebert* addressed by Peter the Venerable around 1140-1150 to a monk of the Cluny order who was living as a recluse. This letter is in fact a small treatise, and as such it appears in many manuscripts where it was copied. To Peter we owe two splendid metaphors in which the basic paradox of this eremitic life is enclosed: first, the recluse is likened to Christ lying in the sepulchre on Holy Saturday, in a condition of death which is the door to life and resurrection; secondly, and consequently, the recluse is invited to find the vastness of the sky in the narrowness of his cell.

1.1. The influence of Aelred's work

If we should look for the reasons why Aelred's work was so popular, I think that we may find them, besides the intrinsic spiritual value of the treatise, in the richness and variety of the materials forming the contents of this comparatively short book, in which a strong personal, and at times overtly autobiographical note strikes the heart of the reader. The possible aridity of the *outer rule* is enkindled with vivid portraits of avid, talkative, restless recluses, a gallery of characters which, according to Jusserand (1895: 124), anticipate Boccaccio's *Decameron*. The severe commendations and warnings of the *inner rule* (practically reduced to the virtues of poverty, humility and chastity) are softened by passages where Aelred unashamedly shows his own shortcomings. The *threefold meditation* on past, present and future benefits of God, given as a sample of what the recluse should think about in her life of silence, is also coloured with personal and family memories, but above all it provides an intensely affective method of visualizing and contemplating the gospel stories. This was to have an extraordinary afterlife, since this part, under the name of Anselm, went almost entirely in Ludolphus of Saxony's *Vita Christi*, sharing thus the immense popularity and diffusion of this work.[6]

A treatise which contains such a variegated material – especially when, as is the case in the Middle Ages, works of literature were often modular in form – is exposed to be split in different smaller tracts. In fact, the radiation of Aelred's rule followed *two itineraries*. One we mentioned above concerns the meditative part of the work, which, if not its very origin, is part and parcel of that new spiritual movement which is customarily called 'affective piety'. The other concerns the outer rule, and it was numerically more relevant, since its presence can be detected in quite a number of works either as direct quotations or silent borrowings, or in some cases as an explicit reference to Aelred as a 'master' on this specific subject, and consequently as an 'authority' to be followed. To give just a couple of important examples, the *Ancrene Riwle* in a chapter on chastity where the *Rule for recluses* is quoted, refers to him as "seint Ailred abbat",[7] while the *Speculum Inclusorum*, when dealing with the outer rule, makes an explicit reference to "the doctrine exposed by the blessed Aelred in his rule for recluses together with the excellent writing of other devout authors".[8]

---

6   For the influence of Aelred's Rule on the meditative literature of the late Middle Ages see Pezzini (2003: 92-95).

7   See Pezzini (2003: 96-98). See also Allen (1918, especially 529-530) and, more recently, Barratt (1980).

8   See Oliger (1938: 140); see also p. 129 where again Aelred is mentioned by name. The text is printed on pp. 63-148. Aelred is also referred to on p. 34 of the Introduction, where Oliger indicates derivations from his *Speculum Caritatis* and *Sermones de Oneribus*, besides, obviously, the *De Institutione Inclusarum*.

2. Eremitic literature in Medieval England

Eremitic literature is particularly rich in England. Here I shall concentrate on works which are specifically recognisable as rules. The major scholar in this field is Livarius Oliger, to whom we owe the edition and study of most of these rules for hermits and anchorites. In an article published in 1928, due to a suggestion made by Hope Emily Allen, he edited three Latin rules which he called, after the place where the manuscripts are now kept, *dublinensis, cantabrigensis and oxoniensis*.[9] The Dublin rule was written at the end of the thirteenth century, and is extant together with other similar texts in a manuscript which Oliger describes as "parvus codex regularum", a collection of rules gathered after 1279; the other two rules belong to the fourteenth century.[10] In 1934 Oliger edited a *Regula reclusorum* by Walter the recluse, written about 1282, for which Grimlaic and Aelred, together with other Christian authors, are used as sources. In 1938 he edited the *Speculum Inclusorum*, in which, as I said, Aelred is mentioned by name as a definite authority in the field. Also the three rules, the first for anchorites and the other two for hermits, greatly depend on Aelred's treatise, a debt neatly documented in the footnotes in Oliger's edition, although none of these rules ever quotes Aelred or his work by name. Especially in the Cambridge rule, which was once attributed to a young Richard Rolle, Aelred's presence is so pervasive that, in Oliger's words, it is "just a new version of Aelred's outer rule" (Oliger 1928: 158).

2.1. The Oxford rule

The Oxford rule, which is the one used by the translators/adaptors of the three English versions, shows clear links with the Cambridge rule

---

9   See Oliger (1928: 151-190 [introduction and *dublinensis*] and 1928: 291-310 [*cantabrigensis* and *oxoniensis*]).
10   The three MSS are respectively: MS Dublin, Trinity College 97 B.3.5, ff. 188ra-192ra; MS Cambridge, CUL Mm.vi.17, ff. 70v-76v, MS Oxford, Bodley Rawl. C. 72, ff. 166v-169v.

(five passages are quoted verbatim), together with references to the Benedictine Rule and the Rule of St Francis. It differs from the Cambridge rule mainly in that it greatly reduces certain spiritual expansions to concentrate on some juridical principles, practical norms of daily life, and the order of prayers. We may say that the balance is heavily in favour of the 'outer' rule, although spiritual suggestions and insights are also present. It may be interesting to know that the extant manuscript of the Oxford rule belonged to a Franciscan community of religious, although this is not proof that it was produced there or by one of the friars. In any case it is interesting to remark that no less than four passages have been identified by Oliger as deriving from the Rule of St Francis.

The Oxford rule has in its present condition 22 chapters, not numbered in the manuscript but marked by underlined headings and initial capitals. However, it lacks the final part, and presumably, by comparing it with one of the three translations, two or three chapters are missing.[11] To give a cursory idea of the contents, here is the list of the chapter headings, to which Oliger has attributed a number:

Prologus
    I. Qualis debet esse vera paupertas
    II. Quod vere pauper Christi sancte possit vivere, licet non ingrediatur religionem
    III. De obedientia quam debet Deo et hominibus
    IV. De voto suo faciendo
    V. Qualiter recipiat res mundi
    VI. De providencia in cella sua
    VII. De humilitate in cibis et potibus
    VIII. De vestimentis suis
    IX. De calciamentis suis
    X. De predicatione et mendicatione
    XI. De sustentacione eius per viam
    XII. De silencio heremite
    XIII. De abstinentia et ieiunio in domo propria
    XIV. Quando licet heremite domi comedere carnem
    XV. De proprietate quam habebit

---

11   I follow the text as edited by Oliger (1928: 312-320).

XVI. De labore heremite
XVII. Quomodo debet iacere et qua hora debet pausare et qua hora surgere
XVIII. De matutinis dicendis
XIX. Quo tempore et qua hora debet dici officium pro defunctis
XX. De modo et tempore contemplacionis seu meditacionis
XXI. De hora prima dicenda
XXII. Hora qua debet heremita sacerdos missam celebrare vel laycus audire

Spirituality and practicalities go hand in hand. Poverty is a major theme. Sobriety in clothing, food, possessions is highly recommended. Preaching implies that this rule is not for recluses, and in chapter VI the fact that the hermit may live in a town or in a village is explicitly mentioned. The chapter titles may be misleading: for example Chapter IX (*De calciamentis suis*) is not particularly about shoes, but concerns a modest and sober way of moving around the country. Rather surprisingly liturgical offices, times of fasting, hours of rest, sleep and work are rather quickly dealt with.

2.2. Versions based on the Oxford rule

There are three English versions clearly derived from the Oxford rule, although they have no connection with each other, and offer interesting variations both in the layout of the text and especially in the translation proper. They are found in MS London, British Library Additional 34193, ff. 131r-136v; MS British Library Sloane 1584, ff. 89r-95v; MS Bristol City Reference Library 6 (dated 1502), ff. 137v-140v. While the source is common, the rendering varies greatly, as can be seen by simply considering the length of the text: while Additional has 4657 words, Sloane has 2231, and Bristol only 1454. The style of the translation also varies: Additional shows a literality which may at times produce awkward and hardly understandable passages, not to mention misspellings, missing words and a rather careless handwriting, which makes the text not always easy to read; Sloane has a better wording and syntax, although its possible use is marred by the fact that the rule is written as a continuous text with no paragraphing or any segmentation whatsoever; Bristol is certainly the best version, to which an elegant presentation of the text should be added, with fine handwriting and decorated initial capitals at the beginning of each clearly distinct chapter.

A brief description of the three manuscripts where the rules are found may raise intriguing questions.

BL Additional 34.193 (ff. 228) belongs to the 15th century.[12] The main pieces it contains include *The Pilgrimage of the Soul*, a collection of liturgical *Hymns* in Latin with an English version in royal stanzas, our *Rule for hermits*, the *Sayings of the Philosophers*, the *Dysticha Catonis* in English with parts in Latin, and smaller pieces such as a fragment of a life of St James the Greater, a vision, a religious poem, a letter of Bernard of Chartres, a report of the Synod held at Westminster on 9 Sept. 1125, and, strange as it may seem, a letter from "Baltizar by the grace of Mahounde... Sowdayn of Surry, Emperor of Babulon..." to the king of England and France and Edward his son, offering the latter his daughter in marriage.

BL Sloane 1584, of the beginning of the 16th century, is a small codex (ff. 95) which seems to have belonged to a parish priest. It is signed "Scriptum per me Johannem Gysborn canonicum de Coverham" (f. 12r). The contents here are even more baffling. There are liturgical pieces concerning the "ministration of deacon and sub-deacon according to the Premonstratensian order", a few medical prescriptions spread in different places, letter forms about how to request ecclesiastical licences, a model-sermon for Easter day, questions for confessors, a form of confession and a small treatise on penances to be given as remedies against the confession of capital sins, instructions about enamelling and engraving, short passages on the pains of hell, on death, the plague and various other illnesses, verses to the Virgin, the angels and the patriarchs, a poem in which a woman complains about the hardness of heart of her lover, after which, as the final item in the manuscript, comes our Rule for hermits!

Bristol Public Library Ms 6 (ff. 140)[13] contains mainly Latin pieces of liturgical matters. Two items are dated, 13 Sept. 1502, and

---

12   For a description of this manuscript see *Catalogue of Additions to the Manuscripts in the British Museum* (1888-1893), London 1894, pp. 225-226.
13   This manuscript is described in Ker (1977: II/203-204).

31 Oct. 1502. The short pieces in English concern tribulations, the discretion of spirits, the Rule for hermits, followed by the "Virtues of Rosemary", of which I like to quote the beginning:

> Fyrst take rosemary leves and bynde hem in a clene lynnen cloth and boyle hem in fayr water tyl the water be half soden a-way and vse thys to drynke, for thys water ys good for many maner of evelys in man-is body. Also boyle rosemary leves in wyn and vse to washe the face therwyth, and thy face shall euermore be clere and the here of thy face and of þi hed shall neuer pyle.
>
> (f. 140v)

2.3. Overview

I shall end this chapter by making some points concerning both the content of the Oxford rule in general and some translational choices of the English rules in particular. In carrying out this analysis, the Additional rule, notwithstanding its drawbacks, is the first choice, since it is precisely for its literalness that it is the best representative of the Oxford rule, featuring a table at the beginning, with single chapters well evidenced on the page. Moreover, since the Oxford text is incomplete and lacks the final chapters, Additional offers the only testimony of what the Latin rule must have been in its integrity.

The Additional version has gathered the text into 17 chapters, of which the last three translate the missing part of the Oxford Latin text. The difference in the numbering is due to the fact that in some cases Additional amalgamates smaller Latin chapters in larger units. Here is the table provided by Additional, slightly simplified and rendered in modern English, with, in brackets, the corresponding chapters of the Oxford Rule in Roman numbers:

1. Of the forsaking of this wretched world (I-II)
2. Of the obedience of an hermit (III)
3. Of his vow (IV)
4. Of his poverty (V)
5. Of his purveyance (VI-VII)
6. Of his clothes (VIII)
7. Of his shoes (IX-X-XI)
8. Of his silence keeping (XII)

9. Of his abstinence (XIII)
10. When he shall eat flesh (XIV)
11. Of his property (XV-XVI)
12. When he shall lie and when he shall rise (XVII-XVIII-XIX)
13. Of the manner and time of his contemplation (XX-XXI)
14. What hour he shall say mass or hear mass (XXII)
15. Of his silence at the table with labour and refection
16. Of his shrift and housel
17. Of the service of a lay hermit

A quick survey of the Oxford rule throws some light on the life of hermits, and on the ideas accompanying that vocation, which was current in the 14th century. Three points made at the start may be of interest, especially if we consider the kind of apologetic tone they have. They mark in fact the necessity of a rule and of an authority, and seem to vindicate a characteristic role for the hermits in the church. These are the statements:

1. Although the eremitic form of life has no canonical acknowledgement, it is good that those who choose to follow Christ in a life of poverty have a rule.
2. Although any state of life can lead to sanctity, marriage as well as celibacy, living a life of poverty in the world or far from it is the best and surest way to reach heaven.
3. Although the hermit has no recognized authority over him and his obedience is due only to God, it is anyway necessary for him to obey his prelate, or even his patron if this is a priest. He must also have a spiritual father in order to be advised and, if the case, corrected.[14] Concerning authority, however, the rule is rather flexible: vows of poverty and chastity are to be taken before God only, and also before the bishop (or abbot or prior, one rule adds), but only if the hermit wants and if he can. Licences on the other hand have to be requested both for dresses and for preaching.

---

14 Old rules, starting from Grimlaic's, had repeatedly warned against the danger of pride, vanity, self-indulgence and other faults a solitary may incur in exactly for being alone.

It is interesting to remark that not so much solitude as poverty is presented as the most peculiar characteristic of hermits' life. This is strongly marked in the first chapters, and it may explain both the Franciscan links shown in one of these texts, and the popularity of such a rule in times when a simple and poor life was perceived as the best testimony to his faith a Christian had to offer. Poverty does not forbid the possession of some goods, which may be needed, for example, to improve the cell, to build a new one, to buy books which are necessary, or clothes : in any case the hermit should give to poorer people what remains (see Chapter V).

The hermits envisaged by this rule do not actually seem to be separated from the life of the people. Jusserand (1909: 137-138) says:

> In the fourteenth century hermits for the most part seldom sought the solitude of deserts or the depths of the woods [...]; they lived by preference in cottages, built at the most frequented parts of the great roads, or at the corners of bridges. They lived there [...] on the charity of passers-by.

This is confirmed by the Oxford rule, where it is said that to provide food for his life the hermit may, if he lives in a town or in a borough, beg every day; otherwise he should buy food once per week.

Shoes, as I said, have to do both with poverty (they must not be "curious", that is "extravagant", neither be boots, but only sandals, including the possibility to go barefooted) and with walking. This gives the occasion to advise sobriety, and this means that a hermit should not go around, use a servant for errands, talk with people along the roads, etc. (see Chapter IX).

2.4. Issues in translation

Now, to show how the same text can evince different responses, I shall quote some points where to compare the three English rules with the source Latin text, not without recalling that at least two of them shorten the text to a considerable extent, and the one which follows it more or less literally, shows some choices of its own, as when a chapter on subjects for contemplation is dryly reduced to a series of indications, while on the contrary, norms about times of prayers, which are rather concise in the Latin, are integrated with many detailed indications of psalms or collects to be said.

Let's start from ch. III, which in the original consists of three smaller units: one about obedience, a second about confession, a third about the necessity of always speaking the truth. Here is the Latin:

(III) Soli Deo debet heremita obedientiam facere, quia ipse est abbas, prior et prepositus sui claustri, idest cordis sui, pro cuius amore omnia mundana non solum reliquit, immo per gratiam Dei voluntatem habendi deseruit.

Episcopo etiam in cuius diocesi habitat et patri suo spirituali, qui noticiam habent condicionum eius, confiteri debet, et patrono loci, si fuerit prelatus ecclesie vel sacerdos bone discretionis, debet, sicut et episcopo, notificare vitam et modum vite sue. Et si aliqua viderint in illo emendanda, obediat consiliis eorum propter Christum magistrum suum qui dicit: *Qui vos audit, me audit et qui vos spernit, me spernit.*

Omni tempore loquimini veritatem et neminem dubitet pro veritate dicenda, *sed* illum solum timeat *qui corpus et animam potest* mittere *in gehennam* ignis; et specialiter contra omnes iudeos, saracenos et falsos christianos catholicam fidem sancte romane ecclesie non credentes, pro huiusmodi erroribus destruendis mortem pro fide Christe subire, si oporteat, non formidet.

Here are the English versions:

Additional 34.193
An herimite also owes to make his Obedience all-only to all-might god for he is abote prior and þe gouernour of his cloister, þat is to say of his hert, for whosse lawe he hase not for-sakyt all-only all wardely thyngis, but also þe varray worlde, and also his owne wylle be þe vertu and grasse of Jhu Cryste.

Also he owis to notyfie and show his lyffe to þe byschop in whos diosice he dwellis, and þe patrone of þe plase yf he be a prelate of þe kyrke, or to a prest of gude dyscression and conuersaccion. And yf so be þat they cane fynde or fele any thynge in hym to be a-mendyd, yet be-fallys hym to obey to there counsellys and theyr correcconys for þe love of Criste hys master, þe wilk says: *[he] tha[t] heris yow [heris] me & he þat dyspicys yow dyspicis me.*

Evyr þat he speke trewth and drede no maner for trouthe to be saide, but þat *he drede him þat may chaste bo the body and sowlle into euer lastynge fyr,* and yet he be-hovys hym not for to drede noder Jves ne Sarsonnys and in aspecyall false Crystyn menn not be levynge in þe feith of holy kyrk for þis erysy and all oþer poyntis of errysy, and to susteyne, maynten and encris þe feith of Criste, yt be-hovys hym to dye. (f. 132r)

And ther-for þilke a hermeytt owght fyrst to be buxun to God allmyghty & to his commawndmentys, fore he ys abbott & prior off his cloister, that ys to say off his hert & off his body, for whos loue he has nott forsakyne onely that he had, butt þat myght haue had yff he had dwellyd in the world.

Hyme owght also to be buxom to the byshope in whos byshopryke he ys wonnynge in, and to his patron in whos place that he wonnys in. And yffe he be a prelate person ore preste & off gud and honest lyff & off dyscrecion, thene awght hyme forto shewe his lyff vnto hyme & wyrke after his cownsell in that att ys gud, for and he here hyme, he heris God hyme-selfe, for so says owre lord Ihesu Crist to his dyscypyllys: *That mane that herys youe heris me, & that mane þat dyspycys youe dyspycis me.* Iff hys patron be no prest, then hyme awght to go to hyme that maid hyme heyrmett and schewe his lyff to hyme.

Ilke a heyrmett awght euer more to say the soothe, & dred non erthly mane fore the sothfastnes, for *hyme awe onely for to dred hyme that has pover off his body and off his sowle & may fore his trespas pyne them bothe in helle.* Agayne Jewys and Saressyns and fals cristyne mene that says owght ore doys agayne cristyne trovthe, thene owght hyme to dye stedfastlye to stond for to maynteyne with all his myght the trovthe off holy kyrke, and yff ned be ther-for to be redy to dye. (ff. 90v-91r)

Bristol MS 6

OBEDIENCE

A heremyte owght to make obedience to god oonly for he ys abbot, pryor and prepositor of hys cloyster, that ys to say of hys hert, for whos loue he hath forsakyn all thing, for who so euer leve well of haueyng, leuith all thyng by grace of our saveoure Jesu Criste

CONFESSYON

Also an heremyte owght to be confessyd at hys enteryng yn to relygyon of the byschope of the dyosyce in the which he doth ynhabyt hym self yn, or to þe patrone of hys place yf he be a prelate of the chyrch, or to a preeste of good dysposycion. To any of thes he owght to shreve hym, wher fore yf ther were any thing yn hym amys, he mought obey to the councell of them for the loue of Criste hys master þat sayth: *he þat heryth hym heryth me and he that despysyth you despysyth me.*

OF TYME OF SCILENCE

For trowth and for our faythe it ys lefull to speke at all tymes yn defence of them and yn thys case dowte no man for sayng trowth But dowte hym oonly that hath power to send bothe body and soule yn to hell. And specially a-gayns Jewes, Sarazens and fals christen men þat beleue not in þe chyrch; for to destroy such errours dowte not dethe yf nede be. (f. 138v)

A few remarks are in order. It appears clearly that *Additional* stands out as expanding on the original text, and this is done either by adding an adjective or a phrase (almighty God; for the love of Christ), or by the generous use of doublets (by the virtue and grace of Jesus; good discretion and conversation; their counsels and their corrections), or by putting a stronger stress (to leave *omnia mundane* becomes 'all worldly things and also the very world', *pro fide* is rendered by 'sustain, maintain and increase the faith'); interestingly *pro cuius amore* becomes 'for whose law'.

Sloane also adds something to the text, as when he says that not only God must be obeyed but also *his commandments*, or when at the end of the second paragraph he specifies what should be done if the patron is not a priest. There are also good examples of rephrasing of the Latin text, as when he amalgamates the rule to notify the hermit's life 'to a priest of good and honest life and of discretion' and then to follow his counsels: 'Then he ought to show his life to him and to act according to his counsels if they are good.'

The *Bristol* version has clearly perceived the three-part composition of the unique Latin chapter, and has accordingly split it into three units, giving a proper title to each part, although to qualify the third one as 'silence' is rather baffling in that the rule is about speaking! Here too we can find nice expansions, as where at the end of the first small chapter *per gratiam Dei* becomes 'by grace of our Saviour Jesus Christ'. The approach to a wise priest to unveil the hermit's life and to ask for counsel has become technically a 'confession' (the title of the third short chapter), rightly expressed by the technical verb *shreve* (shrive). On the whole, the Bristol version is both shorter and clearer than the other two.

Another comparison may be made with a smaller unit, a short chapter entitled in Latin "De voto suo faciendo":

(IV) Omnipotenti Deo faciat votum paupertatis et castitatis cum Dei adiutorio. Votum eiusmodi non debet fieri per preceptum alicuius hominis sive status, sed soli Deo, "cui servire regnare est", faciat votum suum. Aliter enim videretur quod militaret sub regula vel nomine. Sed tamen episcopo si velit faciat votum suum et secundum consilium suum vivat, si potest.

Additional 34.193
Euery hermite be-fallys to make his wowe of pouerte and of chastyte with þe helpe of god. Nevir þe lesse þe wowe of suche a mann owys not to be mad be þe precepte of any mann of his state, but all only be god, whome he serue þat is a kyngdome, or ellis yt shuld seme þe he shuld forfett agayne his rewle or

agayne man*n*. But nethelesse be-fore þe bysshop yf he wyll he may make hys
wow aftyr his dyspocyon. (f. 132r)

Sloane 1584
Hermettis awe to make a vowe off wyllfull pouerte & off chastyte to god
thorowe helpe off hyme-selfe, noght thorowe the bydynge off a-nother off his
order, butt to bynd hyme sadly to God allmyghty. He may make ytt be-ffore
byschope, abbot or priore, and do aftyr ther covnsyll & þer commawndment.
(f. 91r-v)

Bristol 6
OF THE VOWE OF POU*ER*TE AND CHASTITE
To all mighty god vow he hys pou*er*te and chastite wyth the helpe of gode.
Neu*er* the less ther owght not to be no vow made by the com*m*aundmentys of
any man of hys state, but to god alone by fore the byschope, and then yf he
wyll he may make hys vowe after hys owne arbeterment. (f. 139r)

In this case *Additional* is the most literal, although one wonders
whether the Latin phrase *cuius servire regnare est* is accurately translated into 'whom he serves that is a kingdom'! We may notice that the
statement *Aliter enim videretur quod militaret sub regula vel nomine*,
faithfully rendered by *Additional* is not translated either by *Sloane* or
Bristol.

I shall take another example from two very short chapters,
dealing with sobriety in food and drink.

VII. De humilitate in cibis et potibus
Non sit curiosus de cibariis corporalibus, sed pro Dei amore ipsa cibaria sociis
indigentibus largiatur; et hoc est indicium magnum humilitatis et vere
paupertatis

Additional 34.193
He may not be lusty nor lycours to no dilectabyll mete nor drynk*is*, butt for þe
luffe of god be-fallis to gyffe and to a p*r*este w*ith* his pore & nedy fellowys,
for this is þe dome and þe payme*n*t of very pou*er*te and of gret mekenes and
charite. (f. 132v)

Sloane 1584
Hyme awght nott to be besy aftyr sere mettis and drynkis, and yff he haue
more then he nedys hym-selffe, then go gyffe yt gladlye to theme that has
more myster, for that ensampyll off wyllffull pouerte opynly shewynge off
charite & off grett meknes. (f. 91v)

135

Bristol 6
OF HYS METYS
That ys the Jugement of trew poverte and grete mekenes that he be neuer
curyus of hys bodily metys but such as he getys for the loue of god lett hym
depart gladely to the nedy. (f. 139r)

Additional and *Bristol* have taken *indicium* for *iudicium* (*dome*, and
jugement), a rather common error. *Sloane* is correct, and his para-
phrase-translation is a good rendering of the Latin. *Additional*
amplifies *curiosus* (lusty and lecherous), as he does with *sociis*
indigentibus (a priest with his poor and needy fellows), and to poverty
and meekness he adds "charity" as a summary. *Bristol* reworks all the
sentence, and apart from the blunder on *indicium*, the addition of
'gladly' sounds rather pleasant, reminding the reader of the Scriptural
text: "hilarem datorem diligit Deus" (2Cor 9:7).

Another and final example is from the chapter on clothing
(VIII, De vestimentis suis), and deals with forms of bodily penance.

> [...] Et si ex devocione iuxta carnem cilicio uti voluerit, bene licebit, nisi
> fuerit in oratione contemplacionis, ita quod pro nimietate vermium ex cilicio
> proveniecium posset impediri de contemplatione sua, et sic pocius intenderet
> dolori carnis quam contemplacioni spiritus. Cilicium igitur consciencie
> relinquemus.

Additional 34.193
[ch. VI] And yf so be þat of devosyon agayne temptacion of fleshe þat he wyll
were heire, well and lawfully he may yf so be þat be thourgh his owne
devocyon. But yf this be an impediment to stere hym fro þat devocyon, þat yf
it be thurgh bredynge of mykell vermyn be ewyne þe fleshe & þe heyre, rather
or yt shulde be so, as god for-bede, with drawe yt as fortyme and so rather to
þe flesshe þan to þe contemplacyon of þe sprite, and thus we for-sake þe heyre
of his conscience. (f. 133r)

Sloane1584
[...] He may were the heyre, yff he wyll, next his fleych yff ytt lett nott grettly
his deuocion in praynge for bytynge off wormis that bredys thar-vndyr. Here
in his hart weres he euermore whene he thingkis off the passion off owr lord
Ihesu Cryst. (ff. 91v-92r)

Bristol 6
[...] And yf he wyll of devocyon were next hys flesh a cylyce it ys laufull.
(f. 139r)

Additional reveals once more his uncertain grasp of the Latin: he translates *iuxta carnem*, meaning 'near the flesh', by 'against the temptation of the flesh'! And where the rule seems to suggest that, if the haircloth prevents a peaceful exercise of contemplation because of the worms it produces on the skin, this 'torment' should be removed, leaving to conscience to decide whether to use it or not (*Cilicium igitur consciencie relinquemus*), we do not really understand what *Additional* means when he says that 'thus we abandon the hair of conscience'. This seems to be a rather careless literal rendering, when not a positive blunder based on an interpretation of *consciencie* as a genitive specifying *cilicium*, while I think that within this context, taking *consciencie* as a dative connected with *relinquemus*, the correct meaning is rendered by 'we leave the (use of) the haircloth to conscience'. *Sloane* does much better, since he clarifies and spiritualizes the *cilicium* by interpreting it as 'the memory of the passion of our Lord Jesus Christ in one's heart'. *Bristol* does not actually seem to be interested in a rule concerning bodily penance, a rule which he starkly simplifies by noting that this should be intended nothing more than 'a lawful devotion'.

3. Concluding remarks

Leaving a more detailed analysis to a complete edition of these three versions of the *Regula oxoniensis*, I here conclude with a general and simple remark. My findings appear to confirm the conclusion reached by Warren, that all these writings for anchorites, ranging from brief epistles to major mystical treatises, were meant to reach a larger audience than the single hermit or recluse, both as spiritual guides and as practical rules for self-discipline, which could be practised even when not living a solitary life in a hermitage (see Warren 1985: 103-107). This raises the question of what the readership of these literary works was. The miscellaneous contents of the three manuscripts are rather frustrating and not particularly helpful in identifying both compilers and readers. These may suggestively belong to a wide range of people stretching from persons simply wishing to enjoy something spiritual to those wishing to collect literary and spiritual pieces of some value.

CHAPTER 6

The Italian Reception of Birgittine Writings[1]

The title of this chapter should be explained in order to avoid undue expectations. The word 'reception' is here used because it has a broad meaning: it is meant to suggest not a wide scope, but rather a vague horizon. What I am going to present is in fact an initial survey of Italian versions of Birgitta's *Revelations* which does not pretend to be complete, together with some remarks on the type of these translations (which cannot be more than suggestions derived from small samples taken at random); in addition to this presentation I thought it would also be interesting to collect some information on writings connected with the Swedish saint, attributed to or inspired by her, including those produced to celebrate her sanctity.

It is only slightly ironic that in compiling this survey I practically find myself in the uneasy position of one who follows in the footsteps of a scholar who has been for me both a leading light and a favourite target of criticism. In my previous research on English translations of St Birgitta's *Revelations* I have always used as a basis the list of manuscripts which was first established by Cumming (1929) in his introduction to the edition of the Birgittine compilation extant in the Garrett MS. That list has been very helpful, although a few items were missing at the time, subsequently added by Jolliffe (1974a), and there were some inaccuracies in the description of the content of the manuscripts, which a closer analysis allowed me to correct. The most serious objection to Cumming's presentation, however, was his way of evaluating the translations. As I have shown in the comments made on the Birgittine texts I have been editing over the years, Cumming's judgements appear highly disputable today, both in view of our different appreciation of medieval translational practices, and in the

---

1   An earlier version of this chapter was first published in Morris/O'Mara (2000: 186-212).

light of the evidence provided by the edition and the detailed analysis of most of the items he listed.[2]

My task now is a difficult one, especially because no such basic catalogue exists of the Italian translations of Birgitta's *Liber celestis*. I am well aware that my investigation marks the very beginning of a new field of research, which means that, while it may be welcomed as a promising contribution, there is the highest risk for me of falling into the same hasty evaluations which I have often criticised in Cumming's presentation, and into an even greater approximation, since my list of Birgittine translations into Italian is far from being complete, most probably much less complete than his description of the English renderings. Being at a very early stage, the scope of my study is limited, both in respect of the material I present, and in the evaluation of the translational practices I propose. As for the first of these points, I shall consider only the material extant in manuscript form, leaving out the printed editions; as for the second, I want to specify that the remarks made on some examples of translations found in the texts I describe should be taken only as tentative, no more than quick 'glimpses' into a large universe, which a closer and more substantial analysis could modify to a considerable extent, or even reverse completely. This has to be stated both for intellectual honesty and as an anticipated apology for what will be found missing or objectionable.

To start with, it is worth remembering what is well known, that Italy is the only Mediterranean country where Birgitta's work had a wide circulation, as is testified by quite a number of manuscripts of the Latin texts extant or produced in Italian scriptoria.[3] This is hardly surprising, given the very simple fact that Birgitta lived the last twenty-four years of her life in Italy (1349-1373), acting as a public figure; moreover, her spiritual heritage was ensured by the early foundation of two Birgittine monasteries: the Florentine convent of Paradiso in the Pian di Ripoli (1394-1395) and the Scala Coeli near

---

2   For a list of these editions see fn. 8; see, in particular, chapters 1 and 2.

3   Of the most important manuscripts listed by Undhagen (1977) nine are Italian: Napoli (N: pp. 118-120); Palermo (P: pp. 150-152), Roma (R: pp. 152-153), Venezia (V: pp. 153-156), New York (Y, from Napoli: pp. 156-162), Milano (A[a]: Braidense: pp. 162-164), Venezia (S[a]: Marciana: p. 164), Milano (a: Ambrosiana: p. 165); Cremona (I: pp. 179-181).

Genoa (1406).[4] Both were a centre of the diffusion of her cult and of her writings, and many of the manuscripts I am going to discuss, containing full or partial translations of her book, are directly connected with these two monasteries.

As a second important premise, I should like to recall that the study of the versions of the *Liber celestis* into Italian belongs to the vast field of medieval and Renaissance translations, a huge bulk of texts which were instrumental in the diffusion of old and new cultures, and deeply influenced the formation of Italian prose as much as other European vernaculars. A cursory look at two of the best anthologies of Italian literature produced in the thirteenth and fourteenth centuries shows that more than half the texts there collected are translations, mostly from Latin, some from French.[5] But in spite of this impressive phenomenon, it must be said that in Italy a consistent scholarly interest in these translations, or 'volgarizzamenti', is relatively recent, not earlier than the 1950s, and only partially relevant for our topic, in that it seems to be more concentrated on the study of translations of secular classical authors.[6] This can certainly be helpful, in that any study of translational practices is undoubtedly relevant for the whole of the subject. But it is also true that the translation of religious texts is worth special consideration, and this for two reasons at least. The first is the prevalent practical character of the work, with the predictable consequence of clarity as a paramount quality (preference for parataxis, for example), and the large use of technical devices (summaries, repetitions, etc.).[7] This was required by the fact that translations were

---

4   For the foundation of the Italian convents see Cnattingius (1963) and Nyberg (1996), and the bibliography there indicated.

5   I refer to Segre/Marti (1959) and De Luca (1954). In both introductions some interesting remarks are made concerning the literature in translation, particularly De Luca (1954: xx-xxii).

6   See a recent bibliographical survey of the research in the field by Frasso (1997). The limitation of the field to pagan authors is in itself revealing. Folena remarks that for the specific subject of the translation of religious texts "manca un approfondimento e uno studio complessivo soddisfacente" [more research is needed and a comprehensive satisfactory study is still to be produced] (1991: 93, fn.17).

7   See Folena (1991: 11), where the translation of 'sacred texts', principally the Bible, is traced to the necessity of basic religious instruction, for which Augustine is quoted who thought that "it is better to incur the reproach of

141

produced mainly in view of the spiritual reading in a community, where the texts were normally read aloud.[8] The second and most important reason is the shared field of referentiality in Christian literature which must be known and taken into account when we come to analyse and assess a translation: without a Christian background and some familiarity with the language of faith and piety it would be difficult to explain, for example, why in the translations I am going to examine the phrase *virgo Maria* is rendered as *nostra donna* (MS D, Book VII,13) or why such a phrase as *innocens filius meus* can become *Angnello innocente* (MS D, Book VII,8) without causing any problem of interpretation to the reader. The same spiritual background must also be supposed to interpret, for example, the different treatment of the rubrics, which when translated are often starkly reduced and summarized, against that of the text, which, being taken as 'revealed', is much more respected in its integrity.

These short introductory remarks are meant to account for both the difficulty and the necessity of the task I have undertaken. The difficulty frightened me at first, the necessity encouraged me to try; and here are the first results of the enterprise.

Although there are printed editions of the Italian text of the *Revelations*, which I leave as a matter for future research, I shall limit my attention to the early history of Birgittine reception in Italy, examining the translations which were produced between the fourteenth and the fifteenth centuries and are still in an unpublished manuscript form.[9]

Already in 1996 an Italian translation of a book of Birgitta's *Revelations* had been the subject of research by the present author, and the existence of a second one was just mentioned in the same essay.

---

grammarians than not to be understood by the people", and the Council of Tours (813) is mentioned, where it is suggested that homilies should be translated in the Romance or the German vernacular, so that people could more easily understand what is preached.

8   See the numerous remarks I have made in the various editions of Birgittine translations I have published and studied since 1986, listed in References (Primary sources).

9   As an example of a printed edition I would like to mention the translation by Ruscone (1848), which I have come across while exploring old catalogues of Italian libraries.

This last item, a translation of the full text, is chronologically the first. It is now in the Biblioteca Comunale degli Intronati, Siena, with the shelf-mark I.V.25/26 (S). The colophon of the first volume reads: "Questo libro è de la compagnia de la Vergine Maria di Siena. El quale fece scriuare Ser Cristofano di Gano notaio dello spedale de suoi denari e di quegli di Meio di Jacomo che andò al sepolcro per non tornare. Nel mccclxxxxviiij. Pregate Dio per loro. Amen." A similar shorter remark is repeated at the end of the second volume. We know then that the work was finished in 1399, and that Ser Cristofano di Gano Guidini, disciple, friend, and sometime secretary of St Catherine of Siena, paid for the translation.[10]

A slightly later translation of Book IV only is extant in Florence, Biblioteca Mediceo-Laurenziana, MS 27.10 (L). It belongs to the early fifteenth century, and the manuscript was for some time in the private library of the Medici family. I have studied this version in comparison with an English translation of the same Book IV in London, British Library, MS Harley 4800.[11]

Another translation of all Birgitta's work is extant in "a manuscript bound in three volumes, catalogued in the Beinecke Rare Book and Manuscript Library, Yale University, New Haven, CT, USA, with the shelf mark Z111 0141-2" (Y). It contains Books I-VI in volume 1, and Books VII-VIII, *Sermo Angelicus, Quattuor Orationes, Extravagantes, Vita* and Index in volume 2; volume 3 contains no new material, but some 'visions' excerpted from other works of the saint, and again the *Sermo Angelicus, Quattuor Orationes* and *Extravagantes*. The book is connected with the second Italian Birgittine foundation, the convent of Scala Coeli in Genoa. The work was carried out in two years by an unnamed professed Birgittine nun, who

---

10 The manuscript is mentioned and briefly described in Holloway (1996: 37). Holloway says the translation was completed in 1398, then quotes the manuscript where the date she gives in Roman numbers reads 1389, while Feiss dates it correctly to 1399 (1993: 321, fn. 26). She also says that the work was "carried out" by Ser Cristofano di Gano Guidini. This should not be taken to mean that Ser Cristofano is the actual translator of Birgitta's work, since the colophons of the two volumes state respectively that he "had it written" ["fece scriuare"] and "had it made" ["fecelo fare"].

11 See ch. 2, where I describe the two manuscripts and analyse the translation comparing it to some English versions of the same century.

completed it on 26 July 1626. We do not know whether she was the translator or only a copyist, but Feiss suggests that "we may with considerable probability and no less awe acknowledge this Sister N. as the translator as well as the copyist of this Italian version of Birgitta's works". It may be interesting to note that the translation was primarily made, according to the anonymous author, "solely to arouse to greater devotion all our sisters and others, if by chance they should read it": this was said in Latin. The translation itself, in Feiss's words, is "an unadorned and accurate reflection of the rather straightforward Latin of the original texts" (1993: 318, passim).[12]

It remains now to describe and analyse other translations which I have found going through the more than one hundred volumes of the largest catalogue of manuscripts extant in Italian libraries (Mazzatinti 1890-1997).[13] The most consistent bulk of writings (twelve items) is in Florence, at the Biblioteca Nazionale Centrale (hereafter BNC). Since they provide enough matter for a chapter, I shall concentrate on this group of manuscripts, paying special attention to what concerns the *Revelations* proper.

1. Italian translations of the *Revelations*

The huge bulk of Birgitta's text seems to have prompted or even encouraged the practice of translating single books or groups of books.[14] This is in fact what happens regularly. I shall here describe

---

12   Feiss (1993: 319, fn. 21) also mentions the translation made by Ruscone (1848).

13   Henceforth, references are given simply as Mazzatinti followed by the volume and page number.

14   I must specify that I shall consider in this part of the chapter only what is really a rendering of Birgitta's own text. Sometimes in the catalogues of manuscripts there are vague references pointing to some "revelation" which I have not been able to check, and which I mention here just for the sake of completeness. For example, in a miscellaneous manuscript copied by, or belonging to, Roberto di Gaspare da Massa, dated 10 January 1484 (Firenze, BNC, MS II, VIII, 28), we have on ff. 242r-v and 244r certain "Revelationi di S. Brigida" which are said to have been written by Luca del Paradiso in 1420.

144

and analyse the four manuscripts of the BNC, Florence: three of them contain two or more books of the *Revelations*, the fourth one is a compilation of various chapters. For the sake of easy reference I shall name them A, B, C, D, following an approximately chronological order:

(A)   II, II, 393, fifteenth century, ff. 241 (Mazzatinti 9, 116). Content: Book I, part of Book II (chapters 1-3), Book III and IV, and on ff. 235r-236v some "prayers" by St Birgitta. The manuscript was at a certain time in the library of Carlo di Tommaso Strozzi (1587-1670).
(B)   II-130, dated 1494. ff. 154 (Mazzatinti 7, 228-229). Content: Books I-II and two "letters". From the Paradiso monastery.
(C)   II, III, 270, completed on 26 April 1495, ff. 149 (Mazzatinti 9,101). Contents: Book VII-VIII, miracles (ff. 137r-148v) and two "laude". It comes from and it belonged to Paradiso.
(D)   II, II, 391, paper, fifteenth century, ff. 144 (Mazzatinti 9, 115-116). This is a compilation signed by a certain "Antonius" followed by some prayers. Also this manuscript belonged to the library of Carlo di Tommaso Strozzi, together with the one containing the *Vita abbreviata* (II, IV, 517) which will be considered in the second part of the chapter.

I shall first examine MSS A and B, since they overlap to a significant extent (Books I-IV in A and Books I-II in B), and appear to be copies of the same translation. Although I have checked only short samples, I have good reasons to believe that this translation is the one found in the Sienese manuscript (S) mentioned above.

On the Spaniard Lucas Jacobi, or Luca del Paradiso see Feiss (1993: 314, fn. 7), and especially Nyberg (1996: 13-14). I have not been able to read the text of these *Revelations*, and cannot say which part of the *Liber celestis* is translated here. Further investigation is required. Another reference is given for a Bologna manuscript, Biblioteca Universitaria MS 163 (74, Busta VII, n. 5: Mazzatinti 15, 94), of the eighteenth century, which is described as "Rivelatione fatta da Giesu Christo a s. Brigida". I have not been able to examine this so far. In my quotations below from the *Liber celestis* I use the editions by Aili (1992, 2002), Bergh (1967, 1971, 1991), Jönsson (1998), Undhagen (1977) and Undhagen/Bergh (1991).

A. MS A (II, II, 393) is a handsome parchment codex of the fifteenth century. It looks like a presentation copy, having on the first folio two large illustrations in pen (reproduced in Morris/O'Mara 2000). In the upper part of the folio St Birgitta is sitting at a desk on the right-hand side, in the act of writing, her haloed head turned to the left, looking to where is the bust of Christ surrounded by six cherubs. In the lower part there is a nativity scene according to the typical Birgittine iconography: under the triangular roof of a hut we have, starting from the left side, the ox and the donkey, Mary kneeling, the baby laid on the ground, Joseph bearing a lighted candle, Birgitta kneeling; from the top of the hut penetrates a ray, with at the end the dove of the Holy Spirit descending on the baby. All the figures are grouped in twos, using two levels, so that we have three groups, with, in order, from top to bottom: the animals and Mary, the dove and the baby, Joseph and Birgitta. Outside the hut a devout layman is kneeling in adoration: is he the patron who ordered the manuscript to be produced?

The text starts with the rubrics, followed by the prologue of Master Matthias:

> Rubriche del libro primo de le celestiali riuelationi di sancta brigida nouella. Questo è el libro di sancta brigida nouella prencipessa del regno di suetia, el quale libro è diuiso in octo libri, ma in questo uolume non se ne conterranno se non cinque libri. La quale sancta brigida morì a roma nel mille trecento sectanta e due, addi uinti e tre di luglio. Poi fu canonezata adi secte d'octobre mille trecento nouantuno per papa bonifazio nono. (f. 1v)

> [Rubrics of the first book of the heavenly *Revelations* of St Birgitta. This is the book of St Birgitta, princess of the kingdom of Sweden, a book which is divided into eight books, but in this volume there will only be five. This St Birgitta died in Rome in 1372, on 23 July; she was afterwards canonised on 7 October 1391, by Pope Boniface IX.]

It appears that the original project was to gather the first five books. In fact it seems that something has interrupted the work, since the books actually copied are only the first four, and even these are not complete. There is an interruption after f. 67 v, which ends with this passage: "mutare le cose carnagli nelle cose spirituali, e nelle etternagli quelle cose che sono per mancare. Egli reputa che sia dato allui quello che si da a suoi membri": this corresponds to Book II, 3 §36-37 in Undhagen/Bergh (2001): "ideo et in spiritualia voluit commutari carnalia, et in eternalia ea que sunt casura. Illud quoque sibi ipsi fieri et exhiberi reputat, quod exhibetur suis membris". After some blank leaves (ff. 68r-72v), on f. 73r the third Book begins, with thirty-five chapters; on ff 109v-114v there are five prayers taken from various books; Book IV follows on ff. 115r-235v; other prayers are on ff. 236r-v and 239r-241r (ff. 237-238 are missing). The layout of this second part is different from the first one: for example, in the upper margin of each folio there are the running marks of the book in large red Roman numbers, and, unlike the first part, the rubrics gathered in the index before the books are in black, while they appear in red in places, where they introduce the chapters. It seems that the work has been carried out in two stages. The unfinished state of the manuscript is also visible in various places (including the very first chapter!) where space is provided for illuminated capital letters which have never been filled in.

B. MS B (II-130), dated 1494, is a large paper codex, 21 x 30 cm, which starts with the Prologue by Master Matthias "stupende e meravigliose cose sono udite nella terra nostra". It contains Books I and II, each preceded by the rubrics. It comes from the Paradiso monastery, and should be studied together with MS A since the two translations are very similar, most probably being the copy of a common exemplar, which is either MS S or a copy of it. Here is an example taken from Book I, 10, § 31-32:

Appropinquante autem morte, cum cor pre violencia dolorum rumperetur, tunc omnia membra contremuerunt et caput eius quasi modicum se erigens inclinabatur, os eius apertum videbatur et lingua tota sanguinolenta. Manus eius retraxerunt se modicum de loco perforacionis et pondus corporis pedes amplius sustentabant. Digiti et brachia quodammodo extendebant se et dorsum fortiter stringebatur ad stipitem.

(A) Appressimandosi la morte, el cuore suo per la uiolentia e forza de dolori suoi scoppiò; allora tucte le menbra sue tremarono, e 'l capo suo un poco rizzandolo inchinò, *eccosi rende le spirito al padre*, e la bocca sua *era* aperta [...] sanguinosa, le mani sue *si ratraccharono* e un poco si ritrassero dal luogo del pertuso, e *poi* sosteneuano maggiore peso per lo corpo che più grauaua. E i diti elle braccia si distendeuano e più forte stregneuano el dosso a la croce.

(f. 14r)

(B) E apressandosi *l'ora della* morte il cuore suo per la uiolenza e forza del dolore scoppiò. Allora tutte le sue menbra tremarono e il capo suo un pocho rizzandolo inchinò, *e così rende lo spirito al padre.* La bocca sua *rimase* aperta, ella lingua sua era tutta sanghuinosa. Le mani sue *si ratrapparono* e un poco si ritrassono da *chioui* de pertusi: i *piedi* sosteneuano maggiore peso per lo corpo che grauaua più. Le dita elle braccia si distendeuano; e più forte stringeuano il dosso alla croce. (f. 17v)

I have marked in italics words or phrases which do not appear in the Latin: the amplification is irrelevant, and this translation can be described as literal. The only significant addition is the sentence "e così rende lo spirito al padre", which has no correspondence in the Latin, and which further confirms the hypothesis of the inter-dependence of these two translations. Some of these expansions are different in the two versions: the only significant change is "chioui" [nails] instead of "luogo" [place], which corresponds to the Latin *loco*; whereas "poi" [then], instead of the more correct "piedi" [feet] may be a misreading of the copyist, or an interpretation of a difficult reading. The comparison also shows that B cannot be a copy of A, where a line is missing. Since B is a Paradiso volume it is more probable that A is a copy of B, and the presence of the lay figure in the illustration of the first folio would suggest a secular patron for whom the books were copied. In any case I would surmise that they both depend on a common original, very near the Sienese manuscript, if not this very codex, which will be clear if we read the passage as quoted in MS S:

Approssimandosi la morte el quore suo per la uiolentia e forza de dolori scoppiò; allora tutte le menbra sue tremaro, el capo suo un poco rizandolo inchinò: E così rende lo spirito al padre. La boccha sua era aperta, e la lengua sua era tutta sanguinosa, le mani sue si rattracchiaro e un pocho si ritrassero del luogo de pertusi. E piei sosteneuano magiore peso per '1 corpo che più grauaua. E diti elle braccia si distendeuano, e più forte stregneuano el dosso alla croce. (f. 22v)

A comparison shows that in this very short passage the Sienese ver-sion is the most correct, and that the form "piei" for the more common "piedi" may explain the reading of the word as "poi" in MS A. To verify the literalness of these versions I give here the same passage taken from the compilation (MS D) which I shall discuss later:

148

(D) Approssimandosi dopo questo la morte *del mio figluolo*, el cuore suo per lo *soprabondante* dolore rompendoselj, allora tutte le menbra sue tremarono, el capo suo un poco rizzandolo poi *in estanti* s'il reclinò *sul petto*. La bocha sua *rimase* aperta, e la linghua apparue allora tutta sanghuinosa, le mani si ritrassono un poco dal luogo *doue prima stauano e chioui* per lo peso del corpo che cadde all'angiù. Le dite e le braccia tutte erano *stechite* e le *reni* fortemente si stringeuano colla croce. (f. 13r)

The additions are ostensibly more numerous. Besides, the last two sentences provide interesting examples of a translational procedure which complicates instead of simplifying the syntax: four co-ordinate clauses in the Latin are linked in two by the use of subordination indicating in the first case a consequence ("allora" [then]), and in the second a cause ("per lo peso" [because of the weight]). This is only one example of the more original method of this translator.

C. The manuscript II, III, 270 is a paper codex, measuring 29 x 21 cm, bound with leather over boards and closed with clasps. It consists of 149 folios. The text is written in two columns. The colophon indicates that it was written at the Paradiso and belonged to the nuns of the monastery; in 1842 it was bought by Antonino Capacci, and in 1850 it was transferred from the Biblioteca Rinucciniana to the Magliabechiana as a gift by Duke Leopold II, from where it went into the BNC. It contains the translation of Books VII (35 chapters, ff. 1r-35r) and VIII (which begins on f. 50r after the eight chapters of Alfonso's Prologue) followed by "Miracles" (ff. 137v-148r) and two poems in honour of St Birgitta (ff. 148v-149v). At the end of Book VIII, on f. 137v we read:

Fu compiuto di scrivere a di 20 aprile nel M495. Fu scricto con molta fatica e con molto disagio, la maggior parte a llume di lucerna. Et però chill'acacta con diligienza si lo tenga. Et alle monache del paradiso si llo renda. Amen.

[It was completed on 20 April 1495. It was written with much exertion and much hard work, mostly by the light of a lantern. For this reason anyone who receives it is asked to keep it diligently, and to return it to the nuns of the Paradiso].

On the last folio it is repeated that "Questo libro è delle monache del paradiso dette di sancta brigida. Chillo legge prieghi idio per chi la scritto" [This book belongs to the nuns of the Paradiso who are called

149

after St Birgitta. Anyone who reads it is asked to pray for the person who wrote it].

This version follows the early Latin edition known as the 'Alfonso text', without all the additions and declarations which are printed in the modern critical edition. Another difference should be noted, since what in Bergh's edition of Book VII is given as the second part of chapter 13, §8-74 (1967: 153-161) is here chapter 14, so that from here to the end the numbering of chapters is displaced by one.

The translation is literal, but literalness is a slippery label, and should not necessarily be taken to mean a pedantic and uninspired imitation of the wording and the syntax of the original. Although sometimes this is the case, with certain renderings which may be understood as plain blunders, I would rather call the translation 'literal' which shows a basic respect for the original, that is, one where slight omissions or amplifications are allowed, provided they do not substantially alter the text.[15] In short, literalness does not exclude some good reworking of the original, especially in terms of economy, leaving out what may be redundant, or not strictly required, as in the following examples, taken from Book VII, 5, §3 and Book VII, 16 (which corresponds to ch. 15, §17 in Bergh's edition) respectively:

> a. Quattuor igitur sunt, ad que *diligenti premeditatione et assidua sollicitudine* teneris aduertere
> Adunque quattro cose sono quelle alle quali *con ogni sollecitudine e diligientia* tu debbj attendere
>
> b. penetrabatur acutissima *sagitta* doloris immensi
> era trapassato [...] d'uno smisurato e agutissimo dolore.

In (a) above two words are used instead of four, but nothing substantial is missing; the same is true of (b), where the image of the arrow is left out, but the two adjectives are set in inverted order before

---

15   In judging the 'correctness' of a literal translation one should be aware of semantic changes through history. For example, the rendering of "nec eciam *sustineatur* eis propter hoc cum mulieribus coinquinari" (VII, 12, § 21) by "ne che per questo sia loro *sostenuto* d'inpacciarsi con le femmine", is not a blunder: the Italian verb 'sostenere', meaning today 'help, sustain', kept in the fifteenth century also the sense of 'tolerate', which is the Latin meaning here.

the noun ending the sentence, with the undoubted effect of better emphasis.

In other cases this principle of economy may result in more simplicity and clarity, as in the following example taken from Book VII, 12, §35-37, on proud and pompous prelates ostentatiously riding their big horses:

> Ego enim dico vobis, quod prelati qui super magnos equos ascendunt propter superbiam et vanam gloriam, tociens super illorum colla dyabolus ascendit. Nam scio personam, que vidit demones quasi Ethiopes, qui, *quando prelati et cardinales pedes leuabant ex superbia ad equitandum super dorso magnorum equorum suorum*, illi Ethiopes tunc super colla prelatorum *pedes leuabant* et ascendebant ac ibidem irrisorie sedebant, et quociens illi prelati ex pompa calcaribus equos *percuciebant*, tociens Ethiopes *in gaudio suo* capita sua leuantes *illorum equitancium* pectora suis calcibus *impellebant*.

> Per ciò che io vi dico che i prelati i quali usano caualcare i grandi cavagli per superbia e uana gloria, allora il diauolo sale sopra de loro cuori. Per ciò che io conosco una persona che uide i demoni quassi come gezzi, i quali *quando i prelati e cardinali per superbia salgono sopra i loro grandi cauagli*, eglino ghezzi *salgono sopra* i colli d'essi prelati, e per dirisione *salgono sopra* di loro. E quante volte essi prelati per pompa *percoteuano* i cauagli cogli speroni, tante volte essi ghezzi leuauono il capo e *percoteuano* i pecti d'*essi prelati* co calci. (f. 12r)[16]

Some clauses are reduced, but not mistranslated. The impression is that the Italian version, using shorter sentences, lexical repetitions, here italicised, and more paratactic clauses produces an overall effect of a more speedy pace and better clarity.

---

16   The rare Italian word 'ghezzo', which appears in this passage, is the same as the English word 'gypsy', both being a shortening of 'Egyptian'. The word translates as 'Ethiops', a qualification often used in Birgitta's text to describe the devil as a 'black man'. In the Italian *Vocabolario degli Accademici della Crusca* (1893), the word is first described as an adjective, for which two possible origins are suggested: one more widely accepted would derive it from 'aegyptius', meaning 'blackish', but another interpretation is given as "more probable" deriving it from 'ghez' or 'geez', which is the name of a people who in very ancient times passed from south Arabia to Africa, settling on the south coast of the Red Sea. It was later used as a noun, meaning 'a blackish person'.

As I have said for A and B, I found that the translation in C depends on the Sienese manuscript, in which the passage just quoted appears in this form:

> Perciò che io ui dico che e prelati che usano caualcare e grandi cauagli per superbia e uanagloria, allora el dyauolo sale sopra de loro quori. Perciò che io conosco una persona che uede e demoni quasi come gezzi, e quali quando e prelati e cardenali salgono per superbia sopra e loro grandi cauagli, essi gezzi salgono sopra del collo de prelati e per dirisione segono sopra di loro, e quante uolte quelli prelati per pompa percoteuano e cauagli colli speroni, tante uolte essi gezzi leuauano el capo e con allegrezza percoteuano e pecti di coloro com calci. (MS I.V. 26, f. 113r)

Small differences, such as "segono" in S instead of "salgono" in C, the omission of "con allegrezza" (corresponding to *cum gaudio* in the Latin) in C, and "coloro" in S instead of "essi prelati" in C, do not rule out the possibility that this version is derived, with slight adjustments, from the Sienese manuscript. These changes in fact do not affect the phrasing of the text, but rather concern single words, where some innovation is more predictable. To give just one example, the Latin *tunica*, repeated four times in Book VII, 8, § 6-8, is translated in S first by "tonica", then omitted, and finally by "gonella" (twice), while in C it appears regularly as "gonnella".

Expansions seem to be used often to clarify or to make an allusion more explicit. See, for example, Book VII, 4, where "respondens autem *sponsa* dixit" becomes "rispose *quella persona la quale vide questa visione, cioè sancta brigida*, e disse" (S: "rispose chi uidde questa uisione, cioè sancta brigida, e disse"), or the rubric of Book VII, 11, where a vision Birgitta had "pro domina *regina* neapolitana" is translated "che ebbe sopra il regno di napoli *al tempo di madonna giouanna*" (S: "per la reina di Napoli"). However, it must be said that this procedure is by no means consistent all through the book, as we can see in the rubric of the following chapter 12, where the phrase "ad responsionem Domini Bernardi archiepiscopi Neapolitani" is reduced to "pregata dall'arcivescovo di Napoli" (S: "a richiesta di missere Bernardo ariciuescouo di Napoli"), or in chapter 10, where an allusion to Alfonso as "episcopo meo" is simply left as it is: "al mio vescovo". Who this bishop was is probably self-evident in a Birgittine convent. Incidentally, Alfonso's eight introductory chapters to Book VIII are presented in this translation in this way: "comincia il prologo del prouatissimo e spirituale huomo vescovo Alfonso di Spagna" (f. 35v). Without drawing undue conclusions, it seems that the translator shows a freer attitude towards the rubrics than towards the text of the *Revelations*.

D. Of the four manuscripts I am analysing, the compilation of certain chapters of Birgitta's *Liber* by a man called Antonius, MS D (II, II, 391), appears to be the most interesting, both as a translation and as a compilation. Indeed, since at the end of the manuscript the compiler announces another "volumetto" drawn from Birgitta's book, it appears that the rich and various material of the *Revelations* could be used to produce what today we would call 'thematic books'.[17]

The theme of the compilation, at least of the first and by far the longest and most important part, is 'prophetic', by which I mean that the central intention is a repeated call to repentance and the condemnation of various forms of sin, in particular the bad behaviour of bishops, clerics, and friars. This is apparent from the very beginning of the book, which is introduced by these words:

> Incominciano certi Capitoli tratti per uolgare[18] da libri riuelati da dio alla beata Brigida di Suetia, sposa di Cristo nouella, la quale fu mandata da Cristo propheta in questo presente tempo pericolo ad annuntiare agli uomini e femmine del mondo, che si conuertano a loro creatore, come si lamenta dio che le creature sue anno gittata la fede sua, et singularmente dei sacerdoti.
>
> (f. 1r)

---

17   On f. 131v it is said that here is the beginning of "un altro uolume delle celestiali uisioni", which is a compilation of chapters from Book IV 126, 127, 23, 33, 34, 46, 58, 70, 74, 71, 68. The final chapter is numbered 90, but it corresponds to Book IV, 91 of the critical edition, as can be seen in the rubric: "Cristo ammaestra la sposa di quattro mali in cui si debba umiliare".

18   The same incipit occurs in a work mentioned in the Index Aureliensis (1970: 272): "Incomenciano certi capitoli trati in uolgare de li libri di sancta Brigida da dio allei reuelati. Laquale brigida fu de lo Reame di suetia electa da Cristo per sua nouella sposa & da lui come profetiza in questo presente e pericoloso tempo mandata ad anuntiare a gli homini e ale femine del mundo che'ssi conuertano alo loro creatore" (Mondovì, 1518, 4to, 232 pp.). The verbal correspondence, except for a slight rearrangement of the text, would suggest that this book is a printed edition of the compilation extant in this manuscript. The analysis and comparison of these two texts is the subject of chapter 7.

[Here begin certain chapters translated into the vulgar tongue from books revealed by God to the blessed Birgitta of Sweden, newly-wed bride of Christ, who was sent by Christ the prophet in this present time to announce danger to the men and women of the world so that they would turn to their creator, and how God laments the fact that his creatures, particularly the priests, have thrown away their faith.]

While Christ is here explicitly presented as a "prophet", Birgitta is said to have been sent by him to act as a "prophetess", her mission being exactly the same: to call everybody, men and women, and especially the priests, to conversion. We find a similar tone, aggravated by the strong emphasis on the fire of hell and the end of the world, in the conclusion of this first part of the compilation on f. 131v, after the signature "Antonius":

Finiscono in questo uolume le celestiali uisioni fatte alla beata brigida nouella sposa di Cristo, mandata in questo tempo pericoloso da dio a annuntiare agli uomini che si correghino de loro vitii pero che 'l fine del mondo s'approssima. Onde beati quelli della etternale benedittione che udiranno queste diuine parole e metterannole in opera pero che (MS scamperò che) scamperanno dello etternale fuocho dello 'nferno e aquisteranno la celestiale gloria di uita etterna alla quale Cristo crucifixo ci meni per li meriti della sua sanctissima passione. Preghate per Antonio voi che questo leggerete: preghovi che preghiate dio che mi facci quella gratia che io glo più uolte adomandata.

(f. 131v)

[Here in this volume end the heavenly visions revealed to the blessed Birgitta, newly-wed bride of Christ, sent by God in this dangerous age to exhort men to turn away from their vices because the end of the world is getting near. Therefore those are blessed with an everlasting blessing who will hear these divine words and put them into practice, for they will be freed from the everlasting fire of hell and will conquer the heavenly glory of eternal life, to which Christ crucified may lead us for the merits of his most holy passion. Pray for Antonio you who will read this book: I pray you to pray God for me, that he may grant me the grace I have so often asked him.]

The prophetic, one could say apocalyptic tone, is evident in the references to the necessity of conversion, the approaching end of the world, and the final conclusive destination of men either to heaven or hell. In the light of this, it is particularly significant that Antonio starts his compilation with Book I 47: by this choice he transforms into a sort of prologue a chapter devoted to denouncing the bad priests who despise and betray the law of God and are thus worthy to be cursed and damned.

The compiler is careful in giving the references of the chapters he gathers and translates, but he does not follow the order of the *Liber*. This was perhaps the initial project, in that he marks the beginning of a new book, but it seems that the selection, at least after a certain point of the work, is rather loose and follows no fixed sequence. A later hand has marked the beginning of each book in the margin, and continuous numbering of all the chapters.[19]

As I have already noted, this translation is less literal and more original than the other previously examined. I shall illustrate this by a couple of examples, which I give in a rather extended form so that everybody can check what I say. In fact it is my conviction that translations should be analysed not only word by word, but rather using larger units of the text, where the choices of the translator are more evident.

The first sample is taken from Book I, 47, §1-6, which is the first chapter of the compilation:

> Sicut enim mater, que habet infantem in ventre, preparat *vestem* puero, sic Deus preparauit legem, que non erat nisi *vestis* et umbra et signa futurorum faciendorum. Ego autem vestiui me et inuolui me in istis *vestibus* legis. Deinde sicut crescente puero mutatur habitus antiquus et assumitur nouus, sic ego, completa et deposita *veste* antiqua legis, assumpsi nouam *vestem*, idest legem nouam, et dedi omnibus, qui voluerunt habere *vestes* mecum. *Vestis* autem ista non est stricta vel difficilis sed ubique moderata. Non enim precipit *nimis* ieiunare vel laborare vel se occidere vel aliquid *ultra possibilitatem* facere, sed proficua est ad animam et ad corpus moderandum et ad castigandum apta. Corpus enim cum nimium peccato adheret, ipsum peccatum

---

19   The sequence is: I, 47. 1. 2. 6. 8. 9. 10. 11. 13. 14. 16. 22. 25. 26. 34. 35. 32. 56. 59; II, 16. 18. 20. 23. 24. 30. 15; III (f. 43r), 4. 5. 6. 10. 12. 16. 17. 18. 21. 27. 28. 29. 30. 14. 19 (marked as "capitolo molto notabile"); IV (f. 60v: Finisce el uolgarizzato del terzo libro della Beata Brigida. Incomincia el quarto al quale fanno principio il uolgarizzarlo dal xxii capitolo: [Here ends the translation of the third book of the Blessed Birgitta and begins the fourth, whose translation starts at chapter 22] 22. 36. 57. 130. 7. 12. 23. 13. 49. 50. 101. 106. 91. 4. 35. 36. 61. 62. 63; VII, 21, 15, 16, 26; VI, 74. 77. 83. 90. 92. 100. 33. 44. 94; VII, 7. 8. 10. 31 ("ultimo"); IV, 40. 45. 47. 53; VII, 20; VI, 34. 54; VII, 30; VI, 67; III, 1. 2. 3. 7. 15; IV, 125. 17. 8. 9. 10. 1. 54. 28. 11. 14. 16. The selection forming the "second volume" is indicated in fn. 17 above. For a better description see this volume, Appendix 3.

corpus consumit. In lege enim noua duo inueniuntur: primo discreta temperantia et rectus usus omnium rerum anime et corporis, secundo facilitas seruandi legem, quia, qui non potest stare in uno, potest in alio. Ibi inuenitur, quod, qui non potest esse virgo, licite potest esse in coniugio. Qui cadit, potest resurgere. Sed lex ista nunc reprobatur et contemnitur a mundo.

(D) Impero che, come la madre che a il fanciullo nel uentre apparechia le *uestimenta di che il debba coprire quando sarà nato*, così io apparechiai *innanzi la mia incarnatione* le *uestimenta* della legge *anticha* le quali non sono se non ombre e segni delle cose che doueuano uenire, *onde quando io presi carne della humana natura* io mi uestii e inuolsi in questi *uestimenti* della legge. Poi, a tempo, come quando il fanciullo cresce si mutano le *uestimenta* antiche e fannosi le nuoue, così io, *compiuta* e consumata ch'ebbi la legge uechia, presi la nuoua *uesta* della nouella legge e donala *benignamente* a tutti che meco uoglono *essere nella beata uita*.

Questo mio *nuouo e bello e piaceuole uestimento* non è stretto né malageuole, ma a tutto è *abile* e ordinato. Pero che non comanda [di] digiunare *sopra 'l potere*, né affaticarsi *oltre il modo*, né che *l'uomo* uccida se medesimo ne etiamdio che *l'anima* faccia *sopra la sua possibilità*. Ma esso è *sopra modo utile* e proficuo all'anima e al corpo atto a moderarlo e a gastigarlo. Che con ciò sia cosa che 'l corpo ageuolmente vive *nella corruptione* del peccato, esso peccato consuma e *distrugge* el corpo. Nella *diuina* legge nuoua, *cioè cristiana*, due cose ui si trouano, cioè in prima la discreta temperanza / (f. lv) e l'ordinato uso delle cose create all'anima e al corpo. La seconda l'agevolezza d'osseruare essa legge, in pero che chi non è sofficente di stare in uno stato, egli [è] conceduto l'altro. Iui si truoua che chi non può stare *nella bellezza della pura* uirginità pigli il *sacramento* matrimoniale, chi chade *per fragilità* si rileui *con fortezza di uirtù*. Ma che adiuiene oggi *in questo pericoloso tempo* che questa *amabile e soaue* legge è riprouata e disprezzata dal mondo? (f. lr-v)

I have marked in italics all the additions to the Latin. They are meant:

1. to explain (*cioè cristiana*);
2. to better qualify (*benignamente, beata uita, diuina legge, bellezza della pura verginità, pericoloso tempo, amabile e soave legge*);
3. to balance a sentence (e.g., *l'uomo, l'anima*; the positive or negative qualities of clothes; the similarity between *corruptione / consuma*; or the contrast between *fragilità / fortezza*, etc.).

The first two choices have to do with meaning, the third with style and rhythm. Here choices may be different, and I have also marked in italics two cases in which the behaviour of the compiler contrasts with the Latin: the first is the word *vestes* repeated seven times in the Latin, and reduced to six (1 uesta, 5 uestimento) in the Italian; the second is an opposite choice: two expressions of emphasis in the Latin (*nimis* and *ultra possibilitatem*) are expanded to three in the Italian: "sopra il potere, oltre il modo, sopra la sua possibilità"; the idea is thus repeated, but nicely expressed with lexical variety.

Another example comes from Book I, 8, § 2-3, a prayer the Virgin Mary taught to Birgitta:

Benedictus sis tu, Deus, creator omnium, qui in uterum Marie virginis descendere dignatus es. Benedictus sis tu, Deus, qui cum Maria virgine esse sine grauamine voluisti, et de ea immaculatam carnem sine peccato sumere dignatus es. Benedictus sis tu, Deus, qui ad virginem cum gaudio anime eius et omnium membrorum venisti et cum gaudio omnium membrorum eius sine peccato de ea processisti. Benedictus sis tu, Deus, qui Mariam virginem, matrem tuam, post ascensionem tuam crebris consolacionibus letificasti et per te ipsum eam consolando visitasti. Benedictus sis tu, Deus, qui corpus et animam Marie virginis, matris tue, in celum assumpsisti et super omnes angelos iuxta deitatem tuam honorifice collocasti. Miserere mei propter preces eius.

Benedetto sia tu dio creatore del tutto che nel uentre della *gloriosa* uergine maria ti degnasti discendere. Benedetto sia tu dio che colla uergine *intemerata* maria uolesti essere sanza nulla sua gravezza e degnastiti di prendere di lei la inmaculata carne sanza *nullo* peccato. Benedetto sia tu dio che alla *pretiosa* uergine maria uenisti com *smisurato* gaudio dell'anima sua e di tutte le sue menbra [e con gaudio *ineffabile* di tutte le sue menbra] e sanza *macula di peccato* d'essa nascesti. Benedetto sia tu dio che la *dolce* maria uergine madre tua dopo l'ascensione tua in cielo con *infinite e magne* consolationi la magnificasti e per te medesimo *uisitandola la consolasti*. Benedetto sia tu dio che 'l corpo e l'anima della *pretiosa* maria uergine madre tua in cielo collocasti e sopra tutti gli ordini angelici e presso alla diuinità tua *con ogni triunpho d'onore* / (f. 8v) la exaltasti. Abbia misericordia di me per li meriti e preghieri suoi. (f. 8r-v)

All the words in italics are additions to or modifications of the Latin. The reader will not fail to notice the choice of qualifying the Virgin Mary by a different adjective every time she is mentioned. In this way the existing anaphoric tone of the prayer is enhanced through a series of adjectives which form a sort of internal litany in praise of the Virgin:

in uterum marie virginis:	nel uentre della *gloriosa* uergine maria
cum maria virgine:	colla uergine *intemerata* maria
ad virginem:	alla *pretiosa* uergine maria
mariam virginem:	la *dolce* maria uergine
animam marie virginis:	l'anima della *pretiosa* maria uergine.

Curiously, the sentence between square brackets is cancelled in the manuscript, probably by a reader who thought it to be a redundant repetition written by mistake, whereas the repetition exists in the Latin, and the translator cannot be the author of the excision, since he had been careful to vary the repeated phrase by qualifying the simple Latin *cum gaudio* with two different adjectives, "smisurato" and "ineffabile". Other amplifications and variations may be of note here, for example, the choice of concrete nouns which give a more visual effect to the passage: in the part not quoted, where *feruenter* becomes "fire of love", the angels are sitting on their "thrones", while in the prayer sin is qualified as a "stain", and the adverb *honorifice* becomes a phrase: "with every triumph and honour"; moreover *crebris* [many] is turned into "infinite e magne". Even the syntactic inversion of *eam consolando visitasti* turned into "visiting her you consoled her" establishes a better logical sequence. In the translations of MS A and B the choices are much more literal, and are, respectively: "si ferventemente, gl'angioli, peccato, onoreuolmente, molte". Finally, while *assumpsisti* is translated "assumesti" in A, and very literally "assunsisti" in B, D prefers to drop it, merging its sense with "collocasti" which follows, that is to say that an 'adorned' translation does not necessarily imply the amplification of the text.

It may be interesting, for once, to compare these translations with the one found in the Sienese manuscript containing the full text of the *Revelations*:

Benedecto sia tu idio creatore d'ogni cosa. El quale ti degnasti di discen/(f. 18v)dare nel uentre di maria uergine. Benedecto sia tu dio che senza grauezza uolesti essare con maria uergine. & degnastiti di prendare di lei carne immaculata senza peccato. Benedecto sia tu idio. el quale uenisti alla uergine con allegrezza dell'anima sua e di tutti e menbri. & con allegrezza di tutte le sue menbra senza peccato di lei uscisti. Benedecto sia tu idio. el quale doppo la tua ascensione con molte consolationi. rallegrasti maria uergine madre tua. & per te medesimo consolandola la uisitasti. Benedecto sia tu idio. El quale el corpo di maria uergine madre tua l'asummesti en cielo e honoreuolmente lo

collocasti al lato ala tua deità sopra tutti gl'agnoli. Abbia misericordia di me
per li suoi preghi. (f. 18 r-v)

It is on the whole a clear example of a 'literal' translation in the sense
that the original vocabulary is carefully respected; on the other hand
this is not simply a 'gloss' in that the word order of single sentences
does not follow the Latin. The translator in fact demonstrates some
good attempts at reworking the text, especially by a different
organisation of the sentence: whereas the Latin clauses end regularly,
and somehow monotonously, with the verb, they are rearranged by the
Italian translator to form a chiasmus in the third and fifth paragraph.

2. Birgittine literature in Italian

After dealing with the translations of the *Revelations*, I should like to
mention some writings which are more or less directly connected with
St Birgitta's life and works, and are thus evidence of an Italian
'reception' or 'tradition'. The material found, hitherto still unexplored,
belongs to such genres as Hagiography, Prayers, and Prophecies; and
to this list we may add other testimonies of this reception, such as
Poems and Panegyrics composed in honour of the saint.

2.1. Hagiography

A work which, although it does not properly belong to the *Liber
celestis*, was often copied or printed as a prologue to the same, is the
Vita of St Birgitta and her daughter Katarina. In the BNC there is the
autograph copy, dated 6 June 1558, of a translation made by Lodovico
Domenichi at the request of Margherita Acciaiuoli de' Borgherini to
whom a dedicatory epistle is addressed which contains some interesting remarks. This manuscript, marked II, IV, 517 (Mazzatinti 11,
81), consists of 40 folios. The manuscript was in the hands of Carlo di
Tommaso Strozzi (1587-1670) in 1670, the same who also owned the
"Compilation" of MS D. He was a scholar, who started the "Raccolta

159

Strozziana" in which he collected medieval codexes and literary manuscripts.

The *Vita* consists of twenty chapters, and is preceded by a letter to the Christian reader attributed to "Otho Magno Gotho Arcivescovo Ipsalense", who I suppose is Olaus Magnus (d. 1557), the last Catholic archbishop of Uppsala. In his dedicatory letter the translator plainly says that he is not really happy with the quality of the Latin, which he finds "weak and inept", not corresponding to the high standard required by such an important subject, but it seems that, after undertaking the work grudgingly (although he says "molto volentieri"!), he chose to produce a faithful rather than an elegant translation:

> Io ho dunque molto volentieri tradotto la vita di Santa Brigida, et della sua figliuola Catherina, et per quanto ho potuto, se non diligentemente et bene, almeno fedelmente l'ho fatto: doue liberamente io confesso d'hauer durato un poco più di fatica, che l'opera non richiedeua rispetto alla qualità dello stile assai più inetto et debile, che non meritava il suggetto. (f. lv)

> [I have then very willingly translated the life of St Birgitta and of her daughter Katarina, and as much as I have been able, if not diligently and well, I have done it faithfully, but I freely confess to have endured a little more labour than should have been the case, given the quality of the style which was much more inept and weak compared to what the subject needed.]

It would be interesting to study this translation, which implicitly, if not avowedly, is meant to improve the original. The Latin text is that of the so-called *Vita abbreviata* (Uppsala Universitetsbibliotek, MS C 15), which in the Ghotan edition of Birgitta's works was inserted after the *Extravagantes*.[20] To give the reader a small sample of this translation, I quote from the beginning of the text (Ghotan 1492, A):

> Et quamvis sexu de fragili, non tamen fragilem sed mulierem fortem, sanctam scilicet Birgittam, de sanctorum Regum Gothorum regni Swecie oriundam progenie, velut plantulam salubrem, fructiferam semine spirituali multis profuturo, ecclesie sue militanti, in singulare decus et solacium destinauit.

---

20 See BHL, item no. 1356. The incipit "Benedictus sit Deus Pater et Filius et Spiritus sanctus de cuius privilegiata familiaritate..." corresponds to this Italian text: "Benedetto sia Dio padre, e 'l figliuolo, et lo spirito santo. Della cui priuilegiata famigliarità ..." (f. 4r).

> Et benché di sesso fragile, destinò nondimeno per singolare ornamento, et consolatione alla sua Chiesa militante, Santa Brigida, donna non fragile ma forte, discesa dalla progenie de santi Re Gothi del Regno di Svetia, come pianta salubre, et fruttifera, con seme spirituale, il quale era per giouare a molti. (f. 4r)

It appears that this Renaissance translator, unlike what we have seen in the late medieval versions previously examined, looks beyond the smaller units of words and clauses, and builds his text with an eye to the longer unit of the paragraph.

2.2. Prayers

The so called *Fifteen Oes* are no longer recognised as St Birgitta's work, although they have long circulated as hers.[21] The whole collection is extant in a sixteenth-century manuscript now at Ravenna, Biblioteca Classense, MS 16, ff. 14 (Mazzatinti 4, 150). Only the first six have been copied in a manuscript now at Cremona, Biblioteca Statale, MS 47 (A.4.34-12837).[22] This is a miscellaneous manuscript of the fifteenth century. The prayers, preceded by the traditional introduction listing all the indulgences and spiritual benefits derived from reciting them, are on ff. 129r-130r.

Here is the translation of the fourth prayer, together with the Latin text established by Gejrot (2000: 224-225):

> O Iesu, vera libertas angelorum, paradysum deliciarum. Memento terroris et horroris, quos sustinebas, quando omnes inimici tui quasi leones ferocissimi te circumsteterunt et colaphizationibus, conspucionibus, vngulacionibus ceterisque inauditis penis te molestaverunt. Et per omnia contumeliosa verba, dira verbera durissimaque tormenta, domine Ihesu Christe, quibus omnes inimici tui te afflixerunt, te deprecor, ut me liberes ab omnibus inimicis meis visibilibus et invisibilibus et dones michi sub umbra alarum tuarum proteccionem salutis eterne invenire.

---

21   On these prayers, their content and their circulation see, among others, Duffy (1992: 249-256). For ME translations see Meier-Ewert (1971) and Hirsh (1974). For the Latin text see Gejrot (2000).

22   Mazzatinti (70, 39) erroneously says that only "two" prayers have been copied: in fact there are six of them.

O Iesu de li angeli uera libertade. O Iesu delitia del paradiso. Ricordati *de li crudeli flagelli*, del terrore, del horrore quali (su)stinesti quando li toy inimici come leoni ferocissimi fornoti d'intorno, e *ricordeti* di quelle pugnate cum sputamenti e guanziate, e de le *dure* e contumeliose parole, e de le graue e acerbissime 'parole' e tormenti et de li altri supplicij *grandi* et inauditi con li quali da quella gente rea *iniquamente* fusti tormentato; pregoti aduncha Signore mio che tu te degni liberarme da li inuisibili e uisibili inimici, e donarme la perfectione de l'animo e del corpo mio. Pater noster, Aue Maria, Aue dulcissime. (f. 130r)

The translator has evidently confused *verba* (words) and *verbera* (blows), translating both by "parole"; the word "perfectione" for the Latin *proteccionem* is either a mistranslation or more probably the rendering of a different Latin original (a scribal confusion between "*perf*eccio" and "*prot*eccio' is not difficult to explain), to which the translator may have adapted his text by simply cutting the image of "the shadow of thy wings" clearly connected with the idea of protection; he has also rendered the idea of "eternal salvation" by the more concrete image of "the perfection of body and soul". The expansions, which I have italicised, are mostly meant to emphasize the emotional tone of the text; a re-ordering of a sequence is visible in "le graue e acerbissime parole e tormenti" translating "dira verbera durissimaque tormenta", the displacing of "Signore mio" immediately after the expression of request also shows a certain freedom on the part of this translator. It may be interesting to note that the popularity of these prayers has known no interruption, as is testified by their presence in a very recent Italian handbook of devotions.[23]

2.3. Prophecies

Among the 'prophecies' attributed to St Birgitta the most popular one, at least in the Florentine manuscripts, is a poem beginning "Destati o

---

23   See Terrin (1992: 418-427). The text printed in this huge anthology of popular devotions is the same as the one found in an anonymous booklet entitled *Divozione delle Quindici Orazioni di Santa Brigida* (Rome, 1918). The translation follows the Latin closely, showing that the differences found in the Cremona translation ("parole" for *verbera* and "perfectione" for *proteccionem*) are either a mistake or are due to a different Latin original.

fiero lione al mio gran grido" and ending "Perse fortuna il suo splendore surgie / El cielo il mostra e altro affetto il porgie" (103 tercets in terza rima). The poem is known as "la profetia di sancta Brigida", and is extant in six of the twelve manuscripts of the BNC II, I, 249 (Mazzatinti 8, 78), ff. 210r-211v (as an appendix to the Cronica by Giovanni Villani, copied in 1432); BNC II, II, 203 Mazzatinti 9, 57), pp. 355-370 (a miscellaneous manuscript of the sixteenth-seventeenth centuries); BNC II, II, 349 (Mazzatinti 9, 101), f. 241r (Storia fiorentina up to 1336, by Francesco del Rosso), preceded by another prophecy, beginning "Fiero del gran [...] tutti il persi / O quanta grande spesa / fie di gran fiamma aresa nel gran male" and ending "E scioglierassi allora quello animale / e se fatto tanto umile / e già non pare vile per gran percosse"; (the poem "Destati" is on f. 241v). The fourth manuscript is BNC II, IX, 125 (Mazzatinti 12, 13), a fifteenth-century humanistic miscellany ("zibaldone") containing poems, sonnets, quotations. A remark written at the end of the poems apparently provides the name of the author of this rendering: "Finita la profetia di sancta Brigida, la quale tratta di quello à da venire dal 1460 infino al 1470, ridotta in volgare in versi da Iacopo da Montepulciano mentre era nelle carcere del comune di Firenze". The last manuscripts are BNC II, X, 57 (Mazzatinti 12, 47), of the fifteenth century, containing "Destati o fier leone" on ff. 55r-64r; and Magl. Cl. VII, n. 727 (Mazzatinti 13, 159), of the sixteenth century, containing "Destati o fier lione, che sta' tu a fare". The same poem is extant in a collection of "prophecies" kept at Volterra, Biblioteca Guarnacci, MS 252 (5685 – Mazzatinti 4, 233-234), of the sixteenth century ff 15r-20r. The dual quality of the text may explain its use as a prophecy in books of chronicles, and as a poem in miscellaneous collections.

2.4. Poems

Belonging to the same literature inspired by St Birgitta are various works, which I list here only to give an idea of the presence of this saint in the history of Italian piety. One is a "Relazione della Passione del nostro Salvatore fata a s. Brigida, a s. Matilde e a s. Elisabetta", by the Franciscan Angelico da Verona, who died in Udine in 1850, found in Udine, Biblioteca Comunale V. Joppi, MS 81 (Mazzatinti 46, 158-

164, item no.13, p. 159). Another Franciscan friar, Giovan Paolo Iacopini, of the Tuscan province, who died about 1788, wrote a "panegirico di S. Brigida" now in Assisi, Bibl. S. Convento, MS 185, ff. 66r-77v (Mazzatinti 104, 97). To the end of the eighteenth century belongs a sonnet "in lode di S. Brigida", now in Bologna, Biblioteca Universitaria, MS 1817 (3935), under the mark "Caps. C.", beginning "Se a lodarvi m'accingo, o Dea celeste" (Mazzatinti 25, 210). The tradition of writing poems in honour of St Birgitta is an old one: in BNC MS II, III, 270 (1495) of Paradiso provenance there is a "Laude deuota a honore di sancta Brigida" (f. 149r-v) following another "Diuota lauda della nostra madre sancta Brigida".

3. Conclusion

It is not easy to draw conclusions from what looks like a list of items to be studied. But some points can be made. With regard to the Italian translations of the *Revelations*, I think that the translation to start with is the one of the full text of the *Revelations* contained in the Sienese manuscript (MS S), which should be edited and studied. This is all the more necessary because three out of the four versions extant at the BNC (MSS A, B, and C), appear clearly to be based on, if not actual copies of this translation. To these must be added the version of Book IV extant in MS 27.10 in the Biblioteca Laurenziana (MS L), which also clearly depends on the same Sienese translation.[24] The compilation in MS D is most certainly worth an edition and a study of its own. Besides being an analysis of the kind of translation found here, this future study should try to discover the principles, if any, used to extract single chapters from the *Revelations* to produce a new

---

24   See ch. 2. Besides the almost total correspondence in the very wording of the text, a relevant sign of dependence is that this translation of Book IV follows the Sienese version in inserting after chapter 2, which contains an allegorical vision, the explanation of the same vision which is actually chapter 129 of the Book. Again, in ch. 2, §20 (Aili's 1992 edition), both manuscripts have "santo" as a mistranslation of "saucium" (wounded), evidently read as "sanctum".

work. In fact this use of Birgittine material is well attested, from what I know, in England, where spiritual tracts (see Pezzini 1992, 1993a) and even a *Life of the Blessed Virgin* (see ch. 13) were drawn from pure Birgittine texts without any additions. The Italian reception of Birgitta's work and her type of sanctity should also be considered in the literature I have listed above, not forgetting the study of iconography both in manuscripts and in churches.

This chapter was and is meant to be a beginning, an invitation to start an exploration into a still largely unknown field, which appears to be a promising mine for young researchers to dig. I hope that a deeper analysis of the texts, which I have only touched upon here, will yield interesting results concerning not only the Italian reception of Birgittine writings, but also the history of the Italian language, and of translational practices in the fifteenth and sixteenth centuries.

CHAPTER 7

The Prophetic Voice in St Birgitta's Revelations: an Analysis of *Incominciano certi capitoli*, a Late Fifteenth-Century Italian Compilation (Florence, Bibl. Naz. Centrale MS II, II, 391)[1]

It seems that in Italy St Birgitta of Sweden was received mainly as a prophetess, both as one who could forecast coming events (prophecies of political content were falsely attributed to her) and, more properly, as a preacher speaking in the name of God to call people to conversion. Roger Ellis rightly remarks that Birgitta, writing in "a church under attack from without and betrayed from within", produces a spirituality which is "like that of the Old Testament prophets, one of crisis and of judgement, whose central feature is a stark opposition of saved and damned, and whose central note a call to repentance and greater holiness of life" (1982c: 157-158). It is indeed crucial to note that Christian prophecy is not primarily concerned with prediction, since a prophet "is a Christian who through experienced revelations receives a message that he or she is called to hand on to the Church for its edification as part of a firm design in God's will to save, guide, and bless his people" (Hvidt 2003: 153). This salvation has two aspects: "being rooted in social, economic and political reality", the prophet delivers a message in which "God is revealed" within this reality, "either reassuring the people of divine compassion and care or warning them of God's indignation and justice" (Bergant 1993: 783).

In a previous essay devoted to a survey of manuscripts containing Italian translations of St Birgitta's *Revelationes* I drew attention to a late fifteenth century compilation of prophetic content

---

1   This is a largely revised version of a paper presented at the International Symposium on "700 Years of Birgittine Spirituality and Culture", held in Vadstena, 4-9 August 2003. First published in *Aevum* 79 (2005).

extant in a Florentine manuscript (chapter 6: 151-157). In a footnote (fn 18) I suggested the possible connection between the manuscript version and a book printed at Mondovì in 1518, of which, according to the *Index Aureliensis* of books printed in the sixteenth century, three copies are now extant: one in Turin, another in Stockholm and a third copy in Uppsala.[2]

After a careful analysis I established that both the manuscript version and the printed edition go back to the same source, although they do not exactly coincide, neither in the presentation of the material nor in the wording of the text. Moreover, a number of omissions due to *homoeoteleuton* in the manuscript, subsequently corrected, lead one to suppose that the copy we have is not the holograph of the compiler-translator, which makes allowance for at least one original earlier version. A shared mistranslation[3] would suggest a common source which is a further step from the original. On the other hand, the differences between the manuscript and the printed book oblige us to admit that the Florentine manuscript is not the copy used by the Mondovì printer. These facts allow us to conclude that the work must have had a not negligible circulation around the end of the fifteenth and the beginning of the sixteenth century.

The work bears no title, and is referred to by the first words of the long introductory paragraph which describes the content, the tone and the aim of the compilation:

> Incomenciano certi capitoli trati in volgare de li libri di sancta Brigida da Dio a'llei revelati. La quale Brigida fu de lo reame di Svetia electa da Cristo per sua novella sposa et da lui come profetiza in questo presente e pericoloso tempo mandata ad anuntiare agli homini e ale femine del mundo che'ssi convertano alo loro creatore.[4]

---

2   These copies are: Torino, Biblioteca Reale, Rari 2 (20); Stockholm, Kungliga Biblioteket, 1700/1232; Uppsala, Universitetsbiblioteket, Sv. Rar. 10:749. See *Index Aureliensis*, IV, Aureliae Aquensis 1970, 272.

3   The phrase from *Rev.* IV,35 "et intellegerent *calorem* spiritus tui sancti" is translated "sentano el *cuore* del sancto spirito" in the manuscript (f. 86r), and "sentano nel *core* de la gratia del sancto spirito" in the book (f. 63r).

4   This is the first paragraph of the version printed as a book. The wording of the manuscript is slightly different and seems to be less correct. It reads: "Incominciano certi capitoli tratti per volgare da libri rivelati da Dio alla beata Brigida di Svetia, sposa di Cristo novella, la quale fu mandata da Cristo

The author states that he has translated only a number of chapters (*certi capitoli*) of the *Revelations*, he then qualifies Birgitta of Sweden, elected as Christ's bride, as a prophetess (*profetiza*) having the mission to call men and women to conversion, with a special urgency dictated by the fact that the present time is dangerous (*pericoloso*), a phrase which, as we shall see, is often repeated as a sort of refrain throughout the compilation. This is why I have qualified this work as 'prophetic'.

It is not without reason that the compiler chose to start his work with a chapter (*Revelations* I,47) the content of which is to show "how God laments the fact that his creatures, particularly the priests, have thrown away their faith".[5] Here we have the two main complementary characteristics of the prophetic preaching: complaint against what is wrong and a call to conversion, according to the double-faced vocation of a prophet, sent by God "to destroy and to throw down, to build and to plant" (Jeremiah 1:10). To these characteristics a third one should be added, which is in fact the ground on which the other two are based, and this is the unquenchable and always available mercy of God, a chord which is less prominent, a music which may be subdued and sounding in the background, but which resonates in all

---

propheta in questo presente tempo pericolo ad annuntiare agli uomini e femmine del mondo che si convertano a loro creatore. Come si lamenta Dio che le creature sue ànno gittata la fede, e singularmente dei sacerdoti (f. 4r)". The epithet 'the prophet' (a mistake for 'prophetessa', or a noun to be understood as feminine?) seems to refer to Christ and not to Birgitta, and the word 'pericolo' (another mistake?) instead of 'pericoloso' could be taken as an object of the verb 'annuntiare', as if 'danger' were the subject of the prophetic proclamation. Incidentally, in a rubric on f. 41v there is a similar mistake: 'pericolo' was later corrected by the addition of -*so* in black ink. The sense of the manuscript version would be that Birgitta "was sent by Christ the prophet in this present time to announce danger to the men and women of the world", as I translated in chapter 6, 152. In quoting from the manuscript I follow a few editorial principles: single different words written without interruption are separated, modern capitalization, punctuation and diacritic marks are inserted; the graph 'ç' is transcribed as 'z', to which it corresponds; final '-j', whether in words or in Roman numbers, is standardized as '-i'; 'u/v' have been standardized according to their modern Italian usage.

5   This rubric is so important that in the manuscript it has been practically amalgamated in the long title, becoming thus a part of it. In the book version the rubric is more correctly marked by a paragraph and a big initial capital letter.

kinds of genuine prophetic literature, imbuing these texts with a diffuse sense of hope, which is also essential to any true prophecy. This is why the prophetic voice strikes a note of severity and patience at the same time, as can be seen, for example, in the rubric for chapter 18, combining the rubrics of *Rev.* I,55 and 56: "Parla Cristo alla sposa come e iudici e difensori e lavoratori della chiesa sua sono diventati arco maladetto pieno d'avaritia insatiabile. E come esso Cristo gli sostiene che anco non ne fa vendetta" (f. 28v). While denouncing the cupidity spreading through all the classes of his Church, Christ nevertheless tolerates his people (*gli sostiene*) and does not take revenge on them.

It must be remembered, then, that the unquestionable fidelity of God to his promise of salvation is the real foundation of the prophetic voice, a voice which speaks in a space suspended between an ideal past and an ideal future, a point from where renewal is advocated, which is more often than not a return to the old times. This explains why Birgitta's criticism of bishops and priests, and more generally of the Christian people, is set against the pattern of evangelic life established by the apostles, just as her harsh attacks against monks and friars are based on the models of sanctity visible in and provided by their founders, Benedict, Dominic and Francis.

An overall view of Birgitta's *Revelations* quickly leads one to perceive that the theme of prophecy is pervasive in her work, and it is not without significance that she was mainly seen as a prophetess.[6] It is true that her book also contains other literary genres, such as teachings, meditations and prayers, and we know that treatises of spiritual instruction were drawn from the *Revelations*. Nevertheless, the fact that a compilation was made on the basis of her 'prophetic voice' invites us to consider in what sense she was perceived as a prophetess, and to discover what were the themes of her prophetic preaching. In this respect it may be relevant that the compilation was made at the end of the fifteenth century, in a time when voices crying for reform, *in capite et in membris*, were spreading through all the

---

6   There is a considerable literature of 'prophecies', mainly of political quality, falsely attributed to Birgitta: see Pezzini (chapter 6: 161).

levels of the Church, hierarchy and laypeople alike.[7] This may explain why among the topics selected by the compiler of the work there are not only complaints about and violent protests against the bad behaviour of clerics and religious, but also discussions about problems of clerical discipline, such as celibacy (*Rev.* VII,10: f. 101v), and even on more important theological questions about, for instance, faith in the real presence in the Holy Eucharist (*Rev.* IV,61-63: ff. 87r-92r) or the salvation of the pagans (*gentiles*, interestingly rendered by "gentili cioè e saracini": *Rev.* VI,77: f. 96r).[8] This is to say that orthodoxy and morally correct life go hand in hand, and right faith must be matched with right behaviour, and viceversa, in order to belong to the body of Christ in a proper and integral way.[9]

1. The manuscript

The manuscript containing the compilation is now in Florence, Biblioteca Nazionale Centrale, II, II, 391. It was once in the library of Senator Carlo di Tommaso Strozzi (1587-1670),[10] registered as no. 58, and before the present collocation it was marked as Magl. Cl. XXXV, num. 180. The manuscript belongs to the fifteenth century, it measures

---

7   According to Morris, the most peculiar characteristic of Birgitta's spirituality is that "First, she is a prophet of reform. At all stages of her life she observes a decline in moral standards and a falling away from the ideals taught by Christ; and she urges a return to the old values, advocating an ideal which is realisable by an imitation of early Christian modes of existence, and exemplified primarily in biblical models" (1999: 174).

8   References are given by book and chapter to the *Revelations* and to the folios of the Florentine manuscript, where not otherwise indicated. To find the corresponding chapter in the printed book see Appendix 3.

9   For a more general and detailed approach to the prophetic and reforming aspect of Birgitta's writings see Fogelqvist (1993) and Sahlin (2001).

10   On Carlo Strozzi see Frati (1933: 526-528). Another MS with Birgittine material translated into Italian (*Rev.* Book I, III, IV and part of Book II, plus some prayers by Birgitta), now Florence, BNC II,II,393, once was part of the library of the same Strozzi (see ch. 6: 144-145), as well as MS BNC II, IV, 517 containing Domenichi's translation of Birgitta's *Vita* (ch. 6: 157).

mm 290 x 200, it is paper, and consists of 151 folios, with regular catchwords on folios 15v, 27v, 37v, 49v, 61v, 73v, 85v, 97v, 109v, 121v, 133v, 143v.[11] On the last folio it bears a fine, elegant drawing of a face in pencil (f. 150v). Each chapter of the *Revelations* has a progressive numeration in Arabic numbers on the left side of the page, which may be the work of the copyist himself, whose name, Antonius, appears three times (on f. 131v twice, and on f. 150v). The manuscript bears traces of two, or possibly three other hands. Passages omitted through *homoeoteleuton* are restored by seemingly two hands: one very similar to the main hand might belong to the copyist himself or be a careful imitation, while the other (see for example on ff. 51r, 52v, 57r, 103r-v, 106r, 134r) is in clearly different handwriting. Other interventions in a different hand appear here and there in the form of annotations or markings, as on f. 42v, where in the margin we find the remark: "carità ismisurata averso degli ingrati homini" (measureless charity towards ungrateful men). Another hand (Strozzi himself?) shows the later intervention of an active and conscious reader who corrects the text with a clear reference to the Latin original.[12] This presence is particularly evident in *Rev.* IV,7 (chapters 46 and 47 in the manuscript, ff. 69r- 73r), a crucial chapter dealing with afterlife, with

---

11   For a description of the manuscript see Mazzatinti (1890-1997: 9, 115-116). Mazzatinti gives a number of 144 folios, and this refers to the work proper, but a modern numbering (3.7.1972) counting also four flyleaves at the beginning and three at the end of the codex, gives a total of 151 folios. In fact the manuscript has two numberings: the first and older one marks the folios in ink on the top right corner of the page, but the sequence is erratic and full of errors, so this numbering is of no practical use and should be ignored. The second modern numbering in pencil marks the folios in a regular sequence on the bottom left of the page, and this is the one I follow here.

12   The words are written above the original. To give just a few examples: on f. 66v 'dovea' corrects ms. 'potea' (Latin: *debuit*); 'divina' corrects 'amore' in the phrase 'con amore di carità' (Lat. ex *divina* caritate); on f. 67r in the margin 'carità' replaces 'verità' in the phrase 'tu se essa verità' (Lat. Tu vere es ipsa *caritas*); on f. 71r the same hand inserts 'la vergine' (Lat. *virgo*) which had been omitted; on f. 123v in the margin 'iustitia' replaces 'maestà' in the phrase 'della divina maestà' (Lat. in *iusticia* Dei); on f. 124v 'la dispositione del mondo' is written above the phrase 'le cose che vedete e palpate' (Lat. iuxta *mundi disposicionem*).

special attention to the highly controversial topic of purgatory,[13] and in *Rev.* IV, 8 (chapter 95 in the manuscript, f. 123r-v), where Birgitta has a vision of the soul of Nicola Acciaiuoli in purgatory.[14]

Another hand must finally be mentioned, which on two occasions marks the beginning of a new Birgittine book: *Liber secundus* on f. 33v and *Liber tercius* on f. 43v. All this is certainly proof that the manuscript was used and read attentively more than once.

The choice to mark the chapters by a progressive numeration was probably necessary in that the compiler does not present a clear, logical organization of his material: no introduction, no index and no general plan are given. Broadly speaking, the work seems to be divided in two parts, of which 103 chapters form the first, and only 12 chapters the second. This is in fact plainly declared where a break between two 'volumes' is marked by a colophon and a new incipit. The colophon of the first volume reads: "Finiscono in questo volume le celestiali visioni fatte alla Beata Brigida novella sposa di Cristo mandata in questo tempo pericoloso da Dio a annuntiare agl'uomini che si correghino de loro vitii però che 'l fine del mondo s'approssima. Onde beati quelli della etternale benedittione che

---

13   The rubric is starkly reduced: 'Incomincia una visione mirabile che ebbe la beata Brigida stando in estasi di mente secondo che di sotto si contiene' (f. 69r). But within the chapter (from *Rev.* IV, 7, n. 56) the translator inserts a relevant remark: 'Per similitudine molto bella spone qui el modo che si purgano l'anime in questi tre purgatori, e altre cose molto notabili dello stato dell'anime le quali sono stati per li tempi passati assai incognite, ma acciò che l'uomo tema in questo tempo pericoloso le volse Dio revelare a questa beata Brigida' (f. 72r). This remark was taken by a later reader (or by the scribe?) as a 'new' chapter, to which number 47 was given.

14   The specification that the unnamed 'soul' is that of 'messer Nicola A.' is given in a remark: "Questi due capitoli che ora seghuitano si continuano col capitolo vii° nel libro iiii° dinanzi volgharizzato, dove si narra come l'anima di messer Nichola A. fu veduta nel purgatorio dalla Beata Brigida e delle sue pene" (f. 123r). The same remark is found in the printed book, where the name 'Nicola Aciauioli' is written in full (f. 89v). Niccolò Acciaiuoli met Birgitta when she stayed in Naples in 1363 and in 1365. He was a Florentine banker, and at the time Queen Giovanna's chief adviser. He was also a patron of Birgitta's during her stay in Naples (see Morris 1999: 122-123). This clear, explicit interest in the eternal destiny of this famous banker and statesman may allude to the Florentine origin of the compilation.

udiranno queste divine parole e metterannole in opera pero che scamperanno dello etternale fuocho dell'onferno e aquisteranno la celestiale gloria di vita etterna alla quale Cristo crocifixo ci meni per li meriti della sua sanctissima passione" (f. 131v). The beginning of the new part reads: "Al nome del nostro signore Cristo crocifixo per noi e della intemerata e pretiosa sua madre Maria donzella di paradiso e reina di vita etterna. Incomincia un altro volume delle celestiali visioni fatte alla novella sposa di Cristo Brigida 'del reame' di Svetia" (f. 132r). Both colophon and incipit appear in the printed book. In the manuscript the copyist adds to the colophon a request for prayers: "Preghate per me Antonio. Voi che questo leggerete preghovi che preghiate Dio che mi facci quella gratia che io gl'o più volte adomandata" (f. 131v). But, to show that these are only two parts of one and the same work, the numbering of the chapters, in both the manuscript and the book, continues regularly as if there were no interruption.

Other sub-sections can be identified. For example, in the first volume, after an AMEN concluding the selection from Book II, the repetition of the initial formula "Incominciano certi capitoli del terzo libro della beata Brigida delle visioni celestiali a'llei fatte" (f. 43r) and the layout of the page where an unusually large space is provided for the capital L (f. 43v), would suggest that the chapters from Book III (27-41 in the manuscript) may be taken as a unit within the work. Another division occurs between the end of the chapters taken from Book III and the beginning of the chapters from Book IV. This is marked by AMEN written at the end of chapter 41 (f. 66r), and the remark: "Finisce el volgharizzato del terzo libro della Beata Brigida. Incomincia el quarto al quale fano principio in volgarizzarlo dal xxii capitolo" (f. 66v). This indication of a new section does not appear in the printed book. Apart from this, each chapter in the manuscript is indicated by the number of the book and chapter of the *Revelations* from which it is selected. This is particularly helpful for the present day reader, when one wants to study the translational technique, for example, but the method does not facilitate the finding of a particular chapter within the compilation itself. The later numbering in the margin of the chapters as a regular sequential series is certainly an attempt to provide a more useful reference for the reader. It must be said that the references to the source chapters indicated in the rubrics

174

are correct, except for very few cases, 9 out of 115 – see Appendix 3. Other seven cases, all from Book IV, differ by one number from Aili's numeration in the modern critical edition (1992), but this may derive from a different numbering in the original Latin.

2. The printed book

When we turn to the book we may be easily struck by the beauty of the first page, illustrated by fine woodcuts. The largest and most important one, in the centre, shows Birgitta bearing a cross and a book set against a landscape of desert and rocky land out of which, however, leaves, flowers and bushes are sprouting. The setting may hint at John the Baptist preaching in the wilderness, and more generally at the prophetic mission, which, according to Isaiah, consists in making the desert flourish.[15] Smaller woodcuts surround the main scene. We have the eternal Father dressed as a Pope accompanying the beginning of the text proper. The apostles Peter and Paul, St. Christopher, St. Stephen and St. Lawrence are on the bottom band; on the top and on the left margin there are decorations; on the right, we find from top to bottom, four scenes from the life of a saint, alternating with three biblical scenes: the crucifixion, the harrowing of hell, and the risen Christ with two figures (the Emmaus story?). Two other small woodcuts decorate the book: one on f. 4r (ch. 2 of the compilation, from *Rev.* I,1), representing Birgitta with a lily and a book, the other on f. 12r (ch. 11, from *Rev.* I,16) with three figures who illustrate the title of the chapter, concerning a saint who successfully prays God to deliver a woman possessed by the devil. A

---

15   See Isaiah 32:15-16, and also 35:1-2; 41:18-19; 43:19-20. Incidentally, the phrase 'et edificabuntur in te deserta' (Isa. 58:12) is quoted in VI,83, a short chapter on the conversion of the heathen, which is translated in the compilation (f. 96r: 'e luoghi deserti si redificheranno'). It may be interesting to note that, as already shown, the '*gentiles*' are normally translated as 'saracini', which reminds us of the increasing threat of the Turks to the Western world after the fall of Constantinople in 1453, certainly a not insignificant feature of the 'pericoloso tempo' often evoked in the text.

major variation on the text of the manuscript is a long 'addition' at the end, to which neither number nor reference to the source are given, although the passages, except for the first which is simply attached to the final chapter of the compilation, are carefully separated in the page. The first passage comes from *Regula Salvatoris* 280-287 (*RS*, Eklund 1975: 134-135 and 212-213), the second from the same *RS* 306-317 (Eklund 1975: 138-139 and 216-218), the third from *Revelaciones extravagantes* 44 (*Extr.*, Hollman 1956: 160-161), the fourth from *Extr.* 39,12 (Hollman 1956: 157), the fifth from *Extr.* 31 (Hollman 1956: 145-146).

A general table of the 113 chapters is provided at the end of the book. The very concise description of the contents of the chapters does not coincide with the wording of the rubrics within the text itself, but this may be due to the fact that each chapter-heading in the table is allowed only two lines. See for example the different wording of the rubric of chapter 14 (from *Rev.* I,26) compared with the chapter-heading in the general table:

> (*Rubric*) Come la sposa in estasi levata per mirabile modo vedeva l'exercito angelico laudare il signore, e della creatione de l'homo, e de miracoli che fece per Moisé, et come venne nel mondo per la salute humana, e della corruptione pessima della charnalità che oggi si comete, et del matrimonio spirituale. Cap. xiiii.

> (*Table*) Come la sposa posta in oratione vedea l'essercito de li angeli lodare il creatore et de la creatione de l'homo. Capitulo xiiii.

The colophon reads: *Impressum in Montis Regalis per Josephum Berruerium et ad instantiam domini Stephani de Allegro mercator librorum Janue Sub anno domini M.ccccc.xviii. die xv. Mensis Marcii.*[16]

---

16   It may be worth remembering that Genoa, from where this 'mercator librorum' comes, at whose request the work was printed, had a famous Birgittine convent under the title of *Scala Coeli*, the second Italian foundation after the Florentine *Paradiso*, and that not far from the town, at Quarto alla Riviera, Alfonso Pecha of Jaén, the main editor of Birgitta's *Revelations*, had founded a monastery in 1382, where he spent the last years of his life (d. 1389). From this monastery comes one of the best and most lavishly illustrated manuscripts of the *Revelations* (Y), now in the New York Pierpont Morgan Library (see Undhagen 1977: 156-162). From *Scala Coeli* comes a translation in Italian of the full text of *Revelations* completed on 26 July 1626

The book consists of 114 folios + 2 blank folios, with a modern foliation in pencil on the bottom left of the page; the quires are marked a4 b8–p8; it measures mm 205 x 145, and is 1 cm thick.[17] It looks attractive, and one might think that a printed edition ought to be better than a manuscript version. This is not the case. The beauty of the printing is not matched by the correctness of the text. The first embarrassing feature is the decision to follow a sequential numbering for the chapters of the compilation while maintaining the references to the original book of the *Revelations* to which they belong, a mixed criterion producing a situation which, to say the least, is messy and confusing. Thus, while in the manuscript there are originally unnumbered rubrics followed by the indication, for example, of I,32 and I,56, the corresponding chapters in the book are marked as 'libro I, capitulo 17' and 'libro I, capitulo 18', where Book I refers to the Latin text of the *Revelations*, while 17 and 18 indicate the position of the chapter in the new redaction of the translation. To aggravate the confusion, the references to the books are sometimes wrong (first for second, for example, or sixth for third), and the numbering of the chapters is not regular: some are repeated, others are omitted, as can clearly be seen in the list given in Appendix 3. At times it seems as if the printer had a copy bearing the correct numeration which allowed him, when he was more careful, to ignore the mistakes previously made. A table of contents is provided at the end, where, contrary to what happens in the body of the book, the progressive numbering, except for a couple of mistakes, is correct. But the difference with the numbers given in loco makes the use of it not really easy without a table of comparison. In Appendix 3 I have supplied this table, together with the modern foliation related to each chapter.

Another point which makes the book less reliable than the manuscript is the presence of various mistakes due to a wrong or careless reading of the manuscript copy on the part of the printer. Here

---

(see ch. 6: 138, 141). These may be mere coincidences, but they might also suggest a kind of interest in Birgittine writings and consequent editorial activity centred in Genoa.

17   For a description of the book see Bersano Begey/Dondi (1966: vol. II, n. 1050, 492-494, with reproductions of the first page and of the small woodcut on f. 4r representing Birgitta); Sander (1969: I, n. 1021, 182).

are some random examples, where Ms is for the manuscript, and B for the printed book.

Ms (7v): in deità (deity)	B (4r): in dieta (diet)
Ms (48r): l'umilità (humility)	B (35r): la unità (unity)
Ms (69r): indi (hence)	B (52v): vidi (I saw)
Ms (75v): di sé medesima (of herself)	B (49r): dice medesima (she says the same)
Ms (103v): monasterio (monastery)	B (75r): ministero (ministry)
Ms (111r): terza età (third age)	B (80v): sexta età (sixth age)

Other mistakes are less dangerous, as, for example the repetition of words, parts of a sentence, or of an entire line, as is the case, for example, of "e ogni stato del mondo più voluntieri reguardano li dilecti", which is the last line of f. 69r and the first of f. 69v. Unfortunately there are mistakes also in the manuscript version, as can be seen in a large extract given at the end of this essay, although in general the manuscript seems more correct. The conclusion of this first part is that anyone wishing to study this compilation should in preference use the Florentine manuscript, comparing it when necessary with the printed copy extant in Turin and in the two Swedish libraries, which at times has a more correct reading or allows one to restore an omission.

3. The compilation: structure and contents

To structure the Birgittine revelations in a recognisable pattern must have been a problem ever since the first attempt was made. The redaction completed in 1377 by Alfonso Pecha, former bishop of Jaén, became established for various reasons, certainly not because it was the best possible solution to the problem of organizing a shapeless sprawling mass of chapters into a neat, clear pattern, easy to retrieve and to consult. The fact that Alfonso used the same material to compile three other works, the *Liber celestis imperatoris ad reges*, the *Tractatus de summis pontificibus* and the *Celeste Viridarium*, shows that he was not completely satisfied with his first redaction, or that he saw other possible ways of organizing the contents of the *Revelations*.[18]

While it is not easy to see whether any organizational pattern could be found, the reforming intent of the Florentine compilation is evident from the beginning. It is declared in the long title reported above, where two main purposes are described: the conversion of life, and the recovery of the true faith. Morals and doctrine, as I have said, go hand in hand, and this explains and justifies the presence of some doctrinal chapters beside the much more numerous texts dealing with the reformation of life. Even the presence of chapters on pilgrimages to holy places are in order with the declared intent: they end by an appeal to conversion (*Rev.* VII,26: f. 95v), and may implicitly include a criticism of a practice which risked turning into religious tourism with no consequence on the pilgrim's spiritual life. Moreover, the recurring phrase 'in questo pericoloso tempo', both in the rubrics and in the text, rings as a truly prophetic voice, which is not so much interested in the future as in the present. The actualizing translation of some rubrics goes the same way.

If we turn to a possible organization of the book into parts we find no visible clue. There is a clear choice at the beginning: *Rev.* I,47 is a long chapter containing criticism of the church, and it is placed at the start probably as a sort of preface to show the general theme and tone of the book. After that, the compiler apparently proceeds by a regular selection of chapters according to the number they have in the Latin, with a couple of exceptions. But, starting from Book IV, he seems to abandon any order, either of chapters or of books. So, after some chapters picked out at random from Book IV, he presents a selection from Book VI and VII, in inverted order and organized in a mixed sequence, then he goes back to Book IV, then combines a mixture of VI and VII, creates a sub-sequence from Book III, and finally he ends the first volume with 11 chapters from Book IV, which also form the only source of what he calls the 'second volume' (12 chapters). This gives a total of 115, corresponding to 113 chapters of

---

18   See Undhagen (1977: 22-26). Six chapters out of 19 of the *Tractatus de Summis Pontificibus* (Undhagen 1977: 23-25), and specifically IV,10, 33, 57, 49, VI,74, VII,31, are translated in the compilation.

the *Revelations*:[19] 19 out of 60 from Book I; 7 out of 30 from Book II; 20 out of 34 from Book III; 46 out of 130 (in the first Alfonsian redaction) from Book IV (of which ch. 7 and ch. 23 are split in two parts, corresponding to chapters 46 and 47, 49 and 106 of the compilation respectively); 12 out of 109 from Book VI; 10 out of 31 from Book VII.

No one will fail to notice the fact that two thirds of Book III were used. This book deals mainly with the bishop's office, providing a sort of treatise on pastoral care derived mostly from what should not be done: if a play on words can be allowed, I would say that this is a handbook on *cura pastoralis* to be imagined through visions of *pastoralis incuria*. The relevance of the topic, and consequently its position in the compilation, is marked by the compiler himself, who gives this part an autonomous title and ends it with a sort of colophon and a big AMEN, which normally marks the end of a work or at least of an important section of it. The intent is also clearly specified in the 'title', where it is said that in the chapters to follow, Mary mother of God 'complains about the wicked prelates of the church who only seek the honour of the world with its lusts' (f. 43r).

Apart from this, the reason on which the ordering of chapters is based is not clear, except that here and there seem to be some smaller sub-sequences identified by a similar or homogeneous content. In this process rubrics may be helpful.

4. The rubrics

The rubrics are an important way of identifying the intent of a compiler: they may give us his reaction to the text, the reason why he selected a particular chapter, or what he marks out as an important topic. This emerges from the way he translates the Latin: choices, omissions, emphasis, personal comments. I feel that when we analyse the translation of a Latin text in the Middle Ages rubrics tend to be

---

19   A different numbering in the printed book gives a total of 113 chapters. See Appendix 3.

disregarded. They do not belong to the text proper, they have not the same official status, and it is known that the translators accordingly feel rather free in their rendering. But this is precisely the reason why they should be seriously considered when we are looking for the translator's mood rather than his fidelity to the official text.

To illustrate my point I shall quote some rubrics, where we shall find literalness, reductions (this is by far the most normal practice), but also expansions and additions. They are interesting as samples of various translational practices. In some cases they help identify the compiler's intent more easily than the clues he spreads within the text itself.

a. *Predominantly literal translation:*

Rev. I,16 Qualiter videbatur sponse, quod quidam sanctorum loquebatur ad Deum de quadam muliere, a demone terribiliter conculcata, que postea precibus Virginis gloriose fuit liberata.

Chapter 11 Vedeva la sposa *in contemplatione posta* che uno sancto parlava a Dio *lamentandosi* come el demonio terribilmente conculcava una femina *posta nel mondo* la quale poi per le preghiere della madre di Dio fu liberata.

(f. 18v)

The few expansions and the omission of the adverb *gloriose* are not such as to question the basic literalness of this rendering; besides, 'lamentandosi' is only a more precise translation of 'loquebatur', one of the many cases where the translator reveals a more pictorial attitude than the cold Latin words. Another interesting feature is the contrast, created by the translator, between Birgitta 'in contemplatione posta' and the woman possessed by the devil 'posta nel mondo'.

b. *Reduction*

Rev. III,18 Verba matris ad filiam, quod citius fratres nunc audirent et audiunt vocem diaboli quam sui patris Dominici, *et quomodo nunc pauci imitantur eius vestigia,* et qualiter episcopatus desiderantes propter *mundi honorem et* sui quietem et libertatem *non sunt in regula sancti Dominici,* et de terribili sententia contra tales *et de experientia damnationis pro tali episcopatu.*

Chapter 34 Parla la madre di Cristo alla sposa come e frati oggi più tosto odono la voce del demonio che quella del beato Domenico. E come

181

desiderano e uescouadi *per fuggire el giogho della religione.* E della terribile sententia che riceveranno. (f. 53r)

The parts marked in italics in the Latin have been omitted, whereas a sentence, marked also in italics, has been added in the translation. The table at the end of the printed book (ch. 30) allows even greater concision: "Parla la beatissima vergine Maria a la sposa comandandoli la sanctità del beato Domenico." One would say that a more positive note rings here: while the summary rubric of the title stresses a series of negative attitudes, and omits to mention the good example set by the saint who should be imitated, this is instead the only thing selected in the short title. 'Per fuggire el giogho della religione' amalgamates in a shorter rendering the Latin 'propter sui quietem et libertatem non sunt in regula sancti Dominici'.

A more drastic reduction occurs in the rubric for IV,7:

> *Rev.* IV,7: Visio mirabilis et notanda de quadam anima iudicanda et de Dyaboli accusacionibus et virginis gloriose aduocacionibus et de exposicione ipsius visionis, in qua celum per palacium, Christus per solem, virgo per mulierem, Dyabolus per Ethiopem, angelus per militem designantur; et in qua duo loca penarum irremediabilia et tria remediabilia computantur et multa alia mirabilia et quam maxime de suffragiis.

> *Chapter 46* Incomincia una visione mirabile che ebbe la beata Brigida stando in estasi di mente secondo che di sotto si contiene. (f. 69r)

I take a final example of reduction from the very first chapter of the compilation, which is the rubric of I,47, put at the beginning to give the 'intention' of the compiler in planning his work:

> *Rev.* I,47: Verba Domini ad sponsam de legis nove adieccione et qualiter nunc ipsa lex reprobatur et contempnitur a mundo et quomodo mali sacerdotes non sunt Dei sacerdotes sed Dei proditores et de malediccione talium et dampnacione.

> *Chapter 1* Come si lamenta Dio che le creature sue ànno gittata la fede sua e singularmente dei sacerdoti. (f. 4r)

One would expect that the rather emphatic vocabulary of the original (God's law reproached and despised, bad priests, qualified as traitors, worthy of malediction and damnation) would appeal to our compiler.

It is not so. It may be that he thought a title should be clear and concise, especially that opening the book. In fact, in translating the text proper he adopts a rather different attitude, as can be shown from a passage taken a few lines later in this first chapter, where the sentence: "Ma che adiviene oggi *in questo pericoloso tempo* che questa *amabile e soave* legge è riprovata e disprezzata dal mondo impero che dicono *gl'uomini carnali e sensuali* che questa *mia* legge è stretta e grave e sanza forma" (f. 4v) translates: "Sed lex ista nunc reprobatur et contempnitur a mundo. Dicunt enim legem ipsam strictam esse, grauem et deformem."

I discussed some characteristics of this translation in ch. 6: 151-157, and shall add some remarks later on. We could say, in general, that while the rubrics are normally shortened, the text is frequently expanded. This is a regular procedure.

c. *Expansion*

The translation of the first chapter title of the book given above is probably an extreme example of reduction. But there are rubrics where an opposite solution is adopted, as in the translation of the rubric for *Rev.* IV,4:

> *Rev.* IV,4: Verba Dei ad sponsam de duobus spiritibus, scilicet bono et malo; et *de mirabili et utili bello in mente* cuiusdam domine orto ab inspiracionibus boni spiritus et a temptacionibus maligni spiritus; *et quid in istis sit eligendum.*
>
> *Chapter 56* Parla Dio alla sposa come *ogni creatura rationale* à oggi due spiriti: *l'uno è l'angelo celestiale ad inducere l'anima a Dio; l'altro è el demonio a tentare l'anima a peccati acciò che vada all'onferno*; e dello exenplo d'una reina, come e due spiriti le davano suggestioni *l'uno che essa lasciasse el mondo e le sue ponpe*, l'altro, cioè el demonio, *che essa dovesse godere nelli honori e nelle cose temporali.* (f. 83v)

The changes are notable. I have marked in italics both what has been omitted from the Latin, and what has been added in the Italian text. This is an example of explicative rubric, showing homiletic attitude: what may seem an addition is in fact the unfolding of what is implicit and the anticipation of what is to be found in the chapter. The printed book, following the procedure already illustrated, while displaying the same amplification found in the manuscript within the text, in the general table summarizes the content of what is chapter 55 in its numbering thus: 'Parla Cristo a la sposa come ogni creatura rationale sia due spiriti, cioè l'angelo bono e lo rio.'

d. *Additions*

Additions are a particular type of expansion, in that what they add is not necessarily implicit in the Latin, but consists in various forms of personal comment on the part of the compiler. The most obvious of these comments is the addition 'capitolo molto notabile' given to *Rev.* I,10 and III,19. A more implicit expression of the same type is found in the rubric of *Rev.* VII,30: 'una visione fatta a questa beata da Cristo molto notabile e generale a ogni umana creatura, come esso Cristo si lamenti de peccatori ingrati e del iudicio che ne farà': this is not really the translation of the rubric, but a new presentation of it, where both an evaluative expansion ('molto notabile') and a stark contraction ('generale' and 'ogni' for 'de universis peccatoribus omnium statuum et condicionum') are combined.[20] An addition to *Rev.* IV,22 is more impressive: "E della ira di Dio sopra il mondo che verrà se l'anime non si correggeranno" (f. 66v), a text not in the Latin.

One of these comment-phrases, and perhaps the most significant, has already been found in an example quoted: 'in questo pericoloso tempo' recurs frequently both in the rubrics and in the text. In *Rev.* I,1 a short *nunc* is translated: 'ora in questo malvagio tempo' (7v). The same happens in the rubric of *Rev.* I,59 (hora in questo tempo pericoloso: f. 31r) while in the text of the same chapter *credent operibus cum venerint* is translated 'crederrano quando verrà el tempo angoscioso' (f. 31r); again in *Rev.* III,5 (in questo tempo pericoloso: f. 45r), in *Rev.* IV,22, where *modernis temporibus* is rendered by 'ne tempi d'oggi periculosi' f. 63v), and in the text of *Rev.* III,21 (in

---

20 This is the text of the rubric for *Rev.* VII,30: "Iudex conqueritur sponse de vniuersis peccatoribus omnium statuum et condicionum, narrans beneficia, que fecit eis, et ingratitudinem eorum. Comminatur quoque eos cum sentencia terribili ire sue, ammonet tamen eos, quod conuertantur ad eum, et suscipiet eos cum misericordia sicut pater."

questo malvagio tempo: f. 53r), and III,29 ('in questo tempo pericoloso d'oggi': f. 61r).

Another similar actualization occurs in the rubric of *Rev.* III,6 (f. 45v), to which an 'oggi' added to the Latin is a further mark of its meaning for the present time, as is the addition 'del tempo presente' added to 'contra il mondo' in the rubric of *Rev.* IV,37 (f. 67v). A similar choice can be seen in the insertion in chapter IV,7 '[...] E altre cose molto notabili dello stato dell'anime le quali sono stati per li tempi passati assai incognite ma acciò che l'uomo tema in questo tempo pericoloso le volse Dio revelare a questa beata Brigida' (f. 72r) – see fn 13. The focus on the present time is a well-known feature of prophetic literature to mark the urgency of conversion. This is clearly expressed in some rubrics where a general and timeless similitude is turned into a description and value-judgement applied to the contemporary scene. See the one to *Rev.* I,59 below.

5. Organization of the text: survey of the selection from Book I

When we turn to the organization of the text, we can only describe its contents, it being impossible to discover a structuring principle in the selection. The difficulty comes from the fact that, as already noted, on the one hand Birgitta's work is so interspersed with prophetic pages, and on the other the prophetic mission is so far-reaching, that practically any chapter could have been used. In short: it is not easy to draw a prophetic book out of a prophetic work, except in terms of an abstract. Moreover, a fact that may obscure the pattern is the decision not to combine 'prophetic' excerpts chosen from different places, but to translate entire chapters, which at times are surprisingly heterogeneous, since we can find linked together a part in praise of Our Lady followed by a condemnation of hypocrisy and reproaches to corrupt clergy.

To give an idea of the selection we may go through the 19 chapters selected from the 60 in the first book of the *Revelations*. If a design must be identified, the one I can think of is something similar to a musical composition, where echoes and counterpoint play an important part in connecting apparently disparate passages. The main underlying themes are, as already said, faith and morals. Within this broad pattern, we have an introductory chapter against the clergy (I,47), followed by one denouncing how faith is being broken and God's law despised, a sign of great ingratitude on the part of men who are supposed to be believers (I,1). Then a chapter presents the articles of faith and describes how the bride, be it Birgitta, the Church or any Christian soul, should adorn herself (I,2), followed by a chapter on the battle to be fought against the world (I,6).

The chapters I,8-11 form a sort of unit, containing a prayer to Christ (8), praises of Mary (9), a meditation on the crucifixion (10) and an exhortation on how to live in imitation of the crucifix, especially in widowhood (11). Apparently prayer and praise of Mary's magnificence seem to have nothing to do with an appeal to conversion, but this Marian chapter contains a complaint against those who deny Mary's corporal assumption (f. 12r), and so it becomes a warning against unbelief.

The chapters I, 13, 14, 16, 22 and 25 could also be taken as a sort of subsequence where the devil has a central position. Within this sequence a positive note is regularly struck, reminding the reader of God's promise of mercy (13), telling of a prostitute who was delivered from the devil's possession by the intercession of Mary (16),[21] teaching how profitable it can be for the righteous to live among the wicked (22), and illustrating three examples of God's tolerance and three of his forgiveness of sinners (25). A teaching on how to live in a saintly way in marriage is contained in the following chapter (I,26), marked as 'sopralmodo notabile' (exceptionally relevant), where a summary of the history of salvation is presented in order to contrast a carnal to a spiritual way of living in the marital state, showing thus how doctrine becomes the foundation of the spiritual life. To this is linked a chapter on how Birgitta ought to live (I,34), connected with one where Mary describes her total unity with her son during the passion (I,35): that is, sanctity is primarily to be conceived as the

---

21   The printed book has a nice woodcut at the beginning of this chapter, which in the running order bears the number 11.

imitation of Christ, as a life of union with him. The final three chapters of the series taken from Book I start by going back to I,32, describing Birgitta's choice of poverty, which marks a stark contrast with I,56 which follows, where cupidity is the target of severe condemnation (*cupiditas*, rendered emphatically by 'la maladetta cupidità della avaritia': f. 28v). The rubric of this chapter is strange at first. Here is the Latin:

> *Rev.* I,56: 'Verba qualiter Deus capitulum superius immediate dictum declarat et de sentencia contra tales illata et qualiter Deus ad tempus propter bonos sustinet malos.'

> *Chapter 18* Parla Cristo alla sposa come e iudici e difensori e lavoratori della chiesa sua sono diventati arco maledetto pieno d'avaritia insatiabile. E come esso Cristo gli sostiene che anco non ne fa vendetta (f. 28v).

Contrary to what it may seem, this is not pure invention, but nothing less than the retrieval of part of the rubric of the preceding chapter, to which this is an explanatory continuation. The rubric for *Rev.* I,55 actually reads: 'Qualiter Christus similatur potenti domino, edificanti magnam ciuitatem et optimum palacium, per que mundus et Ecclesia designantur, et *qualiter iudices et defensores et laboratores in Ecclesia Dei conuersi sunt in arcum prauum.*' One wonders why the compiler did not also select chapter 55. A possible answer is that chapter 56, although full of threatening phrases much in the manner of an apocalyptic preacher, is mainly concerned with describing God's tolerance and forgiveness, which is also evidenced in the rubric given above, where it is said that god tolerates the wicked and does not take revenge. The phrase 'pieno d'avaritia insatiabile' is an addition of the translator, in which he comments on or anticipates the content of the chapter he is summarizing.

The last chapter selected from Book I is ch. 59, again a harsh tirade against the clergy, the same topic which was chosen as the first chapter, and in this way the selection comes full circle. The Latin rubric is only the description of the similitude used by Christ: "Verba Christi presente sponsa, scilicet qualiter Christus per rusticum, boni sacerdotes per bonum pastorem, mali sacerdotes per malum pastorem et boni Christiani per uxorem designentur et figurentur. In qua figura multa utilia continentur." The translator, by inserting two temporal adverbials, actualizes the text, making it relevant for his own time. 'Presente la sposa, parla Cristo per similitudine come *antichamente* fu retta la chiesa sua per buoni pastori, *hora in questo tempo pericoloso* sono date le pecore nelle mani de lupi per le miserie de mali pastori' (f. 31r). A timeless metaphor has thus been transformed into a contemporary denunciation.

The selection from Book I follows the ordering of the Alfonso redaction, except for ch. 32 which is inserted between 35 and 56. The same happens with Book II, with the sole exception of ch. 15 put at the end. Book III has a relevance of its own. The compiler has split it in two parts. One comes after Book II, and includes 15 chapters, following the order of the Latin except that chs. 14 and 19 are put in final position. Another section, totally devoted to the bishops, is placed towards the end, and contains chapters 1-3, 7 and 15.

When we come to Book IV the compiler starts organizing his chapters in a new and original way, the reason for which is not easy to discover. He goes forward and backward, and he does so even with the *Revelations* Books, putting in sequence VII, VI, IV, VII, VI, VII, VI, III, IV as can be seen in Appendix 3.

6. Book III

As already noted, Book III seems to have a particular relevance for the compiler, since almost two thirds of the chapters are selected. One way to proceed is to consider what the translator does with the rubrics, and read them in order to find the threads that weave the tapestry he offers us. The series starts with *Rev.* III,4-6, which are all about bishops and their bad government of the church. The author almost completely disregards the rubric of *Rev.* III,4, giving a more general title, apparently referred to the whole section, in which he says that 'Mary complains about the bad prelates of the church, who pursue the glory of the world with its lusts'. Ch. 4 is indeed about the difference between a 'corporal' bishop and a 'spiritual' one, that is: the office does not necessarily correspond to the dignity, or the sanctity of the prelate. Ch. 5 simplifies the rubric enormously, to the extent of changing the original completely: it reports words purported to be by St Ambrose on how the saints 'in this dangerous time' pray for the Christian souls who are abandoned because of the bad life of the prelates, a refrain running through all this section. Ch. 6 translates a similitude expressed again by St Ambrose transforming it into a judgment on the present time, a choice frequently made: "come e vescovi e prelati ànno oggi lasciata la legittima e bella sposa loro, cioè la cura della chiesa, e sonsi acostati colla adultera femina, cioè col mondo e con essa si dilettano".[22] This is a good example of how the translator renders a rubric, using simplification, explicitation and actualization at the same time.

The following sequence introduces the intercession of Mary (*Rev.* III,10) seen as a rainbow showing her mercy towards both the good and the wicked: the rubric, again departing from the Latin text in great part, marks how the Virgin is unable to placate Christ and so heal the ruin of the church caused by the bad pastors. *Rev.* III,12 is a prayer of intercession for a bishop, but also a warning against the presumption of an easy final salvation.

According to Jönsson (1998: 36), *Rev.* III,14-19 "is a coherent, interesting group of revelations". In fact, our compiler follows the source text order translating 15-18 as a sequence, but why he puts 14 and 19 at the end of this section we do not know. By a selection in the rubric of *Rev.* III,16 he stresses the fact that 'Christ does not take delight in the damnation of souls' ("Cristo [...] non si diletta della dannatione dell'anime"). This topic could be in harmony with the theme of mercy and intercession seen in the previous chapters. *Rev.* III,17 in fact describes another prayer of intercession, that of Saint Dominic for his friars, a request which was apparently unsuccessful, since the following chapter 18 laments that the Dominicans, not hearing the words of their founder, prefer to look for bishoprics in order to get rid of the yoke of religious life. *Rev.* III,21 illustrates another great religious figure, St Benedict, who is also the subject of

---

22   III,6: "Verba eiusdem Ambrosii ad sponsam quandam similitudinem viri et uxoris et ancille disponentia, et qualiter per adulterum episcopus malus et per uxorem ecclesia et per ancillam mundi amor designantur, et de crudelissima sententia contra adherentes magis mundo quam ecclesie."

Rev. III,20, which was not selected. Praise of St Benedict, however, is not followed by a criticism of the monks. To complete the picture of religious life, the Franciscans are the target of a severe attack in *Rev.* VII,20, here translated on ff. 106r-107v, where the chapter is wrongly indicated as '33', being in fact ch. 83.

A series of four chapters, *Rev.* III 27-30, could also be taken as a sequence. We have a severe tirade against the city of Rome (27), and it is possible that the theme of the 'city' explains the choice of ch. 28, where four cities are described, corresponding to this present world, purgatory, hell and heaven respectively. Ch. 29 contains praises of the Virgin Mary as the true temple of God, and a curious change in the rubric: the Latin *qualiter sacerdotum templa sunt vanitate depicta* becomes "e come e sacerdoti sono vero tempio di Dio" (f. 60r)! Nowhere in the chapter can this sentence be found. It may be either a blunder mixing *vanitas* and *veritas*, or the affirmation of an ideal, against which priests are denounced because they are not what they should be. In fact, the text condemns the vanity of the clergy, although the end is, again, a request for mercy made by Birgitta to Mary, for priests. In any case Mary recalls that intercession, even hers, can be effective only if the soul for whom prayers are said has the will to abandon sin and to progress in doing good. Ch. 30 has no visible link with what precedes: it is a praise of Mary, and an exhortation not to be upset by the tribulations and hardships of life.

The first section gathered from Book III ends, as I have said, with *Rev.* III,14 and 19, which have in common the condemnation of hypocrisy, referred to some bishop.

A second section made with chapters taken from Book III appears at the end of the 'first volume' of the compilation. It consists of five chapters (1,2,3,7,15), all of which deal with the episcopal office, and the way of life a bishop should lead, offering a paradigm of how this office should be performed. Other chapters in this book, for example *Rev.* III, 8,9,11, and above all 13, deal with the same subject, and the reason why they were not selected is beyond my imagination.

7. Some aspects of the translation

In an earlier essay I analysed a couple of large excerpts of this work in order to give a general idea of the kind of translation adopted.[23] In this chapter I have particularly examined the various ways of rendering the rubrics, where much freedom is shown. The treatment of the text proper is considerably different, and one general principle could describe the translator's choices: the changes are normally expansions, of which two types can be identified: one, less frequent, is explanatory; the other, much more prominent, reveals an emotional-devotional response to the text. Suffice it to list some examples of phrases or sentences taken at random which need no further comment.

Explanatory additions:

I,1: *latro pessimus*: uno pessimo ladrone, *cioè il demonio* (f. 8r)

I,1: *quia feci eum et redemi*: imperoché l'o creato *alla immagine mia* e ollo ricomperato *del mio pretioso sangue* (f. 8r)

I,14: *qui in cruce crucifixus*: che in croce fui crocifisso *per la salute della humana natura* (f. 18r)

III,18: *ablata est mitra et ecce apparuit quod latebat subtus*: O. O. O. ghuai *a me* che tolta m'è la mitera e ora s'aprirà quella *ipocrisia* che *mi* stava aghuattata sotto (f. 54v).

Note in this last example, besides the personalization of the text, and the specification of the meaning of *quod* by 'hypocrisy', the vivid figurative lexis, where 'aghuattata' (etymologically connected with *squat*) is more pictorial than *latebat* (was hidden).

Emotional emphasis

I,10: *intime dilexi eum*: con tutto il cuore e con tutte le forze mie si l'amai (f. 12v)

I,10: *ipse filius meus*: esso mio caro thesoro figluolo mio (f. 15r)

---

23 See ch. 6, where I noted that "this translation is less literal and more original" (p. 153) than the other late medieval Italian translations examined in the essay.

I,13:   *inimicus dei* (rubric): l'anima perversa e che mal vive (f. 17r)
        inimicus meus (text): l'anima misera e accecata la quale m'offende
                                                                    (f. 17r)
I,13:   *ad ignem sulphureum*: al fuoco arzente e al zolfo puzzolente (f. 17v)
I,26:   *de corruptione* (rubric): della corructione pessima della carnalità
                                                                    (f. 21v)
III,27: *et rogo te, ut rogare digneris*: E preghovi madonna che dobbiate
        essere avocata al vostro dolce figluolo Jesu (f. 56v)
IV,47: *Filius loquitur*: Lo dolce sposo Cristo parla alla beata Brigida e dice
                                                                    (f. 104v)
IV,53: *Verba Virginis ad sponsam*: Parla la nobilissima madre di Cristo alla
        sposa (f. 105v)
VI,34: *Mater loquebatur*: La gratiosa madre di Cristo Maria dice così alla
        sposa (f. 107v)

In order to give a clearer picture of the final product of this translation I think that nothing can be better than providing a large extract, in which the reader himself can compare the Latin with the Italian, and see the changes that have been introduced. Given the differences in wording between the manuscript and the printed book, here reported in the footnotes, one can also visualize the relationship between the two versions. The excerpt is taken from *Rev.* I,56.

To help the reader to compare the Latin text with the Italian version I have used italics to mark in the Latin text words either omitted (for example *porrige manum*) or not literally translated (for example 'molti' for *illi*), and in the Italian rendering words or phrases which have been added to the original (for example 'cioè dell'amor mio'). As I have already remarked, contrary to the procedure used for the rubrics, where reductions occur rather frequently, the text proper is much more respected, and apparently only expansions are allowed, and even favoured. These are mainly of two types: they are used either to add an explanation or to enhance emphasis. This chapter has been chosen in that it is a good sample of the prophetic genre, combining denunciation of wrongdoings and proclamation of God's patience. A quick survey shows that the translator has chosen to mark the negative side of the message much more strongly than the evocation of God's mercy. The difference consists mainly in quite a number of expansions and additions, meant primarily 1) to explain a noun or a phrase, 2) to better qualify a word, 3) to balance clauses in a sentence. The first two choices have to do with meaning, the third with style and rhythm (ch. 6: 154-155). This tendency to paraphrase, both in terms of explanation and emphasis, is in fact confirmed by the examples I give here, referring not only to single phrases and sentences, but also to larger textual units.

Revelationes I,56
(Undhagen 1977: 423-425)

BNC II,II,391, ff. 28v-29v
(Printed book version: ff. 20r-20v)

1 "Dixi tibi *prius*, quia gladius Ecclesiae abiectus est et pro eo assumptus saccus pecunie, qui ex una parte apertus est et ex alia sic profundus, quod, *quidquid* ingreditur, numquam capit fundum nec umquam impletur. 2 Hic saccus est cupiditas, que omnem modum et mensuram excedit et in tantum inualuit, quod contempto *Domino* nichil desideratur nisi pecunia et propria voluntas. 3 Attamen ego sum sicut dominus, qui et pater et iudex est. Cui *eunti ad iudicium* dicunt circumstantes: 'Domine, procede cicius et fac iudicium!' Quibus respondit dominus: 'Expectate modicum usque cras, quia forte *filius meus* adhuc interim emendabit se.' [...]

(*28v*) 1 Dissiti in uno altro capitolo che 'l coltello della chiesa, *cioè dell'amor mio*, è gittato via e in luogo d'esso ànno preso *e pastori della chiesa* el sacco della pecunia, lo quale da l'una parte è aperto, dall'altra è tanto profondo che avengha che sanza rimedio vi si metta mai non s'empie né dice[24] basta. 2 *La profondità* di questo sacho è la *maledetta* cupidità *della avaritia*, la quale sopralmodo *in questo tempo* excede e sopra ogni misura. E intanto (*29r*) prevale che disprezzano el creatore loro e nulla altra <cosa>[25] desiderano se non pecunia e la propia volontà. 3 Nondimeno io sono[26] *grande* signore lo quale è padre e iudice. A cui dicono quelli che gli stanno dintorno:[27] 'Signore vieni tosto e fa el *tuo iusto* iudicio'.[28] Alli quali esso risponde: 'Aspectate un poco insino a domane, imperoché in questo mezzo forse e figluoli miei si corregeranno'. [...]

7 Dixi eciam tibi prius, quod populum diuisi in tre partes, scilicet in iudices, in defensores et laboratores. Quos enim significant isti iudices nisi *clericos*, qui diuinam sapienciam verterunt in prauam et *vanam*? 8 Sicut *illi* clerici solent facere, qui recipiunt multa verba et componunt in pauca – et illa pauca verba sonant idem, quod illa multa –, sic clerici huius temporis receperunt decem mandata mea et composuerunt in unum verbum. 9 Quid est hoc

7 Dissiti in prima che 'l populo *cristiano* è diviso in tre parti, cioè in iudici, defensori e lavoratori. Che significano e giudici senone e *maladetti* prelati eclesiastici *del tempo d'oggi*, li quali la divina sapientia conuertono in prava e mala[29] sapientia? 8 Costoro fanno come molti[30] scolari che le molte parole le conchiudono in poche, e quelle poche dicono quello che fanno le molte.[31] Così el chericato d'oggi ànno ricevuti e dieci miei

---

24   dicono B.
25   artra cosa B.
26   como uno (Lat *sicut*) add. B.
27   This sentence is omitted in the book.
28   fa il iudicio tuo B
29   vana B (Lat. *vana*).
30   certi B (Lat. *illi*).
31   sig<n>ifichano quele che le molte B.

verbum? *'Porrige manum* et da pecuniam!' Hec est sapientia eorum, loqui pulchre et agere male, simulare se meum *et agere nequiter contra me.*

10 Ipsi denique pro muneribus peccantes libenter paciuntur in peccatis, simplices exemplo suo precipitant. Insuper *euntes per viam meam* odiunt. **11** Secundo defensores Ecclesie, idest curiales, sunt infideles. Qui fregerunt promissionem suam et iuramentum et peccantes contra fidem sancte Ecclesie mee *et constitucionem* libenter tolerant.

12 Tercio laboratores, idest communitas, sunt sicut tauri indomiti, quia habent tria. Effodiunt enim terram pedibus, secundo implent se ad satietatem, tercio complent voluptatem suam iuxta desiderium suum. **13** Sic communitas nunc totis affectionibus inhiat temporalibus. Implet se immoderata gula et vanitate mundi. Complet absque racione carnis sue delectacionem.

comandamenti e ànnogli rechati[32] in una parola. **9** E quale è questa parola se non 'Dammi pecunia'?[33] Questa è la loro sapientia *maladetta*, cioè parlare adornato *con rime* e fare male, simularsi essere de miei e essi sono del dymonio.[34]

10 Essi per doni temporali volentieri sostengono quelli che peccano; e semplici per lo *pessimo* loro exemplo si turbano. E quelli che m'amano e so miei servi si gli odiano e *perseghuitano.*[35] **11** Anco essi defensori della chiesa, cioè e signori mondani, li quali sono infedeli e ànno rotta la promessione e 'l giuramento loro, contra quelli che peccano averso della[36] santa *madre* eclesia volentieri (*29v*) gli portano *sanza nulla iustitia temendo di perdere*[37] *la loro utilità temporale.*[38]

12 Anco e lavoratori, cioè la comunità *de popoli*, sono diventati come tori non domati. Li quali fanno tre chose, cioè che chavano la terra co piedi, secondo che mangiano a satietade, tertio che compiono[39] la concupiscentia loro *carnale* secondo la loro volontà. **13** Cosi fa oggi la comunità *della gente*, imperoché con tutte le forze loro s'affatichano *e spendono el tempo loro* nelle cose temporali *sanza nulla*[40] *memoria di me.* Mangiano con molta disordinatione *e solo a diletto della maladetta ghola.*[41] Compiono *etiamdio*[42] *ogni* loro dilecto carnale *e bestiale* privandosi d'ogni ragione *humana a modo che'lle bestie.*

---

32   ridoti: B.

33   vengano dinari e pecunia B.

34   Questa è la loro sapientia: studio di parlare ornato e bene conposte rime. E simulansi esser me, e sono del diavolo B.

35   In pero che per presenti e doni sostengono i peccatori E gli simplici per loro pessimo exemplo e quegli che m'amano e sono mei servi si schandolezano e conturbano e ànnoli in odio e si li perseguitano B.

36   contro la B.

37   non perdere Ms.

38   Li quali sopportano per non perdere li beni temporali abbandonano la iusticia e equità B.

39   empiano B.

40   nessuna B.

41   Mangiano con grandissima dilectatione pianamente satisfare a la maledetta gola B.

42   Empiono ancora B.

194

8. Conclusion

When I started to think about this contribution I had three expectations or aims in my mind. One was to determine the kind of relationship existing between the manuscript and the printed book. The second was to explore the content of the compilation, to see what corresponded to the compiler's project of prophetic preaching. The third was to identify on which criteria the selection had possibly been made.

As for the first expectation I feel quite satisfied, having established the connection between the two works, and also the fact that the manuscript is normally more reliable and useful than the book. The table provided in Appendix 3, with the correct number of the chapters selected (correcting the few errors of the manuscript) and with the correspondences between these and the sequential numbering of the chapters of the book, will, I hope, be useful for further research.

As for the second aim, I think I have given enough information about the topics dealt with in the work, especially concerning the connection between faith and morals in a reforming project.

As for the third object of my research, my frustration grew deeper and deeper as I advanced through the book. I cannot really explain why some chapters of the *Revelations* were selected while others of similar or the same content were left out. In fact, the prophetic tone is so pervasive in Birgitta's work, so much is her figure seen as a prophetess, that practically any chapter could be selected to compile an exemplary specimen of Birgitta's prophetic voice. Probably the aim of the compiler was merely to produce a manageable book out of the huge corpus of the *Revelations*. The fact that this compilation went into print may prove that he was successful.

CHAPTER 8

How and Why a Translation May Be Revised: The Case of British Library, Arundel MS 197[1]

The manuscript marked London, British Library, Arundel 197 is a small codex dating from the end of the fifteenth century. It measures cm 19x13, and consists of 73+2 folios. It is in parchment, rubricated and written in a clear cursive hand. It contains meditations and tracts of spiritual guidance, of which the longer and most important ones are the *Fervor Amoris* (ff. 10r-38v), a treatise on contemplative and active life from the *Revelations* (VI,65) of St Birgitta (ff. 38v-46v), and an abstract taken from a version of David of Augsburg's *Formula Novitiorum* (ff. 48r-64r). Together with these longer works there is a collection of short tracts, including another chapter from Birgitta's *Revelations* II,6 (ff. 46v-47v), a prayer "to the Sacramente" (ff. 47v-48r), a meditation on the hymn *Veni Creator* (ff. 64r-70r), and another on the *Te Deum* following a tract on tribulations (ff. 70r-73r); folios 1r-10r contain a miscellany of short works.

At first glance it seems just one of the many late medieval compilations of religious texts, save for the peculiar fact that the texts have been corrected in many places. The corrections are numerous: words, phrases, and whole lines have been erased to make place for new words, phrases, and lines, written carefully by a hand very similar to the original one. I shall call this second hand 'the reviser' and indicate him as A1, leaving the siglum A for the original text.

What might have been the reason, if any, for taking such pains to revise and correct texts already established and transmitted in a 'received' form? In fact at least the three longer texts mentioned above and the short Birgittine tract (all, except the *Fervor Amoris,* translations from Latin) are extant in other manuscripts, and the versions in

---

Arundel 197 prior to the revision, as can be reconstructed by comparison, are clearly the same as those found in other codices. Who was this reviser? A philologist wanting to produce a better version in order to prepare a printed edition? Somebody who, after copying the texts, wanted to work on them? Or a later reader who, as Connolly (1994: 63) suggests, shows an "active intellectual engagement with the text"? A theologian, or a spiritual authority intent at producing a 'more orthodox' doctrine for his audience? Or simply a neurotic reader writing private notes never meant to be published?

I must say that I can hardly believe that a parchment manuscript, with rubrics, could be interpreted as a 'rough copy' to be corrected in view of producing a better copy or a printed text. At the same time it is difficult to imagine such pains being taken by a single reader if the cause was simply his dissatisfaction with a text. My hypothesis is that the manuscript was probably produced for a religious house, a community of men and women (*fratres* in *Formula Novitiorum* becomes 'brothers and sisters'), where the texts were read in public, and that the aim of providing a better text, more suited to the ideas of the leader of the community, could be a sufficient reason to justify the effort spent in the revision. Lay readership could be excluded, at least in the mind of the reviser, especially if we consider an addition to the final tract on *Te Deum,* where the reader is described as "called [...] to his [God's] holy vyneyarde by fore thousandis of oþer pepul þat leveþ in þe worlde" (f. 70v).

To further support the hypothesis of a text revised and prepared for public reading, a detail has come now into focus, which I had somewhat disregarded in my previous work on the manuscript. On folio 31v, accompanying the text of *Fervor Amoris,* there is an indication giving the reference of a passage in this way: "In revel. Brigide regine li° .4. ca°. 38°." The reference is in itself remarkable, in that normally only the Fathers of the Church or the biblical passages are given this distinction: this would suggest a Birgittine context for the manuscript. But more relevant is the fact that our reviser has intervened here to rewrite the reference so that it should be inserted and read in the current text. By a red mark in the text, inserted after "for as y rede" and repeated on the margin, a not particularly skilful reader had what he needed to do the operation, since the concise reference is developed in this way: "in þe revelacions of sent Birgit.

þe iiij boke. and. xxxviij chaptur a sethe". But as a warning to easy and quick conclusions, I must say that the same hand has crossed out a paragraph immediately before this one which is of pure Birgittine source, belonging to the same chapter from where the rest of the quotation is taken.

I have wrestled with Arundel 197 three times: twice to edit the two Birgittine tracts (see Pezzini 1988: 292-298; 1994b: 381, fn. 7, and 391-395), and more recently when studying the English translations of the *Formula Novitiorum* (see ch. 4). The messy situation of certain passages (and this seems to go against the idea of texts prepared for public reading, certainly not always easy), and the multifarious quality of the changes have been a challenge since the beginning of my study. Nonetheless, the possibility of reconstructing the psychology of a writer looked fascinating. The drama begins when, thinking that the mind of a writer should be consistent within certain patterns, one discovers that it is not. What remains to think is that there are probably different ideas of consistency.

Since important parts of this MS have already been examined,[2] this time I chose to concentrate on the abstract of David of Augsburg's *Formula Novitiorum,* for the reason that, unlike the *Fervor Amoris,* this is the revision of a translation, as is the case with the Birgittine texts. This would imply three stages: the Latin, which the reviser might have known and used; the first translation; and finally the revision. It is obvious that any edition of this abstract must take all three stages into account. We are lucky enough that Queens' College Cambridge MS 31 contains a complete translation of David's work which is literal, and from which, or from one very similar to it, the text in Arundel 197 has been copied.[3] This allows us not only to see the cancellations and additions which are still visible but also to recover what has been erased and overwritten. I shall indicate the changes in italics when the new words have been rewritten after erasure, whereas apexes mark the words added above the line or on

---

2   See Connolly (1994) for the text of *Fervor Amoris,* and my edition of the two
     Birgittine tracts (*Revelations* II,6 and VI,65) quoted above (Pezzini 1988 and
     1994b).
3   See ch. 4. For the Latin text forming the base of the English versions of the
     Formula Novitiorum see also Pezzini (1997).

the margins. I shall use Q for the QCC MS 31 of the *Formula,* A1 for the revised text in Arundel 197, and A for the supposed or reconstructed original text.

Before proceeding to illustrate some of the changes made by A1, I will list the different types and techniques of correction. The most common technique is the insertion of new words (including grammatical words), phrases, and sentences, or the cancellation of the same by crossing lines. In many places, new words and phrases have been written after erasing the previous ones. The economic attitude of the reviser shows when he erases only part of a word to change only the letters which cannot be retrieved: he uses part of *mayde* to make *mary,* so that 'þat blesful mayde' becomes 'þe *blessed 'virgyn'* ma*ry'* (f. 39r), or he transforms *man* into *person,* where on an erased 'm' he writes *'pers'* using the abbreviation for *per-,* then he rounds *'a'* into an *'o',* leaving the last *'n'* as it is. We can have an idea of the overall effect by looking at a passage of the treatise on contemplative and active life taken from Birgitta's *Revelations* VI, 65. I give the text following exactly the format it has in the manuscript (# indicates line breaks):

> (f. 39r) þen he muste mekeli praie god *that* of his grace *he wille tendurly preserve and kepe*

> (f. 39v) *them to the increse of vertu, and to þe increse of þe growynge of þer saluacion* # ~~sion to his p~~/ and when he wille worship god deuoutly in her # te, he *muste ley a parte alle occupacion as for the time of his prayer* # ~~þat hym bihoueþe without worly besines, he may wel abide and make~~ # *ande then apon þat,* if he be weri *of his longe praynge* and in þe mene time *pera* # *ventur is* trobelid with temptacions, *then hit wilbe necery to geve hym to sum ocu* # *pacion* oþer for his owne nede, *or for þe profete of oþir.*

If we want to recover the probable original text, we may take it from the one extant in Oxford, Bodleian Library MS 423, from which I have edited the tract (see Pezzini 1994b: 397-398, ll. 39-45), integrating a missing line of this manuscript with C.U.L. MS Ii.vi.40, with which Arundel 197 seems to better correspond in this passage. The passage, arranged so to correspond to Arundel 197 format, reads:

> For hem he must mekely praie god of his grace that he suffre hem not to be tempted # ouer that they mowe withstonde. He must haue to al this discre #

cion to his praier, and whane he wil worshipe god deuoutly in her # te, him behoueth [C: also to be wele disposid and ordeynid, for if we haue # þat, him bihouiþ] to be withoute worldly besynesse; he may wel abyde and make # þe lenger praiers. But yf he be wery for to longe praienge, and in the mene tyme # be trauailed wiþ temptacions, than it is spedful to take other besynesse, or # trauaile either for his owne nede, or for profit to other. (f. 151r)

Something new is introduced by A1 in this translation: while the original text invited prayers to help withstand temptations, the new text is preoccupied to specify the meaning and aim of temptations: increase of virtues and of salvation. Also, the original perspective is inverted: the faithful who must withstand temptations practically disappear, and God comes to the foreground: it is he who will tenderly preserve and keep them. The other changes are of a more practical order, but there too we may notice how the new text maintains a certain coherence in that the word 'occupacion', substituting 'besynesse', is regularly repeated.

To give a foretaste of what kind of changes may be expected, I will quote some examples taken from the shorter Birgittine tract, which I have called 'The twelve points', a translation of the second part of Book II, ch. 16 of Birgitta's *Revelations*. The version in Arundel 197 is very similar to that in London, BL Additional MS 37790, f. 236v, with which it can be compared (see Pezzini 1988: 293-298). The first thing we remark in the revision is a tendency to emphasis, both doctrinal and emotional. A couple of examples will suffice. 'Luf all in me', found in Additional, and most probably the first version in Arundel 197, is turned by the reviser into '*love all maner of pepul for mi sake*' (f. 46v), a sentence which is partly written on an erasure, and partly on the margin. This may be taken as an explanatory addition. Another example is the change from 'I will þou haue wakynge to tempyr the to gouerne þe in þy body' to '*y suffur þe to vse wacchynge to worship me so hit be do with temporate gouernaunce of þi body*' (f. 47r). In this case the verb is changed to better conform with the Latin *permitto,* and a motivation is added which was not in the original, and which constitutes a turning of perspective: waking is to be done primarily not as a way of self-mortification but as a way to worship God; the temperance of the body is not an aim but a means. A third example occurs in connection with an invitation to meditate on the last Judgment (Latin: *considera*

201

iustitiam meam et futurum iudicium), which after alteration becomes 'biholde and thinke on my *strayte rightwysnes þat shal be in þe dredful day of* dome that is to come' (f. 47r). I have marked in italics the words that have visibly been rewritten, by which a strong new emphasis has gone into a much plainer text. So, just from this short piece we have examples of amplifications as: 1) explanatory additions to clarify the text; 2) doctrinal rectification to obtain a different balance; and 3) emotional emphasis on Christian themes, much in the mood of a preacher.

Starting from the temporary conclusions derived from the changes seen in this short tract, and considering the vast number of the alterations to be found in the manuscript, I have devised three sections under which to order the work of the reviser:

1. Language (grammar and style)
2. Meaning (details added or cut off)
3. Religion (theology, spirituality, pastoral attitudes)

I am aware that these divisions are not clear cut, and that in some or many of the examples provided they overlap, so that we may find more than one of these reasons to explain the alterations. Grammar and style, for instance, interrelate, and the decision to be specific and detailed, while it may affect meaning, is in itself a stylistic choice. At the same time, the difference between doctrine and spirituality is between what we believe and how we live our faith, but here too it is easy to pass from one to the other, the two being obviously interconnected.

1. Language

Changes related to grammar can be dealt with rather quickly: they are neither numerous nor really relevant. If, for example, the double comparative and the personal pronoun added to the imperative mean emphasis, then our reviser tends to be emphatic. Double negation seems to be preferred: 'nor bere *not* þi hed' (ff. 53v-54r: the catch-word on f. 53v is 'bere þi hed'); 'Be not glad to be in *'no'* company' (f. 54v); 'nor geue neuer' (f. 54v: Q has 'and neuer yeue'); a slight change transforms a 'neuer […] or' into 'neuer […] nor'. Stylistic refinement to avoid repetition may be seen in 'in so miche þat as *ny* as þou maiste' (f. 56r), where 'ny' replaces a previous 'miche'. But perhaps the most important interventions in the domain of syntax are the frequent insertions of 'then', 'therefor', 'yett', 'so' to mark correlation and consequence more clearly, together with a frequent and skilful use of modality (for example 'leste […] þou *'miȝt'* be temptit […] or *'hit miȝt'* drawe fantaȝies', in ch. 30, f. 56r) to soften down certain statements. A good example occurs in chapter 8, on folios 50v-51r, where the additions of such words and phrases as 'may', 'forwhy' [from an original 'for'], 'also', 'shulbe', and 'it is so þat' combine to refine a whole paragraph.

The addition of 'to' before a complement recurs at times, as in 'The woman þat þou gavyste *'to'* me' (ch. 5, f. 49v), or in 'to do *'to'* oure lord grete worship' (f. 56r). 'Of' is inserted after 'maner' in 'alle maner *of synnys'* for A: 'alle maner werkis' (f. 58r), but 'al manere tidinggis' (f. 56v) is left untouched. Other choices are less relevant and more a matter of personal preference, as where 'in wythdrowynge that ys necessary' (Q) is turned into 'in withdrawynge *of þat* is necessary' (A1, f. 51r), or 'behaue' becomes 'behaue *'þe'* (f. 50r), or when in the phrase 'his propur invencions' A1 adds 'owne' to strengthen 'propur' (f. 48v), an addition which occurs quite often.

Attitude towards doublets is contradictory: in same cases the reviser eliminates them, in another he creates a new one. So we have 'þat þou doiste refuse ~~and caste a way~~' (ch. 8, f. 50r) on the one hand, and *'speke and sey'* (ch. 26, f. 55r), where Q has 'saye', on the other.

Linguistic changes may have to do with style but also reveal moral attitudes. Both meanings appear in the following passage from the *Formula,* where the elimination of some repetitions in A1 produce a better phrasing, while the change of the personal pronoun, from a generic 'he' (related to the subject 'a creature') to the more forceful 'þou', involves a more direct way of addressing the reader.

Q: Thou commyste to serue thy god as euery creatur oweth to serue hys god, for he hath no thyng but onely of hys god, and therfor he shuld yeue hys god all that he hath, all that he cane, and all that he may. (cols 5-6)

A1: Thow comiste to serue þi god as euery creatur *is bounde,* for *þou haste* no thinge but only of *hym, and* þerfor *þou shalte* geue *þi* god *agene* al þat *þou* haste, al þat *þou* can, and al þat *þou* may. (ch. 1, f. 48r)

This more aggressive pastoral attitude can be seen in many other places. I choose but one example, taken from chapter 23, where, after some warnings against the evils produced by gossip, the reviser adds rather imperiously: *do þou not so* (f. 54v).

2. Meaning

The addition or elimination of single words and short phrases is a well-practised technique to modify a text at a low cost. The point here is to understand what attitudes lurk behind these changes, since additions can range from a pedantic love of precision to a change in doctrinal or spiritual perspective. I give here a list, which is far from being complete. It is meant only to give an idea of what variations of meaning these changes, which may be easily disregarded, might in fact imply. Here are some examples, listed under headings indicating their possible meaning:

Precision

- A1: *an inheritage of euerlastinge joy* (ch. 1, f. 48r) for Q: an herytage euerlastynge
- A1: (birds singing) riȝt swete in þer *detijs* (ch. 29, f. 56r) for Q: ryght swete in there maner

Restriction

- A1: he shal lede þe the *'riȝt'* way to god (ch. 2, f. 48v) for Q: he shall lede the the waye of god (*te ducat in viam Dei*)

- A1: but if it be *for riȝt a nedeful cause* (ch. 5, f. 49v) for Q: but yf ytt be profitable
- A1: poure not out þi selfe *'in biholdynge'* apon al mete (ch. 7, f. 50r)
- A1: þat þou may aftur þi mete *be disposid to 'pray'* (ch. 7, f. 50v) for Q: that thow may aftyr thy mete pray quikeli
- A1: keper of *'gode'* fame (ch. 16, f. 53v)

Preference for another word with roughly similar meaning

- A1: be not *dulle* (ch. 4, f. 49r) for Q: be not slowe
- A1: a *milde* voyse (ch. 27, f. 55v) for Q: an esy voice
- A1: for þe *kyngdom* of hevene (ch. 2, f. 48v), for Q: for the reaume of heuen
- A1: take no hede of courtly *gyse nor of* courtly po*yntes* (ch. 29, f. 55v) for Q: take noone heyde of courtly goynges nore courtely portes (ch. 32, col. 56)

New emphasis

- A1: as þe drede of god comp*ellethe* […] a man (ch. 16, f. 53v) for Q: the drede of god compowneth […] a man (Lat. *componit*)

Introduction of a missing name

- A1: as þe profete *'davethe'* techeþ us (ch. 32, f. 57v)
- A1: marie *'maudelene'* (f. 38v)

An attitude of reverence

- A1: aftur *diuine service is do* (ch. 4, f. 49r) for Q: aftyr the office and seruice
- A1: *For almiȝti god takyt more* hede (ch. 29, f. 55r) for Q: God taketh heyde
- A1: of al *'holy'* churche (ch. 30, f. 56r) for Q: of the churche

Moralistic attitude

- A1: to be *'holde worly and transitori'* thyngis (ch. 4, f. 49r) for Q: to veyn thynges
- A1: *the trewe serv*ant of god (ch. 6, f. 49v) for Q: the seruante of god

Doctrinal shift

- A1: a ful feiȝthe *'to'* þat holy churche teche þe (f. 45v) for A: a ful feiȝthe as holy churche bileueþe

The most frequent alterations appear to be those which extend or restrict the meaning of a sentence, either by adding a new word or phrase, or by cutting off the existing one. A cutting may in fact enlarge the meaning of a sentence or a clause:

- A1: only þei take hede what ~~gode~~ ensampul thou shewiste þem now (ch. 8, f. 51r)
- A1: loke not ~~myche~~ abovte in þe stretis (ch. 30, f. 56r)

The expansion may be due to the desire to better illustrate a metaphor, as when for Q '(the mind full of idle thoughts) ys made derke wyth a maner of duste', A1 gives '[...] darke *as a thynge þat was feyre and is defowled with* duste' (ch. 32, f. 57r). An expansion meant to give a stylistically more rounded sentence occurs where Q 'or elles thy time spendyde vnprofitably' is replaced by *'or ellis hit miȝt cause* þi time *'to be'* spendid vnprofetabulli' in A1 (ch. 32, f. 57r). A literal translation may be changed to specify the meaning of the text, as in chapter 29 on avoiding vainglory in singing, where Q 'the more that thow fleyst veniteys' (*quanto magis vanitatem fugis*) becomes '*þe more devotelier þat þou syngiste*'(f. 55v) in A1; in the same chapter 'the beholders' (Q) are turned into '*þe hyrerse*' (f. 56r), a more appropriate word in a context of singing. In some cases one wonders whether love of precision is in fact pedantic fastidiousness, as in the following example: 'as þouȝ a man wolde suppose þe *'to be'* a gote, where þou arte *in dede a* man' (ch. 37, f. 62r).

3. Religion

The analysis of the changes which may be referred to as doctrine is by far the most interesting, given the religious content of the texts collected in the manuscript. It is also, predictably, the field in which the reviser's mental attitudes and moral convictions come more evidently to the foreground.

To maintain a certain order I have selected a few items which seem to have some relevance: God, sin, authority, the Eucharist,

206

comments showing the reviser's pastoral mood, virtues and vices, and the evaluation of contemplative and active life.

3.1. God

The absolute primacy of God is regularly stressed and insistently marked, sometimes in strange ways, such as by reducing man's similarity to God, as in the following case: where Q says that God made man 'also lorde of all the worlde and lyke to hym self', A1 reads 'and *'in similitude' y like* to hym self' (ch. 1, f. 48r). To the same intent, substitution can also be used, as where for Q 'ayens any vertue', A1 has 'ageniste þe *wil of god*' (f. 52v).

A curious way of underlining the excellence of God consists in isolating him by cutting off other phrases which become redundant, as in A1: 'we be bounden to serue hym ~~by fore all creaturis~~' (ch. 1, f. 48r). A good example of this procedure occurs in chapter 25, 'Of ydulle wordis': '*þerfor* be glad to speke of god, and more gladde*r* to *do þat may plese hym,* ~~(m)ay stere þi spretis to study vertuis, and to affeccion of deuocion~~'. (f. 55r). Q has: 'more gladde to here such thynge as may styrre' etc. The reviser, by adding 'therefore' and by ruling out any mention of virtues and devotion, lets all the stress fall on God only, which is all the more remarkable in that this is the concluding statement of the chapter.

A high sense of the reverence due to God is shown in the expansion and a commentary following a verse of Psalm 15:8 translated literally in the original version:

I prouidid 'so þat þe drede and reverence of' oure lorde 'was' in my siȝtte euermore [This drede and reverence shulde euery trew lovyng] seruaunt of almiȝti god have by-fore his bodily y, and also by-fore þe y of 'his concience, þat god may pre'serve hym fro al þe perelles of þis lif. (ch. 33, f. 57v)

The words in square brackets are written on a small piece of parchment pasted on the leaf, perhaps an attempt to repair an unsatisfactory correction. We may recover the original text in Q: "I provyde oure lorde in my syghte euer more, for thys werily speketh the herte wythin hym selfe, that he be not mevede frome hym self by veyne gladnes or vnresonable sorowe" (col. 86).

Curiously enough, the reviser is not proposing an image of a stern God, as can be seen in the following changes: where Q reads: (God has taken care of man) 'as a woman of hys lytell chylde', A1 has 'as a woman of her *tendur beloved* childe' (f. 48r). On folio 70v God is called, in an addition, *þi tendur lovynge lorde,* and in the passage from the Birgittine tract already quoted he is prayed that *'he wille tendurly preserve and kepe'* his faithful (f. 39r).

3.2. Sin

The double attitude mixing reverence for God and a sense of his tenderness can be seen in the reviser's treatment of sin, where severity and compassion combine. On the one hand he says that sin is a very serious thing, on the other he asks for a very great compassion towards sinners. In chapter 35, 'Detestacion of notabilite', A1 stresses the sinfulness of self-praising: 'it is a *grete* synne and *but* a vanite' (f. 58v). In the following chapter he invites to have *''over grete'* compassion of synnerse' (f. 59v) because they are in serious danger. A good example is in the following passage, where he expands a simple comparative sentence of the original text which we can see in Q: 'yt ys more ruthfull to be drowned in the lake of helle then in the grounde of the see. Pray for them [...]' (col. 100). This becomes in A1:

> Hit is 'miche' more peti of 'a person' to be drownid in þe bottum of hel by syn then in þe bottum of þe see [in clene lif, for thow a man be drownyd in þe bottum of þe se, yett if he died in clene lif, a may be a-sente in hevene for al þat, but if a die in dedly synne and withoute contricion, þer is no remedi then, but wo apon wo, in euerlastynge payne. Therfor] pray for þem. [. . .] (f. 59v)

The long passage in square brackets is written on the bottom margin of the page, with the caret after 'see' to indicate that it must be inserted there.

This theology of sin is counterbalanced by a theology of mercy shown in another long insertion further on in ch. 37, where the reviser, starting by saying *'yette love þe bodi and þe soule, but hate þe synne'*, mentions King David and Mary Magdalene as being *'sumtyme grete*

208

synnerse', but since they have converted afterwards, *'it is to hope wel of al men levyngge, for thowe þei be bad at one time, yette þei may be gode at anoþer for al þat'* (f. 62r).

3.3. Authority

Together with, and probably derived from, the sustained emphasis on God's absolute primacy, is the stress on the relevance of the 'soverayns', that is, the religious authorities, and of the obedience due to them. The following example may be just a clarification:

> Q: be obedient mekely to thy prelates [...] nor deme them nott [...] (cols 74-75)

> A1: be obedient mekely *to þe prelatis þat beþe þi soveraynis* [...] nor *'mis'*deme þem not [...] (ch. 32, f. 57r)

A longer passage shows the anxiety of the reviser to mark that religious superiors are like doctors:

> Q: Also a seke man that yett suffreth the axcyse or the axcyse of vices oweth to kepe the dyett that hys leche (*medicus*) shewyth hym yf he desyre (*desiderat*) soone to be parfytely heled, so than do thow no thyng nor saye noo thyng that thou supposest that thy mayster (*magistrum*) wolde not that thow shuldest doo nor saye. (col. 8)

> A1: Also a seke man þat suffrethe þe accyse ~~or þe accyse of visis~~ owethe to kepe þe dyete þat his *fesicion* shewethe hym, and if he *purposeþ* to be sone perfiȝtly *y* helyd, so þen do þou *do 'no'* thynge nor sey no thynge þat þou supposiste *þi fesicion 'þat is to sey' þi soverayne* wolde not þat þou shuldiste do nor sey. (ch. 2, f. 48v)

A1 has introduced some grammatical changes, as the imperative form 'do thou do' and the prefix 'y' attached to the past participle of the verb 'heal', a conservative choice, one would say. The most interesting changes are at lexical level, with an overall effect of more cohesiveness; the old word 'leche' (leech) has become a 'fesicion' (physician), and this has been kept to replace 'mayster', linking thus more visibly obedience with inner healing, although the reviser feels obliged to specify ('þat is to sey') that he is speaking of the religious superior, and not of a doctor. The substitution of 'desyre' with 'purposeþ' gives actually more emphasis to the will of being healed. The excision of the word 'accyse' (abscess) may be due to the need to avoid a useless repetition, or to the intention of maintaining the medical metaphor without the following spiritual interpretation, which incidentally exists in the Latin: *accessiones vitiorum*.

3.4. The Eucharist

Although theology is not the main purpose of the tracts gathered in Arundel 197, there are passages concerning theological themes that may be of some interest, such as those dealing with the Eucharist, to be found in the chapter devoted to the service at mass, which is ch. 11 in Q and ch. 10 in A. Here we find a remarkable devotional emphasis:

> Q: For though in all tymes we owe to be besye in all thynges that ar goode, yet that ys moost accordynge when we make vs redy to the receyvynge of Cryste, or when we haue hym wyth vs aftyr the receyuynge. (col. 30)

> A1: For þou in al tymis we ouȝte to be besy to do þo thyngis þat beþ gode, yet it is moste grettiste plesur to our saviour when 'we' make us redy to þe resseuynge of his moste precius body with grete contricion, devocion, mekenis, and with suche oþer stronge and holy vertuis. (f. 52r)

Can we see here the influence of the eucharistic conflicts raging in England as well as elsewhere in western Europe on the eve of the Reformation? In the same chapter another change gives matter for reflection. While Q says that serving at the mass 'ys a werke of charyte promotynge thy neyghtboures in god' (col. 27), A1 changes it into: 'it is a wirke of charite promotynge *al cristyn pepul into grace*' (f. 51v). What to say? Does A1 restrict the fruit of the mass? He certainly specifies it, in that 'neighbour' does not simply coincide with 'Christian people', and 'grace' means less than God.

3.5. Attitudes

At times the reviser shows a strong missionary attitude, as can be seen in the following expansion found in the Birgittine tract on active and

210

contemplative life, where for the much simpler original A: 'in praieng and in techyng', A1 has '*in prechinge and techinge the holi doctryne of almyghty god to alle maner of pepulle*' (f. 39v), oscillating between pedantic precision and theological anxiety. In this capacity he assumes sometimes the attitude of an intrusive preacher, adding his own admonitions, remarks, warnings, etc. For example, a passage in *Fervor Amoris* (ch. Y), which reads: 'whan þei finde a man heuy and grucching' becomes in A1: 'when þei fyn*de any perso*n hevy and gruc*'chynge* when he shuld be meke and pa'ciente' (f. 33r). The reproachful comment is written on the margin, and the phrase 'any person' is derived from 'a man'.[4]

A similar moralistic expansion is found where the phrase in Q: 'for ofte tymes oppinion deceyues' (Latin: *quia opinio sepe fallit*), becomes in A1: 'for ofte time *bi 'misdemyng men be discevid and' synnethe gretely þer-with*' (ch. 5, f. 49v). An even stronger didactic attitude appears in a passage on poverty, where A1 expands the invitation not to have many things by saying that this 'shal make þe notid amonge oþer '*to be a proprietori and covetus in havyngge, þe whiche is contrari to þi profescion and an evil exsampul to oþer*' (ch. 35, f. 60v).

3.6. Moral virtues

When the reviser changes the text, generally he shows more severity, as can be gathered by many examples already quoted. Let us consider the following passage taken from a chapter on vainglory.

---

4   The transformation of 'man' into 'person' occurs quite often, and it may be taken as a use of inclusive language *ante litteram*. In fact, while David of Augsburg's text is addressed to men, this abstract is destined for a mixed community, as it is clear at least from the title of ch. 15 which reads: 'How þou shalte be-haue þe a-monge broþerin and sistris'. Other examples are:

- A1: of any *person* (f. 49v) for Q: of any man (col. 16);
- A1: detraccion [...] is a grete *offence* in a religius *person* (f. 54r) for Q: ytt ys a great vice in a religiouse man (col. 44);
- A1: al foule wordis [...] owethe to be restraynid fro þe mouþe of a religius *person for ever* (f. 55r) for Q: owght to be restreyned fro the mowth of a religiouse man (col. 47).

But, just to show that no complete consistency can be expected, in chapter 8 there is a case where 'a reli[gi]us man' (f. 50v) is left intact.

Q: Wyth all maner of diligence be ware of bostynge and neuer yeue man to knowleghe that ther be in the any thynge commendable, vnneth may ther be in the any laudable thynge but yf other menn vndirstonde ytt. And yf thowe holde thy pease and hyde hit then yt shall please the more. [. . .] (ch. 24, cols 44-45)

A1: Weth alle maner of diligens be ware of bostynge, *and of commend'acion of þi self, nor geue neuer'* to man knolige þat þer is in þe any thynge commendabul, ~~vnethe~~ *for if* þer be in þe any laudabul þynge, *lete neuer* oþer men vnderstande hit, but þat þou holde þi pese and hyde hit, *as myche as þou maiste.* (ch. 22, f. 54v)[5]

Where in the original text what is praiseworthy in us may be seen by others without our showing it (Lat. *vix enim potest in te aliquid laudabile esse quin eciam alij intelligant*), in A1 we are invited to hide it carefully and totally, never to be noticed. In case we want to see how deeply a paragraph may be changed to show a harsher attitude, we may consider the following example:

Q: Also be ware of turpoure of werynesse, vnsayvrynes and sluggydnesse that maketh the sowle lewke, and the body delycate to al maner werkes. (col. 89)

A1: Also be ware of ~~turpur~~ *'al vnclenlynes of þi bodi',* of werines and vnsaverenes of *'devocion'* and sluggisshenes þat makeþe the soule *powre,* and þe body *prowde and prone* to alle maner ~~werkis~~ *of synnys.* (ch. 34, f. 58r)

The reviser may be morally stern, but he is of an equal mind towards men and women, anyway, as can be seen in a change due to the mixed audience he is addressing: for Q 'In alle thynges flee women', A1 has *'In al thingis fle euille wymmen, and wemen oweth to fle euille men'* (ch. 32, f. 57r).

---

5   In MS Arundel 197, what is chapter 24 in Q (Off boystynge) has become part of chapter 22, although the first letter of the paragraph quoted is in red, marking the beginning of a new chapter which has received no title. The numbering of the chapters is different in the two manuscripts.

3.7. Mixed life and contemplative life

It seems that our reviser is convinced that contemplative life is superior to active life. If he was a Birgittine, he certainly maintained his independence of mind, even as regards to Birgitta herself. We have seen that he does not refrain from cutting a paragraph of hers, and in the treatise on contemplative and active life he writes that 'Lazarus was resid *fro depe to life, syngnyfyenge that þe lif of contemplacion is of grete vertu and strengthe above actife lif* (f. 46r). This long addition contradicts in a sense what the text says, and to avoid self-contradiction the reviser is obliged in this case to insert a *'But yett'* at the beginning of the sentence that follows, where the ideal of mixed life is in fact exalted. But he does not renounce his convictions, as may be seen in this addition, for which nearly two lines have been erased and two more have been added on the bottom margin:

> Take hede of þe fourþe witte of þi soule þat is callid gode wille, for þi tendur lovynge lorde shewith þe his gode wille largely, þat biside al his oþer benefetis þis graciusly hath called þe to his holy vyneyarde by-fore thousandis of oþer pepul, þat leveth in þe worlde in grete miseri and punery; ther for loke up lusteli as þou haste grete cause, and sey þes wordis with þe prophete Davethe (f. 70v): Gustate et videte [...] (f. 71r).

The scope of Christian vocation has been somehow restricted, since a more general call to spiritual life appears in the original text, which can be read in the parallel passage in Oxford, Bodley MS 423: 'Take hede to the fourthe witte of þy soule that is cleped good wille, for he weldith gretter delite than thou canst descryue, and it clepith þe and alle thy felowes to the worship of god, seieng: Gustate et videte' (f. 161v).

4. Concluding remarks

In conclusion, I hope to have shown that what Connolly (1994) called the "oddities" of MS Arundel 197 may seem, at closer inspection, less odd. I have tried only to outline some general attitudes which loom

213

through a text that at the start appeared awfully messy and discouraging. In doing so I have tried to resist the drive towards much regularizing. But this said, I think that from what I have shown we know a bit more about this anonymous reviser, his techniques of revision, and probably also his intended audience – precisely the how and the why I had chosen as the subject of my chapter.

Part II

Hymns

Versions of Latin Hymns in Medieval England: William Herebert and the *English Hymnal*[1]

The practice of translating Latin hymns has a long tradition in England, its origins dating back to the Anglo-Saxon Church. Together with the psalms and other biblical texts, hymns were part of the daily office, and as such they had to be learned and understood; moreover, they were considered as ideal models of Christian poetry, and studied in the monastic schools for their literary worth. The surviving OE versions of Latin hymns are, properly speaking, glosses either on the metrical hymns or on their prose versions, meant to help the students understand the hymns by solving the intricate syntactic patterns of the Latin, a fact that further confirms the scholastic use of these texts and of their glosses. Obviously, the primary interest of such texts lies in their rendering of single words, and consequently, and more generally, in their contribution to the development of a Christian vocabulary in Anglo-Saxon England (Gneuss 1968).

When new translations appear in the fourteenth and fifteenth centuries, they are different from the OE versions in two important respects: 1) the hymns are translated as poetry, that is they are cast in rhyming verses and stanzas of various forms; 2) they are put to new destinations, which are neither the choir nor the classroom, but the pulpit of the preacher, the closet of the devout, and possibly extra-liturgical singing. Both these factors are likely to influence the choices of the translator, and a third should be added, that is the predictable shifts in theology and spirituality which intervened between the time of the composition of the hymns and that of their translation, a period which in some cases amounts to nearly a thousand years. Underlying these conditioning factors, which are peculiar to the hymn translation, there is of course the problem of turning liturgical Latin into ME.

---

1   An earlier version of this chapter appeared in *Mediaevistik* 4, 1991, 297-315.

The territory of the English translations of Latin hymns in the late Middle Ages has been charted and illustrated by Gneuss in an excellent comprehensive survey (1968: 207-236). According to the *Index of Middle English Verse* there exist 64 translations of Latin hymns, taking the word 'hymn' to mean a metrical composition in stanza-form intended for liturgical singing. Some of these translations, one or two stanzas long, are used as quotations in Latin sermons, like those extant in Bishop Sheppey's Book (MS Merton 248). Other hymns are found as single pieces in various kinds of manuscripts: judging from the number of translations the most popular appear to have been *Christe qui lux es et dies* (8), *Ave Maris Stella* (6), and *Vexilla Regis* (4). But the bulk of these versions is the work of three people: the Franciscans William Herebert and James Ryman, and the anonymous author of the so-called *English Hymnal*. Herebert wrote in the early fourteenth century, the other two at the end of the fifteenth century. By a happy coincidence these translations are connected with the three new destinations of the hymns: Herebert's versions were to be used in sermons, while Ryman apparently tried to supply English texts to the old Latin tunes, and the *Hymnal* is evidently meant to be read as a sequence of prayers or meditations.

This body of 64 hymns may appear rather small against the total number of ME lyrics, which is more than 1800. It is nevertheless significant. As Gneuss remarks (1968: 214-215), these hymns form only the peak of a larger group: if we take into account the translations of antiphons, sequences and other parts of the service, we reach a total of more than 200 liturgy-based poems, and this, together with borrowings and direct quotations in carols and macaronic lyrics, testifies to the considerable influence of liturgical texts on medieval religious poetry in English. In any case, other factors made the idea of translating Latin hymns less obvious: one was the difficulty of turning into ME verse Latin stanzas written in a tightly-structured syntax and a richly connotated and often highly allusive vocabulary; the other was the fact that the translator could never hope to hear his verses sung in a liturgical service. Moreover, the possibility of using hymns for other purposes was not self-evident, since it is well known that liturgy was far from being a major fostering ground for vernacular expressions of medieval devotion, at least until the appearance of the Prymer. The very fact that before the sixteenth century the hymns in

218

the Prymer are in prose cannot but confirm the complexity of the enterprise. All considered, the decision to translate Latin hymns as pieces of poetry is in itself relevant, and the number of versions we possess appears, against this background, remarkable.

All these hymn translations have been edited, but, apart from Herebert, they have not been adequately studied.[2] We still need a detailed and comprehensive analysis of these hymns as translations, that makes constant reference to their Latin models and does not, as even recent studies do, confine itself to declaring that a word, a phrase or a half-line is not in the Latin original. We must inquire about the reasons lying behind these changes, be they omissions, additions, or expansions and transformations. Attention must also be given to personal style, as far as it can be detected, to conditioning by and fitness for the new destinations of the hymns, and to differences in theological and spiritual outlook which could have influenced the translator.

This study ideally continues the research I started when I published an essay linking Herebert's translations with his activity as a preacher (Pezzini 1974). I propose here a more systematic account of Herebert's hymn versions, which, unlike other liturgical texts he translated, obliged him to face particular problems related to the form and language of the Latin. I shall also analyse the Advent-Christmas hymns of the so-called *English Hymnal*. Ryman's hymns will not be

---

2   We have a modem critical edition of Herebert's translations in Reimer (1987), where his Latin sermons are also published. His poems had been previously edited partly by Brown (1952: 15-29), and partly by Gneuss (1960). Ryman's hymns were published, together with his poems, by Zupitza (1892). The English Hymnal was edited without commentary by Patterson (1927). For all the other hymn translations outside these three main collections see the *Index of Middle English Verse*, and the *Supplement*. Herebert's translations are quoted from Reimer's edition (R) where the reader can also find full reference to the Latin text of the hymns. For the sake of convenience, and to avoid unnecessary repetition, I indicate the source of the hymns quoted according to the volume and page(s) of the *Analecta Hymnica Medii Aevi*, (Dreves/Blume 1886-1922): *Aeterne rex altissime* 51:94-95; *Audi benigne conditor* 51:53-55; *Christe redemptor omnium* 51:49-50; *Conditor alme siderum* 2:35; *Hostis Herodes impie* 50:58-60; *Jesu nostra redemptio* 2:49; *Vexilla regis prodeunt* 2:45. The manuscript of the English Hymnal gives the Latin text together with the English version of the hymns: both are quoted from Patterson's edition (P).

treated mainly for reasons of space, but his versions will be taken into account and cross-compared with the other two to illustrate relevant different choices.

1. Hymns and preaching: the case of W. Herebert

The proper of the hymn was to be sung: "Si sit laus et dei laus et non cantetur, non est ymnus." The first examples of hymn translations we find in the English Middle Ages are illustrative materials for sermons. This is evident in MS Merton 248 (Oxford) where one or two stanzas are anglicized and inserted in sermons written in Latin, whether extempore translations or quotations from existing collections there is no telling. This is also proved in the case of William Herebert's Commonplace Book where we have, in the final quire, verse translations of hymns, sequences, antiphons, responsoria and gospel passages which reveal a neatly devised programme meant to meet the needs of the whole liturgical year, from Advent to Pentecost, including Marian Feasts and the liturgy of the dead.[3]

The homiletic use of the hymns is part of a larger subject, the use of verses in sermons, which has already been studied and illustrated (see Wenzel 1986). In my view, hymns enjoyed in this respect a particular status, especially those written to celebrate the great feasts of the Christian year: they were to a certain extent '*auctoritates*', and although they could not claim the prestige of the Bible, or even of the Fathers, in confirming the preacher's statements, they were none the less important testimonies to the uninterrupted tradition of Christian faith. They radiated the majesty of the liturgy in which they were embedded; they wore the officiality and the solemn fixity of the dogma, according to the ancient saying '*lex orandi, lex credendi*'; they had the beauty of poetry. Hymns were like a bridge linking the medieval preacher's fondness for rhymes with his need to proclaim and prove Christian beliefs. This is admirably illustrated by Herebert's translations, which show a conscious poet at work adapting

---

3   I have drawn attention to this organizing principle in Pezzini (1974: 12-14).

ancient and venerable Latin texts to his medieval audience, trying to keep close to the original (*"non multum declinando"*, he says), and at the same time feeling free to change words and phrases, to add and omit, to explain and visualize what in the Latin remained allusive and abstract.

As a poet Herebert is a good technician, experimenting with various metres and stanza forms, at times even within the same hymn. The best example of variety is the translation of *Conditor alme siderum*, where he starts imitating the Latin quatrain (rhyming aaaa), then he writes a ballad stanza, then two tail-rhyme stanzas (rhyming aab/ccb), and finally two septenary couplets, the first possibly another ballad stanza. These differences should cause no surprise, not only because a medieval poet need not share our modem idea of formal unity in a poem, but above all because single stanzas were treated and quoted as self-contained units, as Bishop Sheppey and Herebert himself show in their manuscripts.

How strong Herebert's sense of rhythm was can be seen in his version of a stanza of the Ascension hymn *Jesu nostra redemptio*:

Inferni clausa penetrans,	Helle clós þóu þorledest
tuos captives redimens,	and bóuhtest þine of bóndes;
victor triumpho nobili	wyht grét nobléye
ad dextram Patris residens	þou opstéye
	to þy Uader ryhthonde. (R 129)

This is his way of working out his favourite septenaries, arranging them in couplets, as here, or in tercets, and occasionally adding internal rhymes (here evidenced by Herebert himself in the MS) and alliterations. As for the language, the use of finite tenses in the translation gives undoubtedly more immediacy to the scene.

Another stanza, from the Lent hymn *Audi benigne conditor*, shows how Herebert was not indifferent to the charm of formal patterns:

Sic corpus extra conteri	Graunt ous pyne wyþouteuorth
dona per abstinentiam,	þe body wyth vastinge,
ieiunet ut mens sobria	þat our gost wyþynneuorth
a labe prorsus criminum.	veste vrom sunnynge. (R 134)

Rhymes are cunningly used to mark contrasts (without/within; fasting/ sinning), the Latin is simplified and reduced to obtain a clearer verbal texture.

Emphasis through formal pattern is reached by the creation of a verbal echo in the rendering of a couplet referring to the baptism of Christ in the Epiphany hymn *Hostis Herode impie*:

Peccata quae non detulit	And of hym was ywasȝe
nos abluendo sustulit	þat sunne nadde nón
	to halewen oure vollouth water,
	þat sunne hauet uordon (R 111)

Reimer misses the point when he remarks that this last line "has no precedent in the source" (1987: 111, fn. 5): it is in fact the expansion / explanation of *abluendo*, which does not refer to Christ, but to us (*nos*) and to the Christian baptism. What Herebert does is to transfer the verbal echo of the Latin *detulit / sustulit* on the word "sunne" (sin), so that sinless Christ, by being washed in River Jordan, sanctifies the water of Baptism making it a destroyer of our sins.

Herebert deals rather freely with the Latin, and can adopt other solutions, as in a couplet from *Jesu nostra redemptio*:

crudelem mortem patiens	so bitter déth to þolien
ut nos a morte tolleres	urom sunne óus uor t'arére (R 129)

Here the Latin correspondence is eliminated, with a certain reduction of meaning, in that the Latin *mors* includes physical death, which Herebert's "sunne" does not. But we may attribute the shift of tone in the image to the preacher's need to draw the attention of his audience to the urgent necessity of leaving a sinful life now, since Christ had suffered death to that end.

Hence we move to consider a second and major conditioning factor which explains some choices in Herebert's translations: his being a preacher. Having already analysed this subject in my previous investigation, I summarize here my main points. In being transferred from the choir to the pulpit, Latin texts are gently arrayed in new colours, so that through them appears the preacher's tendency both to move and to explain, to address directly the audience by strong appeals, to favour concrete nouns and visually effective adjectives, to angle his message constantly towards conversion and penance on the one hand, and to the joys of heaven on the other. To produce these effects through the translation of Latin hymns was a particularly difficult task; however, while it is true that Herebert is more at ease when he translates other liturgical texts, like responsoria and prose passages, he succeeds in printing his personal style even in his hymn versions so that they become useful tools for the evangelical mission of the preacher.

Let us look, for example, at his rendering of a stanza of *Vexilla Regis*, the well-known Passiontide hymn:

Impleta sunt quae concinit	Yvoluuld ys Dauidþes sawe,
David fideli carmine	þat soth was prophete of þe olde lawe,
dicendo nationibus:	þat sayde: Men, ȝe mowen yse
Regnavit a ligno Deus.	hou Godes trone ys rode tre. (R 112)

No idea of singing (*concinit, carmine*) appears in the translation, but a more matter-of-fact "sawe", followed by a didactic addition intended to remind the hearers who David was, a prophet, which, in context, fits better than the much more common "king". Above all we note the remarkable resolution in the second half of the stanza, presenting a preacher who is calling the attention of his audience not to a "saying", but to a concrete object, probably a crucifix he might have been holding to show it while speaking (ȝe mowen yse: you may see). We cannot expect to find many of these direct appeals in hymns, as these poems are mainly invocations addressed to God. But when he has the opportunity, Herebert exploits it, as can be seen in the first two lines of *Hostis Herodes*, or in the rendering of *Popule meus*.[4]

Any preacher knows how important it is to visualize and to actualize the verbal message. Herebert is very clever in producing a wide range of different resolutions to obtain these results. Here I give a list of examples taken from *Christe redemptor omnium* (R 124-125):

ineffabiliter: ouer alle speche and wone
memento salutis auctor: wrouhte of *oure* hele / *nou* haue in þyne múnde

---

4   See Pezzini (1974: 26-29). That "Friar Herebert has some dramatic sense" is also noted by Gray (1972: 14), commenting on Herebert's version of *Quis est iste*.

```
mundi salus adveneris: of sunne make ous sker (clear)
mare: wylde se
Ob diem natalis tui /          Vor þys day singeth a neowe song /
hymnum novum concinimus       and makeþ blisfol mod
```

The new stress is on "us/our" and "now", on colourful adjectives (sker, wylde), to which an emphasis on joy, as proper to Christmas, is added.

Herebert's personal style as a translator can be seen in a better light if we compare his renderings with other versions of the same hymn. Let us take a couplet from *Hostis Herodes*:

```
non eripit mortalia         ne reueth hé nouth erthlich gód
qui regna dat caelestia     þat maketh ous heuene kynges. (R 111)
```

Against the strongly aggressive "reueth" (*robs, plunders*), perfectly corresponding to the Latin *eripit*, Ryman has "claymeth", the translator of MS Sloane 2593[5] a weak "deʒyryt", and the *Hymnal* a sort of philosophical statement: "The hevynly kynge to thyng terrene no nede / may have". Again, where Herebert draws his hearers ("ous") towards the concrete goal of becoming kings in heaven, the other three translations are less personal:

```
Ryman: That geveth kingdomes celestiall
Sloane: þat heuene hast at his ʒeuyng
Hymnal: he yevyth hevynly mede
```

The translation of another stanza of the same hymn provides a good summary of Herebert's characteristics:

```
Ibant Magi quam viderant / stellam sequentes praeviam:
lumen requirunt lumine, / Deum fatentur munere.
```

```
The kynges wenden here way / and foleweden þe sterre,
and sothfast lyʒth wyth sterre lyth / souhten vrom so verre,
and sheuden wel þat he ys god / in gold and stor and mirre. (R 111)
```

---

5   This fifteenth-century MS contains 74 carols and songs, mostly in English, and this hymn translation was certainly intended for singing: see Gneuss (1960: 218). The text is printed in Brown (1939: 130-131).

Two verses of factual narrative can be reduced to one line, at the expense of some words in the Latin (*quam viderant, praeviam*), but as soon as a theological allusion appears, as in the play on the word *lumen*, the preacher intervenes to clarify and distinguish the star-light from the true light, which is God; he goes on to 'objectify' the *munere* by naming the three traditional gifts, and to 'intensify' emotionally the painful journey of the Magi by adding "vrom so verre" (from so far). Here again a comparison with the other translations is revealing: of the two made for music Sloane is more interesting than Ryman, while the *Hymnal* evinces the spiritual meaning of the gifts, by which Christ is acknowledged as "mortall man, prest and heyvyne kynge", a choice which is better suited to the meditative purposes of the translation.

Herebert's choices do not always go in the direction of a stronger poetic vigour, and one may sense at times a sort of conflict between the poet and the preacher. This is particularly evident in his translation of *Hostis Herodes*, where he is not consistently successful. Sedulius's poem is extremely compact and often deeply allusive: Herebert's rendering of the Cana wedding stanza loses the fascinating suggestiveness of the Latin images and yields a plain narrative full of names, things, actions:

> Novum genus potentiae,
> aquae rubescunt hydriae,
> vinumque iussa fundere
> mutavit unda originem.

> A newe myhte he cudde þer / he was at a feste:
> he made vulle wyth shyr water / six cannes by þe léste;
> bote þe water turnde into wyn / þorou Crystes oune heste. (R 111)

A central role is here given to Christ, who lay hidden, so to say, in the Latin original: the English text is certainly clearer, but is a poetic disaster: even the nice detail of colour provided by *rubescunt* has gone.

Together with this tendency towards clarification of an otherwise enigmatic text, other small changes could be attributed to a preacher's attitude. One is certainly an emphasis on 'sin', which is obtained either by addition of phrases or by skewing the translation in this general direction. Examples are: *mortis* / deth of sunfol rote, *a morte* / urom sunne, *languidis* / to sunvol mon, *mundi salus* / of sunne

225

make ous sker (pure), *suspensus est patibulo* / anhonged was uor oure sunne.[6] Another is an apparent anxiety about orthodoxy, evident in certain formulations more precise than their originals, such as "of ryht byleue" for *credentium*, "of ryht leuynge" for *fidelium*, and "Cryst, buggere of alle ycoren" for *Christe, redemptor omnium*, where the idea of universal redemption is restricted to "the chosen ones".

Herebert's consciousness as a poet and translator can be directly observed in his manuscript, where at times he evidences an internal rhyme, or marks the elision of a syllable, or replaces one word by another, as in the change of "mon" to "vlesh", which agrees more literally with the Latin *caro*, or of "gode" (*piis*) to "mylde". Commenting on this last change, Reimer suggests that it "may have something to do with his sense of Franciscanism" (1987: 113, fn.9). I prefer to think this alteration was made to create an interesting verbal echo in the couplet:

> þe mylde sped in rihtfolnesse,
> to sunfole men shéu mylsfolnesse. (R 113)

The connection "mylde / mylsfolnesse" evokes the language of the Beatitudes: "Blessed be the merciful, for they shall obtain mercy" (Matt. 5:7). Nevertheless Franciscanism, and more generally medieval spirituality, colours Herebert's versions, although in his hymn translations we have only small touches and glimpses of it, due to the limitations peculiar to the rendering of these texts. The presence of medieval devotion, largely Franciscan, is much more visible where Herebert can work with more freedom, as in his version of the prose passage *Quis est iste*, or in the poem *Þou wommon boute uére* (Thou woman without peer). But a few changes in his hymn versions may safely be ascribed to his being a friar imbued with the tender affective

---

6   It is interesting to see the same solution adopted by another preacher, Bishop Sheppey, who translates the first stanza of *Vexilla Regis*:
> þe kinges baner bigan to sprede
> on þe crouch sewynde scynys us spede
> wech f(l)esh of flesh makere of mede
> it heng on rode for oure misdede. (MS Merton 248, f. 74r).

Both Herebert and Sheppey stress that Christ died 'for our sins', and both drop the dense theological phrase *crucis mysterium* of the second line (Herebert has either "rode tokne" or "rode troe", Sheppey prefers the more homely "spede").

piety of St Francis. In this respect some of his choices acquire a new meaning, tending towards an emotional intensification which was so typical of the devotion centred on the humanity of Christ. So he prefers the language of mercy ("sheu mylsfolnesse" translates *dele crimina*); he writes "blisse" where the Latin has *gloria* or nothing at all; and he dwells compassionately on the sufferings of the dying Christ, as in the rendering of two lines of *Vexilla Regis*:

Quo vulneratus insuper	þer he was wounded and vurst yswonge,
mucrone diro lanceae	wyth sharpe spere to herte ystonge (R 112)

No one will fail to notice how intense becomes the poet's personal involvement in this rendering of a stanza of *Eterne rex altissime*:

Ut cum repente coeperis	Þat whén þou shalt uerlich comen ous to déme,
clarere nube iudicis,	comen yne cloudebryht with blówinde béme,
poenas repellas debitas,	vrom þe pyne of helle, Iesu, þou ous ʒéme,
reddas coronas perditas.	and ʒeld þe lorene crounes, God wóe to þé réme
	(R 131)

Besides the addition of the blowing trumpets, which may come from *Dies irae*, the English version increases a sense of fear of which there is almost no trace in the Latin (apart from *repente*, here rendered by "uerlich"), and introduces a new feeling of intimate personal relationship with God, who is passionately invoked (réme = cry out) to take care of (ʒéme) and protect the soul from the pains of hell.

The medieval Friars were also known for using the language of secular literature in their religious poems (see Gray 1972: 55-59). This, I think, explains other distinctive features of Herebert's versions. For example, he interprets Mary's womb as "on maydenes bour", a phrase which evokes the world of romances;[7] he translates *Christe redemptor omnium* by "Crist, þat bouhtest mon wyth fyth", which not only reveals how sensitive Herebert was to the Passion motif, but also presents Christ under the image of a traditional courtly lover-knight, a fighting champion, an image which appears in such lyrics as *Somer is*

---

7   On 'bower', "a word which has submerged and delicate courtly and erotic undertones", see Gray (1972: 104).

comen, and winter gon, or in Herebert's versions of *Quis est iste,* a passage from Isaiah read in the liturgy of Good Friday.[8]

This outline account gives only a limited idea of Herebert's poetry. His achievements as a Franciscan preacher and theologian who tries to adapt old texts to new usages and audiences are better seen in his translations of prose texts, where he works much more freely. Yet his characteristics as a poet, a preacher and a Franciscan, also show through clearly in his hymn translations, despite the limitations of the genre: which makes them all the more interesting and revealing.

2. Hymns as meditation: the English Hymnal

When we move from Herebert to the *English Hymnal* we enter a very different world. A century and a half separates the two collections, and this implies changes in poetic taste and style. A comparison between Herebert's choices with Lydgate's may serve to illustrate this change:

> Quis est iste qui venit de Edom / tinctis vestibus de Bosra?
> What ys he, þys lordling þat cometh vrom þe vyth
> wyth blodrede wede so grysliche ydyht? (Herebert)

> Vexilla Regis prodeunt
> Royal Banerys vnrolled of the kyng
> Towarde his Batayle, in Bosra steyned rede (Lydgate)

No contrast could be more striking: a Hebrew word, *Bosra,* which the fourteenth-century friar translates according to its familiar typological meaning, is used by the fifteenth-century Benedictine monk to

---

8   *Somer is comen* is printed in Brown (1932, repr. 1971: 108-111). In the Commonplace Book of John Grimestone (1375), another Franciscan preacher and poet, we find the same language of fight, as for example in "I am Jesu, þat cum to fith", or "I haue þe wonnen in fith", printed in Brown (1924, [2]1952 revised by G.V. Smithers), respectively as nos. 63 (p. 82) and 66 (p. 84). Herebert's *Quis est iste* is admirably discussed by Gray (1972: 12-17). On the theme of the Lover-knight see Woolf (1968: 44-55).

heighten his style and decorate his verses. What had been rejected as a stumbling block, so to say, has been inserted as a precious ornament.

The *English Hymnal* is about half-way between these two extremes in that it shows a curious mixture of solemnity and homeliness which may sound strange to a modem ear. If Phebus and Tytane are evoked to describe dawn and midday, the users of the *Hymnal* are plainly reminded that they must

> one the sondey heren owr seruice,
> observyng hytt wyth perfyt diligence (P 469)

The collection, belonging to the end of the fifteenth century, consists of 22 hymn translations, written in rhyme-royal stanzas, and represents an extremely ambitious project of turning the whole liturgical hymnal into English. As extant it comprises 9 hymns for the Advent-Christmas season, and 13 for the various hours of the daily office; it breaks off after two stanzas of *Ales diei nuntius*: whether the project was ever brought to completion one will probably never know. That the purpose of these versions was private prayer and meditation can be inferred from the *Hymnal* itself, where the line *et ore te canencium* is rendered by "wythe ympnes all þat we mey rede or synge" (P 481); phrases such as *by meditacione contemplatiff* recur quite frequently. This meditative purpose fits well with the choice of the rhyme-royal stanza, which provides more than twice the space of the Latin quatrains being translated. The translator is thus generously invited to use *amplificatio* in all its forms, to decorate and to explore the text, to emphasize a detail and to extract hidden meanings, and even to insert new ideas and images consistent with the basic text which they so expand in order to make it more profitable to the devout reader.

The rendering of the first stanza of *Veni redemptor gentium* may well exemplify the different types of expansion used in the *Hymnal*:

> Veni redemptor gentium,
> ostende partum virginis,
> miretur omne seculum:
> talis decet partus deum.

Come now, gud lord, now come owr savyowr,
Come, shew thy byrth of mary, modyr & mayde;
Discende, gude lord, ryght frome thy heyvenly towre;
Now lat all worldys merueyll & be dysmayde,
How in owr kynd lyst to be areyde,
And os þe son bemes peryth in þe glace,
Thy modyr mayd permaynyng os sche was. (P 450)

The first lines sound almost polyphonic, with the same musical cell (*come*) moving in counterpoint; the expression *partum virginis* is clarified; the wonder of the world (*miretur* [...] *seculum*) is intensified by a doublet; last, and most interesting, the cold and precise theological statement of the last line is dropped, and replaced by two well-known images describing the Incarnation as the wearing of a garment, and Mary's virginity in her conception of Christ as a sunbeam passing through a glass.[9]

Concerning the use of images the attitude of this translator is difficult to define and seems rather inconsistent. It suffices to see how he renders the second stanza of this same hymn to realize that his choices may be the opposite of what we have seen in the first stanza.

Non ex uirili semine	Partles of mannes knolege or mixture ...
sed mistico spiramine	The holy gost by grace did hyt so be ...
uerbum dei factum est caro	Whan god to mane is ioynyd in nature [...]
fructusque ventris floruit.	[...] þe wombe of þe uirgyne
	The frute of lyff tyll vs did sontyfie. (P 450)

Three images are interpreted theologically in the translation, the fourth remains, but qualified as "the frute of lyff", and the colourful verb *floruit* is replaced by the more spiritual "sontyfie". Even the image of the fire of hell, which one would expect to be rather fascinating to a medieval mind, is discarded in favour of a moral explanation:

---

9   For analogues see Gray (1972: 107, "clad in mannis wede" and 1972: 101 for
     the glass metaphor). For an Italian version of this image, see *Le allegrezze di
     Maria* by Fazio degli Uberti (quoted in Mirra 1947: 89):
          E come il sole in sua lucida spera
     Il vetro non corrompe e per lui passa,
     E sua chiarezza riman pura e mera;
          Così la tua verginità, che passa
     E ogni purità e ogni mondezza,
     Col corso natural non si compassa.

per quem averni ignibus   That aftyr ward we bene deputyd to peyne,
Christi crememur acrius.   Wher sowlys bene of all uertu barayne. (P 470)

Against Herebert's tendency towards visualization, the *Hymnal* seems to favour spiritual interpretation and commentary, as we have seen in its different rendering of the Magi's *munera*. This does not mean that the *Hymnal* translator is insensitive to images: when they have no evident theological meaning, he delights in expanding them, and he depicts vivid scenes with a homely gusto:

Presepe iam fulget tuum   The bestys crybbe, the humble assys stall,
                          As pure gold burned most fayr and bryght (P 452)

Feno iacere pertulit,   Thys lord Ihesu wrappyd in a wysp of heye[10]
presepe non abhorruit   The powre oxes stall had not in dysdeyne;
                          Carpetys or kowschonys cam not in hys weye (P 459)

This choice appears more evident in the hymns for the daily office, where an original metaphor may creep in, as when the translator renders *spreto cubili surgimus* by "Owr sluggishe bed no lengar be owr nest", or when he describes at length the calm of the sea after a storm, or when he attempts the solemn diction of a morning opening, translating the line *Iam lucis orto sidere*:

Now the deys sterre in hys hevynly spere,
ffresche as febus, aperyth in owr syght,
Whos bryghtnes gladeth all owre emyspere
Charyng a wey the darknes of þe nyght. (P 474)

A similar solution is found in the rendering of the first stanza of *A solis ortus cardine*. It is only honest to add that we cannot expect our translator to be unfailingly consistent in his choices: contrary to what seems his more regular habit, he may leave unexplained the double meaning of *lumen* in the Magi stanza of *Hostis Herodes*, and on the

---

10   There is an interesting coincidence in the very wording of the hay detail in a fifteenth-century lyric, *Now layde I ame in a wispe of hay* (Brown 1939: 3). The poem is a lullaby in which Jesus tells Mary that it is His Father's will that he must suffer and die on the cross. This connection of the Nativity with the Passion through a common experience of suffering is also present in the *Hymnal*, as we shall see.

231

other hand he may point out a spiritual sense where it is by no means intended, as in the line *noctem canendo rumpimus*, meaning 'we wake up to sing', translated as:

> þe nyght of synne depart owr sowles froo
> þat we ne wandyr in þe clowdy nyght. (P 486)

The *Hymnal* contains a considerable number of translations, and it is not easy to find a viable method of analysis. I chose to concentrate on the nine hymns for the Advent-Christmas season for their more obviously relevant theological and spiritual interest.

The first three versions of the *Hymnal* belong to Advent: they were used at Matins (*Verbum supernum prodiens*), Lauds (*Vox clara ecce intonat*), and Vespers (*Conditor alme siderum*). Taken together they reflect the basic themes and spiritual attitudes of this liturgical season, that is: the sickness of the world, the Incarnation of the Son of God, with a particular emphasis on the virginal conception of Mary, and the waiting for the Second Coming.

As regards the situation of the world before, and without, the Incarnation, *Conditor alme* is of particular interest: the world is said to be in mortal danger, weak and sick, moving quickly towards its night. In the translation all these elements are gathered to signify death, and above all sin: the world is "slomboryng in synne and dedly langwysshyng", "envyryng toward hys end and fyne, / endarkyd by synne approchyng his evenyng" (P 444-445). The connection between obscurity and sin is quite natural, as is the stress on darkness and light with their rich symbolism in the winter season. As for the vocabulary of sin two things are worth noticing: linguistically our translator uses nearly as many words as in the Latin;[11] theologically he enriches the concept of sin as moral guilt with ideas of frailty, ignorance, wretchedness, showing thus a compassionate mood which has a perfect counterpart in his treatment of Incarnation and Redemption.

Another major theme of Advent is the Second Coming. The very naming of Doomsday in a medieval context is likely to convey a

---

11   Against the Latin *crimen, lubrica, sordes, debitum, reatus, infirma, peccatum, delictum, libido, probrum, error, lapsus, culpa, noxae / nocentia*, the Hymnal has *synn, trespace, gylt, infirmite, lust and fowle concupiscence, offence, spottes, errour, laps, noysaunce, iniquite*.

host of images of terror and universal panic. In fact this motif is already present in the Latin hymns, as can be seen in two lines of *Vox clara*:

> Secundo ut cum fulserit
> Mundum horror que cinxcerit

> Whane he shall come and yeue hys last sentance,
> And all þe world shall quak for feer & drede (P 449)

But here too we notice a significant shift: the translator ignores the original image of light (*fulserit*) meant to express the glory of the victorious Son of Man, and prefers to stress Christ as a judge. The emphasis on fear and dread, more a feature of the *Hymnal* than of the Latin, is general. The rendering of the last stanza of *Conditor alme* provides a good illustration:

> Te deprecamur Agie,
> venture iudex seculi,
> conserua nos in tempore
> hostis a telo perfidi.

> We prey the, lorde of mercy and grace,
> Whane thow schalt come & ben owr hygh justice,
> fforgette owr gylt, foryeue hus owr trespace;
> Lett nott þe fende reioice hys entirprise;
> Hys dedly dart thy mercy do venquyse;
> That dredfull dey, gud lord, vs all conserufe
> ffrome thy mercy that we ne flyte ne swerve. (P 445-446)

While the Latin points decidedly to the present, since the coming judgement is seen only prospectively and the prayer is a request only for the time being (*in tempore*), the English version places the stress almost entirely on Doomsday. Fortunately this emphasis on fear is regularly counterbalanced by an equal emphasis on mercy. The version of two lines of *Verbum supernum*, also devoted to the Second Coming, shows the transformation realized in accordance with this new religious sensibility. Against a Latin Christ, impartially distributing punishment and reward (*reddens vices pro abditis / iustisque regnum pro bonis*), the English one is more a stern judge come to treat people with rigour and severity. Nothing in the Latin corresponds to:

233

We ben agast and trembyll ayenst that howre
Whan þu shalt cum to ponysch wyth reddowre. (P 447)

But these lines are enclosed and softened by two significant additions:

Late mercy bene owr conforth and rafuge [...]
We can no more bot to þi mercy leyne. (P 447)

Mercy is presupposed, but never named, in the Latin stanzas. The result is more emotionally charged than the original.

The central theme of the Advent-Christmas liturgy is the Incarnation of the Son of God, which is treated in the hymns along two main lines, one historical, the other theological. The first focuses on the extremely concrete image of Mary's womb, the second describes the reasons for the Incarnation, and the effects of Christ's coming into the world.

The Latin hymns typically use *venter* and *alvus*, or the figurative words *clausula* and *claustra*, which clearly hint at Mary's virginity, to describe Mary's womb. The *Hymnal* translates these words quite literally, but surrounds them with a number of adjectives celebrating cleanness and sacredness. So we have "sacred womb", "clene closet virginall", "þe clere cloystyre consecrate", "cloystyr virginale / Evyr vnwemmed and inviolate"; the metaphorical expression *thalamum* becomes "þe chosyn chambyr of chast clennes". Unlike Herebert and Ryman, the *Hymnal* never uses the word "bower", and rather surprisingly it renders *Caste parentis viscera* by "The chaste bowelys of Cristes modyr deer", a literalism which Ryman, who had much less room in his quatrain, avoids in favour of the colourless phrase "the inwarde partes". We may note in passing that in the case of Elizabeth *alvus* becomes "the cage", a term probably suggested by *clausus* referring to John the Baptist.

Two whole stanzas of *A solis ortus cardine*, one of the oldest Christmas hymns, part of a longer poem composed by Sedulius c. 450, are devoted to extolling Mary's virginal conception. Whereas the Latin simply describes Mary as *parens* and *puella*, the English version celebrates her with a sort of Litany; she is "Cristis modyr deer", "humbyll virgyne benyng and demvre", "Mary modyr of all uirgynes flowre", "modyr and meydyne mylde", and, for the title of *templum*

Dei given to her in the original, "celle celestial", and "the heyvynly towre / off Crist Hiesu" (P 458-459).

All these epithets have an unmistakable medieval flavour, the same we sense when we compare the coldly perfect Latin line, *Enixa est puerpera*, with its warmly affectionate English counterpart, "Now hath thys meyd a blessyd babe yboore" (P 459), an effect which is probably magnified by the rich context of Christmas carols and lyrics against which we inevitably read this verse.

A rich and distinct theology of the Incarnation emerges from the *Hymnal* which is only partially dependent on the Latin original. If the core remains unchanged, new colours appear, and others are intensified, so that we have an overall effect less legalistic and more compassionate. The Incarnation-Redemption, besides being interpreted as ransom, is more readily seen in terms of help and healing, with a consequent stronger emphasis on joy. Christ, who wears our nature like a garment, is celebrated as our brother; the defeat of the devil is stressed with a resulting deep sense of liberation; the Passion motif is more emphasized in these Christmas songs, and is at times expressed by the typically medieval image of the Charter of Mercy.

The three Advent hymns anticipate many of these motifs. So, for example, in *Vox clara* the line *obscura queque increpat*, which Ryman renders by "That alle derknes blameth of synne", is much expanded in the *Hymnal*, and becomes a "gud mesage", saying that

> [...] owr helth shall come frome heyvens hye
> Wyche owr langowr shall lessone and assvage
> And shall vs save from deth and all damage. (P 448)

In the third stanza of *Conditor alme* a line is inserted which has no correspondence in the Latin:

> ffrome all damage owr frealte rauysshynge" (P 445).

Again, in *Vox clara* the line "laxare gratis debitum" becomes:

> To mak for vs raunsone and finaunce,
> Wythe owr trespas frely to dispence,
> And to foryeue owr wrecched ignorance. (P 449)

235

This last verse integrates and softens the rather dry commercial metaphor of the Latin.

The Nativity hymns work out these themes and add other interesting variations. The interpretation of the Incarnation in terms of healing, suggested, it must be said, by the wide use of the Latin word *salus*, seems to have been particularly appealing to our translator. He may expand a hint, or even introduce the motif when the Latin does not strictly require it: both procedures appear in the version of *A Patre unigenitus*. In the fourth stanza the single word *medelam*, together with the image of washing suggested by the verb *ablue*, generates this reworking:

> A soft medicine of pyte and off grace
> Eynoynt vs wyth, lord, have vs in thy cure;
> We ben thy wark, we bene thy oone facture;
> Wasshe awey owr spottes all culpabylle,
> Syth thow art leche and lord most mercyabylle. (P 464)

The Latin is simply: *Omne delictum ablue / piam medelam tribue.* In the same hymn, the line *facturam morte redimens* becomes:

> To saue hys facture frome and all duresse,
> He suffyrd deth and hus reydemyd he;
> Except hys deth ther might no medsyn be
> That might vs all from owr old langowr lesse. (P 463)

The motif reappears in the version of *Eterne rerum conditor*, where *lapsis fides reuertitur* is rendered by:

> ffayth is comyne to bene a gostly leche
> To them echone that grace and mercy seche. (P 473)

The translation leaves its Latin original far behind, and it is certainly not a mere chance that such words as 'leech', 'grace' and 'mercy' have been yoked together to form a different semantic field.

A short summary of the benefits of the Incarnation is found in the rendering of the fourth stanza of *Veni redemptor gentium*. The Latin is highly allusive and refers to Psalm 18:6 in which the sun is likened to a bridegroom coming out of his chamber, a giant who runs from one end of heaven to the other (*ipse tamquam sponsus procedens de thalamo suo; exsultavit ut gigas ad currendam viam*). This was traditionally applied to Christ, seen as the true Sun, his Incarnation a victorious race in the history of the world.[12] The translator expands on this interpretation, which lies hidden in the Latin quatrain, and gives his theology of the Redemption: Christ comes from Mary's womb

> Thurgh hys grace owr myscheff to reydres,
> A myghty gyant off dowbyll substance,
> ffor to reypresse þe feendis fowle pywssance,
> ffrome heyvyne tyl erth hys cowrs hath swetyly tak
> To cause owr joye and owr fynaunce to make. (P 451)

Besides the idea of reparation, which is the very heart of traditional theology, two additions here deserve attention in that they indicate themes more prominent in the *Hymnal* than in the Latin: one is the defeat of the devil (reypresse þe feendis fowle pywssance), the other is joy as a result of the Incarnation (to cause owr joye).

The fiends of hell make their presence felt more in the English version than in the old hymns, and this is realized, as usual, by additions. They have to join the "celestia, terrestria" in acknowledging God's mighty power:

> The fendys also fell for all þeyr bobance
> Mote the obey, it may no nother be. (*Conditor alme*, P 445)

They are not to rejoice at their defeat of the faithful:

> Lett nott þe fende reioice hys entirprise (*Conditor alme*, P 446)

The journey to hell, *excursus usque ad inferos*, where Christ went to deliver the chosen souls, is celebrated as the moment

> Whan he hath putte the feendes to silence (*Veni redemptor*, P 451).

We have thus four instances in the English virtually without parallel in the Latin original.

Happiness is such an important aspect of Christmas celebration, an event which was announced as *gaudium magnum*, that our

---

12   See, for example, the commentary to this verse by Augustine, *Enarrationes in Psalmos*, in Corpus Christianorum, Series Latina n. 38 (Turnhout 1956: 109-110).

translator inserts a line to proclaim "Thys is the fest of owr felicite" (*Veni redemptor*). Christ, called *sidus novum*, is presented as "the lyghtsome sterre raplenyschyth with plesance" (*Vox clara*); he is not only *salutis auctor*, but "Auctor of helth and off all felicite" (*Christe redemptor*); he is "the kyng of blys", and when he is revealed to the shepherds, *palamque fit pastoribus*, "they mey reyioyen all" (*A solis ortus*); his *vexilla virtutum* turn into "baners of blys" (*Veni redemptor*), and a Latin *exultans* becomes "with ioy, gladnes and myrthe" (*Christe redemptor*). Finally theology and spirituality join to affirm that joy is the very essence and the best fruit of moral life:

> clarumque nostris sensibus   And inwardly in to owr hertes sende
> lumen prebe fidelibus   The lyghte of grace that we may gud be
> To thy plesance in owr felicite.
>
> (*A patre unigenitus*, P 463)

In conclusion two further details must be noted, already briefly touched on. Both are traditional metaphors, and reflect influence of the language and traditions of medieval piety. In one the Incarnation is seen as Christ's assumption of the garment of our humanity; in the other, the Passion is pictured as the sealing of a charter, the Charter of Mercy. The first is found in *A solis ortus cardine*, where the line *servile corpus induit* becomes:

> Dysdeynyd not owr freylte in nature,
> Hyt pleysyd hyme owr kynd reyceyue and take,
> The creator took off hys creature
> Liver for luff [...] (P 458)

Certain changes are significant here: not only does the translator replace the idea of slavery (*servile*) by that of frailty,[13] but he also increases the emotional temperature by some of the added verbs (dysdeynyd not, pleysyd hym) and phrases expressive of the divine motivation (for luff) which give the text a very different tone. The same image of the wearing of a livery is used again to extend a Latin

---

13   This is also significantly the language of St Francis of Assisi, who says, that the Word of God received in Mary's womb "the true flesh of our humanity and frailty" (*veram recepit carnem humanitatis et fragilitatis nostrae*): see *Epistola ad fideles* II in Esser (1978: 115).

metaphor in *Veni redemptor*, where the line *carnis tropheo accingere* becomes

> In mannes wed by trophe trivmphall,
> We the besechen, arreaye þi maieste. (P 452)

In a third case, which we have already seen, the image is used to interpret the single word *partus*. This idea of God's wearing our humanity leads quite naturally to the motif of Christ becoming our brother.[14] So the translation of *nostri quondam corporis [...] formam sumpseris* is:

> How thow become of owr fraternite [...]
> In owr nature thow were incorporate. (P 456)

The second metaphor, that of the Charter, appears in a long expansion of one Latin line from *Conditor alme, Donans reis remedium*, which becomes:

> Provydyng remyde be þi grace and myght [...]
> Thys world frome deth to lyffe reconsylyng,
> To gylty sawlys pleyne pardone and remidye,
> Sealyng thy self the Chartyre off mercy.[15] (P 444-445)

As noted earlier, this is not the only reference to the Passion for which the Latin provided no explicit source. Two more instances can be found in the version of *A solis ortus*. In the first, the shepherds, to whom God is revealed as *pastor creator omnium*, may now "lokyne with bere eye / Vpone þe heerd that for hys flok wolde die" (P 460), and the idea of God as creator-shepherd is changed into the more familiar image of Christ as redeemer-shepherd. Of course, both interpretations are correct and biblically founded; but this makes the choice of the translator all the more relevant. The second instance results from a mistranslation of *per quem nec ales esurit*, curiously shared by Ryman. The Latin sings the paradox of a God, who "feeds the fowls of the air" (Matt. 7:29), and now needs a little milk. The two English translators interpret *ales* as "nurse" (probably from the verb

---

14   See Gray (1972: 97), who quotes one of the best carols, *Nowell, Nowell* (in Greene 1977), where Christ is called "blessyd brother".

15   On the Charter of Mercy see Woolf (1968: 210-214) and Gray (1972: 130), who also reproduces one of these Charters on tab. 5 facing p. 86.

aleo, nourish), and the *Hymnal* sees the child relieving his mother ("So dyde the chyld hys modyr aye reylewe", P 460). This could be connected with the motif found in some lullabies, where, anticipating the scene at the Crucifixion with the *Planctus Mariae*, Jesus consoles his mother.[16]

I will conclude with two stanzas of the only original poem in Herebert's collection: *Þou wommon boute uére* (Reimer 1987: 118):

> Dame, suster and moder,
> Say þi sone, my broþer,
>   þat ys domes mon,
> þat uor þe þat hym bere
> To me boe debonere;
>   My robe he haueth opon.

> Soethþe he my robe tok,
> Also ich finde in bok,
>   He ys to me ybounde.
> And helpe he wole ich wot,
> Vor loue þe chartre wrot,
>   þe enke orn of hys wounde.

Many of the motifs pointed out in the foregoing analysis are extraordinarily summarized in these lines, which are the quintessence of Franciscan and medieval piety. That they are also found in the *Hymnal* versions, notwithstanding the wide and relevant differences in style and context, testifies to the strength of this piety, as well as to the liberty of our translators who, though choosing ancient Latin hymns to nourish their preaching or their own spiritual life, were none the less men of their time.

---

16   See the poem *Lullay, lullay, my lityl chyld, slepe and be now styll*, quoted in fn 10. A similar and more diffuse treatment of the Nativity scene as a dialogue in which Jesus consoles Mary is the poem by John Grimestone, *Als i lay vpon a nith*, in Brown (1924: 70-75), comment in Woolf (1968: 150-152). The Passion analogue is the well-known *Stond wel, moder, vnder rode*, printed in Brown (1932: 87-91).

CHAPTER 10

Late Medieval Translations
of Marian Hymns and Antiphons[1]

The corpus of ME translations of Marian hymns and antiphons is rather small in terms of quantity, although when analysed both as a response to a particular theological theme and as providing examples of variety in translational techniques it offers much to interest the reader.

A cursory look at the list of items in the *Index of Middle English Verse* s.v. "Latin hymns (including antiphons)" gives a total of twenty-five poems ultimately linked with Marian Latin hymns and antiphons: if we add another fifteen poems, listed elsewhere, related to Marian antiphons, the total amounts to forty items, which means about 20% of a group of approximately 200 liturgically-based lyrics. In fact it must be said that this list, although helpful for an initial exploration in the field, cannot be used as a reliable tool for research for at least two reasons: on the one hand, it is inconsistent and incomplete, in that it mixes sequences[2] with hymns and antiphons, and excludes the translations of two great antiphons, *Salve Regina* and *Regina Coeli*,

---

1   The Latin texts analysed in this chapter, an earlier version of which was published in Ellis/Tixier (1996: 236-263), are reported in Appendix 4.

2   The 'sequence' has a complicated history and is not easy to define. While the hymn has a regular strophic structure, each stanza being complete in itself, the sequence can have stanzas of different length and form, normally linked in pairs as strophe and antistrophe. In the twelfth and thirteenth centuries it had the form of short stanzas of rhymed lines, with a preferably trochaic rhythm, while the hymn has no rhyme and is normally iambic. In the list given in the *Index* there are six Marian sequences: *Ave gloriosa, Ave Jesse virgula, Gaude mater gloriosa, Gaude flore virginali, Gaude virgo, mater Christi,* and *Virgo singularis* (10 items together), which I do not consider in my essay, and two hymns: *Ave maris stella* (7 items), and *O gloriosa domina* (8 items). The four antiphons are *Alma Redemptoris Mater, Ave Regina coelorum, Regina coeli,* and *Salve Regina* (22 items in total).

which are itemised separately; on the other hand, the precise connection of the poems listed with their Latin originals is not indicated, and if we take the ME poems as being 'translations' of Latin hymns without any further qualification, we will be bitterly disappointed.

In fact, going a little deeper into the *Index* list we discover that the already small percentage of Marian Latin-based poems must be further reduced, owing to the fact that many of these poems cannot be properly termed 'translations', however far we can stretch the meaning of this word. Starting from the very first item, of the four poems listed under the heading *Alma Redemptoris Mater*, only the one by William Herebert (*Index* no. 1232) is a translation, the other three being poems on the Annunciation which use the first words of the Marian antiphon as a refrain, but are related neither to the specific content nor to the imagery of the antiphon, except for obvious references to Gabriel's message and Mary's virginal conception. In these, as in other fifteenth-century lyrics, the Latin hymn or antiphon provides either a Marian title, or a phrase which may function as a refrain, or can trigger a litany of eulogistic expressions which burst out with inexhaustible energy, much as from a slender column in a Gothic chapter house, like spray from a fountain, there spreads out a series of delicate arches, or as a gorgeous fan-vaulting displays its sophisticated tracery. The problem remains, of course, of defining the meaning of the word 'translation' in the Middle Ages, since for example a poem by John Lydgate on *Ave Maria*, consisting of seventy-two lines in nine stanzas, is described as "salutacio angelica per [...] dompnum Iohannem Lydegate translata" (MacCracken 1911: 280). But, while waiting for a comprehensive treatise on the various ideas of translation in the Middle Ages, we can provisionally assume that a poem taking one or two lines from a Latin hymn either as a refrain or as a starting point, the text itself straying in all directions from the original, cannot be properly called a 'translation'.

The versions of Latin hymns in medieval England can be analysed from different points of view. Where there is a significant group of translations made by the same author we can look for the marks of a personal style: this can be done with William Herebert, Bishop Sheppey, James Ryman, and the anonymous author of the so-called *English Hymnal* (see this volume, ch. 9). Another favourable case occurs when we have different versions, the more the better, of the same hymn, since this allows comparison at various levels: language, imagery, prosodic choices, changes due to different spiritual outlooks. Other approaches can be used, as when single translations can be gathered in significant units according to either the content or the destination: we can thus examine, for example, hymns composed for Advent or Christmas, or, as in our case, hymns and antiphons composed as prayers to the Virgin Mary; alternatively we can group translated hymns according to their uses for preaching, meditation, or singing, and analyse them according to the adaptations dictated by their new situation, and possibly evaluate their suitability for their new use. A final approach, which runs through all the others, is to consider the translational techniques applied to the Latin texts in terms of vocabulary and structure – see, for example, chapter 11. In fact, these different approaches cannot and should not be used separately, since the omission of one or other of them could hamper a balanced evaluation.

I shall examine some 'translations' of four antiphons and two Marian hymns according to a pattern I have used in other essays, under three headings: linguistic alterations in terms of words and structure, and changes of emphasis in the theological and spiritual outlook evinced by the same language changes. While the first criterion is always applicable due to the obvious and natural difference between Latin and English, the second and the third can be used in a significant way only with texts produced centuries before their translation, and when a visible shift has occurred, since it can be presupposed that Marian theology and devotion, like any other aspect of Christian faith, may and does change in the course of time.[3]

---

3   The absence of any significant difference in Marian theology explains in part why I do not consider the late medieval Marian sequences in this essay. This does not mean that a comparison is devoid of any interest, at least on a linguistic level (considering, for example, the different connotative force of Latin and English words at that time), but also in terms of 'mood' and 'atmosphere'. In fact, as Wenzel has shown, "much of the intellectual vigour and verbal sophistication of medieval Latin sequences and hymns [...] were lost in the process of translation. Yet such losses in verbal artistry, poetic wit, and structural control were – at least partially – compensated by gains in simplicity and the creation of a more intimate tone with the help of an everyday vocabulary and the dialogue form" (1986: 59-60).

Not everybody may agree in drawing this distinction between theology and spirituality, but I must make clear from the start that while the former, as applied to the Virgin Mary, concerns the meaning and the place of Mary in the wider context of the history of salvation, the latter has mainly to do with the attitudes of the believer towards the Mother of God. That Mary cooperates in the redeeming action of Christ is a theological conclusion; that she is seen as a sorrowful mother at the foot of the cross belongs to spirituality. Ideas and statements are more to be expected in the language of theology, emotions and images in the language of spirituality, although the contrast should not be stressed too much, the two being different aspects of the same faith, and thus naturally interconnected. Moreover we should not forget that hymns and antiphons are poetry, and not simply theology put into verse. This means that they must be read carefully, precisely as a good translator does when decoding a text. A line taken as a whole may state a theological truth, but the wording of the sentence may reveal a particular spiritual attitude: it is here that we can find significant differences between the source text and its translation.

The poems I discuss in this chapter are connected by a unifying theme: the Virgin Mary. Before proceeding to analyse the texts I think it is necessary to draw the main lines of this doctrinal and devotional theme in view of what I have just said.

It is widely known that the twelfth century marks a watershed in the history of spirituality. What is at least partially new is a more emotional attitude in the approach to Christian mysteries, and the consequent foregrounding of the humanity of Christ, and of his mother.[4] The difference should not be thought of in terms of dramatic change, but rather as a gradual shift which cannot always be immediately perceived and becomes more visible in the long term. Of the six Latin Marian pieces which were translated in the English Middle Ages, the two hymns precede this watershed; the *Quem terra,*

---

4   "The twelfth century in the Latin West was both a summation of the patristic past and a new departure that introduced themes, values, and practices that were to be influential in Latin Christianity for centuries. Janus-like, this era sits astride the course of Christian spirituality with an ambiguous glance in two directions" (McGinn 1986: 194). See also Wenzel (1986: 16).

pontus, aethera is ascribed to the sixth century, and the *Ave maris stella* probably dates from the eighth century. The four antiphons appeared in the monastic milieu between the late eleventh and the early twelfth centuries, which means that they overlap between the two different periods, and in some ways mark the dawning of the new era of Christian spirituality. All the pieces can then lend themselves to profitable analysis, although we should not expect, especially as regards the antiphons, a stark contrast of mood or tone between the texts and their translation.

Going back again to the *Index* we find that twelve Latin texts are mentioned, and the mere list of their incipits provides the main lines of the doctrine and the piety we are to find in them. Four begin with *Ave*, three with *Gaude*, and the other three exalt Mary as *Alma Redemptoris Mater, Regina coeli, gloriosa Domina* and *Virgo singularis*. In this we have a clear indication of the dominant laudatory tone of Marian liturgical texts, and of the most common titles which were the ground of the praise: Mother of God, glorious queen of heaven, and virgin undefiled. As a consequence of her being mother of the Redeemer, Mary was also venerated as mother of all Christians, her motherhood being invoked as a source of help in all needs. We find both these motifs in a short passage of Aelred of Rievaulx's *De Institutione Inclusarum*, where Mary is described as "*totius humani generis decus, spes mundi, gloria coeli, miserorum refugium, afflictorum solatium, pauperum consolatio, desperatorum erectio, peccatorum reconciliatio, orbis domina, coeli Regina*" [honour of all mankind, hope of the world, glory of heaven, refuge of the wretched, comfort of the afflicted, consolation of the poor, support of the desperate, reconciliation of sinners, Lady of the world, queen of heaven].[5] This is an excellent summary of early medieval Marian doctrine and piety, since in the monastic theology Mary was seen as

---

5   See Hoste/Talbot (1971: 659). In the two ME versions of this work the passage is translated in this way: "helper of mankynde, ioye of heuen, refuge of wrecches, solace and comfort of disperate, lady of the worlde, queen of heuen" (Oxford, Bodleian Library MS Bodley 423), and "þe fayrnesse of alle mankynde, hope of al þe worlde, ioye of heuene, refut of wrecchen, solas of þo þat beþ in sorwe, cumfort of pouere, and at þe laste, lady of al þe worlde, queen of heuene" (Oxford, Bodleian Library Vernon MS): see Ayto/Barratt (1984: 15-16 and 35 respectively).

"queen of the world, merciful mother of the believers, and mediator between Christ and the church".[6] This is also the basic pattern which we will find in the ever-increasing medieval production of Marian poems, that is, praise and thanksgiving followed by requests for help. The different stress given to these two elements can indicate a different period, and so become a useful criterion in analysing a translation.

A further reason to study the translation of Marian texts as a whole is that they go side by side with an enormous production of Marian vernacular poetry, on which they may be presumed to have had a definite influence: a chapter which belongs to the still largely unexplored field of the relationship between Latin and vernacular lyrics in the Middle Ages.[7]

1. Antiphons

I shall take my first example from William Herebert's Commonplace Book, looking at his translation of the Advent-Christmas antiphon *Alma Redemptoris Mater* (eleventh century). This Franciscan scholar and preacher is not only the best-known medieval translator of Latin hymns, but he is also unique in combining verbal compactness, density of meaning and prosodic ability.[8] All these qualities shine with

---

6   This summary of Marian monastic theology is given by De Fiores (1992: 145). See Johnson (1987: 392), where the figure of Mary is summarized as "beautiful Virgin, merciful Mother, and powerful Queen". For a general presentation of Marian themes in medieval hymnody see Szövérffy (1985). For the English production see Wolpers (1950) and Morgan (1993).

7   "The continuity of this tradition (that of the medieval Latin hymn) and its influence on the vernacular lyric still need to be traced in detail" (Wenzel 1986: 15).

8   See Pezzini (1974) and ch. 9. Given the European extension of the change in spirituality mentioned above, it is no wonder to find the same translational choices we observe in the Commonplace Books of English preachers in, say, the versions of an Austrian monk active in the second half of the fourteenth century. To give just an example, taken from his rendering of the Nativity hymn *A solis ortus cardine*, composed in the 6th century by Venantius

sparkling vividness in the rendering of the first two lines of *Alma Redemptoris.*[9]

> Alma Redemptoris Mater,
> quae pervia coeli porta manes ...

> Holy moder, þat bere Cryst,
> buggere of monkunde,
> þou art ȝat of heuene blisse
> þat prest wey ȝyfst and bunde.

By means of slight amplification Herebert, according to his usual choices, clarifies the Latin text, but he does it only by extracting what is, so to speak, hidden in the dense wording of the original: so we have

---

Fortunatus, the verse "Christum canamus principem" is translated by "wir loben den süessen Jesum Christ" (only one of the four MSS containing this version translates literally the Latin "principem" by "fürsten"), with the evident down-grading of the image of princely power to the more intimate vision of a "sweet" baby. We may also compare a fuller sample, the translation of an entire stanza, with what Herebert did in his hymn versions:

> Castae parentis viscera
> celestis intrat gratia,
> venter puellae baiulat
> secreta quae non noverat.

> Ein slos der kewsche, herzen schrein,
> dar cham des heiligen geistes schein,
> das sie empfieng ein chindelein,
> das trueg verholn die maget rain.

[A lock of chastity, a heart's shrine,/ there came the Holy Ghost's light,/ thus she conceived a little baby/ whom bore secretly the maiden pure.] See Spechtler (1972: 219-221). Against the highly evocative Latin text, the German version, like the more or less contemporary English ones (see ch. 9), prefers to make things more explicit and visually concrete: *celestis gratia* becomes "the Holy Ghost's light", chastity is emphatically stressed, the richly connotative *secreta* is reduced to an adverb and replaced with "a little baby", the phrase *quae non noverat* makes room for the more affective image of "a maiden pure". In this respect a comparative study of translations of Latin hymns in a wider European context would be very interesting.

9   Latin text in Raby (1959: 157); Herebert's version in Reimer (1987: 122-123).

"buggere of al monkunde"[10] for *redemptor*, "of heuene blisse" for *coeli*, and the interesting "prest wey [...] and bunde" for the Latin adjective *pervia*. Here it seems that an etymological awareness can be detected, since the Latin adjective *pervius* [easily accessible] contains the word *via*, which Herebert selects and emphasises with the result of a better visualisation: a "door of heaven easily reached" becomes "a door of heavenly bliss" and "a way which is ready at hand".[11] The choice of the common "holy" for *alma* is in line with Herebert's simplified vocabulary, whereas the long rendering of *redemptoris mater* (Holy mother, who bore Christ, redeemer of mankind) and the foregrounding of "holy moder", with the consequent doubling of the reference to Mary's motherhood, conveys a new idea, since Mary is first and implicitly invoked as our mother, precisely because she is the mother of our Redeemer.

The translation of *pervia* also shows the rhetorical figure of *hyperbaton*, a good example of Herebert's stylistic awareness, which is also visible in the following lines, where *succurre cadenti surgere qui curat populo* is rendered

> rer op þe volk
> þat rysing haueht in munde.

One cannot fail to notice the clever resolution of a Latin intricacy which could not possibly be maintained in English, but what is far more important is the choice to render "succurre cadenti" by "rer op", since it allows Herebert to create a phonic and an (intended?)

---

10   Wolpers confuses two different texts when, quoting this verse as an exception in a context devoted to illustrating the more subjective devotion expressed in vernacular poems against the Latin tradition, he writes: "Ähnlich steht in CB 14/19.2 [Brown 1924] *buggere of mankind* als Übersetzung von *advocata nostra* im *Alma Redemptoris Mater*" (1950: 18). In fact the phrase, meaning "redeemer of mankind", does not translate *advocata nostra*, which belongs to *Salve Regina*.

11   On Mary as a 'way' connecting God and mankind see, for example, Bernard of Clairvaux: "*studeamus et nos, dilectissimi, ad ipsum per eam ascendere, qui per ipsam ad nos descendit, per eam venire in gratiam ipsius, qui per eam in nostram miseriam venit*" [let us try, dearly beloved brothers, to ascend through her to Jesus, who through her descended to us, and through her reach the grace of him who reached our wretchedness], in *Adventu Domini*, Sermo 2, no. 5 in Bernard, *Opera* IV: 174.

etymological link with the following "rysing", obtaining thus an echo effect which is similar to, and perhaps a substitution for, what is found in the Latin *succurre / curat*.[12]

There is another version of *Alma Redemptoris Mater* which lies hidden in a compilation of Marian hymns where it comes as a third part after the translation of *Ave maris stella* and of two stanzas of *O gloriosa virginum*. The text is extant in Bishop Sheppey's Commonplace Book (*Index* no. 3887, in Brown 1924: 55-56), a fact which allows an interesting comparison, since the version, like Herebert's, was to be used in sermons. Here is the text:

> Haly moder, fair and gode,
> of ym þat bowth vs wyt is blod,
> yate of hewen, ster of se,
> þat we ne fall howre help þow be!
> Leche of folke, mary myld,
> wyt ferly kynd þow bare þi chyld,
> maden was and euer sal be,
> has þe angel tald to þe
> wen he gret the wyþe aue mari,
> of synful man þow haue mercy!

A few things should be noted. Emphasis is put on Mary (*alma* is rendered by "haly, fair, gode") and on the redemption (*redemptoris* becomes "of ym þat bowth vs wyt is blod"). The invocation to Mary as "leche of folke" is probably a misunderstanding of *qui curat populo*, in the original a dependent clause linked to *succurre cadenti* and meaning "help the falling people who strive to stand up", but it is nonetheless congruent with, if not prompted by, the idea of the Virgin as one who provides "medycyn, erbes, plastre" to heal a sick and

---

12   Other features of this translation are also noteworthy: for example, the regular choice of finite moods for Latin indefinite ones: *natura mirante* gives "wharof so wondreth kunde", and *sumens* becomes "þou uonge". More interesting is the translation of *peccatorum miserere* by "lesne ous of sunne nouthe", where the marking of "us" and "now" gives a poignant urgency and a more practical goal to the request. Another change, due perhaps to a different sense of order, is the displacement of the wonder of the world, which in the Latin was referred only to the paradoxical situation of Mary having her creator in her womb: in Herebert's rendering, by an inversion of lines, this is also applied to her being virgin and mother. The same solution can be seen in the version by Bishop Sheppey quoted below.

sinful mankind. The same image can be found, for instance, in the lyric "Nou skrinkeþ rose ant lylie-flour", where an entire stanza is devoted to describing our Lady as the best "leche" of the world (Brook 1956: 60-62). The wonder of the world (*natura mirante*) at the paradoxical situation of Mary conceiving her father is transposed and projected in the marvellous way ("ferly kynd") she gave birth to her child. This choice of a simple and affective image instead of a sophisticated theological statement, together with the stresses indicated above, have probably something to do with the situation of the preacher: similar choices are regularly found in Herebert's versions. That no general conclusion should be drawn from these choices is proved by the fact that in a vernacular fifteenth-century lyric we find exactly the paradox ruled out in Sheppey's version:

> Haill! quene of hevin and steren of blis;
> sen þat þi sone þi fader is,
> how suld he ony thing þe warn,
> and thou his mothir and he þi barne?[13]

Another good example of a translation which slightly expands on the Latin is a short poem found in Oxford, Bodleian Library MS Laud Misc. 215 and based on the Paschal antiphon *Regina Coeli* (*Index* no. 2789, text in Brown 1939: 49). The original text is very brief and to the point: Mary is first invited to rejoice at the resurrection of her son, and then invoked as intercessor for us before God. The prayer follows the binary pattern already described, the dominant note being that of joy, marked also by the repetition of "Alleluia" after each of the four verses. The English translation doubles the lines and produces two

---

13   Brown (1939: 37). William Herebert translates "*tu quae genuisti [...] tuum sanctum genitorem*" by "In þe þou bere þyn holy uader", and in his poem *Þou wommon boute uére* he devotes the first three stanzas to the exploration of this and other paradoxes typical of Mary, called "Dame, suster and moder". It is interesting to note that, although he was a preacher, and was writing an original vernacular poem, Herebert reveals himself more intellectually minded than Bishop Sheppey. This fact should make modern readers alert to the danger of making too easy generalisations, derived either from the situation (here preaching) or from the language (here English, supposed more "simple" than Latin). On Herebert's love of paradox see Woolf (1968: 131-134).

quatrains: the expansions are either amplifications of a word or a phrase in the text, or additions congruent with the basic content.

Regina coeli laetare,	Quene of heuen, mak þu murth,
alleluia,	and prays god with all þi myght,
quia quem meruisti portare,	for of þe he tok hys burth,
alleluia,	þat is heele, lyf and lyght.

resurrexit sicut dixit:	He rose fro deth so sayd he.
alleluia,	Save us gode, in nede moste!
ora pro nobis Deum,	pray for vs þe trinite,
alleluia.	ffader and sone and holy gost.

There are two notable changes: the reason for rejoicing is not only, or not so much the resurrection, as the incarnation, although the rising from the dead can be implicit in Christ's being "heele, lyf and lyght", which is the most relevant expansion. On the other hand the request for Mary's intercession is doubled by a prayer for God to save us, much as, at the beginning, Mary is invited not only to "mak murth", but also to "prays (*praise*) god", with a clear echo of the *Magnificat*. A Latin note, prefixed to the English text in the manuscript, informs us that what we may perceive as additions or expansions are in fact the spiritual interpretation of the four "Alleluia":

Nota quod in ista antiphona sumitur alleluya 4 modis, scilicet quod 4 ibi sunt alleluya. Quia alia alleluya tamen valet sicut lauda deum creatura, alia lux vita et laus alia saluum me fac deus, alia pater et filius et spiritus sanctus; sic autem est ista antiphona intelligenda.[14]

[Note that in this antiphon alleluya is taken [translated] in four ways, according to the four alleluyas [of the Latin]. For there is one alleluya which means "praise God, o you creature"; another, "light, life and praise"; another, "save me, o God"; another, "father, son and holy spirit"; so this antiphon is to be understood]

The fact that line 6, "Save vs gode, in nede moste", cannot be addressed to Mary, suggests that the text should be recited in a

---

14　Brown (1939: 49). In the phrase *lux, vita et laus, laus* is probably a scribal error for *salus*, which appears confirmed by the English "heele" of line 4. A parallel comment on the "alleluia" in *The Myroure of oure Ladye* confirms the suspicion that *laus* is an error for *salus* in the present quotation: see Blunt (1873: 83).

responsorial way, to which the alternate rhyme could also direct: this translation, that is, grows out of the gloss on the "alleluia".

Against this sober expansion there are three other poems inspired by the same antiphon which adopt a different procedure. Each Latin verse generates a stanza which draws from the rich tradition of the then growing Marian literature, stemming from biblical roots and theologically based, as can be shown by an example taken from John Lydgate's version (MacCracken 1911: 293-294), where the intercessory role of Mary, the very essential *ora pro nobis* of the original text, is expanded in this way:

> O filia Pharaonis! whom oure lady kept,
> Preseruyd Moyses in hys cage,
> And Iudyth þat sauyd that fayre cyte,
> Fygureth Crystes modyr and Image
> Oure verray resorte, when lost was oure herytage,
> When we shuld apere before the dome,
> Before thy dredefull sonnys vysage,
> Ora pro nobis tunc apud deum.

What Lydgate had lightly done in his version of other Latin hymns, like *Vexilla Regis* and *Christe qui lux es et dies*, that is, produced a translation incorporating text and gloss,[15] is here realised to such an extent that a line becomes a stanza, and a very simple prayer is turned into a small theological treatise. If the biblical figures of Judith and the daughter of Pharaoh belong to traditional mariology, the heavy eschatological stress is unmistakably a late medieval development. To obtain it Lydgate forces the Latin by adding a *tunc* to *ora pro nobis*, which directs the invocation towards the final judgement (compare instead Herebert's insertion of "nouthe" [now] in the same phrase, *ora pro nobis*, in his version of *Alma Redemptoris*) and above all by emphasizing the "dredefull vysage" of Christ at doomsday, a touch which was felt necessary to underline the importance of Mary's intercession, but which was dangerously leading towards a kind of 'mariolatry' which was to provoke the reaction of Luther and of other sixteenth-century reformers.[16]

---

15   See chapter 11. See also comments by Renevey (1996: 265-266).
16   See Hines (1993: 637), item 'Mary': "Her mercy was often contrasted with Christ's harsh justice. She became a mediator between sinful humankind and a

A third Marian antiphon, *Ave Regina coelorum*, is characterised by being strongly slanted in the direction of praise, marked by a hammer-like repetition of *Ave, salve, gaude, vale* at the beginning of each of the four distichs. Mary is celebrated as queen of heaven, lady of the angels, root and door through which the light of the world sprang, glorious virgin, exceedingly beautiful above all creatures; at the end she is asked to pray to Christ for us.[17] Three poems in the *Index* are said to be related to this antiphon; none of them is a translation (see *Index* nos. 1032, 1056 (Lydgate), 2610). If any link is to be found between the Latin antiphon and the English poems, we may only say that the first words, and above all the general tone, function as prompts to the medieval poet, while the connection with the Latin text is quickly abandoned, if it was ever taken into account.

Lydgate's version is a good case in point: in his eight stanzas, giving a total of forty-eight lines, the only traces of the original's eight verses are "holyest root" for *radix*, "to thys worlde a lyghte sprong ys from thy lappe" for *ex qua mundo lux est orta*, "Aboue all women, without comparyson, / Of bewte be thow" for *super omnes speciosa*, and "pray gentill Iesu" for *Christum exora*, to which may be added the mention of "the holy ordres nyne" for *angelorum*.[18] We may note in passing that this "gentill Iesu" corrects and counterbalances the "dredefull visage" of Christ mentioned in the version of *Regina coeli*. Derek Pearsall rightly states that Lydgate's "versions of the antiphon *Ave Regina Coelorum*, with their invocatory Ave-structure and accumulation of 'types' for the Virgin from the rich repertoire of biblical sources, were influential in establishing the main literary modes of Marian praise and celebration in the fifteenth century" (1977: 234-235).

---

distant and sometimes vengeful Christ". Another version of *Regina Coeli* (*Index* no. 2802, in Brown 1939: 52-53) follows Lydgate's procedure in turning each line into a stanza, while at the same time keeping the expansion within a sound theological framework; a fourth version (*Index* no. 2800, in Brown 1939: 49-52) extends to seven stanzas using a highly aureate diction, but the connection it maintains with the original, except in the first stanza, is very thin.

17 Latin text in Daniel (1855/1973: 11/319).
18 See MacCracken (1911: 291-292). The main emphasis of the poem is on Mary's beauty and glory, and in this sense we may say that what is translated is the 'tone' of the original, as evinced in such phrases as *virgo gloriosa, super omnes speciosa*, and *valde decora*.

A reading of the other two poems listed in the *Index* (nos. 1032 and 2610, in Brown 1939: 41-45). cannot but confirm this statement, while testifying at the same time to the high degree of productivity of Marian literature in general: in fact both are based not on the classical text of *Ave Regina coelorum*, but on an altered and reduced version:

> Ave Regina coelorum,
> Mater regis angelorum;
> O Maria flos virginum,
> Velut rosa vel lilium,
> funde preces ad filium,
> pro salute fidelium.

> [Hail, queen of heaven,
> Mother of the angels' king;
> O Mary, flower of the virgins,
> like a rose or a lily,
> pray your son
> for the salvation of the faithful]

The first English poem is a litany of praise, where almost all of the verses begin by "Haile", and the stanzas end with each of the Latin lines of the antiphon. The second appears theologically richer, but the laudatory tone runs throughout the poem, made visible by the salutation "Hayle be þu" repeated at the beginning of all seven stanzas, except the first and the last. The only word which is objectionable in Pearsall's statement is the term "version" used to qualify Lydgate's poem, unless we mean by this also the translation, or the transfer, of a tone and an idea from one text to another, ignoring to a large extent the verbal texture in which the idea is clothed and the tone realised.

A fourth Marian antiphon, reflecting like the other three the monastic theology of the eleventh and twelfth centuries, is the *Salve Regina*, a text in which the petitionary note is more stressed than in the two previously analysed, in common with the *Alma Redemptoris Mater*. Two fifteenth-century translations are extant in manuscripts connected with religious houses: one in Oxford Bodleian Library MS Bodley 423, linked with a convent of nuns,[19] the other in a Carthusian

---

19 *Index* no. 1039, in Brown (1939: 45-47). On MS Bodley 423 see Ayto/Barratt (1984: xix-xxiv).

manuscript, London British Library MS Additional 37049.[20] The first poem consists of eight quatrains plus a distich in alliterative lines. It must be said that, although the prosodic choice allows much room for expansion, the translator does not much deviate from his original, at least in the first five stanzas, although some would probably object to calling a 'translation' the way he deals with the text. Here is a quotation from the beginning:

> Salve Regina, mater misericordiae,
> vita, dulcedo, et spes nostra, salve.

> *Heyl*! comely creature curteys of kynde,
> Chaast *quene* of konnyng, of comfort and counsail,
> The *moderhed of thy mercy* to oure soules sende,
> Worthily to thy worship that we may say *"al heyl"*.
> *Lijf and liking* in the lay allone
> Whan þe *swetnesse* of our saueour þe dide assaile,
> Now helpe vs, *our hope* in oure mykel mone,
> Meue up our myndes to the, and *merciful moder, al hayle!*

In this quotation, the italicised words, representing the translated elements of the Latin original, form so to speak the backbone of a text which grows naturally around and is firmly grounded in it. This procedure is typical of texts produced for meditation in that it helps readers to expand on the hidden meanings of the words they must explore to nourish their prayer. That this reworking, besides being a known and valuable technique, can also result in some nice lines of good poetic quality, is seen in the rendering of *ad te clamamus exules filii Evae*, where an extraordinary emphasis is put on the one word *exules*:

> As careful caitifs and combred we crye,
> Outlawes and outcastes, the sones of synne,
> As the heires of Eue to thy pyte we preie.

The monastic context of this translation can easily account for the insistence on a theme which was at the very heart of a vocation which

---

20 *Index* no. 1073, in Brown (1939: 47-48). On the manuscript see Hogg (1981). Vols. 1 and 2 containing the text have not yet appeared.

was described both as "exire a saeculo" and "habitare in caelestibus", where heaven was home and this world a land of exile.[21]

The other poem, which the editor presents as "An Expansion of Salve Regina", and which is also in quatrains rhyming abab, adopts the curious solution of a line for each Latin word, with the Latin text written on the left column side by side with the English verses.

Salue	Hayl! oure patron and lady of erthe,
Regina	qwhene of heuen and emprys of helle,
Mater	Moder of al blis þu art, þe ferth,
Misericordiae	Of mercy and grace þe secunde welle.

The poem should again be read as an aid to meditation, where the paraphrase is meant to stimulate both reason and imagination to grasp the many riches of the text. The tone is unmistakeably fifteenth century, both in the emphasis on Mary as lady, queen and empress, and in the highly pathetic tone found in such lines as "we sighe, we grone, we wax al faynte" (for *suspiramus*) with a curious mixture of solemnity and homeliness in a Jesus who is called both "þi babe" and "so blyssed a lord". At times a traditional theme, like the well-known 'tears of compunction', forces itself upon the text, showing that the translator is not working in a vacuum: this is apparent in the rendering of *et flentes in hac lacrimarum valle*:

Et flentes	Wepyng for syn and for oure payne,
In hac	In þis derknes oure tyme we spende;
lacrimarum	Of teres þe comforth is a swete rayne,
valle	In þe wayle of grace it will discende.

These two poems are highly sensitive to the verbal content of the source text, both when, in the first example, this provides a series of key-words on which to build a coherent and cohesive new text, and when, in the second, each word is so seriously taken as to be glossed and expanded into a new composition.

---

21   See Leclercq (1957), esp. chapter IV "La dévotion au ciel", pp. 55-69.

2. Hymns

If we want to recover an easier idea of translation and a more sober realisation of it, we must turn again to the fourteenth century and to William Herebert, who tried his craftsmanship on the most popular of the Marian hymns, the *Ave maris stella*, of which six different ME versions are extant. For the sake of easy reference in comparing the various texts, I give here the list according to the *Index*:

1)   454: *Aue maris stella* (London, British Library MS Sloane 2593): Brown (1939: 35).
2)   1054: *Heyl, leuedy, se-stoerre bryht* (Herebert): Brown (1924: 20-21).
3)   1079: *Hayle! se sterne* (BL MS Additional 37049): Brown (1939: 35-36).
4)   1081: *Heil sterre of þe see so briht*: Vernon MS, pp. 735-40.
5)   1082: *Heile! sterne on þe se so bright* (Oxford, Bodleian Library MS Bodley 425): Brown (1924: 58-59).
6)   3887: *Ayl be þow, ster of se* (Oxford, Merton College MS 248): Brown (1924: 55-56).

This group of lyrics presents a unique opportunity of comparison as regards time, destination and technique. (1) The versions span a long period, from the early fourteenth century to the end of the fifteenth. (2) Two poems (nos. 2 and 6), both belonging to the fourteenth century, are found in preachers' books, and were probably used in sermons; one (no. 1) is in a minstrel manuscript, and was intended for singing; the remaining three (nos. 3-5) are texts for private prayer and meditation. This means that we have concentrated in this one group the three main functions of such translated hymns in the Middle Ages. (3) As for prosodic choices, we have quatrains, macaronic distichs, and long stanzas. Let us first consider the content of the hymn.

Unlike *Ave Regina coelorum*, where all the lines but the last one praise the greatness and the beauty of the Virgin, the *Ave maris stella* is much more centred on invocation. Mary is first greeted as star of the sea, mother of God, gate of heaven, mother of Christians, *virgo singularis*, a paragon of meekness. But she is repeatedly invoked to give us peace, to loose our bonds, to restore the sight to the blind, to repel all our evils and obtain for us every good thing, to intercede for us, to free us from sin and make us mild and chaste, to help us live a clean and pure life, to secure us a safe journey towards the everlasting joy of the beatific vision. There are seven lines of praise, and thirteen of invocation, the remaining four referring either to the Annunciation (ll. 5-6) or to the Incarnation (ll. 15-16). The Latin structure is normally very simple, each line corresponding to one title or request, except in the case of the two events just mentioned, where we have a dependent participial clause (*sumens illud Ave / Gabrielis ore*) and a postponed relative sentence including another participial clause (*qui pro nobis natus / tulit esse tuus*).[22]

Let us first analyse the two fourteenth-century versions made for use in sermons. Herebert's amplifications are rare and his changes are few, but, read in the light of his current procedures, they show the consistency of this Franciscan scholar and preacher (*Index* no. 1054, in Reimer 1987: 120-121). He renders *Dei mater alma* by "Leuedy, Godes moder, edy wyth", thus stressing the noble status of Mary, present in the Latin *alma*, but also her blessedness and joy. He translates *funda nos in pace* by "in gryht ous sette and shyld vrom shome", specifying the meaning of peace as security and protection. The contrast *mala/bona* is restricted to *sunne/wynne*, words that may sound more concrete to a popular audience. In the phrase *virgo singularis* the paradox hinted at in the adjective is made explicit in the translation: "Mayde one, þou were myd chylde", and the same explicitness is found in the phrase "in spel / of þe aungeles mouhþ kald Gabriel" for *Gabrielis ore*, and in "Aue [...] þat turnst abakward Eues nome" for *mutans nomen Evae*. The verses referring to the Incarnation undergo a significant shift of emphasis: the shade of a patronising attitude on the part of God, who "condescended" to become the son of Mary (*tulit esse tuus*), is ruled out by Herebert, who translates "of þe oure kunde nom", where "oure" echoes the "vor ous" of the preceding line, stressing thus the relevant fact that to save us (*pro nobis natus*) Jesus became one of us, which means redemption

---

22   Latin text of *Ave maris stella* in Dreves/Blume (1888 : 11/40), and in Raby (1959: 94-95). A long commentary is in Plaine (1893).

interpreted in terms of solidarity. Side by side with this theological awareness Herebert shows the already mentioned rhetorical sensitivity, when he allows himself such poetical nicety as "bond vnbynd" for *solve vincla*.

Sheppey does not translate the entire hymn, but uses only sts 1-2, 5 and 4 (in that order) in his compilation (*Index* no. 3887, in Brown 1924: 55-56, ll. 1-16). He too proclaims Mary "blessed", and in some cases he coincides almost verbatim with Herebert, as in the phrase "sely yate" and in the distich "vs of syn þow lees in haste / and make vs boþe mylde and chast" (Herebert: "Of sinne ous quite on haste / and make ous meoke and chaste"), although here the rhyme "haste/chaste" may be mainly responsible for the choice. But there are interesting differences. Gabriel's message becomes "mysterious", since *illud Ave* is rendered by "þat ilke gretyn vncowþe", although the omission of the word *Ave* conceals the contrast *Eva/Ave* which is the main theme of the second stanza, so that the line "tornand þe name of heue a-gayne" becomes obscure, if not meaningless, to the reader of this text. As for the Incarnation, Sheppey's choice is again different from Herebert's: he simplifies in one verse the two Latin lines referring to it ("þat was borne of þe for vrre sake"), and prefers to insert a line of his own after *monstra te esse matrem*: "þow help vs euer at alle ower nede". His dealing with *virgo singularis* is also different, since he chooses to underline the intervention of God in the conception of Jesus: "onely maden þorow godis gast". A lesson can be drawn from this comparison, and this is that when the Latin leaves the expressions of everyday devotion to enter into theology and mystery we can more easily discover in the translators different attitudes and sensitivities.

A third fourteenth-century version (no. 5) could be compared with the preceding two, especially in respect of theology (*Index* no. 1082, in Brown 1924: 58-59). This translator, like Sheppey, omits *illud Ave*, so that the line "turnand þe name of Eue againe" (identical with Sheppey's) loses its reference: this choice implies that the translator took for granted that his audience was well aware of the classical pun *Eva/Ave*, a central point of patristic mariology. The incarnation is here differently interpreted: on the one hand "sins" are mentioned as what caused the son of God to become man, on the other the personal relationship between Mary and Jesus is particularly

259

stressed: "He þat for vs and for oure mis / be-come þi sone, þou moder his". The singularity of Mary's virginity is simply stated in a colourless "Onely maiden and no more". Some small amplifications are worth noticing, like "sterne [...] so bright", or "Ihesu [...] so shene", or peace intended as being "out of paine". Unlike Herebert, who favours finite moods and paratactic construction, this author adheres more strictly to the Latin original: he has "takand" for *sumens*, and "þat we Ihesu seand so shene, / euer faine we vs be-twene" for *ut videntes Iesum / semper collaetemur*. The doxology, which, when not totally omitted, is normally rendered by matter-of-fact and stock sentences, is rather original as translated in this version:

Sit laus Deo patri.	To god fadir be louyng,
Summum Christo decus,	til holy crist wurschipe als king,
Spiritui Sancto	þe holi gost wold of hem spring:
Honor, tribus unus.	þise þre haue oure wurcheping.

Notice *summum* applied to Christ (but there is the variant reading *summo*, which might therefore account for the translator's use of "holy") who is consequently spoken of as "king", and the theologically perfect mention of the proceeding of the Holy Ghost, not present in the original. That the author has one word, "worship", for both *decus* and *honor* means on the one hand that English was still striving painfully to challenge the far richer Latin vocabulary; on the other that, like other translations already noted in this chapter, this English uses a restricted vocabulary as a specific aid to meditation by the deliberate creation of links between words wanting in the Latin original.

The three remaining versions, all belonging to the fifteenth century, present some problems, in that none of them displays strict adherence to the Latin: one (no. 1) is a kind of macaronic poem, another (no. 3) is a short version 'inspired by' and built around some selected images, the third (no. 4) is an extraordinarily expanded version of ten 12-line stanzas against the six 4-line stanzas of the original.

Sloane 2593 is a song-book containing seventy-four carols and lyrics.[23] Only the first two stanzas of the hymn are used, but they can hardly be called a translation. In the first quatrain the Latin lines of the hymn alternate with English verses so that the whole makes sense, according to the well-known technique of macaronic poetry:

> Aue maris stella, þe sterre on þe see,
> dei mater alma, blyssid mot xe be,
> atque semper virgo, prey þi sone for me,
> felix coeli porta, þat I may come to þe.

It appears to be a skilful rearrangement, especially if we consider the good balance between praise and invocation which receive two lines each in the English verses, and the particular congruity between the final request and the image of Mary as *coeli porta*. The second stanza is entirely in English, but instead of *funda nos in pace / mutans nomen Evae* we find a line with an echo typical of songs ("heyl be þu mary! be þu, mary"), and a repeated praise of the Virgin "ful of godis grace and qwyn of mercy". Again this translator shows a total disregard for the intellectual pun *Ave/Eva*, and prefers choices more appropriate to his musical aims. Rather practically the lyric ends by a distich granting "forty dayis of pardoun" to the people who say, or sing this prayer, provided they are "wiþoutyn dedly synne".

Another version of the hymn is found in the same BL MS Additional 37049 where we found the expanded *Salve Regina* mentioned above (*Index* no. 1079, in Brown 1939: 35-36). Few traces of the original text survive in this version: "meke and mylde" for *inter omnes mitis*, or "mayden vnfyled" for *virgo singularis* (but the English adjective underlines Mary's virginity instead of her singularity in being mother and virgin at the same time). On the other hand, the phrase *maris stella* is selected as a governing image and developed to an incredible extent:

> Hayle! se sterne, gods modyr holy,
> pray þu þi swete son safe vs fro foly
> þat walks in þis warld lyke vn-to þe se,
> ebbyng and flowyng ful of vanyte.

---

23   On this MS see Robbins (1952: xxvi-xxvii) and Gneuss (1968: 218) and other references there quoted. The poem is *Index* no 454, in Brown (1939: 35).

Hor to al wretches þat wil for-sake þair syn
þow schynes as a sterne þaim redy to wyn,
and euer-more redy for vs to pray
to gytt vs forgyfnes withouten delay.

The final effect, given the sustained insistence on sin and forgiveness, is that a Marian hymn of praise and petition is transformed into a penitential prayer, of which, in truth, examples are not lacking in vernacular Marian poems, although they are "comparatively few" (Woolf 1968: 119-121). The fact that this poem is extant in a Carthusian manuscript is sufficient explanation of its tone and of echoes of a famous Bernardine sermon on Mary as "star of the sea".[24] It is also worth noticing that in the manuscript the poem is accompanied by a miniature showing the Virgin kneeling before Christ, and below them a man struggling against the waves (see Brunner 1943: 144-145; and Plate 2 in Ellis/Tixier 1996: 251). The fact adds further interest to the highly suggestive meaning of the metaphor in itself and to the crafty realisation of it by our anonymous translator. One wonders whether this is a casual coincidence, or the miniaturist and the translator are the same person.

The value and the meaning of the last and longest version of *Ave maris stella* is not easy to assess (*Index* no. 1081, in Vernon MS, pp. 735-740). Despite its length, 120 lines against twenty-four of the original, it is not a poem that takes only an initial suggestion from a Latin hymn and then strays far from it. The very fact that the original text is reproduced at the beginning of every two stanzas declares the intention of keeping in touch with the source. At times one gets the

---

24   See Bernard of Clairvaux: "*In fine autem versus 'Et nomen', inquit, 'Virginis Maria'. Loquamur pauca et super hoc nomine, quod interpretatum 'Maris stella' dicitur, et Matri Virgini valde convenienter aptatur. Ipsa namque aptissime sideri comparatur, quia sicut sine sui corruptione sidus emittit radium, sic absque sui laesione Virgo parturit Filium....*" [At the end of the verse he says: 'The virgin's name was Mary'. Let us say a few things on this name, which rightly interpreted means 'star of the sea'. This name is most conveniently given to a mother-virgin. In fact she is very aptly compared to a star, since as a star emits a beam without being corrupted, so the Virgin bore her son without any lesion]. *In Laudibus Virginis Matris*, Homilia II, no. 17, in Bernard, *Opera*, V: 34-35. On Marian monastic theology in general see also Amédée de Lausanne, *Huit homélies mariales*, Sources Chrétiennes 72 (Bavaud/Deshusses/Dumas 1960).

impression that of the two stanzas the first is devoted to expanding the original, while the second is meant to explain and comment on it, but this is far from regular. The petitionary tone seems more diffused than in the Latin, but again we may find a request enveloped in titles of praise, as in the following lines:

> Ladi, qween of paradys,
> To þe we schullen calle,
>
> Godes Moder, wommon wys,
> And Mekest most of alle. (ll. 45-48)

What is only too predictable is that in a text which transforms four lines into twenty-four a certain amount of repetition can hardly be avoided. But in a text for meditation this may be a valuable quality, although perhaps not one in tune with modern expectations. For the sake of comparison I think it useful to quote in full the first stanza translating the lines devoted to the incarnation (*qui pro nobis natus / tulit esse tuus*):

> Scheuh þat Moder art, enclyn
> To him þat dyȝd on Roode;
> He, þorow þe, tak preyer myn,
> þat bouȝt us wiþ his bloode;
> Boren for us was he so fyn,
> Hit com al vs to goode;
> He bi-com heere sone þyn,
> þi Milk þen was his foode.
> Godus Modur, þou him beere,
> þi Milk nas non Ilyche,
> Ladi, him to fostren heere;
> þat Burþe was ful riche. (ll. 73-84)

We may remark the highly affective tone reached through the marked stress on the Passion, only implicit in the *pro nobis* of the original, and the moving and delicate expansion on the detail of Mary's milk not present in the Latin: this shows how the language and imagery more proper to the vernacular poetry of the time could flow into the much more essential verbal texture of a Latin hymn.

A similar remark can be applied to the version of the oldest Marian hymn of the Western tradition, the *Quem terra, pontus, aethera*[25] belonging to the sixth century, once attributed to Venantius Fortunatus. Three stanzas of this hymn were part of the office of the Purification of Our Lady: they appear translated twice in Bishop Sheppey's Commonplace Book, once in full, and once in part (two stanzas incorporated into the middle of a compilation of Marian pieces, starting with parts of *Ave maris stella* and ending with *Alma Redemptoris mater – Index* nos. 1832 and 3887, in Brown 1924: 53-56).

A few examples will give a clear idea of the matter-of-factness of Sheppey's translations compared with the high style and lexis of the Latin. In the first two examples both translations are given:

> lactas sacrato ubere
> 1. þou ȝoue hym souken of þi brest
> 2. he soked þyn pappis þat wor ful rith
>
> tu reddis almo germine
> 1. þow hast i-ȝolde þorow by sone
> 2. þow yeldus vs þorow þi haly birth
>
> vitam datam per virginem
> gentes redemptae plaudite
>
> lif þorow Marye is i-wrouȝt
> alle ben glade þat crist haþ i-bouȝt.

Although inclined to simplify and make explicit what is understood, as is proper to a preacher, this translator is not insensitive to the potentialities of his source text, and can even, on occasion, make virtue out of misinterpretation:

> intrent ut astra flebiles,
> coeli fenestra facta es.
> Lat in þe wepand as ster of day,
> als tow art wyndow of hewen mirth.

He clearly understood *ut* as an adverb, not as a conjunction of purpose, so that the resulting line is somewhat awkward, but on the other hand the addition of "mirth" makes a wonderful contrast with

---

25   Latin text in Dreves/Blume (1886-1922: 11/38), and in Raby (1959: 79-80).

the "wepand" of the preceding verse. These two lines appear in the version inserted in the *Ave maris stella*. The misinterpretation remains unexplained, since in the other version of the same manuscript the author shows a perfect understanding of the text, together with a certain originality and a more idiomatic arrangement:

> þow art in heuene an hole i-mad
> þorow which þe senful þorow-geþ glad.

Notice that *flebiles* (weeping) have become "senful", but the note of joy remains in the "glad" creeping in of the redeemed sinners despite the reduction of the *fenestra* to a "hole", somewhat reminiscent of the severe warning of Jesus: "Struggle to get in through the narrow door" (Luke 13:24).

3. Conclusions

I have now come to the end of my journey, and I think that a few conclusions can be drawn, although no striking novelty has emerged from the investigation. I believe nonetheless that this careful analysis has confirmed the general picture we already had; it also reveals how often the translator made intelligent and elegant choices and gives us the feeling of being behind the translator at his work, enabling us to glimpse his supple intellectual and emotional responses to texts.

1. What is evident from this study is that in the late Middle Ages Marian hymns and antiphons were often 'translated' in many ways: by a more or less close rendering, by paraphrases substantially faithful to the ideas and images of the source text, by expansions to which a Latin line or a stanza functioned as an initial prompt only, by being 'transferred' and used as a refrain in many Marian carols.
2. As a result of the processes outlined in (1) above, the Latin texts we have been studying had considerable influence on the growing Marian poetry between the thirteenth and fifteenth

centuries, an influence which worked within the Latin literature itself, where single lines of the old poems stimulated the creation of new ones, often in the form of sequences. Needless to say, this influence need not be thought of simply in terms of single phrases or images, but can be also one of mood, atmosphere, style.

3. The success of this whole translational enterprise has a whole variety of causes: the familiarity engendered by the recurrent use of these antiphons and hymns in the liturgy of the church, where they still keep their place; the simplicity of their dogmatic content and their basically eulogistic and petitionary structure; the rapid growth and spread of Marian devotion.

4. The language of the translations shows that these poems, which were composed in a different period of the history of Christian spirituality, were in a sense 'updated', taking in the vocabulary and imagery of the new 'affective spirituality', which was visible also in the contemporary Latin religious poetry.

5. The different destination of the versions is an important element which must always be taken into consideration. If texts for preaching look for simplicity and clarity, both in wording and structure, texts for meditation take for granted the need to paraphrase: expansions are realised by an easy reference to the vast corpus of Christian literature, from the Bible to monastic theology and poetry, via the well-known patristic literature.

6. Finally, and most important of all: without an eye constantly kept on this large frame of reference, the translation of Christian texts cannot be properly understood and evaluated.

Translation as Interpretation and Commentary: John Lydgate's Version of *Vexilla Regis prodeunt* and *Christe qui lux es et dies*[1]

In the vast corpus of Lydgate's poetry there are several versions or paraphrases of Latin pieces which have a more or less direct relationship with Christian worship. Of these only two are translations of 'hymns' if we use the word to mean a poetic text written in stanza form, normally a quatrain, intended for public singing in the liturgical office: *Vexilla Regis prodeunt*, and *Christe qui lux es et dies*. These two hymns have a common connection with the Passion, since *Vexilla Regis* was used in Holy Week, and *Christe qui lux* was the ordinary hymn for Compline during Lent. If we judge by the number of versions still extant, the hymns Lydgate chose to translate were among the most popular in late medieval England: the *Index of Middle English Verse* and the *Supplement* register eight versions of *Christe qui lux es et dies*, and three of *Vexilla Regis prodeunt*.[2] The study of Lydgate's renderings may be of interest and shed some light on the history both of the widely practised genre 'versions of hymns' and more generally of the concept of translation in the Middle Ages.

So far literary critics have not been particularly sympathetic to Lydgate's enterprise, their opinions ranging from "anemic" attributed to a line, or "completely losing the flavor of his Latin original" said of the first two stanzas of *Vexilla Regis* (Manning 1962: 139), to "lacking originality and freshness" applied to his translations as a whole

---

1   An earlier version of this chapter was published in Crivelli/Sampietro (1994: 73-98).

2   See Brown/Robbins (1943), hereafter *Index*; and Robbins/Cutler (1965), hereafter *Supplement*, s.v. "Latin Hymns". Although for *Vexilla Regis* the *Index* registers four items, it must be said that Skelton's so called version of this hymn (*Index* No. 3404, now *Supplement* No. 1119), cannot be properly considered a 'translation' in any sense of the term.

(Gneuss 1968: 224). A more favourable appreciation is expressed by Pearsall, who praises the "attractive simplicity" of the version of *Christe qui lux*, and the "lofty tone" of the opening lines of *Vexilla Regis*, but goes on to say that this tone is "not maintained [...] and in the rest the impetus of the work, and sometimes its very sense, are lost in the cross-currents of allusion and aureation" (1970: 260-261). Schirmer deals very briefly with these two translations, which he describes as "paraphrases" (1961: 180, 186),[3] but I find that the word is too vague, and if it means a new text created by a mere amplification of the original, in the usual sense of "telling the same thing in other words", it is certainly misleading. What Lydgate does is actually something more complex, and I hope to show, through a detailed analysis, what the term 'paraphrase' may mean when applied to his renderings of these ancient texts of Christian prayer.

Previous studies have shown that Latin liturgical hymns were anglicized for at least three purposes: to be used as quotations in sermons, to be read as private prayers or meditations, to be sung in extra-liturgical services (Gneuss 1968: 217; Pezzini 1974 and ch. 9). Lydgate's versions seem to belong, in common with most fifteenth-century translations, with the possible exception of James Ryman's, to the domain of private prayer.[4]

The numerous ME versions of the two hymns present us with the opportunity of making interesting comparisons, for which several factors must be taken into account if we want to correctly evaluate the response of the various authors to the Latin original: the different destination, the prosodic means chosen to structure the version (e.g. quatrain or ballade stanza), the personal spirituality of the translator and, possibly, the different devotional background. Although in the

---

3   On translational practices in late medieval England, with particular regard to John Lydgate, see also Rossi (1964: 9-84).

4   In fact the version of *Vexilla Regis* has such a grand tone that it seems to evoke more properly the solemn context of a public proclamation, and I feel inclined to agree with Pearsall who, talking of Lydgate's translations of Latin hymns, sequences and antiphons, suggests that he may have been encouraged by Henry V "to develop a high style in liturgical composition in which English could match Latin" (1977: 234). In this light the two hymns, besides being texts for private devotion, could also be taken as experiments in liturgical language.

case of Lydgate the sample is rather small, it is nonetheless worth investigation for at least two reasons: the first is the opportunity to compare his response to the Latin and his translational style with those shown in other renderings; the second is the remarkable difference in content, and consequently in language, between the two hymns, from which we might expect a different translational attitude. No clear-cut distinction can obviously be made, but it is to be noted that whereas *Vexilla Regis*, dealing as it does with the redemption, consists largely of theological statements expressed through paradox and some powerful images, *Christe qui lux*, being a prayer for the end of the day, is more simple in content and more devotional in tone, allowing thus less elaboration and reworking.[5]

1. *Vexilla Regis prodeunt*

If we want to explore what a translation, or a paraphrase may be, there is perhaps no better example than Lydgate's version of the old and venerable Passion hymn composed by Venantius Fortunatus towards the end of the sixth century.[6] Of the three ME translations of this hymn (*Index* No. 3403, No. 3405, besides Lydgate's No. 2833), the one which is ascribed to the monk of Bury amplifies the Latin original to such a remarkable extent that his version should be more truly described as a text inspired by. Evidently the poet reads and elaborates on the hymn in the light of the theology of Christian redemption, of which the *Vexilla Regis* is a known outstanding example, but by so doing he reinforces the idea of translation as rendering with those of

---

5   For a general presentation of the two hymns, their history and liturgical use, together with their modern translations, see Julian (1957: I/227-228 [*Christe qui lux es et dies*], and II/1219-1222 [*Vexilla Regis prodeunt*]).

6   Text in Dreves/Blume (1886-1922: II/45, L/74). For a full critical and theological commentary see Pimont (1874: II/2/30-ff). See also Raby (1953: 89-90); Messenger (1953: 4-5); Szövérffy (1976: 15-18; and 1985b: 21-24).

interpretation and commentary, so that text and gloss are not kept distinct and separate, but merge to create a new richer textual web.[7]

Some knowledge of the basic concepts and images of the Latin hymn is needed to understand and appreciate Lydgate's treatment of his source text. The dominant theme of *Vexilla Regis* can be summarized in the line *regnavit a ligno Deus*, that is Jesus, who is man and God, becomes king by dying for the salvation of mankind, and the cross is his throne. Death and life, humiliation and glory are so interconnected in the Easter event that the first element of these sharp contrasts becomes the way to reach the second, so that death leads to life, and glory is achieved through humiliation. Lots of hymns, antiphons, sermons and poems proclaim this basic paradox of the redemption which combines the two opposite sides of the Passion in a balance so delicate that it can hardly be maintained. In fact in the early centuries of Christianity and in the High Middle Ages the weight was heavily on glory, whereas after the twelfth century suffering and humiliation came to the foreground. *Vexilla Regis* belongs to the first part of this story and the text, right from the beginning radiates glory and triumph. Fortunatus' hymn vividly suggests in the wording of the very first line the image of the people of God as an army marching behind the banners of his king (*Vexilla Regis prodeunt*), a king who rules from the tree of the cross (*Regnavit a ligno Deus*), a tree which is elegant and radiant with light (*Arbor decora et fulgida*), adorned with the royal purple (*Ornata regis purpura*), victorious over the power of hell whose prey he has snatched (*Praedam tulitque tartari*). Christ's suffering is obviously mentioned, but never indulged in. The terrible pain of the crucified body is counterpointed by the glorious side of the event evoked in various ways: we are reminded that the flesh which hangs on the cross, now itself a shining trophy (*fulget*), is the body of the creator of the flesh (*Quo carne carnis conditor /*

---

7   See Ellis (1989: 7). Two of the essays collected in this volume are particularly relevant to the topic discussed here: Burnley (1989), and especially Savage, where the translator of Lactantius's poem *De Ave Phoenice* in particular is seen to use the same procedures later to be adopted by Lydgate, that is "the 'translation' is actually a translation plus commentary which points us to other Latin texts: the Scriptures and commentaries on them" (1989: 124). However, while in the OE poem the commentary follows the translation, in Lydgate's hymns the expansion-commentary is incorporated in the text.

Suspensus est patibulo); the sad spectacle of a miserable death is elevated into its theological meaning since the hymn proclaims that the body pierced by nails is actually the victim offered in the solemn context of liturgical sacrifice for the redemption of mankind (*Redemptions gratia / Hic immolata hostia*); a horrible wound is transfigured into a positive image: the right side of Jesus transfixed by the spear becomes a healing and washing fountain of water and blood (*Quo vulneratus* [...] *Vt nos lavaret crimine / Manavit unda et sanguine*); what had been the scaffold where Christ died is transmuted into a balance on which the hanging body becomes the price that outweighs the original fall and the sins of all mankind (*Beata cuius brachiis / Pretium pependit saeculi, / Statera facta est corporis / Praedam tulitque tartari*); the cross is rightly invoked as the only hope (*spes unica*), source of justification and forgiveness.

The conclusion is perfectly in tune with the theology of the hymn: God is prayed to "rule" the people he "saves" through the mysterious and paradoxical event of the crucifixion (*Quos per crucis mysterium / Salvas, rege per saecula*). The occasion which prompted the composition of the hymn, and the circumstance in which it was probably first sung, a solemn procession in Poitiers to enthrone a relic of the Holy Cross offered by the Byzantine Emperor (Szövérffy 1976: 8), could only strengthen and emphasize the tone of magnificence and triumph already dominant in the theological vision of the time.

The reading of what is improperly called the translation John Skelton made of this hymn gives us a good idea of how different was the spiritual attitude towards the cross at the end of the Middle Ages:

> The kinges baner on felde is [s]playd,
> The crosses mistry can not be nayd,
> To whom our Sauyour was betrayd,
>   And for our sake;
> Thus sayth he,
> I suffre for thé,
>   My deth I take.
>   Now synge we, as we were wont,
>   *Vexilla Regis prodeunt.*[8]

---

8   Text quoted from Dyce (1885: I/168-171). Henderson (1959: 16-19) provides an edition with modernized spelling.

Only the first two lines of the Latin hymn are translated, the first is then repeated in the original at the end of each stanza in a carol-like refrain, the rest of the poem consists of the long list of pains endured by Jesus and the recurring invitation to abandon a sinful life which form the well-known stock of so many medieval English lyrics devoted to the Passion. To give just an example, here is the second stanza of Skelton's poem:

> Beholde my shankes, behold my knees,
> Beholde my hed, armes, and thees,
> Beholde of me nothyng thou sees
>   But sorowe and pyne;
> Thus was I spylt,
> Man, for thy gylte,
>   And not for myne.
>   Now synge we, &c.

In this version the Latin hymn becomes a pretext for something largely unrelated to its content, and deeply alien to its language. Lydgate's procedure is remarkably different. He does not adhere to the letter of the original as William Herebert more or less did in his rendering, nor does he totally go astray as Skelton. His translation is a text which combines the ancient theology testified in the Latin, a few sparks of medieval devotion couched in a language and imagery typical of the time, and many additions which, although absent from Fortunatus' text, belong nevertheless to the best Catholic theological tradition. Whether this blending is a heavy larding of the original, mere "wit" employed "to appeal to his audience's grasp of the mystery involved without either deepening their understanding of it or enhancing their emotional response to it" (Manning 1962: 139),[9] or a skilful solution which succeeds in being both faithful to the spirit of the source text and at the same time capable of striking a familiar chord for contemporary ears, as I think, the reader will judge.

Before proceeding to analyse Lydgate's version, two observations are in order. Unlike Herebert who, having chosen the very economic structure of the quatrain of tetrameters, was obliged to compress his rendering into few well selected words, Lydgate uses the

---

9   I must admit that this was also my opinion when I analysed Herebert's version comparing it favourably with Lydgate's: see Pezzini (1974: 36-37).

eight-line stanza of the ballade (rhyming ababbcbc), which allows him plenty of space for amplification. The other important point is the use Lydgate makes of Latin: normally line 6 and 8 of the stanza repeat ll. 3 and 4 of the original, but other words are inserted here and there, presumably to heighten the diction, according to the well-known devices of the aureate style.[10]

While at a first reading Lydgate's version[11] seems loose and erratic, a more careful consideration reveals a clear web of words and images aimed at emphasizing throughout the hymn certain ideas, of which two are basic and intrinsically connected: that of the crucifixion as a triumph won out of a hard and cruel battle, and the salvation gained for all mankind through this struggle. Lydgate's choices, which to some critics appear to suffocate the compact and concise *splendor* of the Latin, do in fact enhance the expression of the theological truth affirmed in the original. The duel Christ engaged in against the powers of evil is recalled in every stanza through the sustained use of military and fighting vocabulary: royal banerys, batayle, capteyne, standart, conqueste (st. 1); purple weede, lyff sleyng deth, lyste his blood to schede, his trivmphal mede (st. 2); was sleyne, slough the Tyrant, ffaught for our liberte (st. 3); woundyd to the deth (st. 4); deth and his woundes scharpe, coote armure (st. 5); al bloody, batayle inperyal, palme of this conqueste (st. 6); ranson incomperable, spoylled hell (st. 7); scheeld and proteccyon (st. 8); conquest and victorie vnto the sone (st. 9). In doing this Lydgate is perfectly faithful in content and tone to his source text. Where he adopts a different approach is in the images he chooses to render the idea of salvation. In the Latin we find the image of cleansing (*ut nos lavaret crimine*: st. 2), that of the price paid to redeem the world (*pretium pependit saeculi*: st. 6), and that of a court of justice (*auge piis iustitiam / reisque dona veniam*: st. 7), which is indeed consistent with the idea of sin as "crimen". Lydgate leaves the first image in the Latin original, only adding that from the heart of Christ "Blood and watur ran out in habondance", translates

---

10   Pearsall rightly observes that in the case of Lydgate's "more ambitious religious poetry, as it is evidenced in the translations of Latin hymns [...] his audience is likely to be a narrower circle of the higher clergy, and one furthermore with a taste for fine writing" (1977: 234).

11   Lydgate's translation of *Vexilla Regis prodeunt* is quoted from MacCracken (1962: 25-27).

pretium by "ranson", but in the case of the third image, while inserting in stanza 8 the two Latin lines just quoted, he prefers not to expand on the legal metaphor in favour of a medicinal one: "Cristus Cros" is invoked as "oure medycyne, our bawme in al sikenesse, oure rycheste triacle geyne al goostely poyson", an image which overflows back into stanza 7 where the cross is seen as a "blesset stoke" from which hangs a "ryche frute" which is "restouratyff [...] geyne all oure hurtis and soorys incurable". This theological view which tends to interpret the redemption as healing better than a judicial absolution, implicitly connected with the idea of sin as fragility rather than crime, seems to be more in tune with late medieval devotion, and can also be found, for example, in the so called *English Hymnal*, a collection of versions of Latin hymns composed in aureate style some time during the fifteenth century (see ch. 9).

A third point, and a governing theme of Fortunatus' hymn, is the relationship between the cross and the salvation of the world illustrated by a detailed elaboration on the paradoxical aspect of the redemption. This truth is repeatedly proclaimed, as shown, even in what seems a stark statement, by a richly iconic language: the blood merges into the majesty of the royal purple, gaping wounds become healing sources, what was the tree of death is now the tree of life. Lydgate follows his source text in emphasizing the glorious and saving aspect of the crucifixion, expanding on the same paradoxes of the original and adding some nice images which, while consistent with the general theme, are not in the Latin. He too sees the cross of Christ the King as "his standart celestyal of schynyng / wyth purple hewe depeynt", proclaims that "Lyff sleyng deth deyde vpon the crose", and addressing himself to the *arbor decora et fulgida / ornata regis purpura* invokes the cross as:

> Fayrest of trees celestial fresche schynyng,
> Wyth Royal purplys al bloody was thyn hewe...

The paradoxical way leading to a triumphant upturning of a miserable condition of slavery is clearly stated and cunningly suggested in a stanza which deserves to be quoted in full:

> (Confixus clauis Innocens...)
> Sone of kyng Dauit was sleyne, and his ayre (*heir*)

274

Pure Innocent, nayled to a tree,
Moriens ful hygh vp in the Eyre,
Slough the Tyrant for al his cruelte,
Pride was bore downe with humilite,
Seuum[12] tirannum vinciens,
Where we were thrall ffaught for our liberte,
Et nos ab morte liberans.

Lydgate underlines that a man of royal blood and innocent life is outrageously slain, but it is precisely his death that kills that cruel tyrant which is our death, from whose jaws we are now completely free. This is all in the Latin, even the image of fighting which can easily be extracted from the verb *vinciens*. What cannot be found in the Latin is the line "Pride was bore downe with humilite", an expression which hints at the vast literature on the seven deadly sins and their remedies typical of the late Middle Ages, as does the appeal "O synful man! haue this in remembraunce" in the following stanza 4, so characteristic of many Passion and penitential lyrics. But another hint lies hidden in the text, which should not be overlooked: pride is "bore downe" by a humble man who is "Moriens ful hygh vp in the Eyre", where the contrast high/down and its reversal is another way of expressing the paradox of the redemption, besides being an evident reminder to a *locus classicus* of the biblical theology of the cross, when Christ speaks of his coming crucifixion as an elevation both in literal and figurative sense (cf. John 12:32-33).

The image of the Passion as a battle, as I have shown, was undoubtedly very attractive to Lydgate, and while composing his "ymne", he may have had in his mind the splendid lines of an old and

---

12   MacCracken (1962) prints *senum*, which is clearly nonsense, a mistake which is probably due to the fact that the letters <n> and <u> had quite often the same form in the manuscripts. A similar error of transcription occurs at 1. 40 where *aliguo* should evidently be intended as *a ligno*. This stanza differs considerably from the original text of *Vexilla Regis* by Fortunatus; the Latin text translated by Lydgate is *Confixus clavis innocens / Moriens in alto vertice / Sevum tyrannum vinciens / Et nos ab morte liberans*. The whole text, apart from *in alto vertice*, is incorporated in the English translation. Other changes occur in the version of the hymn current in the late Middle Ages, the one Lydgate translated: the original seventh and eighth stanzas (*Fundis aroma cortice* and *Salve ara, salve victima*) are replaced with two new ones, *O crux, ave spes unica*, and *Te summa Deus Trinitas*.

well-known sequence: *Mors et vita duello conflixere mirando: dux vitae mortuus regnat vivus.* This is in fact what comes to mind when we consider what he makes of the image of the *"Vexilla Regis"* which in the original, besides evoking the cross as a trophy, referred most probably to the standards actually displayed in the procession carrying the relic of the cross through the city of Poitiers, much in the form of a Roman triumph. In Lydgate's version the cross becomes the standard Christ raises to go "Towarde his Batayle" to fight the forces of evil as a self-sacrificing leader: "Vita was Capteyne, whech lyste hymselff be ded / And to slee deth his conqueste to termyne". This military tone, which is but mildly suggested in the Latin, is totally the work of Lydgate, and is, as I have said, consistently diffused all through his version.

If the fighting atmosphere can be said to be derived from the source text, it is not so with three images which Lydgate adds of his own, and which are worth some comments. Two describe in explicit terms the fruit of the redemption, the third is but another metaphor to illustrate the paradoxical aspect of the Passion. The first image is found in stanza 4 where, to translate the Latin *vulneratus*, it is said that Christ was "woundyd to the deth, / To scowre the Ruste of our mortal grevaunce". The metaphor is theologically important in that it declares that sin has not destroyed the image of God in man, but has only defaced it much as rust does on iron or other metal objects. To show how this is part of the best Catholic tradition I would recall two texts belonging respectively to the fourth and to the nineteenth century. Here is what Gregory of Nyssa says:

> Anyone who has expurgated his heart from every wicked attachment to the created things will see in his own beauty the image of divine nature.

And he goes on to compare this expurgation of the heart exactly to what we do when we scour a piece of iron: by taking away the rusty dirt of our sins we recover the brightness of the sun and our original resemblance to the face of God (De beatitudinibus oratio VI, in *Patrologia Graeca* 44, cols 1270-71). At the other end of the story Gerald Manley Hopkins views suffering and fatigue, as Lydgate saw Christ's wounds, as purifying factors, when, using again the image of a blade of iron made radiant by rubbing, he says that "sheer plod makes plough down sillion / shine" (*The Windhover*), an image reinforced by that of "blue-bleak embers" gashing "gold-vermilion", which, although in a very different poetic language, shows how Hopkins works in the theological tradition of Fortunatus and Lydgate.[13]

Another image which has an unmistakably medieval flavour appears in stanza 5, where it is said that Christ's "Coote Armure was lyke a bloody skye". If "bloody" evokes the wounds, and "Coote Armure" the rude fighting, "skye" introduces an antitethic element capable of transforming blue-bleak wounds into gold brilliant stars. An analogue is found, though in a predictably more didactic language, in the *Meditations on the Passion* attributed to Richard Rolle:

> Than was thy body lyk to hevyn. For as hevyn is ful of sterris, so was thy body ful of woundes; bot, Lord, thy woundes bene bettyr than sterris, for sterres shynen bot by nyght, and thy woundes bene ful of vertu day and nyght....[14]

It may be interesting to remark that in another poem, *The dolorous pyte of Crystes passioun*, Lydgate uses again the image of the coat of arms in connection with the wounds of Christ, but in this case it has become "best proteccyoun [...], brest plate and harbirioun, / Yow to dyffende in al adversyte" (MacCracken 1962: 251, ll. 20-22). The cost and the resulting benefit of the redemption here coincide.

The third original insertion is in fact a group of images centered round the basic motif of the cross as a tree. Fortunatus had interpreted this *arbor decora et fulgida* first as a royal trophy, or a *labarum*, then as a balance on which Christ paid the price of our rescue. Lydgate maintains these two meanings, with a strong emphasis particularly on the first (the cross is said to be the "Palme of this conqueste" after a "Batayle Inperyal"), and adds two other ones rightly derived from the vegetal nature of a tree. In one the cross is called "Cheeff gryffe of

---

13   Mackenzie (1990: 144); see also the commentary on the poem, p. 384, for other analogues to the image. John Donne can also be quoted to show the persistence of this image. In "Goodfriday, 1613. Riding Westward" he writes: "punish me / Burne off my rusts, and my deformity, / Restore thine Image" (see Gardner 1952: 31, ll. 39-41).

14   Allen (1931: 34). For other iconic interpretations of the wounded body of the crucifix see also Gray (1972: 69-70).

Paradise": this may be either a reference to the *arbor vitae* of Eden (Gen. 2:9), or perhaps a hint at the *Legend of the Holy Rood*, according to which the cross had been made of the tree which had caused Adam's fall,[15] meaning that God had wanted to redeem us by using exactly the instrument of our ruin. This connection is also strongly marked by the second image Lydgate adds to the text: after stating in stanza 2 that "Frute of a tree caused al our lose", in stanza 7 he portrays Christ as a "ryche frute" which becomes our food, "repaaste" and "restouratyff set in oure feyth moost stable", a possible allusion to the same *arbor vitae* which reappears twice in the Apocalypse, first in the "Paradise of God", to be eaten by "him that overcometh" (Rev. 2:7), then in the new heaven, where its fruits and leaves are "for the healing of the nations" (Rev. 22:2). Again, to show the persistence of an iconic tradition, I cannot help quoting a modern poem where the same image of fruit recurs and the same paradoxical language of the redemption is used:

> Was he balked by silence? He kneeled long,
> And saw love in a dark crown
> Of thorns blazing, and a winter tree
> Golden with fruit of a man's body
>
> R.S. Thomas, 'In a Country Church' (1979: 42)

A final remark concerns the use of biblical names which, except for David, are all an addition of Lydgate. If poetically they may be taken, together with the Latin lines and words, as exotic jewels set in rich ornamentation to produce an effect of solemn and visionary distance, theologically they undoubtedly serve to mark the timeless and universal meaning of the cross by fitting the murder of Jesus into the entire web of the history of salvation right back, through the prophets,

---

15   A short summary of the story of the tree of the cross can be found in the *Golden Legend*, 'De inuentione sancte crucis', where it is said that when Seth, Adam's son, went back to the gates of the earthly paradise to ask for the oil of mercy to heal his father, *"angelus de ligno in quo peccauit Adam eidem tradidit dicens quod quando faceret fructum pater sanaretur"* (in Maggioni 1998: 459-460). For some versions of this legend see Napier (1894), Lazar (1960), and Hill (1965). It is worth noting how skilfully Lydgate exploits the rich referentiality of the tree image against the background of the Christian theological tradition.

to Isaac and Abraham. We may also add that the Latin lines and words work in a similar way: they testify to the uninterrupted course of the Christian devotion which has come, via Venantius Fortunatus, down to John Lydgate. The first biblical name we meet with is "Bosra". It refers to Isaiah 63:1-7, a passage read in the liturgy of the Wednesday in Holy Week. In it the prophet presents a mysterious man, "glorious in his apparel, travelling in the greatness of his strength", coming from Edom, "with dyed garments from Bozrah": his garments are stained red because, he says, he has trodden the winepress alone, a metaphor, the man explains, of the violent struggle he had had to fight against his people. The passage was interpreted typologically as referring to the passion of Christ, and it is in this sense that Lydgate inserts the reference in the first stanza of his version, where he depicts Jesus going to Calvary as a king going "Towarde his Batayle", displaying his "Royal Banerys [...] in Bosra steyned reede", a colour which evokes both purple and blood, as can be seen in the following lines. We have an admirable version of the whole passage of Isaiah by William Herebert,[16] and it is interesting to remark that the Franciscan preacher rules out of his rendering any mention of the two biblical place-names, whereas Lydgate uses one of them to enrich his text: the two poets had obviously a different audience in mind, besides living in two different centuries and in a changed spiritual climate.

In the first stanza Isaac is named, together with his father Abraham, a reference which is self-evident given the central place the sacrifice of Isaac has in the Bible as one of the main events which, together with the killing of Abel, prefigured the redeeming death of Jesus. David is mentioned twice, first in stanza 3 to recall the royal ancestry of Jesus, called "Sone of kyng Dauit [...] and his ayre", then in stanza 5, to translate the *David fideli carmine* of the original, amplified in "The ffuneral compleyntis Dauit songe with his harpe, / With wepyng tvnis". This same stanza is packed with names: Isaiah,

---

16   Text in Reimer (1987: 132-133); comments in Gray (1972: 12-17) and Pezzini (1974: 29-32). The influence of this celebrated passage can also be seen in Lydgate, since *The dolorous pyte of Crystes passioun* referred to above is "but a learned unwinding of the traditional image of the grapes and winepress of the Passion" (Woolf 1968: 198-202).

Jeremiah and Esdras concur, together with David, to proclaim the central message of Easter: *"Regnauit a ligno dues."*

For the *Vexilla Regis* the only possible comparison is between Herebert and Lydgate.[17] At first glance one is struck by the compact conciseness of the fourteenth-century friar, and the loose diffusedness of the fifteenth-century monk. But once we consider the different destinations of the two versions (preaching in Herebert's, probably meditation in Lydgate's case), the different poetic form chosen (the quatrain against the ballade stanza), and allow people to write in different styles, we may appreciate both and admire their achievement. Certainly, immediacy and vividness matter a lot in oral delivery, and this is what Herebert manages to create in his translation. A text to be read again and again in private prayer admits more decoration and amplification as a way of extracting and underlining some of the many implicit meanings of the text. This is what Lydgate does, and I hope to have shown, by my close analysis of his version of the ancient hymn, that he has been successful.

---

17   In fact, the third version (*Index* No. 3403) is only a translation of the first stanza found in Bishop Sheppey's manuscript (now Oxford MS Merton 248) within a Latin sermon: this quatrain, which is registered as "unpublished" in the *Index* and the *Supplement*, has been edited by Pezzini (1974: 36 and ch. 9, fn 6). In these two essays I make several comments on Herebert's version of *Vexilla Regis*, particularly with regard to the translational choices connected with and derived from his activity as a preacher, which I need not repeat here. Pearsall is right when he remarks that in translating "Regnavit a ligno deus" as "Men ye mowen y-se / Hou godes trone ys rode tre" "Herebert was skilful enough to capture the paradox of the last line, which Lydgate misses" (1970: 261), but the point is that the two versions cannot be judged by comparing line to line, since they use a different prosodic structure and are intended for a different audience. It is true that Herebert's rendering is marvellously vivid (see ch. 9: 223) as it is also true that Lydgate does not translate that line, but it is false that he misses the paradoxical aspect of the Passion, which he may omit in rendering a single line, but which he abundantly illustrates, as I have shown, throughout his version.

2. Christe qui lux es et dies

This hymn, which also belongs to the golden age of the Fathers, dating back to the sixth century at least,[18] has neither the theological compactness nor the celebratory solemnity of the *Vexilla Regis*; it is essentially devotional in content, and follows the simplest pattern of the prayer of invocation: God, or Christ, is firstly described in one of his attributes, and then accordingly invoked to meet particular needs of the faithful. The hymn is built around a theme which rings out in the very first line, that is Christ celebrated as "light", followed by and developed into a series of petitions mainly centered on the request for help against the perils of the "night". The verbs are mostly in the imperative, hinting thus at the urgence of Christ's intervention to defend (*Defende nos in hac nocte*), to protect (*Dextera tua protegat*), to keep and direct his servants (*Guberna tuos famulos*), and to repress their threatening enemies (*Insidiantes reprime*). Christ is also prayed to as giver of quiet and peace (*Quietam noctem tribue*), and although he is always invoked as a "lord" (*domine*) to whom his disciples address, themselves as "servants" (*famuli*), there are glimpses of a more intimate relationship in the verbs of the final stanzas: "look at us, remember us, be with us, o lord" (*adspice* [...] *memento nostri* [...] *adesto nobis domine*). This last verb cannot but recall the story of the two disciples who, having met on the road to Emmaus the risen Jesus as an anonymous traveller, did not want to part with him, and asked him to stay with them: "Abide with us, for it is toward evening, and the day is far spent" (Luke 24: 29). But, apart from this reminiscence of a friendly companionship in a domestic atmosphere, it must be said that the danger of temptation, and the consequent call for help, are indeed the dominant themes of the *Christe qui lux*. Although intended as a prayer to be said before going to rest, evoking thus images of quiet and tranquillity, the hymn should in fact be read against the evangelical scene of the agony of Christ on the night of his betrayal,

---

18   For the Latin text of the hymn see Dreves/Blume (1886-1922: XXVII/111, and LI/21). The hymn is mentioned by Caesarius of Arles, who died in 542 (Dreves/Blume 1886-1922: LI/xx and 23), so that the first half of the sixth century can be safely taken as *terminus a quo* for its composition.

when entering the worst hour of his life he strongly urged his friends and followers to be on the watch: "Why sleep ye? rise and pray, lest ye enter into temptation" (Luke 22: 46). In the *Christe qui lux es et dies* the life of the believer is starkly reduced to the contrast light/night mirroring the eternal war between good and evil, a struggle whose dramatic quality is underlined by the repeated request for defense (*defende* occurs once, and *defensor* twice, besides other synonyms such as *guberna* and *protege*) against an enemy whose wickedness is all the more dangerous by being surreptitious (*Nec hostis nos surripiat*) and insidious (*Insidiantes reprime*). In the background another battle looms, the duel Christ engaged in against the powers of evil, when he had to shed his blood in order to redeem his servants (*Quos sanguine mercatus es*). In this respect the only mention of peace (*Sit nobis in te requies*), with its Augustinian echo (*inquietum est cor nostrum donec requiescat in te*), appears in a landscape largely inhabited by fear and anxiety. The heart of the devout must therefore be alert (*Cor semper ad te vigilet*) for the flesh not to succumb to the overwhelming and shrewd force of the devil (*Ne caro illi consentiat*).

It is with such a pattern of ideas in mind that we must evaluate Lydgate's response to this text, and since the choice of the ballad stanza offers the poet double the space provided by the Latin quatrain, amplification is predictably the poet's favourite device. This technique is quite often seen as mere repetition: that this is not so is proved by the fact that it may be used either to select and emphasize a theme, or to comment on a single word to point out some of its possible connotations. Let us consider the rendering of the first stanza:

> Christe, qui lux es et dies,
> Noctis tenebras detegis,
> Lucisque lumen crederis,
> Lumen beatum predicans.

> Cryst, that art boothe daye and light,
> And soothefaaste sonne of al gladnesse,
> That doost awey derknesse of night,
> And souereyne light of al brightnesse
> Beleved art in sothefastnesse,
> Preching this blissful light of pees,
> Be oure socour in alle distresse,
> Christe qui lux es et dies. (MacCracken 1962: 235-237)

Lydgate's task was particularly hard in this case, since the short Latin quatrain contains itself some repetition, with the key words *lux* and *lumen* used twice. The poet rightly chooses to emphasize the theme of Christ as light, and in this respect even the fact that the antagonistic motif of darkness is given only one line may be relevant. In doing so he introduces two new elements, one to underline the regality of Christ celebrated as "sonne" and "souereyne light", the other to specify that happiness means above all peace when he expands *beatum lumen* into "this blissful light of pees". The motif of joy is doubled by the phrase "sonne of al gladnesse", the relationship between joy and peace anticipates the double request of the second stanza (*Sit nobis in te requies / Quietam noctem tribue*). The line "Be oure socour in alle distresse" has no correspondent in the Latin, but must not be taken as a mere addition in that it too anticipates what is going to be, from the second stanza on, the main theme of the hymn: the haunting presence of Satan and the consequent call for help against any kind of temptation.

An attentive reader, as a devout believer meditating on a spiritual text is supposed to be, cannot fail to notice the emphasis Lydgate puts on the night devils and their tricky suggestions. Against two mentions of this presence in the Latin, Lydgate has five, of which two are to be found in stanzas where the original has none. So, probably prompted by the simple verb *defende*, they appear in the second stanza as "alle foon that vs werraye", much as the verb *protegat* may have suggested the "whanne oure foomen vs manace" of the fourth stanza. In the other three cases they translate the Latin: *nec hostis nos surripiat* becomes "Ne that oure foo vs vndermyne" (st. 3), and *insidiantes reprime* is rendered by "oure wayting enemys thou represse", repeated by a prayer "that the feonde vs nought oppresse" (st. 5). It seems only too natural to find a similar emphasis on the opposite theme of rest and quiet, where again we have four mentions in three different stanzas against two in one stanza of the Latin: the two additions are to be seen in the rendering of *lumen beatum* by "blissful light of pees" in st. 1, and possibly in *somnium* translated by "rest" in st. 4 against all other versions where "sleep" in its various forms is preferred.

Another predictable expansion is on the motif of the Passion occurring in the fifth stanza, where the Latin *quos sanguine mercatus es* becomes "Whome thou boughtest in gret distresse / With thyne hooly bloode moost fre", a stress reinforced by the rendering of *defensor* by "chaumpyoun" in the first line, and the double evocation of the "enemys" already mentioned. The theme is repeated in the following stanza, where the invocation to Christ for him to keep and preserve us is supported by "Sith thou boughtest vs so deere". On this and other points it may be interesting to consider the version found in the Bannatyne MS (*Index*, No. 612) which, being in eight-line stanzas, is of the eight versions extant the one more easily comparable with Lydgate's.[19] Here is, for example, the translation of the same stanza 5 just examined:

> Defensor noster aspice,
> Insidiantes reprime,
> Guberna tuos famulos
> Quos sanguine mercatus es.

> Defensor noster, aspice,
> our anely god and defendowr,
> behald our enomus, and se
> ay watand ws fra howr til hour.
> Thow send ws help fra hewynis towr
> to brek his power and his press,
> and saif ws fra his saltis sour,
> Et nos sanguine mercatus es. (Stevenson 1918: 20-21).

Practically only the first two lines have been translated and expanded into six English verses: the stress is entirely on the dramatic and cosmic fight between God and the legion of the devils, to the point that even the verb *aspice*, which is normally intended, and accordingly translated as "look at us" said on the part of the praying community of believers, is here turned to mean "behald our enomiis", whose anger (*wratht*) and destructive violence (*bailful bratht*) are recalled in the second stanza and connected with the arch-devil "balial". The Scottish poet uses the first and last line of the Latin quatrain to open and close his stanzas, and this may explain why "*quos sanguine mercatus es*" remains untranslated. But it is nevertheless worth noting that he does

---

19   A full detailed list of the ME translations of this hymn together with some comparisons and the text of two previously unpublished versions (*Index* No. 616 and *Supplement* No. 620.5) can be found in Robbins (1954).

not address his appeal to the crucifix, but to a victorious Christ whose help does not descend from the cross, but from a "heavenly tower". All in all, it seems that this version tends to dramatise and inflate the text beyond its simple meaning, so that a prayer for the incoming night is projected towards the end of the world and the final meeting with Christ: "Thow grant ws all [...] / of thi wisage til hef ane sycht" is said in the first stanza, and "one dumisday, quhen we sal dred, / Adesto nobis, domine" is the anxious cry concluding the sixth stanza. These eschatological accents, though congruent with the Christian interpretation of night as a metaphor of death, and well present in other liturgical evening prayers, are in fact outside the literal meaning of the hymn. That the translator felt himself free to insert them only means that he was working in the larger context of Christian devotion, and it is against such wider pattern of ideas that his and other translations of hymns are to be judged. On the other hand, to prove the unpredictability of any translation, and to recall how far our sense of uniformity of tone can be from the mind of the late medieval translator, it suffices to look at the second stanza, which opens on the quiet atmosphere of a domestic interior, with the devout believer kneeling beside his bed to say his prayer, specifically "this empne", that is the *Christe qui lux*:

> and gyf ws grace that we may say
> this empne so plesandly to the,
> to bed quhen that we bown ws ay,
> noctem quietam tribue.

This quotation brings us back to the third protagonist of the hymn, the Christian believer torn between his allegiance to God and the temptations of the devil. The only word used to describe him is *famulus*, which appears twice, in the fourth and fifth stanzas. Lydgate accordingly picks up this image of service, and as he does with other key words, rightly underlines it by anticipating the idea ("in thy servyce oure lyff to spende", st. 2), doubling its expression ("thee for to serve yche houre and space" and "defende thy servantes", st. 4). or simply translating it ("gouverne thy servantes", st. 5). If *famulus* renders man's tension towards God, another key word is used to express his reluctance to follow his vocation and the consequent weakness which exposes him to the wiles of the devil: *gravis*. The adjective appears also twice in the hymn, applied to sleep (*Ne gravis somnus irruat*) and to the body (*In gravi isto corpore*). Sleep may be dangerous in that it dulls the spiritual senses which should always be alert, and so is the body in its being heavy and slow to follow in the footsteps of Christ. Lydgate seems not particularly responsive to this image, since he renders it straightly by "greuous" in both cases. The Bannatyne poet more originally speaks of "dully dremys" in the first case, and of "friuell flesch" in the second, while James Ryman in his three versions of the hymn tries different solutions to grasp the various implications of this adjective conveying images of heaviness, slowness, torpidity, and, consequently, spiritual fragility: "this body fraell of kyende" (*Index*, No. 618). "(of us) that be of kynde so ponderous" (*Index*, No. 619), "(of us) so heuy that be and frayll of kynde" (*Index*, No. 617).[20] We may notice that after two attempts he manages to keep together the two meanings he has extracted from the word, and that his stress on human 'fragility' has the flavour of Franciscan compassion, which can hardly be found in the "frivolous flesh" of the Bannatyne poet. Ryman tries the same variation with *gravis somnus*, rendered respectively by "synfull slepe", "ne slepe oppresse us", "slepe, that is vile". The connection between a torpid sleep and sin is prompted by the Latin stanza in which Christ's helping light is invoked to prevent the flesh from consenting to the enemy, and so fall into sin (*Nec caro illi consentiat / Nos tibi reos statuat*). Lydgate's translation of these two lines is worth quoting:

> Ne that oure flesshe of frowardnesse
> Assent the spyrit to enclyne,
> For to bring it to ruyne,
> Thee to gilt thorough theire debate...

There may be an echo of *gravis somnus* in the "frowardnesse" of the flesh, but what is more interesting is that the fight against the devil is turned into an inner struggle, a "debate" between the flesh and the

---

20   Ryman's versions are published in Zupitza (1892). The three versions of *Christe qui lux* are on p. 196 (*Index* No. 618), pp. 325-326 (*Index* No. 619), and pp. 326-327 (Index No. 617).

spirit[21] and that the idea of sin as "guilt" is enriched by the two expressive images of the spirit drawn downwards and brought to ruin.

One point of my analysis was to compare Lydgate's renderings with other versions. In the case of *Christe qui lux es et dies* the difficulty lies in the fact that, apart from the one in the Bannatyne MS, all the versions are in four-line stanzas, which means that no amplification is allowed, with the consequent elimination of the very ground on which comparison can be made. It is only possible to compare different solutions adopted for certain key words, as we have seen in Ryman's translations of *gravis*. But to show how, even with a narrower space available, a good translator can be both faithful to the Latin and original in the choice of words and in the emphasis put on certain motifs, I quote from the version extant in MS Harley 665 (*Index* No. 616) one of the best renderings of the same stanza 5 analysed above:

> Behold to vs, defender god,
> Put doon oure enmys wyld and wood;
> Thou governe hem that bawghtyst on rood,
> Lord Iesu, with thy swete blode (Robbins 1954: 60).

Lydgate's version is not always successful. There are phrases which to a modern reader sound commonplace, only good at filling up a line, as can be seen in such expressions as: "thy servantes yonge and olde", "preserue vs euery membre", "as bookis leere", "in mescheef boothe fer and neere". Particularly disappointing is the rendering of *famulos qui te diligunt* by "thy servantes in yche a place".[22] But these appear to be minor faults compared with his achievement in transforming a hymn of ancient origin composed to be sung in public worship into a text to be used for private meditation by his fellow Christians.

---

21   This may be another suggestion of the evangelical episode of the agony of Christ which forms, as I have said, the spiritual background of the hymn: "Watch ye and pray, lest ye enter into temptation. The spirit truly is ready, but the flesh is weak" (Mark 14:38).

22   Compare "thy seruantys that the love and pray" of the Harley version just quoted, or one of Ryman's renderings: "Thy seruauntis, lorde, that the dothe loue."

3. Concluding remarks

As a conclusion I should like to remark that while it is true that Lydgate's translational technique relies heavily on amplification, it remains to be seen what this means, and to what purposes this method is used. From my analysis of the versions of these two hymns I can say that the text is extended in at least three ways:

a)   more or less synonymous repetition, or mere amplification: e.g.,

   royal banerys   standart celestyal
   soothefaaste sonne   souereyne light

b)   specification, which in a sense restricts the meaning: e.g.,

   ave spes unica   O only hope to wrecchis in distresse
   lumen beatum   blissful light of pees

c)   expansion of an idea or a theme either by clarifying its implicit meaning or by recourse to the wider theological and devotional context of the Christian tradition: e.g.,

   ornata regis purpura   wyth royal purplys al bloody was thyn hewe

   qui es defensor anime, / adesto nobis, domine.
   Keepe and preserue vs euery membre, / Sith thou boughtest vs so deere, /
   Which art defence, as bookis leere, / Of the soule thorughe the pytee...

This last example shows all the three methods at work together: synonymous repetition (*keepe and preserue*), specification (*thorughe the pytee*), addition (*sith thou boughtest vs so deere*). It is with special reference to this third technique of amplification, predictably more widely used in the *Vexilla Regis* given the dense theological quality of the hymn, that I have described Lydgate's translations as including both "interpretation and commentary". To understand how this can be done, and why, it is necessary to remember that we are dealing with Christian texts for prayer, in our case Latin liturgical hymns, which are embedded in a rich and unbroken tradition of thought and devotion shared by the translator and the users of his versions. As for the utility

288

of Lydgate's methods of amplification I need not prove how much repetitions, specifications, and explanatory additions can help when meditating or praying a text. Finally, we should also consider the linguistic value of anticipations and echoes together with the varied use of words and phrases belonging to the same semantic field to give cohesion and coherence to a text.

In his study on John Lydgate, before analysing his religious poems, Derek Pearsall (1970: 256) rightly observes that

> Medieval religious poetry is all practical, and its practical purpose is always to sustain faith and aid devotion [...]. The immediate interest of medieval religious poetry for us, therefore, is as poetry, products of literary art not as documents of individual psychology, and their wider interest is in their profound and often complex reference to a structure of thought and belief which dominated and, in enfeebled form, still affects the Western mind.

I have tried to show some of the "complex references" Lydgate makes while translating, and the efficacy of his various translational techniques for the "practical purpose" he had presumably in his mind. That the modem reader finds it difficult to appreciate these poems is most probably due to the fact that he has lost many of these references, not to mention his practical purpose when reading them, of which the least we can say is that it rarely corresponds to that of the medieval user of these prayers. Once we recover both these references and purpose Lydgate's poems may be judged in a more correct light, and above all they may come to life again.

Part III

Saints' Lives

Bede's *Vita* of Gregory the Great in the Old English version of *Historia Ecclesiastica Gentis Anglorum*[1]

1. Introduction: Gregory the Great and the conversion of the Anglo-Saxons

Anglorum iam apostolus / nunc angelorum socius (Once apostle to the Angles / now companion to the angels): these are the first two lines of the hymn Peter Damian wrote in praise of Pope Gregory the Great (see Dreves / Blume 1886-1922: vol. 48, no. 45). The wordplay on *Angli / Angeli* echoes a famous anecdote which, according to a long tradition, is at the origin of the mission sent in 596 A.D. by Pope Gregory to evangelize the Saxons who had settled in England. This initiative is so relevant in the pastoral activity, or better in the whole biography of Gregory that it forms what is probably the best known of his epithets: he is 'the apostle of the Angles', as Peter Damian's hymn shows so well right from its first line. The enterprise is in fact relevant for at least three reasons. The first concerns the spiritual profile of Gregory in that it reflects his missionary passion; the second is related to the conversion of the German peoples, of whom the Anglo-Saxons themselves were an important section, and of which they were to become the main protagonists in the persons of Willibrord and Winfrid-Boniface; the third is connected with both the strategy of the expedition and the evangelizing methodology as can be seen in a group of letters and instructions with which the Pope accompanied the mission, which taken together constitute a sort of wise and balanced

---

1 An earlier version of this chapter was published in Italian in Cipolla/Nicoli (2006: 1-23).

treatise by which Gregory can be rightly qualified as "a great precursor of practical theology" (Seumois 1953: 84). In a very concise way Bertram Colgrave affirms that the meeting between Gregory and some young slaves from Anglia in the Roman market place, marked by its famous sequence of word-plays, of which the one on *Angli / Angeli* is only the first, "forms a picturesque if legendary beginning to a train of events that was to alter the whole face of Europe" (1968: 1).[2]

All this is confirmed by the constant and widespread popularity enjoyed by Gregory as 'father of the English Christianity',[3] not only in the 'Roman' sees of Canterbury and York, but also at Malmesbury and Whitby, whose origins are strongly linked to the Irish mission. One of the first witnesses of this popularity is Aldhelm of Malmesbury, who describes the Pope as "a highly vigilant shepherd, *our* pedagogue, *ours* I say, since he eliminated the error of bleak heathenism from our ancestors, and gave them the law of the regenerating grace" (*De Virginitate*, 55). In the same vein the anonymous monk of Whitby, author of the first *Vita* of Gregory, calls him "our master", "our doctor", repeatedly qualifying him by the adjective "our" (*passim*). The highest praise can be found in Bede, who in the hagiographic profile devoted to Gregory in his *Historia Ecclesiastica* (hereafter *HE*) declares that the Pope is rightly entitled to be called "apostle" since, he says, "nostram gentem [...] Christi fecit ecclesiam" (he made our nation... into a church of Christ) (*HE* II:i).[4] In his historical commentary to Bede's work, J.M. Wallace-Hadrill rightly remarks that "This making of the Church of England is seen by Bede as something else: the making of the English people" (1988: 49).

The delightful anecdote telling Gregory's encounter with the Anglian slaves, a story so famous that it went into the *Golden Legend*, will be examined later in more detail. First it is important to focus on

---

2   In fact, the Christian faith brings to England "le latin, les éléments du droit
     romain, les écoles épiscopales et monastiques, c'est-à-dire la civilisation.
     L'Angleterre devint rapidement un réservoir de la latinité [...]. Par la mission
     d'Augustin, Grégoire a arrimé l'Angleterre à l'Europe chrétienne et scellé son
     destin pour tout un millénaire" (Chélini 2000: 53). See also Gameson (2000).
3   See Meyvaert (1977: 1) and Dales (2005).
4   I quote Bede from Colgrave/Mynors (1969). For practical reasons the quota-
     tions are indicated within the text.

the place and relevance Gregory the Great holds in Bede's *Historia*. His significance in the whole plan of Bede's account is immediately perceived when we consider that the long chapter devoted to illustrating Gregory's hagiographic profile, including his death and epitaph, is positioned right at the beginning of the second book of *HE*, that is in a strategic place, apparently purposely chosen, since in the chapters following the first Bede narrates events which took place before the death of the Pope.[5] Bede himself gives reason to think of a deliberate choice since he says: "De quo (Gregorio) nos conuenit, quia nostram, id est Anglorum, gentem de potestate Satanae ad fidem Christi sua industria conuertit, latiorem in nostra historia ecclesiastica facere sermonem" (II:i).[6] Bede inserts other *Vitae* in his work, such as, for example, those of the monk-bishop Aidan (III:5) or the saintly king Oswald (III:6),[7] but it is absolutely evident that "Gregory is his hero, as Benedict had been for Gregory" (Leonardi 2004: 137).

The very use of the word 'hero' suggests a hermeneutical category bordering on mythology. Without entering into complex debates on the subject, we can safely posit that the genre of hagiography has some mythical elements in it, but this does not prevent the genre from being used even in history books, as Bede himself shows. The main point to be considered is that on the one hand hagiography does not coincide with sheer invention, and on the other stories of saints have first of all a paradigmatic and exemplary value. This second aspect can even be more important, and it certainly lies behind the strong emphasis put on the virtues of the saints, and can also produce imaginary details in the narration proper, especially in the 'miracles'. Suffice it here to recall in passing that the governing model for Christian historians, of whom Bede is one of the best, is the biblical book of the *Acts of the Apostles*, where history is understood

---

5   Meyvaert remarks that in the Leningrad manuscript of *Hist. Eccl.* the 'Life' of Gregory starts on f. 26v with a big illuminated capital letter, unique in the manuscript, containing the portrait of the Pope: the miniature is reproduced in Meyvaert (1977: 3).

6   "Well indeed may we, the English nation converted by his efforts from the power of Satan to the faith of Christ, give a somewhat full account of him in our *History of the Church*": Colgrave-Mynors (1969: 122-123).

7   See, among others, the *Vitae* of King Sigbert (III:18), Saint Chad (IV:3), Abbess Hilda (IV:23), Saint Cuthbert (IV:27-32), Saint Wilfrid (V:19), etc.

as the unfolding of God's plan of salvation through human events. This means that the writer adopts not a casual but a 'providential' interpretation, and this implies as a natural consequence the fact that quite often the tone becomes hortatory and homiletic by the use, among other materials, of a hagiographical model of saintly life. To quote just a well-known example in the same area dealt with by Bede, it is certainly not surprising that in his *De excidio et conquestu Britanniae* the British priest Gildas presents the Saxon invasions as a punishment for the sins of the Britons. This way of interpreting history was perfectly in line with what saint Augustine had already done in his *De Civitate Dei*, not to mention Eusebius, whom Bede acknowledges as his master and model – see Markus (1983a).

To Bede, Pope Gregory is, then, first of all the Father of the English Church, since he is at the origin of the mission which under the leadership of Augustine reached Kent in 597 and started the evangelization of that Saxon kingdom. In fact Gregory did not only inspire the initiative: he remained the true guide, the organizing mind, the man who in his fervour urges and supports a monk who right from the beginning appears rather reluctant to engage in the enterprise and seems to move entirely in the shadow of the Pope. It is Gregory who prepares the way to Augustine, entrusting him to bishops and kings who are asked to support him with their comfort (*solacium*); it is he who praises him and at the same time invites him to remain humble in his success, gives him instructions about practical pastoral problems, and at the end provides him with the needed juridical authority by establishing him as the Head of the English Church. The historiographic interpretation evident in Bede's *Historia* stresses the crucial importance of the Roman mission in the conversion of the Saxons to such an extent that it obscures any other possible contribution. The Frankish Church seems to offer no help, while the British Church is shown as having an attitude of open hostility at least towards Augustine. I will not go into greater detail here, but I think it is useful to report that the more recent historical research tends to integrate the dominantly Roman vision offered by Bede with signals of an apparently rather active participation of the Frankish Church in the mission. Even the British clergy, who according to Bede allegedly first refused to evangelize the invading Saxons out of an understandable resentment, and later opposed Augustine's authority out of a pride which could hardly be evangelically justified, seems to have offered some form of collaboration.[8] In any case it is evident that Bede writes from a perspective proper to his people, the Angles, and that in this perspective nothing can diminish the decisive role Gregory had in their conversion, a fact which had as its main consequence the entrance of a people living at the farthest northern corners of the western world into the great 'watercourse' of classical Romanitas.

As for Gregory himself, there is, in Bede, another aspect which comes to the foreground in the *Vita*, and this is his exemplary significance as a saint, in particular as pastor and master interpreter of the Scriptures. To quote, once again, Wallace-Hadrill: "This famous sketch of the life of Gregory the Great is more than a summary of facts culled from well-known sources. It embodies Bede's view of the ideal episcopal career, such as was seldom seen in his own day in England. Gregory was at once the contemplative, the ascetic *doctor* capable of expounding the mysteries of the Bible, and the man of action, the *pastor*" (1988: 48). These words only confirm what has been said about the hagiographical genre being a mixture of facts and ideals.

2. Gregory's *Vita* in Bede's *Historia Ecclesiastica*

It is time now to outline the hagiographic profile of Pope Gregory drawn by Bede as a solemn entrance to the second book of his *Historia*. Starting from the Pope's family origins, Bede underlines at the start Gregory's choice to be a monk, a condition understood in the well-known terms of 'angelic life', anticipating thus the 'true' life we shall have in Heaven, compared with which this earthly life is almost a death – see Markus (1983b). This is the reason why Gregory often

---

8   See Meens (1994) and Wood (1994). Wood remarks: "There is in his (Bede's) narrative none of the complexity which is being unravelled by current scholars, with British communities surviving in the East, and with British clergy even assisting in the conversion of those Saxons who settled further West" (2000: 176). In this short paragraph I summarize what I have described in a much more detailed and documented way in the item 'Inghilterra' due to appear in *Enciclopedia Gregoriana*.

complains about the "distractions" caused to him by his worldly duties, although Bede is eager to remark that "nos credere decet nihil eum monachicae perfectionis perdidisse occasione curae pastoralis" (we need not believe that he had lost any of his monastic perfection by reason of his pastoral care), rather the opposite! We have here a crystal-clear presentation of the ideal of a perfect union between active and contemplative life. In fact Gregory, even during his pontificate, as he had done in important public missions such as the one he led in Constantinople, had turned his own house into a monastery (*domum suam monasterium facere curauit*).

Gregory's being at the time mystic and pastor shows up clearly in his writings. Bede presents in some detail the great works of the Pope: the *Moralia in Job*, the *Cura pastoralis*, the *Homiliae in Evangelia*, those on *Ezekiel*, the *Dialogues*, the *Letters* and, obviously, the famous *Libellus* containing Gregory's answers to a set of pastoral questions posed by Augustine in connection with his missionary activity, a booklet which, together with a group of letters related to the mission, Bede thought appropriate to insert in his *Historia*. In describing the spiritual portrait of the great Pope we find some polemical remarks, as the one concerning the use of money: "Nam alii quidam pontifices construendis ornandisque auro uel argento ecclesiis operam dabant, hic autem totus erga animarum lucra uacabat."[9] After this we find the praise of the virtues proper to Gregory, mainly charity, materialized in works of bodily and spiritual mercy. The mission to the Angles is set in this light: "Ad cuius pietatis et iustitiae opus pertinet etiam hoc, quod nostram gentem per praedicatores, quos huc direxit, de dentibus antiqui hostis eripiens aeternae libertatis fecit esse

---

9   "Other popes applied themselves to the task of building churches and adorning them with gold and silver, but he devoted himself entirely to winning souls" (Colgrave/Mynors 1969: 129). This remark, as Wallace-Hadrill observes, is hardly justifiable in the light of the *Liber Pontificalis*, where the rich donations of Gregory to the Basilica of St Peter are registered. We have here a typical specimen of hagiographic writing: "Bede omits what does not contribute to the picture of the Pope he wished to present to his readers; and that picture is a piece of hagiography, and not biography in our sense" (Wallace-Hadrill 1988: 50).

participem."[10] Bede quotes, here, the highly poetic description of the success of this enterprise Gregory himself gives in his *Moralia* (xxvii,11,21), following which Bede takes the opportunity to remind his reader that, according to Gregory's witness, "sanctus Augustinus et socii eius non sola praedicatione uerborum sed etiam *caelestium ostensione signorum* gentem Anglorum ad agnitionem veritatis perducebant".[11] The words I have italicised show that, according to hagiographical rules, there is no sanctity without miracles: it has been proved that, since there was no *Liber miraculorum* at Canterbury, Bede inserted in his *Historia* two miracles attributed to Augustine which he took from another source.[12] The profile registers also an addition which Gregory is said to have made to the Canon of the Mass.[13]

After this ample illustration of the Pope's personality, the *Vita* ends by the death and burial of Gregory, followed by the transcription of the epitaph laid on his tomb in St Peter's Basilica, three small fragments of which have been recently discovered; the famous anecdote of Gregory's meeting with the young English slaves concludes the profile. The collocation of the story is apparently rather strange. It might be a sort of picturesque and effective rhetorical *conclusio*. More probably this choice can be explained by the fact that the story has no sure historical foundation, since Bede qualifies it as an 'opinion' "which has come down to us as a tradition of our

---

10 "To his work of piety and justice this also belongs, that he snatched our race from the teeth of the ancient foe and made them partakers of everlasting freedom by sending us preachers" (Colgrave/Mynors 1969: 131).

11 "St. Augustine and his companions led the English race to the knowledge of the truth, not only by preaching the Word but also by showing heavenly signs" (Colgrave/Mynors 1969: 131).

12 See Wood (2000), who remarks that "For Bede Augustine was indeed a charismatic, and he was unquestionably a miracle worker" (p. 158), adding anyway that "While Augustine and his colleagues were known to have been wonderworkers, Canterbury, mindful of Gregory the Great's fear of vainglory, made no attempt to keep record of their miracles [...]. Faced with the absence of any record, Bede borrowed two or three miracles from elsewhere to give the earliest archbishops their due" (p. 168).

13 Wallace-Hadrill remarks that this addition to the Eucharistic anaphora could not have been derived, as Colgrave thought, from the *Liber Pontificalis*, where there is no complete registration of the petitions added to the Canon (1988: 50).

forefathers" (opinio[14] quae de beato Gregorio traditione maiorum ad nos usque perlata est), and it is on the basis of this tradition, received from the ancestors (ab antiquis), that he thinks proper to insert (oportunum inserere) the episode in his *Ecclesiastical History*. The same story appears in a slightly different version in the anonymous *Vita Gregorii* (Colgrave 1968: 90), a text written by a monk of Whitby between 704 and 714 (Colgrave 1968: 48), that is about ten years before Bede. Both writers refer back to a Northumbrian tradition whose meaning is something which modern historians, by using the testimony of Gregory's letters, acknowledge as a real fact; i.e. the decision taken by the Pope to evangelize the Anglo-Saxons was not an unpredictable stroke of genius, but part of a project he had nursed for a long time. This is clearly suggested by what Bede writes at the end of the Pope's profile, when he says that by the mission to the Angles Gregory fulfilled the task which he had *long* desired (perfecit opus *diu* desideratum).[15] The anecdote then would be a delightful and lively 'narration' materializing a dream coming true on the part of the Pope. If the story was 'invented', the desire expressed by it was not.

---

14   Both Sherley-Price (1978) and Colgrave/Mynors (1969) translate *opinio* by 'story', a term I think is too strong and could be misleading. On what Bede himself may have thought of the factual truth of this episode see what Wallace-Hadrill observes in his Commentary: "Both the beginning and the end of the story, as Bede tells it, suggest that he wanted his readers to understand that it was traditional and generally accepted. He thus places it in a category that would be understood. As to its historicity, he is still in the realm of hagiography, and it may be irrelevant whether or not he considered it to be a 'fact'; but at least he is quite sure that the story ought to be related" (1988: 51).

15   "La mission d'Augustin n'est pas un geste isolé. Elle s'inscrit dans une politique missionnaire à la fois hardie, mais aussi réaliste, asseoir plus largement l'autorité du pape chez les Barbares, devenus les maîtres de l'Occident" (Chélini 2000: 43).

3. The Old English translation of Gregory's *Vita*

When we come to consider the OE translation of this chapter of Bede's *Historia*[16] my first remark is that within the very famous corpus of the so-called "Alfredian" translations, the adjective being now taken to mean "made in Alfred's time"[17], that of Bede's work has not received much attention among the scholars, as can be seen when surveying the bibliography of the last decades – see Waite (2000: VI/ 42-46, 321-353). The point most frequently discussed is whether Alfred was the real translator of the *Historia*, a point which, although clearly stated by Aelfric,[18] was first called into question in 1876 by Henry Sweet in the first edition of his well-known and often reprinted *Anglo-Saxon Reader*.[19] The problem of the authorship has been analysed again and again, with predictable stances for or against Alfred, often based on linguistic arguments, such as the prevalent Mercian quality of the dialect, not congruent with Alfred's West Saxon, or on the quality of the translation. The dominant linguistic approach appears in many studies dealing with lexis, dialect characteristics, syntax and style.[20] In my approach I will consider the possible criteria lying behind the re-writing of Gregory's *Vita* on the part of the translator, and present a short analysis of his translational practices in terms of lexis and syntax.

When one compares Bede's Latin text with the OE version, the first impression one gets is almost shocking: the extended eulogy

16   All the quotations are taken from the modern edition (Miller 1890); the mark
      7 has been regularly expanded as *ond.*

17   That the OE version of Bede's *Historia* was made by Alfred himself or not is
      relatively unimportant. More relevant is the fact that it is part of Alfred's
      'cultural programme' together with the translation of philosophical and
      theological (Augustine's *Soliloquia* and Boethius' *De consolatione*), pastoral
      (Gregory the Great's *Dialogi* and *Cura Pastoralis*) and historical works
      (Orosius' *Historiae adversus paganos*). On the influence of Gregory's thought
      on Alfred the Great see Crépin (1986) and Gameson (1995).

18   "Historia Anglorum, ða ðe Ælfred cyning of Ledene on Englisc awende": 'On
      St Gregory's Day' (in Godden 1979: IX/ 72).

19   One of the most informed and well documented surveys of the entire problem
      is Whitelock (1980). For a different opinion see Kuhn (1972).

20   See an excellent and practical summary in Waite (2000: 44-45).

praising Gregory as father and apostle of the English Christianity, placed with clear emphasis at the heart of the profile to justify the ample space given to the great Pope in the *Historia*, has totally disappeared. The translator structures his own *Vita* in three parts: he links the introductory paragraph with the one about Gregory's death and burial; this is followed by the epitaph, and by the story of the English slaves; the very long central section describing the spirituality, the writings and the charity of Gregory is omitted. Of the 212 lines which the text occupies in Colgrave's edition, only 64 have been translated, that is a little more than a quarter. Such a stark 'reduction' is surprising and not easily explained (see Whitelock 1980: 72; 87, fn 130). If it is true, as has been said, that the translator is primarily interested only in what concerns the English church,[21] his omission of Gregory's eulogy for what he did precisely for the Anglo-Saxons appears strange, unless he thought it superfluous, given the great stress he puts on the story of the young Angles which can be read as a 'narrative' condensation of Gregory's profile. Whitelock suggests that the translator works in a period of cultural decadence, where the historical and documentary consciousness is no longer as high as it was in Bede's time: this shows for example in the need he feels to explain many biblical references which Bede could take for granted. This supposition does not appear entirely satisfactory to explain the 're-writing' produced by our translator. Besides, we must be careful not to equate the possible cultural decadence of the audience with the cultural poverty of the translator, who in our case seems to be a clever and subtle writer, as will be shown in the analysis of the *Vita*. We must not forget that in any translation project the target may be as relevant as the source text, or even more so. Whitelock affirms that the project of the translator seems to be the production of an edifying work: his omissions seem to be dictated not so much by the need to reduce the space of a long work (in fact he translates all the miracles but one) but should be rather ascribed to a poor interest in the sources (1980: 75). This may be true. I think that this OE translation of Bede's *Historia* is primarily a 'compendium', not so bad after all, a sort of

---

21   Whitelock (1980: 62) says: "His tendency to confine himself to English affairs explains […] the omission […] of the parts of the chapter on Gregory which do not relate to the English Church."

popularization which makes Bede's book more readable and thus available to an audience which must have been larger, although less sophisticated culturally and linguistically.

4. An analysis of the Old English *Life of Gregory the Great*

Turning now to the specific analysis of the chapter devoted to Gregory's *Vita*, we may remark that this 'compendious' translation has been cleverly made, and with a clear sense of organization. In fact Bede's longer text has been reduced and re-composed around three main points: chronicle information on Gregory's birth, pontificate and death; the epitaph containing the eulogy in praise of his sanctity; the story of the young slaves marking in a direct and picturesque way the connection between Gregory and the English Church. Such connection is indeed specifically celebrated in the final statement, which after taking up Bede's text literally, adds a significant concluding clause, here italicised, declaring that Gregory's mission had realized God's project and the salvation of the Angles:

> Ond he Sanctus Gregorius mid his trymnessum ond mid his gebedum wæs gefultumende, þæt heora laar wære wæstbeorende *to Godes willan ond to ræde Ongolcynne*
>
> [And by his exhortations and prayers St Gregory gave his help, that their teaching might bear fruit according to God's will and to the salvation of the English people.]

The conclusive force of the clause is emphasized by the omission of Bede's final sentence concerning the origin of the story, given as an "opinion received from the ancestors". So we have a 'new' *Life*, where the reduction produces a sort of medallion in which different linguistic genres are combined: annalistic prose, celebratory poetry and a narrative including dialogues. It is precisely this difference that invites the study of the translation to see whether we have also different linguistic responses on the part of the translator.

It must be said that on the whole the OE translation of Bede's *Ecclesiastical History* has not received many compliments. It has been dismissed as 'over-literal', and the rich presence of doublets led to the suggestion that the translator was in fact primarily a glossator, rarely able to creatively face the syntactic complexities of a true and proper translation. Moreover, the passage we are going to examine had the chance, both felicitous and infelicitous, to be used by Aelfric in his homily for the feast of St Gregory. The result of the comparison between the anonymous translator and the master of OE prose was largely predictable. We can see this in what Dubois said in a study in which, after analysing this passage against what Aelfric writes in his homily, qualified Aelfric's style as "coulant et limpide" [fluid and clear] contrasting it with that of the OE Bede as "confus et souvent lourd" [confused and often heavy] (1943: 228). Fifty years later we find that the evaluation is reversed by St-Jacques (1983: 86, 101), who thinks that this translator has a "sure grasp of prose styles and a fine narrative craftsmanship", contributing to a "true heightening of the readers' emotional response to the people and situations Bede depicts". Such contrasting assessments give me the opportunity to remark that in evaluating the quality of a translation, a mixture of emotional, contingent or ideological factors can be influential in a more or less decisive way, and these are, among others, 1) the temperament of the scholar; 2) the sample chosen to analyse; 3) above all the idea of what a translation is, or should, or can be. It is always terribly hard to evaluate translations made centuries ago adequately, and the risk of deriving generalizations from few samples, perhaps chosen at random, is very high and should be carefully controlled.

Bearing this in mind, I should like to present some examples taken from the three parts of the OE *Vita* I have identified. For a more general judgement on the version of Bede's *Historia* I refer to Whitelock who, after a detailed analysis of the whole text, says that "the Old English Bede is not consistently an overliteral rendering. Beside passages which are stiff and clumsy can be set others which are vigorous and idiomatic. One may cite the account of Gregory's meeting with the Anglian youths for sale in Rome (even the stylist Ælfric did not disdain to borrow from this)" (Whitelock 1980: 76). What follows is a concise analysis of the entire passage subdivided into the three parts above identified.

4.1. The chronicle introduction

As I have remarked, the translator forms the initial paragraph of his *Vita* by combining the incipit of *HE* ii.1 with the news of the death and burial of Pope Gregory put by Bede at the end of his profile. Here is the first part of this paragraph:

> BEDE: His temporibus, id est anno dominicae incarnationis DCV, beatus papa Gregorius, postquam sedem romanae et apostolicae ecclesiae XIII annos menses sex et dies decem gloriosissime rexit, defunctus est, atque ad aeternam regni caelestis sedem translatus.

> OE: *Đissum tidum, þæt is fíf winter ond syx hund wintra æfter þære Drihtenlican menniscnesse, se eadiga papa Gregorius, æfter þon þe he þæt setl þære Romaniscan cyricean ond þære apostolican þreottyne gear ond syx monað ond tyn dagas wulderlice heold ond rehte, þa was forðfered ond to þam ecan setle þæs heofonlican rices læded wæs.*

The matter-of-fact register, typical of chronicle prose, would appear to lead to a literal translation. Only a few remarks on lexis are here in order. A technical term like *incarnatio* is rendered by "menniscness" (becoming man), a word more widespread than the more literal "geflæscness" (becoming flesh). The doublet "heold ond rehte" for *rexit* shows a frequent choice on the part of the translator, to the extent that it has been suggested that he may have been a glossator. The more idiomatic word order in the final sentence proves that this is not a 'literal' version in a pejorative sense. In the second sentence of this paragraph, not quoted here, it is worth noting the translation of another technical word, *secretarium*, where Bede says Gregory was buried. The term may indicate either a sacristy, or a parlour, or a room where a bishop deals with the affairs of his ministry.[22] Colgrave observes that "Ordinarily Bede seems to use the word in the sense of sanctuary" (1968: 165, fn 142). The term appearing in the OE version is "husulportic", that is a sacristy ('husul' is preserved in the now obsolete 'housel', a term meaning the Eucharist).

---

22 This seems to be the meaning suggested in the *Vita* of the monk of Whitby, where it is said that the pope "sepultus est ante eius officii secretarium" (Colgrave 1968: 138).

305

4.2. The epitaph of Pope Gregory

The text of the epitaph, translated as "byrgenleoð" (tomb-elegy), as is proper to a celebrative composition, is written in classical distichs. The sophisticated lexis and the compact structure of Latin poetry might have posed some problems to an awkward translator. It is not so. The choice of this only text in a long chapter devoted to illustrating Gregory's virtues and achievements is probably to be read in the logic of the compendium: in fact the epitaph is a good summary of Gregory's sanctity, except for his writings which are only implicitly evoked. We may surmise that the Pope's literary output had a lesser relevance to a reader for whom Gregory was not so much the author of widely appreciated biblical commentaries as the father of English Christianity, as is stressed in the concluding clause of the OE version, and this precisely because of his sanctity.

The translation is a correct rendering of the Latin verses, with some simplification of the syntax and little expansion in some clauses. This is, for example, the first distich:

BEDE: Suscipe, terra, tuo corpus de corpore sumtum
         Reddere quod ualeas uiuificante Deo.

OE: *Onfoh þu eorþe lichaman of þinum lichaman genumen,*
         Þæt þu hine eft agyfan mæge, þonne hine God liffæste.

This means: "Receive thou, o earth, a body which was taken from thy body, / that thou may give it back when God quickens it." The crucial verbal echo between the two "bodies" is maintained; the attention on Gregory's body is emphasised by the repetition of two "hine" (him) in the second line where the Latin has no pronoun at all, although this may be required by the English grammar; the absolute ablative cast in a participial form (*vivificante Deo*) is elegantly turned into a simpler temporal clause, with the added effect of a new rhythm in the second line. This solution compares favourably with a modern translation of Bede's work: "Receive, O earth, the body that you gave, / Till God

306

lifegiving power destroy the grave" (Sherley-Price 1978: 99).[23] This is an example of imaginative re-creation of a text, probably due to the decision to maintain the rhythm and rimes of a poem.

The translator's intention to produce a lexically simplified text is evident. In the line "Spiritus astra petit, loeti nil iura nocebunt", for example, *astra* is rendered by "heofon", and *letum* by "deað", a word which is found again in the following line to translate *mors*. The emphatic Latin poetical lexis built on subtle variations is abandoned in favour of more common words, even if this implies repetition.

The search for clarity is even more visible in the translation of another verse:

Esuriem dapibus superauit, frigora ueste
Earmra hungur he oferswiðde mid mettum, and heora cyle mid hrægle

Literally: "of the poor the hunger he overcame with food, and their cold with clothes". The Latin personifications Hunger (*esuriem*) and Cold (*frigora*) are replaced by the persons of the poor ("earmra"), and this gives a more emotional touch to the new sentence, which becomes also more transparent for being cast in perfect paratactic parallelism.

An example of expansion occurs in the translation of another line:

Esset ut exemplum mystica uerba loquens
Wæs he gerynelico word sprecende, þæt he lifes bysen wære haligra manna

This literally means: "Was he mystic words speaking, that he a life's example might be to holy men." Incidentally, this is the only mention in the epitaph of Gregory's preaching as reflected in his writings. A similar attitude of lexical simplification appears in the choice to translate *Dei consul*, one of the most fortunate qualifications of Gregory, by "Godes bysceop".

---

23   Compare also what I would call a 'poetical' translation of this distich in Colgrave/Mynors: "Earth, take this corpse – 'tis dust of thine own dust: / When God shall give new life, restore thy trust" (1969: 133).

4.3. The anecdote of the young Anglian slaves

A story is predictably more open to invention and re-writing, and it is in this part of the *Vita* that we find the most interesting choices of the translator, who renders the rather formal and cold style of the Latin text with a certain vivacity and, we may say, a happy narrative gusto.

The fact that we are 'hearing' a story, possibly due to the predictable context of its oral delivery, comes out clearly in some added or explicative clauses, such as "Þa gelomp" (It happened) not in the Latin, or "Þa gyt he furðor frægn ond cwæð" (Then he further asked and said), or "Þa gyt he ahsode" (Then he asked), or even the short "cwæð he" (he said), all translating the Latin short formula *at ille*. One may observe that Aelfric, dealing with the same material in his Homily for St Gregory's Feast, in which he seems to partly depend on this OE version, is more clear and precise,[24] but the point is that 'style' is not something existing in a vacuum, but should also be considered in relation to the intended audience. The remarks I will make mainly concern lexical and structural choices meant to render the text more comprehensible. These are the preference for parataxis together with repetitions and explicative additions so that the text receives a better cohesion, and can be better retrieved by people who were more likely to be listeners than readers.

On the status of the episode the translator apparently does not emphasize Bede's conviction: "hlisa", by which he translates *opinio*, means rumour, opinion, fame, but also glorious memory and renown, and one wonders whether this ambiguity is intended. In fact Bede concludes the episode by repeating that it is just an *opinio* although supported by an ancient tradition, but the translator omits this repetition, and prefers to end his *Vita* with the previously quoted addition

---

24   See Dubois (1943: 226-230), where the story of the young slaves is analysed by comparing in detail the OE version of Bede and Aelfric's Homily for the Feast of St Gregory. Dubois finds in Aelfric "clarté et netteté", stating that "AElfric vise surtout à la concision, afin d'éviter les lourdures et les répétitions" (p. 226). It is out of question that Aelfric masters a more refined style, not forgetting that he can use a language which in the meantime (he writes a century later) has developed in a significant way. But the problem is not well posed, especially if we think of a possible different destination and intention which can be hypothesised in the case of the Alfredian translation.

stating that Gregory's initiative was according to God's will and bore the fruit of the salvation to the English nation.

The comparative length of the passage and its literary genre allow quite a number of remarks on the choices of the translator. These may be summarized as repetitions, specifications and various additions together with a constant preference for parataxis. Although what results from the analysis should not be improperly extended to the whole translation of Bede's work, I have good reasons to think that these choices give a sufficient idea of the translational practice used in the OE version.

Here are some repetitions and expansions which, though not numerous, are worth paying attention to:

quos cum aspiceret
ða he ða heo geseah and beheold

de qua regione uel terra essent adlati. Dictumque est quia de Britannia insula *of hwelcon londe oðpe of hwylcre þeode hy brothe wæron. Sægde him mon, þæt heo of Breotene ealonde brothe wæron...*

accedens ad pontificem
he [...] eode to ðæm biscope and to ðam papan

si tamen apostolico papae hoc placeret
gif ðæm apostolican papan þæt licade, and ðæt his willa and his leafnis wære

Such repetitions may disturb the stylist, but are not necessarily to be intended as a pointless emphasis, rather may be justified if we think in terms of the passage being orally delivered to an audience not particularly intellectually refined according to the above mentioned hypothesis by Dorothy Whitelock. A good example of a similar choice is a sentence where both the use of a 'poor' vocabulary together with the addition of an explanatory phrase undoubtedly 'clarify' the more compact Latin:

BEDE: cum, aduenientibus nuper *mercatoribus*, multa *uenalia* in *forum* fuissent conlata

OE: come *cypemen* [of Brytene] and monig *cepe þing* on *ceapstowe* brohte

The two subordinates (absolute ablative and temporal proposition) are solved and put in the indicative; three different Latin words, here marked in italics, become practically one for being reduced to a single lexeme, "ceap" (today 'cheap', in OE meaning 'cattle' and 'goods'), from which "cypemen" (chapmen: merchants), "cepe þing" (goods), and "ceapstowe" (market-place) are derived; moreover it is specified that these merchants come from Brittany, a relevant element of the story which the translator has decided to evince.

Other expansions are meant to simplify the text, as can be seen in the clause *quod esset uocabulum gentis illius* translated by "hwæt seo þeod nemned wære þe heo of cwomon" (how was the nation named *from where they came*). Paraphrase in any case is not frequent, and there are also cuttings and reductions. An example is *ut aiunt* (as they say), inserted by Bede just before recounting Gregory's encounter with the slaves, as if to recall that the story is after all an *opinio*, a phrase that is not translated. Another reduction occurs in the rendering of a long sentence:

> BEDE: Heu, pro dolor, quod tam lucidi uultus homines tenebrarum auctor possidet, tantaque gratia frontispicii mentem ab interna gratia uacuam gestat!

> OE: *Wala wa: þæt is sarlic, þætte swa fæger feorh ond swa leohtes ondwlitan men scyle agan ond besittan þeostra aldor.*

> [Alas, it is grievous that such fair forms of men of such bright faces should be owned and possessed by the prince of darkness]

The sentence has been re-formatted in two ways: on the one hand by means of a doublet expanding *lucidi uultus homines*, on the other by ruling off the second part of the sentence built on the technical term *gratia* with its double meaning of physical and spiritual beauty, which Bede cleverly exploits by contrasting the external grace of the face to which no interior beauty corresponds. The translator has preferred the more physical contrast between light and darkness, which is marked in the person of Satan by another doublet, since he "owns and possesses" (for *possidet*) the souls of men having "such bright faces". Even a micro-unit such as this sentence may show a condensation of choices which are in themselves revealing.

There are other examples proving that this translator is not an awkward and careless craftsman who follows his source text literally. Two are at the end of the story. After mentioning Gregory's mission led by St Augustine he adds that this has already been told ("þe we ær beforan sægdon"). The other example is the choice to compose a concluding clause rather different from Bede's, who had ended the chapter by repeating that the episode was, anyway, an *opinio*. The translator, although faithful to the Latin, replaces Bede's concluding remark by a finale which has the solemn cadence of a doxology:

BEDE: alios quidam predicatores mittens, sed ipse praedicationem ut fructificaret, suis exhortationibus ac precibus adiuuans.

OE: *ond þa halgan lareowas hider onsende, þe we ær beforan sægdon. Ond he Sanctus Gregorius mid his trymnessum ond mid his gebedum wæs gefultumende, þæt heora laar wære wæstembeorende to Godes willan ond to ræde Ongolcynne.*

[and he sent here the holy teachers, of whom we spoke earlier. And St Gregory was helping by his exhortations and prayers, that their teaching might be fruitful according to God's will and with benefit to the English people.]

The Latin subordinate expressed in two verbs in the participial form (*mittens, adiuuans*) depends on and explains the preceding *opus perfecit*. By putting *mittens* in the indicative mood (onsende) the translator foregrounds and emphasizes the mission to the Angles as the subject of the sentence. On the other hand the second participial *adiuuans* and the final subjunctive *ut fructificaret* are both rendered by a progressive form ("wæs gefultumende": was helping; "wære wæstembeorende": were bearing fruit), as if what had already been acted (the mission) should be, and was in fact being continued in the English Church.

311

5. Concluding remarks

Before concluding I will focus my analysis on two passages which I suspect were adopted, or at least looked at by Aelfric who must have seen this translation and taken it into consideration.

The first is a sentence describing the young Angles:

> BEDE: candidi corporis, ac uenusti uultus, capillorum quoque forma egregia

> OE: *wæron hwites lichoman ond fægres ondwlitan men ond æðellice gefeaxe*

> AELFRIC: *wæron hwites lichaman and fægeres andwlitan menn and æðellice gefexode*

This is hardly mere coincidence. Aelfric certainly did not need to borrow from another translation. If he did, then, as Whitelock (1962) implicitly suggests, he must have appreciated the solution provided in the OE version in which three perfectly parallel clauses, each with two stressed words, correspond to a Latin structure where the three clauses are arranged in a rhythm of 2-2-4.

The second passage is an expansion meant to explain why the people of Rome did not want Gregory to leave for England as a missionary according to a request he had made to the Pope while he was still a priest:

> BEDE: etsi pontifex concedere illi, quod petierat, uoluit, non tamen ciues romani, ut tam longe ab urbe secederet, potuere permittere.

> OE: *þa ne wolde se papa þæt þafian ne þa burgware þon ma, þaette swa æðele wer ond swa getungen and swa gelæred swa feor fram him gewite.*

> [But the Pope would not allow that, nor yet the citizens, that a man so noble and so excellent and so learned should go so far from them]

> AELFRIC: *ða romaniscan ceastergewaran noldon geðafian þæt swa getogen mann and swa geðungen lareow þa burh eallunge forlete, and swa fyrlen wræcsið gename.*

The OE version amplifies the simple phrase *tam longe* by adding a triple clause to stress how important Gregory was for the people of Rome, a man defined in terms of great nobility, virtue and doctrine. This has the effect of better explaining the opposition to his departure, a refusal which the translator, changing Bede's text, attributes also to the Pope of the time. Aelfric does not, here, follow the OE version literally as in the previous passage, but it is difficult to imagine that he was not familiar with it, since he too uses the triple amplification by adopting practically the same terms, since for "æðele", "getungen" and "gelæred" he uses "getogen" and "geðungen lareow".

If what has been said sounds convincing, we have at least two conclusions to draw. The first concerns the personality of the anonymous translator of Bede. As recent research has proved, and as this brief analysis confirms, he works with precision and clarity, and he can also decorate his text here and there with rhetorical elegance. The second and more important conclusion throws further light on what we already know: i.e., that in the Middle Ages 'translating' quite often means 're-writing'. The *Life* of Gregory the Great produced by the anonymous Alfredian translator is surely to be evaluated with regard to its source text, but also with an eye fixed upon, we can safely hypothesise, a different destination and audience. When judged by these criteria, the work is a success, especially as a cleverly patterned 'compendium' in which various registers are used in a wise and balanced combination. Starting from some bare chronicle data, the story rises to a celebratory eulogy in the central part, to end in the more domestic atmosphere of a lively anecdote, neither irrelevant nor superfluous, since that casual encounter of Pope Gregory with the Anglian slaves in the Roman market was to be the manifestation of "the will of God", and had as a result the "salvation of the English people".

CHAPTER 13

"A Life of the Blessed Virgin" from the *Revelations* of St Birgitta[1]

The manuscript Oxford, Bodleian Library, Rawlinson C. 41, contains a *Vita Beate Marie* written in English, in spite of what the Latin title may suggest. As Cumming (1929: xviii) and more recently and in far more detail, Ellis (1982a)[2] have observed, it is the result of a compilation of extracts from almost all the books of St Birgitta's *Revelationes* (only Book V is missing), and especially from Books I, VI, and VII. Examination of this text unpublished until now, is interesting for three reasons:

1. it contributes new documentation to the history of a literary genre that was most popular in the late Middle Ages: the lives of Christ, and to a lesser extent, of Mary;
2. it broadens our knowledge in the vast area of studies on St Birgitta's work that concern the reception of the *Revelationes* in West Europe;
3. more particularly, it offers us a sort of summary of St Birgitta's mariology,[3] or at least discloses which of the images of Mary present in the Swedish saint's writings were received through the anonymous fifteenth-century editor/translator.

---

1   An earlier version of this chapter was published as Pezzini (1993b). I am grateful to the authorities of the Bodleian Library for having allowed me to quote from a manuscript belonging to them (MS Bodley Rawlinson C. 41).
2   A precise indication of the passages of the *Revelations* used in the *Vita Beate Marie* can be found in Appendix I of the Ph. D. dissertation of Ellis himself. I thank him here for his kindness in putting the material of his research at my disposal.
3   For a general presentation of Marian doctrine in the work of the Swedish mystic see Roschini (1973).

A fourth motive of interest, at least for scholars of historical linguistics, concerns the concept and method of translation in the late Middle Ages: new elements or the confirmation of features already noted may emerge from an analysis of the editor's approach as regards his source: what he chooses, how he organizes the material selected, and how he translates the original Latin.

1. The genre *Vita Christi* in the Middle Ages

Of the 'lives' ultimately based on biblical material, Christ's is by far the most important and widespread in comparison with the lives of Mary or the apostles. To better understand the plan and treatment of the birgittine *Vita Beate Marie* it is then necessary to outline the main characteristics of the genre 'Vita Christi' seen in its making and in its late medieval developments. It is well known that a literary form does not evolve without a reason and does not develop by chance. In his study on the *Myrrour of the Blessed Lyf of Christ* by Nicholas Love (d. 1424), Salter (1974: 55-118) has clearly summarized the gradual formation of this type of literary work whose major and best known results are embodied in two fourteenth-century masterpieces: the *Meditaciones Vite Christi* by John De Caulibus, of which Love's *Myrrour* is the translation, and the *Vita Christi* by Ludolf of Saxony[4]. It is sufficient here to briefly record the various stages of this process.

The idea of a 'life of Christ' in the sense of an unbroken narrative dates back to the initiative of Tatian who in the *Diatessaron* (c. 170 A.D.) combines the narratives of the four evangelists in a single history; the work was to be imitated and widely exploited by Victor of Capua, whose *Harmonia Latina* (c. 545) was circulated in the Germanic countries by St Boniface of Fulda. Together with this kind of compendium whose prime purpose seems to have been as a means of study, another highly important element contributes to the idea of the life of Christ as a chronological sequence of significant

---

4   The *Meditaciones* are edited by Stallings-Taney (1997). The *Vita Christi* by Bolard/Rigollot/Carnandet (1865, reprint 2006).

events. This is the gradual emergence of the liturgical year as a series of feasts that run through the whole range of events of Christ's earthly existence from the nativity to the resurrection. It will be necessary to take liturgy and its great celebrations into account when one considers that the lives of Christ, at least those that are not in encyclopaedic form, and likewise, iconography, the theatre and religious poetry, end up concentrating almost exclusively on the two great poles of the nativity and the passion, leaving one virtually in the dark as to the whole part about Christ's public ministry.

In addition to the two basic elements mentioned above (biblical material and liturgical celebrations), the twelfth century brought the new contribution, however relative, of heightened attention to the human nature of Jesus and consequently on the use of his earthly life as a basic ingredient for meditation. The series of spiritual masters who contributed to describing what is generally called 'affective piety' is well known: Anselm, Bernard, Bonaventure. I believe nevertheless that the most typical and accomplished expression of this contemplation of the various episodes of Christ's life with the "eyes of the heart" and with all the senses, remains the work of Aelred of Rievaulx, who in the third part of his *De Institutione Inclusarum* and in the *De Jesu Puero Duodenni* expounds his method for meditation and at the same time provides admirable examples of how it should be applied.[5] The *Lignum Vitae* by St Bonaventure, and the popular and highly influential *Meditaciones Vite Christi*, attributed to him for a long time, are so to speak the most significant result of this interpretation of the literary genre, which we can define with Salter as "a meditative life in a narrative framework" (1974: 61). One approaches the story of Jesus with one's own imagination and emotions, which, with a reasonable elaboration on the basic biblical material, enable one to harmonize with the situation under examination, to be able to assimilate the very feelings of Jesus and of those close to him: to 're-live' the Gospel in the mind and in the heart, in order to relive it in life.

In the course of the thirteenth century, another of the Church's preoccupations is precisely reflected in the history of this genre: the

---

5   On the meditative method of Aelred of Rievaulx see what has been written by Dumont (1961: 17-32) and Pezzini (2003: 81-89).

need to re-evangelize the masses, an urgency that with the Fourth Lateran Council (1215) was to become the pastoral programme for all Christianity. Collections of homilies were produced, planned for the celebrations throughout the liturgical year, based on the Gospels for Sundays and feast days, followed by comments and explanations, and a series of *exempla*, aiming to illustrate a particular moral passage from the biblical readings. Lives of Christ compiled with a specific view to preaching, like the one in the encyclopaedic *Cursor Mundi*, have their own peculiar aspects. These consist in frequent recourse to typological approaches, appeals of a moral kind, and a strong didactic tone translated into a language which combines the plain style of the popular homily with forms of dramatization and the use of images of secular literature, romances in particular. From this type of literary product the cycles of mystery plays finally emerged. These were in fact a dramatized history of salvation, in which the life of Christ plays a central and decisive role.

This development culminates in the work that gathers the various rivulets of this literary genre in a single great stream, the *Vita Christi* of Ludolf of Saxony (second half of the 14th century) in which the biblical stories, theological comment, moral doctrine, mystical interpretation, affective meditation and also a few holy legends converge to make a compact narrative. The same can be said of the *Meditaciones*, which paved the way to Ludolf's great work but had the advantage of being less encyclopaedic and more 'popular'. This is also demonstrated by its success, witnessed by the large number of manuscripts widely scattered over Europe both in the Latin version as well as in the main vernaculars. According to Salter, they constitute "a clearly arranged interpretation of biblical material, the basic account serving as a nucleus of doctrinal and affective energy" (1974: 105).

In his preface, the author of the *Meditaciones* exhorts the reader to fervently apply himself to meditating on the life of Jesus, since this is "the most necessary and the most profitable spiritual exercise":

> Super omnia namque spiritualis exercicii studia hoc magis necessarium est magisque proficuum credo, et quod ad celsiorem gradum perducere possit. Nusquam enim inuenies ubi sic edoceri possis contra uana blandimenta et

caduca et contra tribulaciones et aduersa, contra hostium tentamenta et vicia
sicut in uita Domini Iesu, que fuit absque omni defectu perfectissima.
(Stallings-Taney 1998: 7)[6]

After explaining his intention, the author declares that his language
will be "simple and unrefined" (*loquar rudi et impolito sermone*), because one ought not to bother about "satisfying the ears, but rather
about nourishing the soul" (*ut non aurem sed mentem studeas inde
reficere*: Stallings-Taney 1998: 9). Finally he proposes his method:

> Tu autem si ex his fructum sumere cupis, ita presentem te exhibeas his que per
> Dominum Iesum dicta et facta narrantur ac si tuis auribus audires et oculis ea
> uideres, toto mentis affectu diligenter, delectabiliter et morose, omnibus aliis
> curis et sollicitudinibus tunc omissis. (Stallings-Taney 1998: 10)[7]

The generalized use of the vernacular both in original works and in the
numerous translations of works originally written in Latin suggests
that the readers of these 'lives' were female religious communities and
laypeople. The formal organization of the texts in numerous short
chapters indicates daily reading, silent or aloud to a small group.
Various versions of the same work lead one to suppose that they were
intended for different types of readers: in this respect it is not without
significance that the *Meditaciones* have reached us in a brief version
of 40 chapters and a long one of 95, in which "besides the part
devoted to Christ's life, there is a doctrinal section formed of
passages, especially by St Bernard, which perhaps the same author

---

6   This is Nicholas Love's translation: "For among alle gostly exercyses I leue
     þat þis is most necessarye & most profitable, & þat may bringe to þe hyest
     degre of gude lyuing þat stant specialy in perfite despysing of þe worlde, in
     pacience, suffryng of aduersitees, & in encrese & getyng of vertues. For
     soþely þou shalt neuer finde, where man may so perfitely be taght, first for to
     stable his herte aȝeynus vanitees & deceyuable likynges of þe worlde, also to
     strengh him amongis tribulacions & aduersitees, & forþermore to be kept fro
     vices & to getyng of vertues, as in þe blissede life of oure lorde Jesu, þe which
     was euere withoute defaut most perfite". (Sargent 2005: 11-12).
7   Wherefore þou þat coueytest to fele treuly þe fruyt of þis boke, þou most with
     all þi þought & alle þin entent, in þat manere make þe in þi soule present to
     þoo þinges þat bene here writen seyd or done of oure lord Jesu, & þat bisily,
     likingly & abydyngly, as þei þou herdest hem with þi bodily eres, or sey þaim
     with þin eyen don, puttyng awey for þe tyme, & leuyng alle oþer occupacions
     & bisynesses. (Sargent 2005: 12-13).

eliminated in a second edition to make his work more supple and more within the reach of lay readers" (Levasti 1935: 997). The English version of this work, Love's *Myrrour*, organizes the text according to the seven days of the week, and indicates the liturgical seasons in which the various sections are to be read, so that the work becomes a daily exercise to sustain one's spiritual life within the framework of the liturgical year.

2. The *Vita Beate Marie* of MS Rawlinson C. 41

What has been said both about the contents and the organization of the material in the lives of Christ of the fourteenth-fifteenth centuries, is also true of the *Vita Beate Marie* contained in the Rawlinson MS C. 41, ff. 2r-43v.[8] The work results from a compilation of passages found in the *Revelationes* of St Birgitta, arranged by the author in a prologue and 36 chapters of various lengths, each with a title which summarizes the contents of the chapter itself.[9] The subject of this compilation constitutes one of the two areas that witness the relevant influence of Birgitta's writings on the religious literature of the late Middle Ages: the other includes the translation of chapters or parts of chapters containing teachings on spiritual life.[10] The aspect that characterizes the writings about Jesus and Mary and distinguishes them from those concerning spiritual instruction, is precisely the technique of the compilation for which different passages of the *Revelationes*, from single sentences or parts of sentences to whole chapters or sections of chapters, are assembled and integrated with a most intelligent

---

8   In regard to the natural similarity between the Life of Jesus and the Life of Mary, Cola observes that the *Meditaciones* appear to be "the life of Christ seen by Mary, written with the heart of Mary" (1982: 12), since the presence of Our Lady penetrates all the text in a very strong way.

9   The texts used to compile the *Vita* are from *Rev.* I, 9, 10, 27, 35, 37, 42, 45, 58; II, 21; III, 8, 25; IV, 70, 99; VI, 1, 2, 11, 26, 49, 55, 56, 57, 58, 59, 60, 61, 62, 94, 112; VII, 1, 2, 8, 21, 22, 23, 24, 25, 26.

10   See Ellis (1982a). For texts of the *Revelations* which contain spiritual teachings, see also Pezzini (1986, 1988), and ch. 1.

technique to form new units. This procedure is founded on the very character of the *Revelationes* as a work more like a collection of material rather than a tightly structured text. It is also based on a precedent work by Alphonse of Pecha who, using the numerous references to Mary scattered throughout the work, shortly after 1380 compiled the *Celeste Viridarium*, which is actually a life of Mary set out in books and chapters clearly destined for meditation, as is proved by the presence of a prayer at the end of each chapter which is also derived from Birgitta's writings.[11] Pecha's work establishes a model which, without servile dependence, inspired both the author of a meditation on the incarnation and passion of the Lord that appears in MS Lambeth 432,[12] and the author of the *Vita Beate Marie*, a work that can be situated halfway between the notably more extensive *Viridarium*, and the meditation of the Lambeth MS that is based only on *Rev*. I, 10 integrated with IV, 70. It goes without saying that the anonymous fifteenth-century English compiler/translator is in a sense the 'author' of the *Vita*, if not for the 'text', at least as far as the 'organization and translation' of the basic Latin material is concerned.

The text of the Rawlinson MS has reached us without f. 1, which should include the Prologue, and of which only the last sentence remains: "Show to the how moche my son hath honourde my name, my body, and my soule" (f. 2r). The text corresponds to I, 9: "Ego volo tibi dicere, quam dulciter ipse dilexit corpus meum, quam dulciter animam meam, quantum eciam honorauit nomen meum."[13]

It will be noted that the English translator has simplified the Latin text: he usually does the opposite, but what counts most in this case is that the sequence *corpus, animam, nomen* appears reorganized as "name, body, soule", which corresponds exactly to the editor's own

---

11   On *Viridarium* see Colledge (1956: 33-34), Eklund (1972: 20, 42) and Ellis (1982a: 167-168). So far this work is unpublished and is in the British Library, MS Harley 612, fols. 133r-160v, and Bodleian Library, MS Canon. Misc. 475.
12   See Pezzini (1993a). In this work, beside the edition of the text, the various techniques of compilation of the material extracted from the *Revelationes* are analysed in detail.
13   For the Latin text of the *Revelationes* I have used the volumes of the modern critical edition: Book I (Undhagen 1977); II (Undhagen-Bergh 2001); III (Jönsson 1998); IV (Aili 2002); V (Bergh 1971); VI (Bergh 1991); VII (Bergh 1967).

plan. According to this plan the first chapter is devoted to illustrating "the most excellent dignyte of the holy name of this Virgyn Mary", ending with the glorification of Mary's body and soul in heaven. This will be enough to immediately perceive the intelligence of our editor's use of the text on which he has based his Life of Mary.

To give a general idea of how this *Vita* is organized, I would say that it concentrates on the two poles already identified as the main reference points of medieval piety: the childhood of Jesus and the passion, with an introduction that concerns the life of Mary before the birth of Jesus, the so-called 'proto-gospel', and a conclusion that describes the glorification of Mary after her death.[14] Only two chapters out of 36 are dedicated to the public life of Jesus, but they are not about his ministry. Surprisingly, even the wedding of Cana, an event in which Mary plays no secondary role, is omitted. I will add that two basic emotions are constantly evoked which correspond to the events of the nativity and the passion: joy and pain, through numerous phases in which these two feelings appear confused and in some way inter-related.

After the first chapter of homiletic tone, devoted to the dignity and strength of Mary's name, the author spreads the life of the Virgin to the birth of Jesus over nine chapters, treating in one sequence the wedding of Joachim and Anna (ch. 2), the immaculate conception of Mary (ch. 3), the nativity of the Virgin (ch. 4), her childhood and adolescence (ch. 5), the presentation at the temple with her vow of virginity and poverty (ch. 6), her marriage to Joseph (ch. 7), the annunciation (ch. 8), the visit to Elizabeth (ch. 9), the announcement to Joseph with the invitation to take Mary as his wife (ch. 10).

While so far Mary has been narrating her own life, it is now Birgitta who tells of the birth of Jesus according to a vision she had during her visit to Bethlehem, a change marked by the compiler who inserts a "Brygyt speketh" at the beginning of ch. 11. So one is told how Mary prepares for the birth (ch. 11), how Jesus was born (ch. 12), of Mary who adores her baby and swaddles him (ch. 13), of the visit of the shepherds who adore Jesus with Mary and Joseph (ch. 14). At

---

14   It can be interesting to note how such a four-part scheme finds an exact similarity in the composition of altar-pieces of the late Middle Ages which depict the life of the Virgin: see Kieckhefer (1987: 92).

this point Mary returns as narrator to confirm Birgitta's vision (ch. 15) then to speak of the circumcision (ch. 16), and the visit of the Magi (ch. 17). A chapter follows which is devoted to the Purification of the Virgin and combines a vision Birgitta had during the liturgical feast and words spoken by Mary (ch. 18), a description of the pain Mary feels when looking at her child and foreseeing his coming passion (ch. 19) and finally of the hardship of the flight to Egypt and the massacre of the innocents (ch. 20).

Two chapters are dedicated to Christ's life up to the passion: in one we find Mary afflicted, imagining the pain that her son will suffer, while Jesus explains it as necessary that he should die for men's salvation (ch. 21); in the other, the form of Jesus' body as an adult is described (ch. 22).

The narrative of the passion includes the agony and the sweating of blood (ch. 23), the flagellation (ch. 24), the mounting of Calvary and the crucifixion (ch. 25), the *compassio Marie* (ch. 26), the entrusting of Mary to John (ch. 27), the suffering of Jesus and his friends who are beneath the cross (ch. 28), the death of Christ and in a certain sense even that of Mary (ch. 29), the cosmic earthquake (ch. 30) and the deposition from the cross (ch. 31). The ending of this section is a chapter far more extended than all the others (97 lines in the transcription, as compared to an average of 25/30 lines) which explains how sinners crucify Christ today far more cruelly than the Jews did at the time of Jesus' death (ch. 32).

The four final chapters illustrate respectively the resurrection of Jesus and his apparition to the Virgin (ch. 33), Mary's life after the ascension (ch. 34), the death of Our Lady and her assumption (ch. 35), the final glorification of Mary seen as the mirror of the Trinity (ch. 36).

3. Themes and motives of the *Vita Beate Marie*

The analysis of a work of this kind, so varied in its material, approaches and linguistic registers, is not an easy task. I do not believe it is possible to do more than provide a series of annotations, postponing a more detailed study to a future edition, in order to appreciate the text more fully. Taking into account what has been said of the literary genre 'life of Christ' and applying it to the life of Mary, material is found in the work we are examining that could be described as biblical, theological, moral and meditational in general, even though it is not always easy to verify these qualifications because of their relative uncertainty and possible overlapping in some parts of the work.

Given the fact that biblical data on Mary's life are scanty, one is all the more surprised to see that even the rare New Testament references to her seem to be neglected. The absence of the Cana episode has already been mentioned, but also where the Gospels could have offered a wealth of interesting suggestions, we find a very poor treatment instead: see, for example, the episode of the shepherds, who seem concerned more than anything else to check the sex of the announced Saviour, or that of the Magi whose gifts are not even mentioned, or the arrival of the adolescent Jesus in Jerusalem that is rapidly condensed into two lines. An observation to be found in ch. 20 may help to explain such neglect that seems to us at the very least inexplicable. This chapter is entitled "Off the persecucyon off Herode and the deth off the Innocentis", but this subject occupies only two of the thirty-one lines of the transcription. What may be of interest is that to the question about what Jesus did from his adolescence to the time of his passion, our Lady replies observing that it is not necessary for her to reveal these things, "for as muche as the myracles off hys godhede and hys humanyte be openly declaryd in the gospell, whych may ryght wel edyfey and instructe the and many other" (ff. 23v-24r). The observation is relevant to the extent that it leads to an interpretation of the *Vita* not as an elaboration of the biblical text that is presumably known and in any case remains otherwise accessible, but as its integration, both through 'revelations' and through the reflections suggested by pious meditation.[15]

---

15   This indication appears in the preface of Love's *Myrrour* already quoted: "we mowen to stiryng of deuotion ymagine and þenk dyuerse wordes and dedes of him & oþer, þat we fynde not written, so þat it be not aȝeyns þe byleue". (Sargent 2005: 10-11).

Theological data are present, both as the affirmation of truth and as the analysis of the problems arising in the *intellectus fidei*. Mary's immaculate conception, her virgin birth and her bodily assumption to heaven are clearly affirmed. The theological meaning of the death on the cross is explained by Christ himself to his mother: "Yt ys the wyl off my fader that I shulde suffer deth, ye, sowthly yt ys my wyl with the fader that yt shulde be. That that I have off the fader yt may not suffure payne nor deth, but the flesshe that I have takyn off the, that shal suffer deth, that other mennys bodis and soulis may be redemyd and sauyd" (ch. 21, ff. 25v-26r). Elsewhere the ancient problem of the passibility of an impassible nature is discussed, with the question of how angels could feel upset at the death of Christ (ch. 30).

But the material that is much more used has a moral and meditative character. Concerning these two aspects of the spiritual life we could introduce a distinction: the reflections that suggest a model of behaviour can rightly be called 'moral', while we can take as 'meditative' those passages that, making use of the field of affectivity, aim at involving the reader emotionally in the scene described. This difference has an especially practical purpose, because the intention is in fact unique: to make Mary's life a picture that simultaneously exalts her glory and offers a model for imitation.

No one will be surprised by the fact that the virtues most insistently stressed upon, first in Mary but as a reflection in Joseph and Jesus too, are chastity, poverty and obedience; to which may be added patience in affliction, the subject of a very rich literature in the late Middle Ages. Emphasis on chastity can even appear unpleasant to a modern reader, as when it is repeatedly affirmed that Joachim and Anna were united not for the pleasure of the flesh that for them was dead (ch. 2: "for the plesur of the flessh was ded and mortyfyed yn them" f. 3r), but in strict obedience to the will of God who had ordained it thus. However, this could assume another aspect if it is considered that the fruit of this obedience is a creature free from original sin, free, that is, from that wound inflicted precisely by an act of disobedience. It is impossible here to expound at length on the moral profiles offered from time to time in Mary, Joseph, and Jesus. It will be sufficient to observe that Birgitta's ideal itself radiates through their attitudes of meekness, self-restraint, love of silence and prayer, submissiveness, obedience and mutual attention, patience in adversity, discretion in penitence and fasting and the ability to be content with the essentials, giving any surplus to the poor.

As has been stated, the emotions aroused by this 'Life of Mary' are chiefly the joy and pain on which the whole narration proceeds. In fact, one could read the *Vita* as a rhythmic sequence from the appearance and convergence of these two basic feelings: joy rules from Mary's birth, greeted as "the begynnyng of al trew yoyes" (ch. 4), to the overflowing exultance of the annunciation and the meeting with Elizabeth (ch. 8, 9), to the joy that Mary communicates to Joseph, the shepherds and the three kings at Jesus's birth (ch. 14, 15, 17). From the purification appears the motive of pain together with the vision of the angel who bears "a grete sworde long and brode" (ch. 18): the shadow of the passion looms over the child Jesus (ch. 19), that is to mark the rest of the *Vita*. But waves of joy will not be lacking, as where it is noted that Christ's presence alone gave constant joy to Mary and Joseph "contynually fulfyllyd with a mervelous grete yoye and swetnes" (21). The whole section on the passion is obviously distinguished by great suffering. Mary's participation in the suffering of the one who formed "a single heart" with her is so intense that, with an extraordinary pictorial effect, the sagging of the dead body of Jesus on the cross is echoed in the sagging of Mary, oppressed by bitterness and grief (ch. 29). At the very moment of her deepest sorrow, Mary declares : "And yet my heuines was mixte with summe yoye, for I saw hym that neuer synned that of his grete charite wolde suffer suche thyngis for sowles" (f. 34r). And the *Vita* actually ends on a note of joy and triumph since Mary dies of joy, while contemplating "the grete wonderfull love and charite of God", a joy and sweetness so great that the soul cannot contain it, a death that is like a gentle dream, from which Mary awakens in "everlastyng yoye" (ch. 35).

Much more could be said of this *Vita* of Mary, beginning with the notable variety of language that can switch from the solemn tones of apocalyptic visions, as in the chapter on the purification (ch. 13), to the vocabulary of intense maternal tenderness with which Mary describes how she wrapped Jesus in swaddling clothes shortly after he was born (ch. 13) or how she accepted his dead body deposed from the cross (ch. 31). But I should like to focus on what seems to me perhaps the most peculiar aspect of this 'Life of our Lady', a recurring series of mirror-like reflections whose focal point and mother

326

metaphor is in the encounter of eyes. I can only make a brief reference to these moments. Sometimes this encounter materializes in verbal echoes expressed by perfect parallelism, as in the meeting between Mary and Elizabeth, who fill one another with their marvel and joy:

> When Elizabeth sawe this, she marvelyd gretely the fervour off my spyryte that spake in me, and I lykewyse mervelyd as gretely the specyal grace of god in her. (ch. 9, f. 10r-v)

More often, as I have explained, it is the meeting of eyes: as in ch. 19, where Mary in tears, gazes at the child Jesus thinking of the passion, and Jesus replies, looking at the tears in her eyes with as much pain "as he wholde have dyde"; or at ch. 21, where while Mary is still thinking about the passion, Jesus looks at her and tries to comfort her, explaining the benefits that his death will bring; or as in ch. 26, where the words succeed in communicating the meeting of the two gazes through repeated and almost obsessive verbal echoes:

> Then, when my sonne lokyd to me from the crosse, and I lyke wyse to hym, then the terrys ranne owte of myn eynn, as though thei had renne owte of my vaynes. And when he belde and sawe me so gretly oppressyd with payne and sorow, then he was so gretly trowbled and payned of my sorowe, that all his paynes and sorowes were to hym as thei had bene no payne for the grete sorow that he sawe in me. (f. 31v)

It is also necessary to remember how Mary feels all her son's agony in the passion, almost to the point of dying with him. In the light of what has been said, the editor's choice of using a passage from the *Revelations* that portrays the Virgin as a mirror in which the Trinity is reflected appears all the more appropriate.

> And now my soule and my body be more pure and bright then the sonne, and more clere then the cristall stone. And lyke as iij persons may be seen in a myrrour or a glasse, yf they stonde present nyʒe to hyt, so in my puryte and clerenes may wel be seen the father, the sonne, and the holy gost. I had the sonne of god in my wombe with hys godhed, and now he ys seen in me with hys godhed and hys manhode, as in the most pure myrrour or glasse, for I am nowe gloryfyed. And therfore he that seyth me, may see the godhed and the manhode in me as in a myrrour, and may lyke wyse se me in god.
>
> (ch. 36, f. 43r-v)

There is nothing more to add except that Mary is shown here as the perfect realization of the purpose for which 'lives' of Christ and the Virgin were compiled in the last centuries of the Middle Ages: to attain, through a long and sustained visual and emotional contemplation of the mysteries of Jesus and the Virgin, a communion of life with him and his mother, and through them, with God.

4. A comparison of the English text of the
Vita Beate Marie and the Latin text of the *Revelationes*

It has already been suggested that the editor/translator of the *Vita Beate Marie* has a certain flare of originality as regards the Latin text he uses: though the basic material remains undoubtedly typical of Birgitta, on the other hand, not only the way the original has been translated into English but especially the work of selecting and re-organizing the original text must be attributed to the anonymous author. To give an idea of such a task, I shall quote some examples concerning both the translation technique used in the *Vita* as well as the methods of compiling passages drawn from the various books of Birgitta's work.

The first observation is also the most predictable since it is what one expects: following an established ME fashion, our author generously relies on the doublet, frequently translating one Latin word by two English words. This is such a well-known device that examples are not really required, even though it is worth mentioning since not all translators use this technique or practice it as frequently as our author does. Just to show the way he works, in a few lines of ch. 3 he translates *retia* by "nettis and snarys", *timendum* by "to be dred and feryd", *munditia* by "clennes and purite", *amici dei* by "the louers and frends of god", *expectatione* by "hope and trust", *gaudendum* by "to be glad and joyful", etc. If it is a valid hypothesis that these texts were to be read aloud at a sort of spiritual reading session to a small group in a home or convent, it is easy to see how such a system of verbal emphasis could contribute to a more effective communication of the message. A certain quest for emphasis, usually obtained by the amplification of the original Latin, appears common in the *Vita*. This is apparent, for example, in the following passage:

> Ioseph vero sic servivit mihi, quod numquam audiebatur in ore eius verbum scurrile, numquam murmuriosum, numquam iracundum. (VI, 59)

> He seruyd me so devowtly and mekely that ther was neuer hard of his mought any wylde or unsemely worde, neuer grogyng, neuer murmuryng, neuer angry. (ch. 7, f. 6v)

Apart from the two doublets on *scurrile* and *murmurosum*, an expansion of a simple *sic* to "so devowtly and mekely" can also be noticed in the interpretation.

It should however be explained that after a process of enlarging the vocabulary, a somewhat contrary technique appears which simplifies the complexities of syntax, as can be seen in the following example which shows the translator's two basic choices in a single sentence:

> Cum intellexisset me impraegnatam admirans.... (VI, 59)

> When he persevyd that I was with chylde, and sawe my wombe grete, he mervelyd gretly....(ch. 10, f. 10r)

It would certainly not be a case for increasing the documentation: it is more important to note that both these translation techniques probably have something to do with reading aloud in public, when there is a greater need to emphasize the concept or the image, and this is certainly facilitated both by groups of words from a similar semantic field, and by setting them out in paratactical structures.

Another field in which the editor intervenes with his own originality should be indicated: the organization of the text itself. According to well-known methods already adopted by others,[16] he uses the text of the *Revelations* as a mine from which he extracts various stones to be arranged in new combinations, as a repertory of

---

16 See what has been said in fn. 11 and 12 above in regard to *Viridarium* and the *Meditacion* of MS Lambeth 432.

material to be treated freely. He makes use of various techniques to reassemble it, but they can all be traced to a triple procedure:

1. the inversion of the sequence of the original Latin;
2. the combination of parts of different chapters;
3. the dismemberment of a chapter of the Latin, and its use in different parts of the *Vita*.

One example of the first procedure is found in ch. 22, where the Latin: "Filium meum qualis est in caelo videre non poteris. Sed qualis erat secundum corpus in mundo cognosce" (IV,70) becomes: "Loo, dowghter, such was my son in his manhode when he was in erthe, as I haue now declaryd and shewyd vnto the. But how and of what maner he is now in hevyn, thou mayst not see nor vnderstonde" (ch. 22, f. 27v).

The inversion of the sequence of the two sentences corresponds to the way the editor has arranged his chapter. A similar choice has already been noted in the last sentence of the Prologue quoted at the beginning. However, respect for the structure of the way it is set out does not always dictate the rearrangement of the sentence. Sometimes it appears that rather a sense of rigour, or correctness, intervenes in rearranging Birgitta's Latin. This could be the case of ch. 30, derived from IV,11, and devoted to describing the disturbance of the universe upon the death of Christ which strikes consecutively angels, elements, pagans, crucifiers, souls in limbo, and finally devils in hell: in the original however, the *immundi spiritus* came first, and then the "illi autem qui erant in sinu Abrahe", significantly rendered by "they also that were in lymbe, that is to sey the soules that were in Abrahams bovsome" (ff. 35v-36r). The same hierarchical sense could explain how in ch. 7 the editor overrules the sequence of the Latin (VII,25) that puts Joseph first, then Mary, as those who were aware of Mary's vow of virginity, re-establishing what was evidently a more logical order for him: first Mary, then Joseph.

The technique of conflation is so well known and used that it does not need to be further illustrated: above all, it would require a lot more space. I limit myself to a single passage from ch. 26:

For lyke as that prikketh and grevyth more paynfully that is niȝthe to the harte, so his sorowe was to me more grevous then to all other. / There-fore I may boldly say that his sorowe was my sorowe, for his hert was my hert, / and lyke as a mother, yf she shulde see her sonne to be kutte in pecys, shulde be moste greuously trowbled, so was I in the tyme of hys passyon when I sawe the bytterness of his paynes, / for his payne and sorow excedyd the passyon of all martyrs of sayntis in bytternes of payne. / For lyke as man synned and offendyd in all the membyrs of his body, so my sonne made satisfaction and sufferd payne in all his membyrs. (f. 31r-v)

The English text combines four passages of the *Revelations* found in three different chapters of Book I, as can be seen by the comparison:

Et sicut hoc grauius pungit, quod vicinius est cordi, sic dolor eius grauior erat pre ceteris michi (I,35,5b). Propterea audacter dico, quia dolor eius erat dolor meus, quia cor eius cor meum (I,35,7a). Sicut enim mater, si filium suum viuum incidi videret, amarissime turbaretur, sic ego in passione filii mei visa amaritudine eius turbabar (I,58,1b), cuius passio omnium sanctorum passionem in amaritudine superauit (I,58,1a). Sicut enim in omnibus membris homo deliquit, sic ipse filius meus in omnibus satisfecit. (I,45,2b)[17]

The process of conflation requires a dismembering and recomposing operation. There is a very good example in the *Vita*, where this tech-nique is blatantly visible: it is found in the way the compiler treats VI,57, a chapter that, from the image of the sword that transfixes Mary's heart according to Simeon's prophecy, lists all Mary's great sorrows in chronological order. The editor of the *Vita* literally chops up the chapter and associates the relative phrases with the single sorrows in the various chapters where they occur.

It is obviously impossible to embark on a more detailed analysis of the work. But to confirm the freedom the author feels as regards the base text that he chose for his compilation, one happens to discover that he 'corrects' the Latin, as where a reference is made to St Jerome and to his doubt about the bodily assumption of the Virgin into heaven. The Latin text reads: "Hieronymus maluit *pie dubitare* quam diffinire non ostensa a Deo". (I,9). This is the corresponding English text: "for as muche as god had not shewyd openly the trewth therof, therfore Iherome wolde rather *mekely beleve* yt then for to determyn

---

17   The numbers and letters after the chapter number refer to the numbering system adopted in the critical edition of Book I (Undhagen 1977).

that thyng that was vncerteyn and vnknown". (ch. 36, f. 42v). What was a 'pious doubt' is plainly translated as 'gentle belief' by the English author!

5. Concluding remarks

My purpose at the beginning of my work was to rescue from oblivion a text that up to now does not seem to have awakened much curiosity in scholars. Above all, MS Rawlinson C. 41 is in fairly poor condition, and of the two Birgittine texts that it contains, the first lacks the beginning, and the second, which is more serious, both the beginning and the ending.[18] As far as I have been able to record, the *Vita Beate Marie* is a work worth publishing. It would make a further useful contribution to shedding light on the distribution of Birgitta's *Revelations*, and spiritual literature in general, on the growth of English prose in the fifteenth century, on the techniques of editing and translation so typical of the same century, and consequently, on a vast public who used works of this kind: their spirituality, their demands and their ideas. Once again, even in a badly put together and badly organized manuscript, one can glimpse a whole world that is no less fascinating than the one that appears in the great masterpieces.

---

18   For an edition of the second Birgittine text, together with a detailed descrip-
      tion of the manuscript and an analysis of the compilation and translation
      techniques used in the tract, see Pezzini (1992).

CHAPTER 14

The Genealogy and Posterity
of Aelred of Rievaulx's *Vita Sancti Edwardi*
Regis et Confessoris

If one wants to verify how productive a successful literary work can be, resulting in a series of numerous and different translations and transpositions, the story of the many *Lives* of Edward the Confessor written in medieval England is one of the best study cases. A brief survey of the state of this literature may at first be frustrating. The versions are so many and so various that they create the same effect as a late gothic fan vaulting: you turn your eyes round and round, in a state of dizziness which is exciting and painful at the same time. Research in this corpus of writings is consequently not easy. The length of the text and the differences of treatment, although suggestive and fascinating, present many obstacles to anyone wishing to gather the meaning of this variety into a clear and comprehensive pattern. In fact we have to do with nine or ten redactions in three languages, some in poetry and some in prose, produced over more than four centuries. To add a further difficulty, the corpus has been only partially edited, and not always according to modern scientific criteria. But I think that it is possible, and certainly useful, to present an ordered and possibly complete panorama of this rich and complex literary landscape. This is what I will try to do in this chapter.

The central pillar of this literary tradition is the *Vita Sancti Edwardi Regis et Confessoris* written by Aelred of Rievaulx in 1161-1163, who was asked to re-write Osbert of Clare's *Vita beati Eadwardi* produced in 1138, itself based on a preceding *Vita Ædwardi* by an Anonymous clerk who composed it shortly after the death of the king on 5 January 1066, apparently between 1066 and 1067. Very soon, probably before 1170, Aelred's work was transformed into an Anglo-Norman poem, subsequently rewritten as prose in the fourteenth century. Aelred's *Vita* was then used to compose two Latin poems, one in the thirteenth century, and a shorter one in the fifteenth century, under the reign of King Henry VI to whom the work is dedicated. Finally, in the course of the fifteenth century, two other works were derived from Aelred: a ME prose *Vita* inserted into a manuscript of the *Gilte Legende* (1438), later used by William Caxton for his *Golden Legend* (1483), and a ME *Verse Life*. The final step of this incredible journey was a reduced version of Aelred's Latin *Vita*, which as such reached its definitive consecration in the *Acta Sanctorum*. Also Matthew Paris's *Estoire de Seint Aedward le Rei* in Anglo-Norman should enter the list, a work largely based on Aelred's text, although it is not strictly speaking a 'translation', but is better qualified as a 'compilation', using, as it does, materials 'translated' also from other sources. Keeping Aelred in the central position, the literary history of this *Life* can thus be divided into two parts, corresponding to the genealogy and posterity of the work.

Before outlining a presentation of these different versions, it is useful to recall that in the case of the life of a saint who was also a king, who happened to live and die in a troubled age ending in a dramatic turning point in the history of England, any version, although hagiographical in intent, can be analysed from at least three points of view. The first is the political relevance of the subject, the second is the idea of sanctity transmitted by each hagiographer, and the third concerns the stylistic choices of the different authors/translators, which can either be considered by themselves or in the way they contribute to illustrating the political meaning and/or the virtues which are underlined in drawing the saint's profile. Behind these remarks lies the commonly acknowledged principle that saints' lives tell more about their writers and readers than about the saints themselves. This is why, although not ignoring history, my perspective is predominantly textual.

334

1. The genealogy of King Edward's *Vita*

1.1. The first anonymous biography

The first step leading to Aelred's *Vita* is an anonymous biography written immediately after the death of King Edward, which was probably even begun during his life. It survives in a single and mutilated manuscript (London, BL MS Harley 526, ff. 38-57) of c. 1100. The unnamed author is usually designated as 'The Biographer' or 'The Anonymous'.[1]

The work is not easy to describe. It is written in a mixture of poetry (elegiac distichs for the two prologues and hexameters in other cases) and prose, it has no titles or subdivisions of chapters that may reveal a plan conceived as such from the start. Barlow has divided the work into two 'books': the first is then further subdivided into seven, and the second into eleven 'chapters'; moreover, the missing parts of the work, due to the loss of some folios in the manuscript,[2] have been supplied with passages from Osbert of Clare's *Vita* and other works. In the first book the real protagonist seems to be Edward's wife, Queen Edith, and the related House of Godwin: it has the pace and tone of a chronicle contemporary to the events it narrates. After the death of King Edward a dramatic change occurs in the story: the work starts again, "independent in structure and different in form" (Barlow 1992: xxiv), and in this case the text concentrates on the figure of the

---

1   The work is published in *The Life of King Edward*, attributed to a monk of Saint-Bertin (Barlow 1992). Two famous monks of St Bertin Abbey, Goscelin and Folcard, have been indicated as possible authors, but the modern editor of the text says that "In the present state of our knowledge it is impossible to make a completely convincing case for either" (Barlow 1992: liv). For more information about date (the book may have been started "in the autumn of 1065" [Barlow 1992: xx]; book ii was probably written in 1067 [Barlow 1992: xxxii]), author, historical value and manuscript tradition of this work I refer to Barlow's ample and detailed Introduction (1992: xvii-lxxxi). Quotations of the Anonymous are from this edition referred to as 'Barlow'. For practical reasons within the same paragraph only page numbers are indicated.

2   Barlow hypothesizes that the manuscript "has lost folios between fos. 40 and 41 and between fos. 54 and 55, probably the two centre folios of both the first and the last gatherings" (1992: lxxix).

king, underlining his sanctity which is proved by a series of miracles, so that "only for this part is the manuscript title in any way appropriate" (Barlow 1992: xxv).[3] This raises intriguing questions: what is the cause of this change? Why does Edward, who is not particularly exalted in the first part, suddenly become a 'saint'?

One reason may be the tragedy into which England precipitated after the death of the king. In the prologue to this second part the Anonymous seems to lie prostrated in a very sad plight, and indeed he asks his Muse for consolation. The Muse's answer is that "this sadness lacks a reason", since "even nobler pages wait to be unrolled", in which the author is requested to "paint / King Edward fair in form and worth, what he / did in his life and what when dying said" (Barlow 1992: 88-89).[4] Edward's sanctity seems to be an invitation to turn away from contemporary hard times by looking back to a reign of peaceful prosperity and upwards to the glory of heaven now enjoyed by the holy king.

In this presentation, however, two questions remain unresolved, especially in order to explain the events that followed Edward's death. The first problem concerned the childless marriage of the king, with its sinister foreboding of coming disaster; the other was to determine where the responsibility lay for the miserable collapse of the Saxon monarchy. The first answer was obtained by turning a lack into a virtue, that is, by extolling the perfect chastity of the royal couple. The second answer can be extracted from the attempt of the Anonymous to separate Edward from the house of Godwin, a family who had been instrumental in saving England from the Danes, but who was also the main cause of the subsequent ruin provoked by the harsh quarrel between Godwin's two sons, Harold and Tostig (Barlow 1992: lxii). This is the reason why, in the second part of his work, the Anonymous chose "to emphasize the other-worldly aspects of Edward's life – his detachment from the base cares of politics – and to lift him from the

---

3   The complete title runs: *Vita Ædwardi Regis qui apud Westmonasterium requiescit* (The Life of King Edward who rests at Westminster). Barlow remarks that the title "looks like one added to an anonymous tract, but at an early date, for it ignores Edward's sanctity and (by implication) distinguishes him from the King Edward who rests at Shafestbury": p. 2, fn 1.

4   For practical reasons, I normally quote the English version, except when the wording is important, e.g. in parallel passages or in relevant phrases.

squalor of the theatre of the world into the triumphs of heaven" (Barlow 1992: lxiii). Here too, the gloomy prophecy of the truncated tree pronounced by Edward on his deathbed, interpreted as a dramatic end of the Saxon lineage, realizes at the same time two aims: on the one hand it underlines the fact that the king is not responsible for the fate that follows; on the other, he is painted as a 'prophet', i.e. a 'saint'.[5] The conclusion is that the Anonymous "inaugurates the hagiographic tradition, without however completely obeying to the laws of the genre" (Folz 1984: 92), or, in Barlow's words, within a clear historical frame "has been constructed what must be regarded as a rudimentary and perhaps slightly hesitant saint's life" (1992: xxx).

1.2. Osbert of Clare's Vita beati Eadwardi regis Anglorum

In the *Vita* written by the Anonymous we have something which can be aptly and rightly described as a book of history, with the known characteristics of the genre, including an overt political bias in the interpretation of the events and their protagonists. In the work produced in 1138 by Osbert of Clare, prior of Westminster Abbey, the perspective is entirely hagiographical right from the beginning.[6] About the author we have a highly appreciative judgement expressed by the man who was to re-write Osbert's work. In a miracle added at the end of his *Vita Edwardi*, Aelred of Rievaulx speaks of him as "frater quidam, cujus sincerissimam vitam decorabat scientia, illustrabat facundia, philosophia tam secularis quam ecclesiastica sublimis extollebat" [a certain brother called Osbert: knowledge adorned and eloquence illumined his utterly upright life, and worldly and ecclesiastical philosophy highly exalted him].[7] Although we know

---

5   Folz summarizes the contribution the Anonymous gave to the construction of Edward's sanctity as three facts: his virginity, his gift of prophecy, and his miracles (1984: 91-101, esp. 93-94).

6   The work has been edited by Bloch (1923). Quotations are from this edition (hereafter referred to as 'Bloch').

7   Aelred's *Vita Sancti Edwardi Regis et Confessoris* is quoted from *Patrologia Latina* (PL) 195, here 784D-785A. English quotations and chapter numbering are from the translation of Aelred's *Historical Works* by J.P. Freeland (2005), indicated as 'HW 2005'.The passage quoted here is from ch. 39, p. 233.

nothing about his birth and death, we have sufficient information about his rather troubled life. He was a man of some literary worth, a prolific writer who left a good number of Letters, a sermon on the Immaculate Conception, a treatise on chastity and, beside the *Life* of Edward for which he is famous, the *Lives* of other English saints, Edmund, Eadburge and Ethelbert, all belonging to the Anglo-Saxon royal house (Bloch 1923: 10-12).

It is certainly thanks to his literary ability that he was charged to write an official *Life of King Edward* by some *"seniores"*.[8] Osbert's *Vita* was written to secure the canonization of Edward, and the prior took the opportunity of the presence in England of the papal Legate, Cardinal Alberic of Ostia, to address him the request in a highly emphatic and eulogistic Letter prefixed to the work he submitted to him. Osbert's project had also a double political intent: the consolidation of the still fragile right of Stephen to reign by putting him under the protection of a holy ancestor,[9] and the religious and economic interest of Westminster Abbey. King Edward had in fact offered generous funds to rebuild the abbey and to ensure its future economy, he had been able to see it consecrated and dedicated to St Peter about two weeks before his death, and moreover he had wanted to be buried there. If the king was canonized his body was to become a glorious relic, enhancing the importance of the abbey.

The cardinal delayed the answer and suggested that Osbert himself should go to Rome to present his request to Pope Innocent II. Osbert's project failed, probably because this initiative of ecclesiastical policy was frustrated by incidents of secular politics: the infelicitous decision of King Stephen to arrest the bishops of Lincoln and Salisbury exactly at the time when Osbert was in Rome to plead his cause, and the arriving in England of Empress Matilda, the daughter

---

8   According to Bloch (1923: 68) these *seniores* were plausibly the son of the king, Gervase, Abbot of Westminster, King Stephen, and his brother, Henry Bishop of Winchester. Not so for Scholz, who argues convincingly that the *seniores* "were, in fact, Osbert's brethren of the convent of Westminster" (1961: 42).

9   This is the interpretation favoured by Bloch (1923: 68) which is widely received. Scholz argues that this reason was not so relevant, and that the initiative for the canonization of Edward was almost entirely due to Westminster (1961: 42-45).

of King Henry I Beauclerc and legitimate heir to the throne. The pope thought it was prudent not to engage in a risky initiative with a king he had no reason to trust or to appreciate. So he preferred to postpone his decision giving as a reason the fact that the 'miracles' were still not sufficient, and that the request had to be supported by the whole English Church.[10] In the end, Osbert's *Vita* was the best result of this enterprise, and the book was one of the most important contributions to accompany a second and more felicitous request some years later.

The change of perspective between the first and the second *Vita* comes almost like a subversion: what the Anonymous had treated as little more than an appendix, becomes in Osbert the centre and the very object of his work: Edward's sanctity. The Prior of Westminster collected some miracles, both from the Anonymous and, he says, from some 'schedules' which may be a kind of *Liber miraculorum* relating facts which had occurred at the king's tomb.[11] The change occurs both in the political and the hagiographical outlook. If we take either history or hagiography as an interpretative pattern, looking at things in a very concise and somewhat simplified manner, we can say that the Anonymous is history with a quasi-hagiographical appendix, Osbert is hagiography almost without history, Aelred is a happy combination of the two, although, as is to be expected, the hagiographical aspect prevails in his work. A comparative analysis would show very different choices, once we take into account the fact that both history and hagiography are to be read according to the ideology of the time. This means that history is mainly a narration and interpretation of events in the light of divine providence, in which defeats and disasters are easily explained as a punishment from God chastising the sins of an

---

10   According to Scholz, the suggested political reasons were not so important for the pope's refusal to canonize Edward. Innocent II appears to have really pondered the question at the canonical level with the Roman Curia (1961: 47). Summarizing the first phase of this process, Scholz concludes that "When one sums up the events leading to the attempt of Edward's canonization and its failure, it seems that the initiative was not with the king and his advisors; that Edward was not envisaged as a national or political saint; but that the abbey of Westminster, with its prior, Osbert of Clare, as instigator and main actor, proceeded on its own (though it secured an official endorsement) in the endeavour to gain a special patron for Westminster and thus to increase the sanctity of the place" (1961: 48-49).

11   For the various sources of Osbert's *Vita* see Bloch (1923: 45-46).

unworthy people; hagiography on the other hand is the illustration of *mirabilia Dei* revealed in the life of some people, especially through virtues and above all miracles, occurring both during the saint's life and much more after his death and preferably at his tomb.

1.3. Aelred of Rievaulx's Vita sancti Edwardi regis et confessoris

The canonization of Edward, which was refused to Osbert and his patrons, was rather easily obtained twenty-three years later under the reign of Henry II, who had sent a petition to Alexander III together with twelve other petitions, among which those signed by the two papal legates and the bishops of York, Norwich, Chichester, Ely, Winchester, Salisbury and Hereford; other petitions, above all that of Westminster Abbey, may have been lost (Scholz 1961: 49). The main reasons put forth for the canonization of the king were Edward's holy life, his virginity, the good relations he had with the Roman Church and his miracles (Folz 1984: 98). The papal bull was a gentle reward for the support the king of England had given to Alexander against the antipope Victor IV.[12] The need lying behind Henry's request was the same as Stephen's: to have a national patron saint in whom a symbol of union could be seen between Saxons and Normans in an uninterrupted line of succession.

Edward was canonized on 7 February 1161. Any new saint needs a *Vita*. In the case of King Edward Osbert's *Life* already existed, and it may be that this was the text submitted to the pope in view of Edward's canonization (Scholz 1961: 49-50), but it seemed that this was not a satisfactory solution. So Lawrence, Abbot of Westminster, gave Osbert's book to his relative Aelred of Rievaulx charging him to write a new and definitive *Life*. This was solemnly presented on 13 October 1163 when Edward's body was placed into a new shrine, on which occasion Aelred is also said to have preached the celebratory sermon.

---

12 The support of King Henry II to the legitimate pope is mentioned in practically all the petitions as a reason for granting the canonization "as an appropriate reward" (Scholz 1961: 50).

The Cistercian monk Aelred, third abbot of Rievaulx (1110-1167), is a much better known figure than Osbert of Clare.[13] He was called, and with reason, the "Bernard of the North", and among the writers of the first Cistercian generation he is undoubtedly the most versatile. His large literary production includes important ascetical works, a good number of liturgical sermons, a collection of homilies (*De Oneribus*) in form of a biblical commentary on a section of the Book of Isaiah, a treatise on the soul, historical and hagiographical works. His *Vita Edwardi*, together with his *Genealogia Regum Anglorum*, both dedicated to Henry II, enjoyed a wide diffusion testified to by the number of manuscripts still surviving.[14] Unfortunately there is no modern critical edition of these works, although recent translations[15] have made them known and certainly help to better assess the importance and relevance of Aelred's writings and show the multi-faceted and brilliant variety of his style.

Aelred's contribution to this third version of the Life of King Edward falls into three categories: he added new narrative materials, he subverted the general political outlook and coloured the presentation of Edward's sanctity with his own personal sensitivity; finally he gave the *Vita* his own particular literary style, which was very different from Osbert's, as we shall see.

As for the material Aelred added five new miracle stories which occurred after the king's death, and within the life "four new stories, two concerning the family of earl Godwin, and two whose picturesque

---

13 The most comprehensive presentation of his figure is still Squire (1969).

14 Hoste lists 18 manuscripts of the *Genealogia* (1962: 111-112), and 29 of the *Vita Edwardi* (1962: 123-125). According to Squire "there are three families of manuscripts. MS Laud Misc. 668 is typical of those which are associated with the north of England. MS Digby 59 is characteristic of the larger group [Ten MSS in England and Avranches MS 167, at least] some of which indicate a connection with Westminster. Of the third group MS Harley 220 is typical. Probably the first group would have come originally from one at Rievaulx. Twysden was using an MS of this family. (Almost certainly now Trinity College Dublin MS 172)" (Squire 1960: 376, fn 92). Twysden was the first to print Aelred's 'Vita Edwardi' in Twysden/Selden (1962); this is the text now in *Patrologia Latina* (PL) 195, 737B-790B, from which the Latin quotations are taken.

15 See Aelred of Rievaulx, *The Life of Saint Edward King and Confessor* (1997), and more recently the *Historical Works* (2005), pp. 123-243, quoted above.

character ensured their future repetition and popularity. One of these tells how Edward watches a thief stealing from the treasury in his bedchamber and encourages him to make good his escape before he is caught. The other recounts how the king receives back from saint John the Evangelist a ring he had given in alms in his honour" (Squire 1961: 96). This episode is the best known in Edward's life also because it came to characterize Edward's iconography, as shown, for example, in the Wilton Diptych.

The main reason for dissatisfaction with Osbert's *Vita* seems related to politics. In this respect the work was irremediably linked with the reign of King Stephen, who, to say the least, was not particularly popular with Henry II and his court. Moreover, Osbert's text lacked what is instead very central to Aelred's new *Life*, a topic already crucial in his *Genealogy*: the vision of Henry II as the man who was called to reconcile the Saxon inheritance with the new Norman monarchy. The very request for the canonization of Edward went the same way. The translation of Edward's relics on 13 October 1163, the new *Vita* and the sermon Aelred was asked to deliver at the feast[16] were, in fact, the celebration of the Plantagenet dynasty as the right and legitimate heir of the English monarchy. As Squire writes, Aelred regarded this commission "as the opportunity to set the seal upon the conciliatory work for England which he had initiated in his *Genealogy of the Kings*" (Squire 1969: 92). But another aspect was even more important. In line with this previous work, Aelred wanted to show King Edward as a model of sanctity and of peaceful collaboration with the church that some of his predecessors had so well illustrated in their lives.[17] Since my purpose is predominantly textual, for this aspect of the life I refer to some recent studies in which this profile of sanctity, showing the king as being deeply imbued with monastic and priestly qualities, is clearly outlined.[18]

Against such a serious historical background, stylistic reasons for producing a new *Life* are obviously not as relevant as political

---

16   This sermon was apparently lost; however, it may be the text published by Jackson (2005).
17   See Scholz (1961: 55) and Dutton (1993: 116-123). More generally, on Aelred's view of history and his work as historian see Freeman (2002: 31-87).
18   See Lemoine (2006), where the monastic, messianic and sacramental qualities of Edward's model of royal sanctity are particularly emphasized.

perspectives, but in a study of various forms of 'translation' they are of paramount importance. The comparison between Osbert and Aelred is not easy, and different evaluations have been proposed. Bloch, although qualifying Osbert's writing as a "langue travaillée et savante", says at the same time that the language is "verbeux et souvent obscure" (1923: 17) and finds in it a "prolixité prétentieuse" to which he opposes "le latin incolore et facile d'Ailred" (55), an evaluation which is frankly surprising. In Södergård's words, the editor of one of the French *Lives*, Osbert's style is described as "lourd et prolixe", full of "allusions bibliques et classiques" (1948: 41). Squire qualifies Osbert's Latin as "baroque" (1969: 97), and Barlow labels it as "flaccid rhymed prose" against "the style intense and direct" of the Anonymous (xxviii).

I am aware that to assess a medieval translation has proved to be very slippery ground, especially because it is difficult to resist the temptation to generalize from small excerpts. Both the personal attitude of the scholar, and the time of the edition, lead inevitably to evaluations that can easily be criticised and even reversed. But I think that we have to run the risk, as I will show in some examples I am going to propose. In any case we are probably right when we think that, from a stylistic point of view, the reason for Aelred's popularity is exactly the opposite of what the glory of Osbert was: clarity and concision were the qualities that prompted a long series of translations and adaptations which form the posterity of Edward's Life.

2. A comparison between the three early Lives

2.1. A few general remarks

It is commonly acknowledged that in the road leading to the construction of Edward as a saint king the pivotal event is the Norman Conquest, just like Aelred's *Vita* is the founding stone in the diffusion of his legend.[19] It is also clear that both the Anonymous and Osbert, to whom William of Malmesbury should be added,[20] saw the Conquest as the beginning of a series of disasters for England, with, in retrospect, the vision of Edward's reign as an era of peace (Bloch 1923: 103; Barlow 1992: xlviii). Aelred's main contribution, in this respect, is the interpretation of the Plantagenet dynasty, especially through Henry II, as the reconciliation of the two races into one people. This was the realization of Edward's prophecy, which Aelred, as we shall see, interprets in a totally different way from his predecessors. But other details become significant. One of the clearest is the presentation of the figure of Earl Godwin, the father of Edward's wife, Queen Edith. For the Anonymous he is a hero, frequently called "*inclitus dux*", the man who saved England from the Danes, and, although a 'natural' king, did not pretend the throne or overthrow Edward. Osbert totally ignores Godwin, and Aelred paints him as a negative figure, a murderer and a traitor, worthy of the horrible death he suffers, as told in chapter 25 of his *Vita Edwardi*.

As for sanctity, we see again a progress in these three early lives. I leave out the description of Edward's virtues, important as they are, and certainly presented by Aelred to Henry, as he had done in the *Genealogia Regum Anglorum*, as an example to imitate (Scholz 1961: 55). The texts dealing with this topic are too generic to be of particular interest. What comes to the foreground, instead, is Edward's chastity or virginity. The childless marriage was a terrible problem since no succession was assured, and troubles were to be expected at the death of Edward,[21] who historically seems to have even complicated a potentially tragic situation by promising the throne to different people at different times (Barlow 1992: xviii). In a hagiographical perspective this social drawback was a marvellous opportunity to underline one of the most important virtues required for sanctity,

---

19   A summary description of this hagiographical process through the three early Lives is given by Folz (1984: 91-101).

20   William did not properly write a Life of Edward, but in his *Gesta Regum Anglorum* (1124-1125) he incorporated a lot of material from the Anonymous Biography.

21   Robert Folz rightly thinks that this is one of the two main problems Edward had to face during his reign; the other was his relationship with the great Saxon aristocracy, in particular with the Godwin family (Folz 1984: 91-92).

transforming what might have been a physical difficulty into a spiritual choice, which was to be confirmed by the body remaining incorrupt.[22] Edward's chastity, which is barely mentioned in the Anonymous (Barlow 1992: 92), becomes part of a chapter in Osbert (ch. IV, Bloch 1923: 74-75), but covers the whole of chapter 8 in Aelred (HW 2005: 145-149) with an intense dramatization of an interior conflict on the part of Edward. This is just one of the choices by means of which Aelred depicts the profile of a king-monk, uniting in himself the most important virtues of a ruler and of a spiritual man.

If we want to understand the 'construction' of Edward's profile as a saint, and a saint king, we have to consider both figures, in the light of both state politics and ecclesiastical policy, the two concurring in presenting a complex figure of a saint who happened to rule England in a moment which was to introduce a dramatic change in the history, both of the monarchy and of the kingdom. To illustrate how this figure grows, and changes, in the three early lives, three points may be selected, in connection with politics, church policy and sanctity, seen respectively in Edward's role in the development of the English history, the connection of his cult with Westminster, and an aspect of his sanctity which was to become central, that is his 'virginity'. To this we may add the 'miracles' narrated in growing number within his lifetime, passages that in a textual perspective can be read as a collection of short stories in which to test the capacities and analyse the different narrative styles of the three authors.

2.2. The political interpretation of Edward's figure

The main problem in this field was where to locate the meaning and relevance of Edward before and after Hastings, which put an end to the Anglo-Saxon rule. In other terms, the point was how to interpret the ways in which the Saxons and the Normans are related. Two points are paramount here, one concerning the past, materialized in the figure of the Saxon earl Godwin, and the other about the future, to be seen in the light of Edward's 'prophecy' on his deathbed. Keeping in

---

22   John (1979) is convinced that this was the real reason for the beginning of the cult around the king's tomb at Westminster.

mind that Aelred's *Vita*, being the last stage in this process, in a sense collects what his predecessors had written, the two points are developed along this path. Earl Godwin is presented as a hero in the Anonymous, practically ignored by Osbert, who is not interested in Edward's political role, and turned into a totally negative person, almost a 'villain', in Aelred. As for the 'prophecy' of the truncated tree, this is understood by the Anonymous and Osbert (and, for that matter, by William of Malmesbury as well) as a forecast of disasters without remedy, while in Aelred it becomes the announcement of a coming reconciliation between the two peoples and dynasties, a union personified in Henry II, the addressee of the work.

2.2.1. Earl Godwin's changing portrait

To illustrate these points in more detail, we observe that in the Anonymous Godwin appears to be the main character and the true ruler of England, with the king in a sort of subordinate position. Right from the Prologue, after the presentation of King Edward as "fair in form, and nobly fine in limb and mind", during whose reign "a golden age shone for his English race", and of Queen Edith as "his other part, alike in probity, profound, intelligent, prompt counsellor", Godwin, Edith's father, comes forth as the subject of the book, described as "renowned for loyalty", an "Elysian spring" from whom four children have come to show how "heavenly goodness holds the English realm" (Barlow: 6-9 passim).[23] It is true, as Barlow has remarked, that this work is not in the first instance a Life of Edward, but a history of his reign, in which the Godwin family acts as the real protagonist, to the point that the main cause leading to the Norman Conquest lies in the tragic struggle between the two brothers, Harold and Tostig, without which, the Anonymous seems to say, England would have enjoyed a period of peace. An ideal portrait of Godwin comes at the very start of the book: he is described as "the most cautious in counsel and the most active in war", and "because of his equable temperament, most acceptable both to the people and to the king himself (Cnut at the time); incomparable in his tireless application to work, and with

---

23   For practical reasons, in the quotations that follow I give only the page number of Barlow's edition.

pleasing and ready courtesy polite to all" (9). Throughout the work Godwin is variously qualified as "having the first place among the highest nobles of the kingdom" (10), "regarded as father by all" (15), as an earl "*gloriosus*" (32), "*inclitus*" (38), "*fidelis et deo deuotus*" (42). He patiently tolerates the attacks by Robert of Jumièges, then archbishop of Canterbury, who had accused him of scheming against the king after killing Alfred, Edward's brother (32). He is greeted as a new David, sparing Saul's life (44), a compliment which may hint at the hope that Godwin's descendants were to rule England, as David's family took the lead in Israel after King Saul's death. Finally, "after the earl and his sons had been reconciled to the king, and the whole country had settled down in peaceful tranquillity", Godwin died in Winchester (15 April 1053), mourned by all who saw in him "their father and the kingdom's protector" (46).

In Osbert's *Vita* Godwin is still a "*clarissimus dux*", but this is the only mention he receives. The portrait is totally subverted in Aelred's *Vita*. In a new historical interpretation, meant to include the Normans in the Saxon dynasty, Godwin becomes the 'villain' of the story, flatly accused of killing Edward's brother, of disturbing the peace of the kingdom, and as such worthy of a horrible death. In fact Aelred adds two chapters to Osbert's *Life*, one which is a prophecy about the tragic struggle between the two brothers ending in ruin for both (ch. 24), the other to recount the miserable death of Earl Godwin (ch. 25). Aelred's view is so hostile to the Godwin family, that he relates a vision to the Abbot of Ramsey prophesying Harold's victory at Stamford Bridge (25 Sept 1066) against his brother allied with the Norwegian king, but specifying that this is achieved only thanks to the intercession of King Edward, who after his death continues to love his people, as a realisation of the prophecy the king had pronounced concerning the destiny of the two sons of Godwin (ch. 34).

2.2.2. Edward's prophecy

The second point where the contrast between the Anonymous and Aelred cannot be stronger is the so called 'prophecy' about the future of the kingdom that Edward pronounced on his deathbed. The king is shown as recounting that when he was exiled in Normandy, he saw in a vision two monks who were his friends. These men prophesied ruin and calamity for the English nation, a misery which would end when "a green tree, having been cut from its trunk and set apart from its own root at the space of three yokes, returns to its trunk and is restored to its old root, [...] and with its sap restored, flowers again and bears fruit. Then some comfort in this tribulation and a remedy for the trouble we have foretold is to be hoped for" (HW 2005: 205-206).

Clearly, this has to do with Edward's succession, and at the very least what can be clearly understood is that part of the Saxon blood would have to flow again in the veins of an English king, after "three yokes", that is three kings not in the direct Anglo-Saxon line of succession. These three kings were Harold (r. 1066), William I (r. 1066-1087) and William II Rufus (r. 1087-1110). This reunion of the truncated tree with its original stock was apparently realised when William was born, the son of the Norman king Henry I Beauclerc and the Saxon queen Edith of Scotland, afterwards called Matilda, a prince who was to be the third king after the Conquest. But the prince died in 1120, taking away with him any hope of 'normal' succession. So the problem remained open. This is why both Osbert of Clare and William of Malmesbury, following the Biographer, interpreted the prophecy only in the negative, alluding to the Norman Conquest as the total destruction of English rule. The wonderfully concise description of William is the best illustration of this point:

Nullus hodie Anglus uel dux, uel pontifex, uel abbas: aduenae quique diuitias et uiscera corrodunt Angliae, nec ulla spes est finiendae miseriae.

[No Englishman today is an earl, a bishop, or an abbot; new faces everywhere enjoy England's riches and gnaw her vitals, nor is there any hope of ending this miserable state of affairs] (Mynors/Thomson/Winterbottom 1998: 414-17)

Osbert, after recalling the death of Harold, the victory of the Normans, the deposition and imprisonment of archbishop Stigand, writes as in echo:

Neque enim hodie regem aut ducem aut pontificem ex eadem gentem cernimus aliter originem ducere quam arborem succisam ut reuirescat et fructum proferat suo stipiti denuo coherere. (ch. 22, Bloch: 109)

[Today we do not see any king or duke or bishop of the same people as we cannot see how a truncated tree may newly be attached to its trunk in order to live again and bear fruit]

For the three of them, this prophecy is, in the Biographer's words, a "*reuelatio impossibilitatis*" (Barlow: 120), something announcing a situation which cannot be changed. It is not so for Aelred, who on the contrary seems to write exactly as a response to his predecessors, whose interpretation he harshly contradicts:

> Quidam praemissam similitudinem dicunt, pro impossibili regem statuisse, illi maxime qui totam Anglorum nobilitatem sic deperisse lugebant ut ex ea gente nec rex, nec episcopus, nec abbas, nec princeps quilibet vix in Anglia cerneretur. (PL 195 773C-D)

> [Certain people, especially those who grieved that the whole nobility of the English had perished so that no king, bishop, abbot, or prince from this people could be found in England, say that the king put forth the above allegory as something impossible to realize] (HW 2005: 207).

Aelred then presents his own original interpretation, saying that the tree represents the kingdom of the English, whose root "was the royal seed that descended by a direct line of succession from Alfred [...] to Saint Edward" (HW 2005: 208). The tree was cut when the kingdom was transferred to another seed. But after three kings not in the direct line of the Saxon dynasty, the first reunion of the trunk to the root occurred when King Henry I married Matilda, Edward's niece, uniting thus the Saxon and Norman seeds. The tree flourished when from them Empress Matilda, daughter of Henry I and his wife Matilda, the only surviving heir of the couple, married Geoffrey of Anjou, and it bore fruit when from them "noster Henricus velut Lucifer matutinus exoriens, quasi lapis angularis utrumque populum copulavit" (PL 195: 774C) [our Henry rose from it like the morning star, joining the two peoples like a cornerstone] (HW 2005: 209). The result is that now

> Habet (nunc) certe de genere Anglorum Anglia regem, habet de eadem gente episcopos et abbates, habet et principes, milites etiam optimos, qui ex utriusque seminis conjunctione procreati aliis sunt honori, aliis consolationi.
> (PL 195: 774C).

> [Now certainly England has a king from English stock, and it has bishops and abbots from the same race, it also has princes, the best soldiers, too, who have been brought forth from the union of the seed of both races, for honour to some and consolation to others] (HW 2005: 209).

Aelred needs to distinguish 'flowers' from 'fruit', creating thus a further 'step' in order to reach Henry II's reign beyond the highly disputable reign of Stephen of Blois, 'illegitimate' successor to Henry I. At this point the 'rewriting' of the prophecy comes full circle, and as such it passes into the various translations of the *Vita*. Aelred is so convinced that his interpretation is right and conclusive, that he closes the chapter he says he has "inserted" into the order of the narrative by flatly dismissing any different solution of the problem: "If this explanation displeases anyone, let him either explain it otherwise or await another time when it may be fulfilled" (HW 2005: 209).

2.3. King Edward and Westminster

What was to become the royal abbey of Westminster, intrinsically connected with the Confessor's cult, is mentioned in the Anonymous as a foundation by the king, with nothing particularly relevant. This monastery which stood upon the Thames outside the walls of London, dedicated to St Peter, "but insignificant in buildings and numbers", with very poor endowments, was looked upon by the king because it lay near the town, was a delightful spot, and above all because it had as his patron St Peter. Out of his love for the Prince of the Apostles, the king decided to have his burial-place there, and accordingly he "ordered that out of the tithes of all his revenues should be started the building of a noble edifice", so that God "would look kindly upon him, both for the sake of his goodness and because of the gifts of lands".[24] The decision is followed by an architectural description of the building (Barlow 1992: 67-69). Interestingly, this story is 'mirrored' by the similar decision of Queen Edith to erect and endow Wilton Abbey. But, apart from these historical facts, almost nothing is said concerning the relevance of Westminster in the legend of the king.

From this rather slender source, Osbert of Clare creates a sort of story within the story, devoting to the building of Westminster a large

---

24   Barlow remarks that "It is possible that Osbert of Clare manufactured charters simply because the untimely death of the king had defrauded the monastery of authentic instruments" (1992: 68, fn 167).

section (chapters VI-XI) of his *Vita*. If we add narrations of visions and miracles connected with the presence of Edward in the abbey (chapters V, XII, XVIII, XXVI, XXVIII, XXIX), or those relating the dedication of the church (XIX), the endowments of it (XX), the burial (XXIV) and the translation of the relics (XXX), we reach a total of sixteen out of the thirty chapters of the work which have to do with Westminster.[25] The reason is easy to find. The fact that the body of the king was buried in the abbey he had contributed to build, was certainly enough reason to work for Edward's canonization.[26] Apart from any other consideration, in the medieval ecclesiastical policy a church possessing an important relic, the whole and 'uncorrupted' body in this case, could easily become a shrine capable of attracting crowds of pilgrims, and the corresponding income (Folz 1984: 95).

The various stages of the story told in Osbert's *Vita* could be listed in this way. First there is the vow of the king, taken when he was still young in Normandy, to go on a pilgrimage to Rome to thank St Peter for the peace achieved during his reign and to pray to him for the future welfare of the kingdom (ch. VI). This announcement gives rise to a sort of panic in the nation, in which all classes of society fear that the departure of the king might bring back the disorders he had contributed towards ending. Ambassadors are sent to Rome to ask the pope for the solution of the vow. Pope Leo IX agrees, on the condition that the king promises to use the money he had collected for his pilgrimage to build a new monastery or to restore an old one (VII). A vision received by a recluse of Worcester suggests that this place

---

25   Scholz wittily remarks that "The glorious history of Westminster and its privileges sidetrack the author so much that, occasionally, he has to remind himself of his original intent: 'But, since our purpose was to narrate his (Edward's) life and not to talk about privileges, let us start again our narration' (Bloch 91)" (Scholz 1961: 42).

26   See Appendix D in Barlow (1992: 150-163). It is true that, as Folz remarks, after Edward's death "no one was found to promote his canonization. The silence, if not the indifference of Westminster Abbey are surprising. No hagiographical note is found in the history of the abbey written by the Norman monk Sulcard about 1080-1085" (1984: 94). John, while acknowledging that "Edward's status as a saint owed nothing for a long time to either the Westminster monks or the Angevin court", maintains a more optimistic view of the king's sanctity saying that this status "rested on a continuous cult that may even have begun in his lifetime" (1979: 178).

should be Westminster (VIII), and then a miracle of the healing of a cripple, obtained through the 'collaboration' of the king with St Peter, makes the decision inevitable (IX). Then another marvel occurs: a fisherman tells how in a vision he had seen the church standing on the bank of the Thames being miraculously consecrated by St Peter himself at the time of Mellitus, the first bishop of London (X). A second legation is sent to another pope, Nicholas II, carrying a letter by Edward in which he renews his promise to re-build the Westminster monastery, asking at the same time for the renewal of the donations and privileges granted by his predecessor, to be confirmed forever, including especially independence from the local bishop and the guarantee that any fugitive reaching the church should be saved in his body and his life (XI). What, according to the Anonymous, was a simple decision taken by Edward emerges from this reconstruction as an enterprise decided by God himself who manifests his will through visions and miracles, partly realised by St Peter, and with the support of two popes, as expressed in documents probably forged by Osbert. King Edward does not appear to be much more than a humble and obedient executor. Westminster comes again to the foreground at the end of the *Life* through the description of its consecration, and, after the death of the king, as the place of his burial where many miracles occur. These important additions point to a sort of canonization of the building itself, and link its construction with Rome, giving an aura of universal relevance to the abbey.

This story flowed into Aelred's *Vita*, where all the subject-matter produced by Osbert was included, not without Aelred's personal touches visible both in the narrations and in the description of Edward's feelings about the circumstances. To give an example of the king's strong emotional involvement in the enterprise, see how Aelred describes the consequence of the miracle of the crippled man the king accomplished with the aid of St Peter: "This miracle gave the holy king a great incentive to love and venerate the merits of blessed Peter, and it inflamed his desire and increased his eagerness to complete the work he had begun in his name" (HW 2005: 165). Nothing of this sort can be found in Osbert, who prefers to mark a biblical allusion by connecting the miracle with one of the same kind performed by St Peter (Acts of the Apostles 3:2-8). Another typical Aelredian touch and a clear mark of his Cistercian attitude is found in the fact that, while Osbert praises Edward's generosity in showering the abbey with his gifts, not only in terms of gold and precious stones to decorate the church, but also in meadows, pastures, woods, waters, fields and arable land left to the monastery as a personal endowment (*quot prata, quot pascua, quot siluas, quot aquas, quot rura, quot sata contulit ecclesie!*: ch. XX, Bloch: 105), Aelred, on the contrary, turns this generosity to the giving of alms and gifts to the poor, using Luke 16: 9-11 to give his remark an evangelical ring: "With a lavish hand – he writes – he also distributed his treasures, *by means of the mammon of iniquity* making for himself *friends who* would *receive him into the eternal dwellings*" (ch. 28, HW 2005: 200).

2.4. Edward's sanctity: his virginity

Barlow stresses that for the Anonymous Edward was not a 'saint', at least not in book i (xxiii), although in the narrative there are more than a few glimpses leading in that direction. Using a rather formal language, the king is described as "*piissimus*" (Barlow: 52), "*deo dilectus*" (80), "*deo carus*" (82), a man who "used to stand at the holy offices with lamb-like meekness and tranquil mind", who liked to converse with holy monks, not really interested in displaying "the pomp of royal finery" and ready to show mercy and give help to the poor and the sick, having a powerful support in his wife, who often anticipated him in his actions of mercy (63-65). But the Biographer does not hide features which a hagiographer would probably have omitted: he says that the king was "of passionate temper and a man of prompt and vigorous action" (43), and that he "spent much of his time in the glades and woods in the pleasure of hunting" (63), adding significantly that this was the "only worldly pleasure" that the king enjoyed. More decisive proofs of sanctity were the gift of prophecy and the making of miracles. The Anonymous deals with these aspects of sanctity rather sparingly, and his testimony is hampered by the fact that the manuscript is mutilated, so that the modern editor has had to fill the big gaps of the final and more 'hagiographical' part of this Life with material taken from Osbert and other writers. We must be content with two miracles, one concerning the healing of a woman with a smelling disease and the other of a blind man; to this we may add the concise final paragraph, in which we are told that "Having revealed him as a saint while still living in the world, at his tomb likewise merciful God reveals by these signs that he lives with him as a saint in heaven. For at his tomb through him the blind receive their sight, the lame are made to walk, the sick are healed, the sorrowing refreshed by the comfort of God" (127).

Edward's celibacy is first mentioned by the Anonymous in a vision sent to Brithwald, bishop of Wiltshire, who in answer to his weeping because of the Danish ravages saw St Peter "consecrate the image of a seemly man, assign him the life of a bachelor (*celibem ei uitam designare*), and set the years of his reign by a fixed reckoning of his life" (Barlow 15)[27]. The Anonymous identifies this king with Edward, whose celibacy reappears in the short portrait of Edward's sanctity placed in the first paragraph of the so called 'second book', where he says that the king "preserved with holy chastity the dignity of his consecration, and lived his whole life dedicated to God in true innocence". This was gladly accepted by God, who glorified him by 'signs' the Anonymous has "learnt from the joint testimony of good and fitting men" (93).

But the real creator of the 'virginity' theme is Osbert, in a trend which was to be greatly developed and emphasized by Aelred, with a transparent connection with the Gregorian reform of the clergy and the implied great glory of celibacy as a particular sign of sanctity (see Huntington 2003). The fact is that Edward's marriage had produced no children. The explanation given by Osbert is that the king, having in his heart the memory of Mary Virgin and mother, had become "the house of virginity" (*uirginitatis factum domicilium*), and that, notwithstanding his marriage, "God in his mercy preserved holy king Edward in the purity of his flesh for all the days of his life", with Queen Edith imitating him "as a daughter". The consequence of this was that "as he had a virgin conscience, so his body has remained incorrupt in the sepulchre until these days" (ch. IV, Bloch: 74-75). The statement is repeated when, thirty six years after his death, Edward's body is translated for the first time: since his limbs had not suffered any

---

27   The story of this prophetic vision of St Peter's consecrating Edward as king is also present in Osbert (ch. III: *uitam ei designare celibem*: Bloch: 72) and Aelred (ch.4: *precipue celibem vitam commendans*: PL 195:703B; 2005: 136).

damage to his purity, so his body remained in the glory of the resurrection. The integrity of the body is so marked that we read of a rather comic episode, in which the bishop of Rochester tries to steal a hair of the king's beard without succeeding. The conclusion of Osbert sounds like an epitaph: "Let him rest in his palace (that is the abbey of Westminster) uncorrupt and virgin" (ch. XXX, Bloch: 121-123).

Aelred's treatment of this subject is somewhat more dramatic. First, the single chapter (IV) in which Osbert describes both the king's sanctity in general terms and the celebration of his "chaste marriage" is divided into three chapters (6-8) forming a sort of sub-unit. Ch. 6 is devoted to the illustration of Edward's sanctity in typical hagiographic terms, in a way which is very similar to Osbert's. Ch. 7 is intended to show a concrete aspect of Edward's sanctity, his mercy and generosity, and relates an event proper to Aelred in which the king, seeing a thief stealing his treasures, stops him from being too greedy, and then lets him run away without denouncing him, so that "the boy fled, neither betrayed by the king nor pursued" (HW 2005: 144). Three virtues are thus illustrated in this story: the king's love of sobriety, his merciful attitude towards a poor man, and the easy way of forgiving. The king's chastity is singled out and becomes the only subject of ch. 8 (146-149), which right from the title specifies that it will deal with "His chaste marriage, and His and the Queen's virginity".

Aelred's emphasis on the virginity of the royal couple is ostensibly stronger than Osbert's, and the development of the topic is even more so, both in length and strategic narrative. The starting point is similar: the problem of the succession to the throne for which a wife was needed. Right from the beginning Aelred shows himself to be a fine psychologist and an acute observer. Implicitly saying that Edward had taken a vow of chastity, he creates a dramatic situation in the king's mind, torn between the necessity of keeping his vow secret, and the unavoidable decision to take a wife for the good of the kingdom. The way out of the dilemma passes through an intense prayer in which Edward beseeches some Old Testament heroes of purity, such as the three children in Babylon, "unharmed in the Chaldean flames", the patriarch Joseph, the chaste Susanna, holy Judith, and "surpassing all of these", the Virgin Mary, a perfect icon, "both a wife and a virgin so that the bond of marriage should not destroy the seal of chastity" (HW 2005: 146). Confiding in God's help, Edward gives then his consent to the thanes, and Edith, Earl Godwin's daughter, is chosen as a wife. Aelred's political stance creeps in here again, since while in Osbert the earl was still qualified as *"clarissimus dux"*, in the rewritten story he becomes "a man of singular cunning, a betrayer of kings and kingdom, skilled in deceit and accustomed to dissimulation, someone who could easily turn the people to any faction at all", and finally "a thorn" from which Edith, "a rose", had been engendered. The celebration of the marriage follows, in which Godwin is again described in very hostile terms, as a man wanting to "bind the king's mind more tightly to himself; he had no little fear of the king because of the murder of his brother, and more than a few betrayals". On the other hand, the nature of Edward and Edith's marriage is beautifully described by Aelred:

> When they came together as one, the king and the queen covenanted to preserve chastity. They did not think that they needed any witness to this bond beside God. She became a bride in spirit, not flesh, he a husband in name, not act. The attachment of marriage continued between them apart from the marriage act, and an embrace of chaste delight without the deflowering of her virginity. He loved but he did not corrupt her; she was loved but not touched. Like a kind of new Abishag (1 Kings 1:4), she warmed the king but her love did not weaken him with lust, soothed him by her submission but did not soften him with desires. (ch. 8, HW 2005: 148)

The language of the passage is highly revealing of the medieval attitude towards sexuality and virginity, which Aelred shared with his contemporaries. The last biblical reference, mentioning the young girl who was hired to warm king David in his old age, may hint at the difference in age between the king and the queen, although the more marked emphasis of the reference seems to underline the similarity between Edward and David. Anyway, the abbot of Rievaulx is so anxious about Edward's chastity being real and true that in a sort of appendix he refers that this "was so widely known and believed throughout England that many, being certain of the fact, argued over their intention"[28]. Some people thought that the king did not want to

---

28   See, for example, William of Malmesbury: "The king's policy with her was neither to keep her at a distance from his bed nor to know her as a man would; whether he did this out of hatred for her family, which he prudently concealed

"beget traitors" (again, Godwin's shadow is looming in the background!), an opinion which Aelred dismisses, but which in any case he reports to conclude that "no one doubted the king's continence, even though they quarrelled over its cause" (HW 2005: 148-149).

2.5. Miracles and the art of narrative:
the story of the scrofulous woman

Edward's miracles, which incidentally constitute by far the largest part of the *Vita*, cannot of course be discussed very extensively in this chapter. As two folios are missing in the last gathering of the manuscript, we have only two miracles which can be ascribed to the Anonymous; my choice was therefore to select one of these and compare this version with the ones found in Osbert and Aelred. Although the sample is small, it may be sufficient to illustrate the different approaches of the three biographers to such stories.[29]

The story tells of a young woman, "already provided with a husband, but gladdened with no fruit of the marriage", and with "an infection of the throat", which "had so disfigured her face with an ever-smelling disease that she could scarcely speak to anyone without great embarrassment" (Barlow: 93). Advised in a dream that King Edward could cure her, she went to him, who, by anointing her face with water several times and by making the sign of the cross, healed her. The miracle was so extraordinary that not only did the woman recover all her health and beauty through the king's touch, but she also became pregnant, and "lived henceforth happily enough with all around her" (Barlow: 95).

Osbert, while following at times almost verbatim the Anonymous' redaction, inserts some details of his own meant to link the

---

to suit the time, or whether from a love of chastity, I have not discovered for certain" (Mynors/Thomson/Winterbottom 1998: 353-355).

29   A detailed analysis of this miracle can be found in Yohe (2003). The article focuses on three miracles. The other two are that of the cripple carried on the king's back and that of the king and the young thief, already mentioned. The first is read as a sign of "honoring the poor and suffering", the second as "simplicity and alms for the sake of the poor", and that of the scrofulous woman as expressing "affectionate relationship and prayer".

miracle more visibly with the king's sanctity. It is perhaps not without significance that the miracle (ch. XIII) is introduced by a passage in which Edward's chastity is recalled as a glorious accompaniment to his sacred dignity, a glory not to be turned into ruin by a carnal intercourse although licit, a state of innocence approved by God and visualized by "shining signs in this corrupted flesh". One of these signs stands out in the story of the scrofulous woman who is both "corrupted in the flesh" and unfertile in her marriage. This connection would suggest that this sickness in a sense manifests visually something which is unchaste, and/or that only the king's chastity can restore the flesh of the woman to health and integrity. The detailed description of the healing is directly derived from the Anonymous, as the following comparison will show:

> ANONYMOUS: Liniente rege morbus medicatus a crusta mollescit et soluitur, ducenteque manu a diuersis foraminibus uermes plene cum sanie et sanguine egrediuntur. Item pius rex sancta dextera premens, et educens saniem, nec abhorret in infirma muliere hunc pati fetorem, donec medicante manu omnem illam noxiam elicuit pestem.

> [Those diseased parts that had been treated by the smearing of the king softened and separated from the skin; and, with the pressure of the hand, worms together with pus and blood came out of various holes. Again the good king kneaded with his holy hand and drew out the pus. Nor did he shrink from enduring the stench of the sick woman until with his healing hand he had brought out all that noxious disease.] (Barlow: 92-93)

> OSBERT: dum sancta regis dextera foramina linit, soluitur crusta et mollescit; glandule cum uermibis egrediuntur; sanies et sanguis dextera regis premitur; et mulier in breui integre saluti reparatur. (Bloch: 93)

> [while the holy right hand of the king is smearing the holes, the crust softens and dissolves, the glands and the worms come out; the pus and the blood is squeezed out by the right hand of the king; and in short the woman is wholly healed]

The connection of the healing with the king's chastity, which, together with his humility, seems to be the source of his miraculous power, reappears at the end in an exclamation by Osbert: "O, how holy and humble is the innocence (*innocentia*) of such a prince, who did not disdain the stench of a killing (*noxius*) humour and by doing so gave the young woman back to health" (Bloch: 93). No one will fail to notice the healing counterpoint established by the contrast *innocentia / noxius*. The happy end is even more marked than in the Anonymous, since the woman "lost the shame of sterility and from then on lived in joy with her husband in her house for a long time".

Aelred's narration is striking because of the intense emotional participation by which, as seen in Edward's dilemma concerning his marriage, what in the other authors are general statements become deeply felt personal problems. See, for example, how the pain of the sick and unfertile woman is dramatised in Aelred's *Vita*:

> A certain young woman, given in marriage, was suffering from two misfortunes. Illness had deformed her face, and unfruitfulness in childbearing had deprived her of her husband's love. Something like acorns had grown under her jaw, and this unsightly swelling had marred her whole face; the fluid under her skin putrefied and corrupted her blood, and worms breeding in it gave off a disgusting odour. The disease struck her husband with horror, and her sterility weakened his affection. The unhappy woman lived on, despised by her husband and a burden to her parents. Her friends seldom approached her because of the stench, and her husband seldom looked at her because of his horror. Sorrow, tears, and sighs resulted, day and night, while her sterility brought hatred on her and her infirmity contempt. Helplessness deflected the skill of the doctors. What could the wretched woman do? What alone was left her when human help failed? She prayed for divine aid, blurting out as if in the voice of that equally wretched woman, 'I beg you, Lord, to loose me from the chains of this reproach, or else take me from the earth'.[30] (HW 2005: 179).

This short sample shows how a matter-of-fact narration can become emotionally intense under the pen of a skilled writer, so that both the painful isolation of the sick woman, and the even more painful relationship with her husband, here mentioned four times while practically invisible in the other versions, contribute to the readers' involvement. In this light it is also revealing that Aelred chooses to further reduce the slow-motion description of the miracle by the Anonymous which Osbert had already shortened. All he has to say is that

> Subito rupta cute, cum sanie vermes ebulliunt, resedit tumor, dolor omnis abscessit. (PL 195, 762A)

---

30   The quotation is from Tobias 3:13, referred to the daughter of Raguel, whose seven successive husbands had died the first night after the marriage.

The quick and perfect sequence of the Latin comes out inevitably a bit diluted in the English version: "Her skin suddenly cracked, worms came bubbling out along with the corrupted blood, the swelling subsided, and all pain left her" (HW 2005: 180). It seems that Aelred is less interested in wonders than in human suffering, an attitude of compassion which is so typical of him as is shown in his sermons and ascetic treatises.

If we compare the description of this miracle in the three versions we can easily draw some general conclusions about the style of each author. Looking at the short quotations taken form this story, we may remark that, while the Anonymous uses many subordinates, Osbert has only one, although he writes rather long sentences; Aelred on the contrary is clear and concise, creating also a quick and very effective rhythm by a clever use of stresses. Apart from other merits, it was probably the lively narrative style that granted Aelred's *Vita* the great popularity it endured for centuries, as the following part of this chapter will briefly show.

3. A survey of the Lives derived from Aelred's *Vita*

The success of Aelred's version was immense, since his *Vita* superseded the other two and became the obligatory reference for all subsequent treatment of the subject. In this chapter I can do no more than list the Lives derived from this one, and give some glimpses of the ways in which they are related, to which I will add some short remarks about the kind of version they represent.

Here is the list of the Lives derived in different forms from the Aelredian archetype:
1. First Latin rhythmic *Vita* (13th century)[31]
2. Second Latin rhythmic *Vita* (15th c. – Luard 1858: 361-377)
3. Third Latin *Vita* 15th c. – Horstmann 1901: 330-349)
4. Anglo-Norman poem (before 1170 – Södergård 1948)

---

31   An extract from Cambridge, Caius College MS 153 is printed in Luard (1858: 381-383).

5. Anglo-Norman prose *Vita* (14th c.)[32]
6. *La Estoire de Seint Ædward le Rei*, (? Matthew Paris – 13th c.)[33]
7. ME prose *Vita* (15th c. – Hamer/Russell 2000: 3-38)
8. ME poetic *Vita* (15th c. – Moore 1942).

3.1. The Latin Lives

3.1.1. First Latin rhythmic Vita

The first Latin rhythmic Life belongs to the thirteenth century and it is so similar to Aelred's *Vita* that it was for a time attributed to him (Södergård 1948: 42-43). It is now extant in two manuscripts: Cambridge, Gonville and Caius College MS 153, and Rome, Vatican MS Reg. Lat. 489, ff. 35v-60v, in which it follows the Anglo-Norman poem produced by a nun at Barking Abbey in the same century.[34] There is no edition of this work, but we can have an idea of its relation to Aelred's text by comparing a few lines of the passage about how the nation reacted when the king announced his intention to go on a pilgrimage to Rome to solve a vow he had taken:

> AELRED: Ad hanc vocem tota illa multitudo contremuit, et interiorem produnt lacrymis suspiriisque dolorem. (PL 195: 750D)

> POEM:
> Talia tractanti plebs obviat, atque dolorem
> Anxia quem patitur mens pia, voce probat.
> Effluit in lacrymas caeco terebrata dolore,
> Suspiransque tremit, tacta timore gemit. (ll. 1-4: Luard 1858: 381)

The rules of poetic diction can explain the lexical sophistication and the intensification of stress given to the more concise language of Aelred. This seems to be a general and natural trend in the poem. The same passage shows how the anonymous author can dramatize a prose text by turning it into a speech directly addressed to the king, as in the following lines:

---

32 Extracts from London, BL MS Egerton 745 printed in Meyer (1911).
33 First edited by Luard (1858), re-edited by Wallace (1983).
34 Luard (1858: xxx-xxxi) gives a short description of these MSS, and lists six chief differences between the poem and Aelred's *Vita*.

AELRED: Tunc omnes in commune vociferantes in regem, se non deserendos, se non exponendo gladiis, patriam hostibus non prodendam, nec dimittendum pacis obsidem quem Deo dante receperant, nec pro uno, ut putabatur, bono tot admittenda pericula allegabant. (PL 195: 750D-751A)

POEM:
[...] Unus pro multis haec recitando gemit:
"Quid tibi mentis ait, pater inclite, quo rationis
    Jure paras populum linquere, quaeso, tuum?
Quae, vel quot maneant, te discedente, pericla,
    Quanta, quis expediet, sint peritura bona?
Quae tecum venit, te pax abeunte recedet,
    Quae nequit absque suo sceptra tenere pari.
Succumbet certe regni status iste ruinae,
    Quem sublimavit lingua manusque tua.
Agmina multa quidem procerum populique relinquis,
    At tua prae multis millibus una manus.
Pro dolor! Exponis patriam, pater, expoliandam,
    Quam premet ad nutum Barbara turba suum.
In jugulum nostrum descendet Barbara ensis,
    Quippe tuos cives sternet iniqua manus.
Ire paras Romam, laudabile, non tamen unum
    Pluribus aequandum credimus esse bonum. (ll. 25-40: Luard 382).

Another feature of this Latin Life, apart from the differences already listed by Luard (xxx, note), was signalled by Södergård (1948: 43), who remarks that the poem gives a very shortened version of three miracles (ch. 39-40-41) described in much detail in Aelred's work. But these are only few annotations, since a more extended comparison would require the availability of a complete text.

3.1.2. Second Latin rhythmic Vita

The second rhymed Latin Life was produced in the fifteenth century and was dedicated to King Henry VI. It is extant in two manuscripts, datable to 1440-1450: Oxford, Bodleian Library, Selden Supra 55 and Digby 186 (ff. 16r-22v)[35].The text, edited from Selden 55, has been published by Luard (361-377). This Life seems to bear no direct relation to the earlier one. It is clearly based on Aelred's *Vita*, but in this case the rewriting takes the form of an extreme condensation, as can be seen in the passage corresponding to the one quoted above:

---

35   See the description in Luard (1858: xxvii-xxx).

Ipse quidem vellet, proceres contraria suadent,
impediunt, retrahunt, allegant mille pericula,
quae sibi, quae regno, sine rege timenda fuere;
fletibus et precibus quamvis invitus obedit [...] (Luard 368-369)

The abridgement is stark in that only four lines are used to relate an even larger part of the story, including the king's desire and his decision to obey the request presented to him by all his people, here significantly reduced to the 'chief men' (*proceres*)! The way these 'reductions' are carried out could be a subject of research, since, for example, while the story of the king's chaste marriage takes 37 lines against 42 in prose (Luard 366-367), the miracle of the scrofulous woman is described in 12 verses against 19 lines in prose (Luard 371-372).

The following quotation shows how Aelred's clear, concise and perfectly balanced prose could easily be turned into verse:

AELRED: Fit ille coniux mente, non carne; ille nomine maritus, non opere. Perseverat inter eos sine actu coniugali conjugalis affectus... (PL 195, 748A)

POEM: Conjux mente fit haec, non carne; salute maritus Ille fit, haud opere; sed amor ligat unus utrumque. (ll. 207-208; Luard 367)

3.1.3. Third Latin Vita

To these rhymed Latin *Lives*, a third one should be added, which was produced in prose at the end of the fifteenth century and inserted in the *Nova Legenda Angliae*, long attributed to John Capgrave, although now it is recognised as the work of John of Tynemouth (see Lucas 1970).[36] This is the first 'printed' Life of Edward, published in 1516. The author has simply reduced Aelred's original text by generous

---

36   The *Nova Legenda Angliae* was printed by Carl Horstmann in 1901. Saint Edward's Life is in vol. 1, pp. 330-349. Horstmann remarks that "It is hardly fair to name Capgrave with our Collection, his share being, at most, restricted to the change of the original arrangement – and yet it is his name by which the Collection was known in modern times. The earlier Bollandists, not having access to English sources, give the lives of our Collection under Capgrave's name [...]. Their testimony can have no value. So Capgrave's share in the work, within the limits indicated, remains an open question which I have no means of deciding" (p. lxvii).

cuttings. It is this text that was chosen to be inserted in the *Acta Sanctorum*, where it appears for 5 January.[37]

3.2. The Anglo-Norman Lives

3.2.1. First Anglo-Norman Life

On the basis of Aelred's *Vita* an Anglo-Norman poem was written very soon after the original between 1163 and 1170 by a nun of the abbey of Barking who decided to remain anonymous[38]. The text is extant in two manuscripts: Welbeck Abbey, MS ICI, fol. 55c-85c (4239 lines); Vatican Library, Reg. Lat. 489, fol. 1r-35v (5222 lines). A very long section of this Life appears in a manuscript containing Wace's poem *Roman de Brut*, in which ll. 14763-14774 have been replaced by 3879 lines, corresponding to ll. 69-4482 of the poem.[39]

The author describes herself as a humble nun, whose French she qualifies as poor. Her linguistic self-consciousness is worth quoting:

> Un faus franceis sai d'Angletere
> Ke ne l'alai ailurs quere.
> Mais vus ki ailurs apris l'avez,
> La u mester iert, l'amendez. (ll. 7-10: Södergård 109)

> [Un faux français je sais d'Angleterre
> Que je n'allai chercher ailleurs.
> Mais vous qui ailleurs appris l'avez
> Là où besoin sera amendez-le.][40]

She is also very uncertain about the worth of her translation, to the point of accusing herself of presumption!

> Merci crie, si quiert pardun
> Qu'el' emprist la presumptïun

---

37 *Acta Sanctorum*, Paris: Victor Palmé 1863, Januarii Tomus Primus, 290-304: the *Vita*, divided in xi chapters, is on pp. 293-302, followed by a *Translatio* on pp. 302-304.

38 On the author and her work see Wogan-Brown (2001: 249-256).

39 See the description of these manuscripts in Södergård (1948: 46-48).

40 Anglo-Norman is rendered into modern French, so as to facilitate comparison.

De translater iceste vie.
Des qu'ele n'est mielx acumplie,
Or emblasmez sun numpueir
Kar aquité s'ad sun vuleir. (ll. 5318-5323: Södergård 1948: 273)

[Merci elle crie, si cherche pardon
Du fait que'elle a entrepris la présomption
De traduire cette vie.
Si elle n'a été mieux réalisée
Blâmez son impuissance (non-pouvoir)
Car elle s'est acquittée de son désir.]

The best known nun-writer of the abbey is Clemence of Barking, who wrote a *Life of Saint Catherine*, but it seems that her authorship can be safely excluded. The date is inferred by the modern editor from the dedication of the work to Henry II, in a period when the fratricidal struggles between his sons (1172-1189) had not yet begun, and certainly before the murder of Thomas Becket (1170), after which it would have been difficult to honour in such eulogistic terms the king who was behind that event, especially in a monastery where Becket's sister was the abbess (Södergård 1948: 16-26).

The modern editor of the poem describes some characteristics of this version in relation to the original Latin text. These are digressions and expansions mostly in the form of moral comments and religious reflections. To give just one example, in the story of Edward's chaste marriage, a very short sentence in which Aelred expresses the king's fear that the treasure of his virginity might be destroyed, is followed by a commentary about the fragility of human heart according to a well-known metaphor taken from St Paul's 2 Cor 4:7:

Stupet rex *thesauro* metuens suo, qui *in vase fictile* reconditus, facile poterat calore dissolvi. (PL 195 747A)
[The king was shocked, fearing that his treasure, which was hidden in an earthen vessel, could easily be destroyed by heat.] (HW 2005 145)

The Anglo-Norman poem takes up the image of the fragile vessel to expand on it after explaining the sense of the metaphor:

Cest vessel est le cors humain,
En ki nul bien nen est certain
Et ensurquetut chasteté
Relment i trove seürté. (ll. 1109-1112: Södergård 1948: 144)

365

[Ce vase est le coeur humain,
En qui nul bien n'est certain,
Et surtout la chasteté
Réellement n'y trouve sureté.]

The expansion is 22 lines long (ll. 1109-1130: Södergård 1948: 144-145). A new miracle, not in Aelred, concerning the healing of a nun of Barking (ll. 6442-6545: Södergård 1948: 304-307), has been included. Some historic annotations have also been inserted. Personal expressions in form of direct addresses ("Lords", "hear", "look") or of phrases introducing dialogues are used to mark the passage from one chapter to another.[41] Many of these features, above all the very frequent verbal repetitions, would suggest that the text was meant to be orally delivered. The result is that Aelred's style, already rapid, acquires an even more lively and personal tone in the Anglo-Norman poem (Södergård 1948: 34).

3.2.2. Second Anglo-Norman Life

The poem was subsequently reduced and simplified in a prose version, which, according to Södergård (1948: 36), is mostly a re-writing through a process of 'de-rhyming':

> The method consisted in suppressing rhymes and rhythm, changing some words, altering or omitting phrases and expression used to create rhymes. All this was intended to hide the fact that the original was in verse.

3.2.3. Third Anglo-Norman Life

A third earlier *Life* in Anglo-Norman can be added to the list. This is a poem attributed to Matthew Paris and dedicated to Queen Eleanor of Provence. It is entitled *La Estoire de Seint Ædward le Rei*, and is now extant in Cambridge, University Library MS Ee.iii.59, a lavishly illustrated manuscript of the thirteenth century, written "with some degree of certainty" between 1236 and 1245.[42] The work was first

---

41   All these additions, together with the difference of the prose version of the poem, are usefully signalled in the introduction of Södergård's edition (1948: 26-34).

42   On this beautiful manuscript see Binski (1990), in which some of the sixty-four pen-and-wash illustrations are reproduced. Aelred's influence is visible in

published by Luard in 1858 and re-edited with modern scientific criteria by Wallace in 1983. This is not a translation of Aelred in a strict sense, although the author draws a large amount of material both from Aelred's *Vita* and from his *Genealogia Regum Anglorum*.[43] It suffices to look again at the passage concerning the king's chaste marriage to see that, while a verbal quotation in Latin is taken from Aelred and inserted into the Anglo-Norman poem (*Sicut spina rosam / Genuit Godwinus Editham*), the treatment of the story is much more expanded, a sort of free elaboration which closely follows the pattern of the story set by Aelred, but in the verbal description goes very far from the model (ll. 1058-1278: Wallace 1983: 30-37).[44]

3.3. The ME Lives

The fact that the two ME versions are the last to be produced may come as a sort of surprise, since they appear only in the fifteenth century: is this a problem of readership? We have a prose *Life* contained in two manuscripts and a poem extant in three, all except one dating from the fifteenth century.[45]

---

fig. 3 (Binski 1990: 142), portraying Edward advised by his barons to take a wife and pondering their advice before an altar; fig. 4 represents the death of Godwin, choked by a morsel, who is being dragged away from dinner; an anti-Saxon reader has erased Godwin's face. The mainly political perspective of this *Estoire* also appears in the obsession about the king's succession and in the growing presence and power of the barons around him, to the point that Binski concludes that "St Edward [...] emerges as a paradigm of a form of constitutional monarchy" (1990: 347-348).

43   For a detailed comparison between Aelred's *Vita* and Paris's *Estoire* see Wallace (1983: xxiii-xxvii).

44   In this respect, to write, as Wallace does, that "Those passages which are based on Aelred's *Vita* follow it closely" (1983: xxix) sounds ambiguous: while this is true of the 'pattern' it is certainly not so if we consider the largely different wording of the text. The work is better described by Binski as "a vernacular versification and adaptation of an earlier *vita* of Aelred of Rievaulx", with "numerous thirteenth-century interpolations" (1990: 334).

45   See a good description of all these manuscripts together with their relations in Södergård (1948: 44-45).

3.3.1. ME Prose Life

This prose *Life* is preserved in Oxford, MS Trinity College XI, a small parchment codex of 52 folios containing only this item. A longer and more detailed version is found in London, BL MS Additional 35298. This last manuscript is in fact the most complete version of the so called *Gilte Legende*, written in 1438, which Caxton says in his prologue he has used, together with the Latin and the French versions, for his edition of the *Golden Legend* printed in 1483 (Hamer 1978: 24)[46]. It is highly probable that either Additional 35298 or a parent or sister manuscript now lost was the codex used by Caxton (Kurvinen 1959: 364. 371). Unsurprisingly, the two texts correspond, as both go back to Aelred's *Vita*, but it is right to give the priority and the originality of the version to the anonymous author of the Life which was included in this manuscript of the *Gilte Legende*.

The Additional Life follows Aelred rather closely. I give first an excerpt taken from the chapter about the king's marriage in which we can see to what extent the translator is faithful to the original:

> AELRED: Confirmato Edwardi Regis imperio, omnibusque summa pace ac prosperitate compositis, proceres de successione solliciti, regem de uxore ducenda conveniunt. Stupet rex thesauro metuens suo, qui in vase fictili reconditus, facile poterat calore dissolvi. Sed quid ageret? Si obstinatius obniteretur, timebat ne proposi sui proderetur dulce secretum: si suadentibus praeberet assensum, naufragium pudicitiae formidabat. (PL 195: 747B)

> PROSE LIFE: When the reame was made alle sure and stedefast, the councelle of the londe drewe them togeder tretyng of a mariage for the kyng. And when it was mevid to the kyng he was than gretely astonyed, dredyng to lese the tresoure of his virginyte, the which was kepte in a bretelle and a fulle frayle vesselle. And what that he shulde do or saye he wyste not, for if he shulde obstynately denye it he drad leste his avowe in chastite shulde be opynly knowen, and if he consentid thereto he drad to lese his chastite.
>
> (f. 49ra; Hamer/Russell: 9)

A second example is taken from the beginning of the chapter dealing with the miracle of the scrofulous woman. In this case the original Latin is shortened and simplified, although at times additions can be

---

46   The "Lyf of saynt Edward kynge and confessour" is on ff. 322v-332r. Under the title there is a woodcut in which the king shows the ring he had given to a beggar, who later revealed himself as Saint John the Evangelist.

found, like when the translator specifies that the woman had been given in marriage to a 'noble man':

AELRED: Adolescentula quaedam tradita nuptiis duplici laborabat incommodo. Nam facies eius morbus deformaverat, amorem viri sterilitas prolis ademerat; sub faucibus quippe quasi glandes ei succreverant, quae totam faciem deformi tumore foedantes, putrefactis sub cute humoribus, sanguinem in saniem verterant, inde nati vermes odorem teterrimum exhalabant. Ita viro incutiebat morbus horrorem, sterilitas minuebat affectum. Vivebat infelix mulier odiosa marito, parentibus onerosa. (PL 195: 761C-D)

PROSE LIFE: There was a yong woman yovyn in mariage to a noble man, and not longe after she had .ij. misfortunes. Furste she was bareyne, and also there rose vp vnder hir cheke manye foule bouchis and kyrnels fulle of corrupte humors, þe which engendrid foule wormes and made hir flessh to stynke, so that she was abhomynable and hatefulle to hir husbonde and to alle hir frendis.
(f. 50ra; Hamer/Russell: 17)

The text contained in the Oxford manuscript has some verbal similarities with the ME Verse *Life*, but since it has some details extant in the Latin which do not appear in the poem, which moreover gives more recent historical references, we may conclude that this prose *Life* precedes the verse *Life*. Södergård goes so far as to suggest that the source of the English text might be the Anglo-Norman poem he edits (65).

3.3.2. ME Verse Life

The ME Verse *Life* does not seem to be a work of particularly high quality: one would think that in this case 'poetry' means only 'rhymes'. But, apart from its literary value, we can read it as a text in which political and religious perspectives undergo a further change, not to speak of stylistic choices, concerning which Aelred remains unsurpassed. Two examples are offered to illustrate my argument.

The first is taken again from the chapter about the king's chaste marriage. Reading the ME poem one is immediately given the impression that the author is not really interested in either extolling the king's chastity or exposing Edward's inner struggle before taking his decision, a passage that has simply disappeared. The main concern of the poet is the political problem of providing an heir for the good of the nation, a point certainly not ignored by Aelred, who writes that the

369

barons were *"de successione solliciti"*; although this is by no means the focus of the chapter on Edward's marriage. Here is the poem:

> [...] grede on him for þer nas non eir after wille
> to nyme a wif leste he lete þet lond folliche aspille
> for ʒif he hadde an kende eir biʒute be his wif
> þe sikeror hi wolde be to liue wit-oute strif. (ll. 291-294: Moore 10)

The political stance is clearly emphasized by the many expressions in which Earl Godwin is portrayed as "fals & traitor", the man "þet the kings brother slou", a phrase repeated twice, "þis traitor þet fel was y-nou", followed by "þe traisons mony on þet he dude in englond". A patriotic tone appears in a curious addition to Aelred's text, as when the poet, speaking of Edith, says that one of her merits was that she was not "brought from *another* land":

> [...] heo was so clene maide & of so holi liue
> þet beter him were in holinesse nyme hire to wiue
> þan an hei kings douter of another lond ibroʒt
> þet to his holi liue acordi nolde nout (315-318: Moore 11)

The anxiety about the lack of an heir reappears threateningly at the end of the passage, curiously enough as a commentary to the couple's chastity:

> [...] þer nas neuer bituen hom noʒt bote clannesse
> boþe hi were at one accord to libbe in clene liue
> so þet hi were wit-oute eir me þincþ for al his wiue
> so þet heiemen of þe lond bispeke hit wel faste
> & for defaute of eir of him of worre were agaste (324-328: Moore 11)

The second example has been chosen for a stylistic comparison, by which it can be easily shown how difficult it was to imitate Aelred's narrative vivacity. It is the story in which Aelred relates the miserable death of Godwin choked by a morsel he pretended to swallow with no consequence, in order to demonstrate that he was not responsible for the murder of Alfred, Edward's brother:

> As he spoke he put the morsel into his mouth and got it halfway down his throat. He tried to draw it further in but could not; he tried to spit it out, but it stuck more firmly. Soon the passage by which he drew breath was blocked, his eyes rolled back, and his arms stiffened. The king regarded the man dying

so unhappily and, perceiving that divine vengeance had overtaken him, spoke to those standing by, saying: 'Take this dog away'.

(PL 195: 767 A-B; ch. 25, HW 2005: 191-192)

The poetic translation appears to be rather poor, having reduced it all to a death by choking, and omitting the dramatic reaction of the king:

þe mossel he dude to his mouth ac þe king hit blesseþe er
hit bileueþe (*stopped*) amidde his þrote; astrangleþ he was riȝt þer
& deide ate borde al stif wit schamnesse ynou (870-872: Moore 29-30).

The long story of Aelred's *Vita* ends in two remarkable achievements which may be read as a sort of consecration: its landing in two classical works of Christian literature. The first is Caxton's *Golden Legend* (1483) which incorporated the ME translation. The second is the collection of *Acta Sanctorum* where we can read Aelred's Latin *Vita Edwardi* in a reduction produced and printed in 1516. To complete the picture we should not omit the fact that Edward's celebrity extended beyond the boundaries of England: a *Vita* written in Old Icelandic is preserved in two interdependent manuscripts, edited in 1852 and 1868.

4. Concluding remarks

A *Vita* is a long text to analyse, and when, as in our case, we have eleven versions of this work the landscape to explore is hugely vast and terribly complicated. What I intended to do in this chapter was first to offer a possibly readable map of this rich constellation of works, and secondly to give some glimpses of what can be found through a cross-comparison of different versions produced at different times in different languages and various literary genres. The challenge is fascinating. What I have gained is a personal relish in chasing after the personality of the various authors and translators, their political stance, their different types of spirituality, and last but not least their different stylistic choices and abilities. This is particularly true of the early three *Lives*, where the point was to construct a credible figure of a holy king who reigned in a crucial period of English history, right at the watershed between the Saxon and the Norman rule, a king that was finally seen as a conciliator and a peacemaker, caring for the good of his people, to the point of being a mirror and an exemplar to all his successors. Once the figure had been so to speak 'canonized' in Aelred's *Vita*, the various responses found in the many translations are no less interesting. Judging by the sparse examples I could offer, we may see how any translation is in part a rewriting, and this includes changes in the vocabulary, phrasing and emphasis which may be required by a new destination, as is the case with the Anglo-Norman poem by the nun of Barking, or due to the personal preferences of the translator, as is the case with the ME poem. Through the study of these changes we can reconstruct the personality of the translator, his social background, his political stance, etc. Indeed, a whole world looms through a translation.

Much remains to be done exactly because this constellation of *Lives* is so large. To start with, a modern critical edition of Aelred's *Vita sancti Edwardi Regis et Confessoris* is badly needed, even if I realise that the enterprise, given the number of manuscripts, may be discouraging. The same is true for other versions for which a reliable edition or even an edition at all is still lacking: I am especially thinking of the two rhymed Latin *Lives*. Deeper and more extended comparisons are to be made in order to have a more articulate and better founded profile of the translators.

In the end, what is clear to me is that research in the field of translation studies is both exciting and rewarding. Apart from the scientific contribution the scholar can provide by editing and analysing these texts, he can be sure of one result: the pleasure of discovering that it is through the study of translations, as much as of original works, that we can get to know living persons, their ideas, their feelings, their responses to subjects which, beyond the passage of time, continue to be interesting precisely because they have to do with human life, albeit that of a 'saint'.

Conclusion

The fourteen chapters of this book may be read as the record of a personal journey made over the last twenty years. Any journey is triggered by curiosity and desire. My journey has been an exploration of that particular way of 'reading' a text, when not struggling with it, which is normally called 'translation'. Within this vast topic, I have chosen to focus on the literature of the Middle Ages, and in particular on texts of a religious nature. A choice that was in fact the natural sequel to a series of studies that began with my dissertation, discussed in 1967, on the tenth-century Northumbrian glosses to the Gospel of Luke accompanying the Latin text of the so called "Rushworth Gospels" produced in the eighth century.[1]

The starting point in this field of research was the need to understand what problems a fourteenth century preacher, in this case William Herebert, had to face when deciding to use liturgical hymns produced in Latin about a thousand years earlier in order to enliven his sermons with the testimony of the uninterrupted tradition of Catholic doctrine and prayer, so that his contemporary English hearers might enjoy the full power of that tradition (Pezzini 1974). While seemingly promising, this study had no immediate follow-up and was for some years abandoned in favour of other explorations. What finally prompted a definite return was the first Conference on "The Medieval Translator", held at Gregynog Hall, University of Wales, in August 1987, where I delivered a paper on the "Birgittine Tracts of Spiritual Guidance" (here chapter 1). It was especially the kind welcome, the warm response and the friendly support of Roger Ellis that encouraged me to pursue my research in the field of translation studies. The Medieval Translator conferences, eight so far (2007), have actually been the leading light of my journey: five (1, 4, 8, 9, 10) out of the fourteen chapters of this book originated as papers read at these conferences. Having established the principal direction of my research, I have

---

1   The most relevant and original parts of the dissertation have been published as Pezzini (1977).

managed to follow it in different ways, and this book is the fruit of this work. In fact, while responding to 'opportunities' prompted either by conferences or by requests of contributions to particular volumes, I have explored the field along three main lines, each with its own state of coherence. These lines now form the three parts of the book: tracts and rules, hymns, and saints' lives.

The Medieval Translator Conferences are subtitled "The Theory and Practice of Translation in the Middle Ages". Though perfect in its wording, this balance is not easy to maintain. In my opinion the study of translation practices comes first, and this for the very simple reason that medieval translators were not theoreticians as much as they were practitioners. I have always been deeply convinced that before being able to elaborate theories, one has to have analysed texts. Or better, any theory which is, in any case even implicitly, indispensable at the start, must be substantiated and, if needs be, revised in the light of what actual translation practices reveal. This is why the studies collected in this volume are above all analyses of texts.

There is probably another reason that explains the choice to favour analyses, and this has to do with my personal attitude. I must say that the more I get involved with the real relish in chasing the translator's personality, indeed his 'humanity', through his choices, the more I become suspicious of general theories. This is also why this final chapter should not be taken as a 'general' conclusion. In fact, every chapter has its own 'particular' conclusion. This is undoubtedly due to the fact that many of them originated as papers delivered at conferences, where a 'conclusion' is expected and in order. This also means, however, that what comes out as the fruit of research on one text is not necessarily applicable to another of the same genre, or even to another translation of the same text. In fact, the more we explore medieval translations, the more we encounter variety, and this too may frustrate and cast doubts on any attempt at producing a general theory.

The choice to consider only religious works does in a sense limit further the scope of the analysis. Religious texts have, after all, their own peculiar status and consequently their own characteristic 'rules'. I have already mentioned this in the Introduction, but allow me to recall that a difference in status may explain, for example, why in visionary literature translators feel much freer when they deal with the rubrics, which are editorial, than when they translate the very text

374

of revelations, whose significance/importance verges on that of the Bible's. On the other hand, while having a high status because of their origin and their use, liturgical hymns are nonetheless treated in a manner which seems 'free', but which is not completely so, in that elaborations and expansions are strictly linked to and derived from the linguistic 'macro text' formed by the Bible, the liturgy in general and the Patristic literature which constitute their theological, spiritual and literary background.

All this said, I can summarize the results of my research in three very general points: the study of medieval translational techniques first enriches and enlarges our idea of translation, it then helps us understand translation as a way of reading, and finally as a form of writing.

The first point concerns the *idea of translation*, a practice that in its medieval version has come to cover such a vast area that it stretches from very literal and at times pedestrian renderings to a deep and creative reworking of the source text, which should be more properly called 're-writing'. This may more frequently be the case with narrative texts, where much freedom is allowed, either in expanding or adding details to the story or in the choice to vary the rhythm, pace, dramatization, and so on. The sensational 'genealogy' and 'posterity' of the Life of St Edward the Confessor is one of the best cases in point. The three essays on the saints' lives provide three very different examples of translation: the first is a form of clever 'reduction', the second is overtly a 'compilation', and the third and most impressive one is a series of 'new versions' in three different languages, both in poem and in prose, of the same story along a considerable stretch of time.

But this freedom in dealing with the original text can also creep into rules and spiritual tracts, where the criterion of adaptation is paramount. Indeed this attitude visualizes and underlines an aspect of translational work which is common in every age, but which was particularly marked in the Middle Ages: books and texts were translated to answer a need, and the urge to provide a proper response to the need mattered much more than the fidelity to the original work. In the balance between the source and the target, quite often, if not always, it was on the target that the heavier weight lay. This implies that it is important to determine the intended readership of the translation produced, which at times includes a new 'use' of the text. When this intention is not explicitly stated, it can be recovered by an attentive reading of the various translator's choices, whether in lexis or syntax, or in more visible alterations of the original text. It is only natural to add that this intended readership must be seriously taken into account when evaluating the meaning of a translation. To ask ourselves whether a translation is successful or not, implies that we consider not only its relationship with the original text, but also its aptness to the new audience and use.

The second point is a direct consequence of the first. To explain the extraordinary variety of techniques employed in medieval translations, it is important to keep in mind that, besides being conditioned by the new language, the new readership and the new use of the text, the translator is first of all *a reader*. This means that he transfers into the target language what he perceives as relevant in his source text. We shall certainly better understand his work if we think of what happens in our mind when we read, an action in which the same processes are at work. We skip, we select, we underline; in a sense we translate into our own idiolect words, idioms, phrases, and sentences expressed in different ways in the text being read. The translator does not do anything that is very different when, before transferring a text into his own or another language of his choice, he freely chooses to omit and cut or to add and explain, accordingly. The difference between the modern translator, who experiences the same mental processes, and his medieval counterpart is that in the Middle Ages texts represented more of a 'common good',[2] to be used and in case reworked, than an objective piece of work deserving as much respect as possible.

Against this background it is easy to understand that such categories as literalness vs. freedom, or omission vs. expansion, or pedestrian rendering vs. creative rephrasing, when rigidly applied do not say much about the quality and the meaning of a translation. To give an easy verifiable example, a literal translation of a word may

---

2   Blake (1977: 21) states: "Texts were copied and adapted by anyone; they were treated as though they were public property. Once available they were part of the common good. It would be difficult for a reader or scribe to know whether what he was reading was the author's original or not."

retain in a more visible way its iconic content or its structuring function, while an interpretative transposition inserts, so to speak, an explicative gloss into the text itself. Both choices are obviously valid in themselves, and where one or the other choice is consistent throughout the text, it may help in assessing not so much the 'correctness' as the 'type' of the translation, and, whenever possible, may allow to draw a profile both of the translator or of his readership.

This idea of translation as a way of reading can be better highlighted when we have examples of translations that have been corrected and revised (see chapter 8). But another more subtle evidence of this 'aggressive attitude' towards the text can be seen in various forms of marginal annotations which some 'readers' employed either to replace words or to mark out particular passages, as I have evinced in some manuscripts (see chapter 7). Incidentally, this is the reason why a careful reading of the codex should accompany the study of the translation contained in it.[3] This is in fact what I have done in some detail, a choice commanded by the fact that more than half of the chapters of this book deal with material still in manuscript form or which I have edited.

The third point derives from the second, in that the translator from being a reader becomes himself *a writer*. We have long known that in medieval literature the boundaries between different kinds of writers are not as clear-cut as they are today. Burrow writes, with reference to a passage from St Bonaventure,

> Men 'make books' by writing. Some do no more than copy an existing text, or else combine existing texts into new compilations; others add words of their own, either for 'purpose of clarification' or else 'in prime place'. But all are *writers*. Scribes, compilers, commentators, and authors are all, in different ways, doing the same thing: making books (1982: 30).

In a continuum spanning between two very distant extremes, the translation occupies a large space, itself very diversified, between the work of the glossator, where each word is interpreted either with one or two or more other words, and that of the creative author in the

---

3   See in this respect the interesting reconstruction of eight 'Reader Profiles' from the marginal annotations in BL MS Additional 37790 (Amherst Manuscript) by Cré (2007).

modern sense, who, incidentally, is never so creative as to build a text from zero since he writes within a literary tradition. It is precisely because of this intermediate position that the practice of translation might be used as a means for learning how to write: a sort of training before encroaching upon personal compositions.[4] In this way the translator learns first how to 'read' a text, then how to 'transpose' it into his own native language, so that he may finally be able to 'compose' originally, having learnt how to master words, syntax and the colours of rhetoric. Translation can thus be taken as a practice in between reading and writing. As reading practice, translation increases the sensitivity to the various aspects of a text not only in terms of words and forms, but also in terms of many suprasegmental features such as sounds and rhythms; unashamedly considered as a form of writing, translation practice can improve one's compositional skills too.

In the light of these considerations it is probably not so strange that in England the fourteenth and fifteenth centuries "witnessed a great vogue in translation" and at the same time "a pronounced upsurge in the production of works in English" (Blake 1977: 15). This is a kind of virtuous circle, which makes the study of translation so exciting and so rewarding. And the very practical conclusion of this book is that, paradoxical as it may seem, I know no better introduction to the study and practice of creative writing than the study and practice of the art of translation.

---

4   Introducing a second collection of papers delivered at the first Medieval Translator conference, Roger Ellis could write: "This volume shares with its predecessor a spirited rejection of the common assumption that translation is inferior to 'original' writing, and reacts in very similar ways against the equally common distinction, regularly forced and frequently unhelpful for the study of medieval translation, between translation and adaptation" (1991: xv).

Appendices

Appendix 1

Manuscripts containing Italian translations of the *Revelations* of St Birgitta. Sigla as appearing in ch. 2.

A.   BNC, II, II, 393, 15th century, ff. 241. Contents: Book I, part of Book II (chapters 1-3), Books III and IV, and on ff. 236r-v and 239r-241r some "prayers" by St Birgitta.

B.   BNC, II-130, dated 1494, ff. 154. Contents: Book I-II and two "letters". It comes from the Paradiso monastery.

C.   BNC, II, III, 270, completed on 26.4.1495, ff. 149. Contents: Book VII-VIII, miracles (ff. 137v-148r) and two "laude". It comes from and it belonged to the Paradiso monastery.

D.   BNC, II, II, 391, 15th century, ff. 144. Contents: a compilation from various books.

L.   Firenze, Biblioteca Mediceo-Laurenziana, MS 27.10, early 15th century. Contents: translation of Book IV.

S.   Siena, Biblioteca Comunale degli Intronati, MS I.V.25/26, dated 1399. Contents: Books I-V in volume I (I.V.25); Books VI-VIII, *Sermo Angelicus, Regula Salvatoris, Vita, Miracula, Orationes* in volume II (I.V.26).

Y.   Yale University, New Haven, CT, USA, Beinecke Rare Book and Manuscript Library, MS Z111 0141-2. Completed on 26 July 1626. Contents: Books I-VI in volume 1 and Books VII-VIII, *Sermo Angelicus, Quattuor Orationes, Extravagantes, Vita* and *Index* in volume 2; volume 3 contains no new material but some 'visions' excerpted from other works of the saint, and again the *Sermo Angelicus, Quattuor Orationes,* and *Extravagantes*. From the Birgittine convent of Scala Coeli in Genoa.

Other MSS containing translations of Birgittine material are in Florence, Biblioteca Riccardiana. Here is the list:

MS 1336, paper, 15th century, ff. 161. Contents: Books V-VIII (Morpurgo 396).
MS 1345, paper, 15th century. Contents: *Sermo Angelicus* (ff. 90r-114v) (Morpurgo 405-407).
MS 1397, parchment, 15th century, ff. 79. Contents: Books I-II (Morpurgo 440).

MSS containing the so called 'Birgitta's Prophecy'

MS 1251, paper, 15th century. ff. 108. Prophecy on ff. 100r-102v (Morpurgo 313).
MS 1258, paper, 15th century. ff. 136. Prophecy on ff. 54v-58v (Morpurgo 321).
MS 1312, paper, 15th century. ff. 151. Prophecy on ff. 140r-143v (Morpurgo 379).

Appendix 2

Chapter titles of Book I of David of Augsburg's *Formula Novitiorum* in Quaracchi, with variants from three Latin MSS (CC, D and J1), and with the chapter titles of the major Middle English translations (A, Q and U) given in full. Sigla as appearing in ch. 4.

Quaracchi edition

1. Quid novitiis semper considerandum
2. De obedientia
3. De pace cum praelatis habenda
4. De disciplina in dormiendo servanda
5. De sollicitudine in divino Officio habenda
6. De disciplina in Capitulo servanda
7. De disciplina servanda in mensa
8. De disciplina servanda in dormitorio
9. De disciplina in labore manuum servanda
10. De disciplina circa Missam servanda
11. De disciplina circa confessionem servanda
12. De disciplina in cella et circa obedientiam servanda
13. De lectione et praedicatione
14. De disciplina in occulto servanda
15. De disciplina inter Fratres exterius servanda
16. De verbis
17. De otiosis verbis cavendis
18. Quod de Deo libenter loquaris
19. De otio cavendo
20. De meditatione Domini Iesu
21. De ostentatione cavenda
22. De disciplina extra domum servanda
23. De oratione et meditatione in via facienda
24. De feminarum familiaritate vitanda
25. De libertate et custodia cordis servanda et de subiectione erga praelatum
26. Compendium supradictorum

Variants in Latin MSS

i. Corpus Christi College Cambridge MS 256 (CC). Note that the titles are as given in the body of the text. In the Table of Contents they are sometimes slightly different: those in square brackets, lacking in the text, are from the Table of Contents. The numbering, lacking in CC, is taken from MS St John's College Cambridge G.2 (J2)
1. [Quare veneris]; 2. [De obedientia]; 3. De pace cum prelatis; 4. De surgendo a sompno; 5. Quomodo in choro gubernare te debeas; 6. Qualiter te in capitulo habeas; 7. De correccione; 8. Qualiter in mensa te habeas; 9. De dormicione; 10. De obsequiis; 11. De missa. Seruire ad missas salubre est; 12. De confessione; 13. De cella et obediencia; 14. De leccione; 15. De predicacione et confessionis audicione; 16. De disciplina vbique seruanda; 17. Quomodo inter fratres te habeas; 18. De verecundia; 19. De incessu; 20. De sessione; 21. De risu; 22. De verbis; 23. De detraccione cauenda; 24. De rumoribus; 25. De iactancia; 26. De multiloquio; de verbis ociosis (in J2 "De multiloquio et verbis ociosis" from ch. 26); 27. Quod de Deo libenter loquaris;[1] 28. De ocio; 29. De exemplo Christi; 30. De vana gloria et modo cantandi; 31. Qualiter te habeas iuxta domum (Table of Contents, "de egrediendo foras"); 32. De visu; 33. Quomodo te habeas cum socio in via; 34. De oracione in via; 35. De bono exemplo dando; 36. Quod mulieres sunt vitande (Table of Contents, "de feminis fugiendis"); 37. De libertate cordis; 38. Epilogus siue compendium omnium supradictorum.

ii. St John's College Cambridge MS D.9 (J1). Only chs 8-29 are numbered, in the margins. Variants are as noted from the titles in CC.
5. Quomodo in choro te debeas seruare; 6. Qualiter in capitulo te habeas; 8. Qualiter in mensa sit habendum; 11. De missa, quod in ea ministremus deo; 15. De predicacione et confessionum audicione; 20 (brings together titles for CC's chs 20-22, so that numbers are two less than CC's thereafter); 22 (brings together titles for CC's chs 24-5, so

---

1   Under this heading other subjects are gathered, which the MS indicates by adding the titles in the margin, "de auditu et disputacione", "de contencione" and "de modo loquendi", though the last is not relevant to the material in the chapter. The marginal titles also occur in J2 as "de auditu et disputacione et contencione" and "de modo loquendi".

that numbers are three less than CC's thereafter); 23. De maledictis – De verbis ociosis – Quod (Ms de) libenter loquaris de deo; 24. De auditu et disputacione et contencione (corresponding, with the last phrase of 23, to CC ch. 27); 25. (brings together titles for CC's chs 28-9, reading "De bono exemplo Christi quod sit sequendum" for the latter, so that numbers are four less than in CC thereafter); 26. De modo cantandi et vana gloria cauenda; 27. De egrediendo foras quomodo se habebit; 28. De visu reprimendo; 29. Quomodo te habeas in via cum sociis; 30. De meditacione et oracione in via; 31. De exemplo bono dando; 32. De feminis fugiendis; 34. Epilogus predictorum

iii. Durham Cathedral Library MS B.iv.42 (D) Up to ch. 22 each chapter is given a title and a number; thereafter neither title nor number was written, though space was left for this purpose. Chapter numbers have been written in the margin by a later hand, used here for missing numbers. Missing titles have been supplied from MS St John's College Cambridge D.9. Variants are as noted from the titles in CC.

1. no title in the MS; 4. De surgendo a sompniis; 6. Qualiter in capitulo te habeas; ch. 10 "De obsequiis" is missing, but the numbering continues as if it were included; 11. De missa; 13. De claustro et obediencia; 15. De confessione vel predicacionis audicione; 26. De maledictis (cf. J1 ch. 23); 27. De verbis ociosis (26-7 correspond to CC ch. 26, so that numbers in D are thereafter one less than those in CC); 28. Qualiter de deo libenter loquaris; 29. De auditu et disputacione et contencione; 30. Qualiter sit loquendum (28-30 correspond to CC ch. 27, so that numbers in D are thereafter three less than those in CC); 32. De bono exemplo Christi; 33. De modo cantandi et vana gloria cauenda; 34. De egrediendo foras quomodo se habebit; 35. De visu reprimendo; 36. Quomodo te habeas in via cum sociis; 37. De meditacione et oracione in via; 38. De exemplo bono dando; 39. De feminis fugiendis; 40. De libertate cordis; 41. Epilogus predictorum.[2]

---

2   D's titles for chs 33-41 precisely match those of J1 chs 26-34.

Chapter titles in Middle English MSS

i. Queens' College Cambridge MS 31 (Q). Except for the first chapter, the numbering is in the body of the text.
1. [wanting]; 2. Of obedience; 3. Off pece wyth thy prelates; 4. Of risynge fro slepe; 5. How thow shalte gouerne the in the quere; 6. Howe thowe shalte gouerne the in the chapitre; 7. Of correccion takynge; 8. How thou shalt haue the atte table; 9. Off slepyng; 10. Of obsequies and seruices; 11. Off masse; 12. Off confession; 13. Off the celle and of obedience; 14. Off redynge; 15. Off prechyng and herynge of confession; 16. Off disciplyne to be kepte in euery place; 17. How thow shalte haue the amonge thy brethren; 18. Of shamefastnes; 19. Of goynge; 20. Of syttynge; 21. Off lawghyng; 22. Off wordes; 23. Off detraccion to be fledde; 24. Off boystynge; 25. Off tithynges; 26. Off moche spekynge; 27. Off ydell wordes; 28. Off fleynge contencion in disputacion; 29. Off maner of spekynge; 30. Off ydelnesse; 31. Off the ensample of Cryste; 32. Off veyne glorye and maner of syngynge; 33. Off goynge owte; 34. Off syght; 35. How thou shalte haue the to thy felowys in wayes; 36. Off prayers in the wey and meditacion; 37. Off gode ensample to be yevyn; 38. Off eschuynge of womens company; 39. Off liberte of herte; 40. A compendiouse rehershaile of the matiers aboue towched

ii. CUL MS Dd.ii.33 (U)
The Prologue; 1. How a religiouse person shuld consyder; 2. Of obedience; 3. How we shuld haue peace with our prelatis; 4. Of rysyng from slepe; 5. How þou shalt order the in the quere; 6. How þou shalt behaue the in the chapiter howse; 7. How þou shuldist take correccion or rebuke for thyne offencis; 8. How þou shalt behaue the at the table; 9. Of slepyng in the dortour; 10. Of laboures or servycis; 11. Of confession; 12. Of kepyng of thy cell and sewyng; 13. Of devout redyng; 14. Of good religiouse maner; 15. How to behaue the among thy sustrys; 16. Of shamefastnes; 17. Of goyng; 18. Of syttyng; 19. Of lawghyng or smylyng; 20 Of wordis and spekyng; 21. Of spekyng or heryng of detraccion; 22. Of tydyngis of the world; 23. Of boostyng or praysyng; 24. Of moche spekyng; 25. Of idyl and vayn wordis; 26. Of heryng without contencion or stryfe; 27. How and after what maner þou shalt speke; 28. Of idylnes; 29. How we shuld folow

the example of criste; 30. How to avoyd vayn glory in syngyng or redyng; 31. Of goyng forth from home; 32. How þou shalt kepe thy syght; 33. How þou shalt behaue the goyng by the wey with thy suster or other company; 34. Of prayer or meditacion by the wey; 35. How þou shuldist geue good example; 36. Of eschewyng of mens company; 37. Of lybertye of the hert; 38. A compendiouse rehersall of the firste part

iii. BL MS Arundel 197 (A): "An abstracte owte of a boke þat is callid formula nouiciorum"
1. [no title]; 2. Of obedience; 3. Of rising fro slepe; 4. How þou shalte gouerne þe in þe quere; 5. How þou shalte gouerne þe in þe chapter; 6. Of vndernemynge and blamynge; 7. How þou shalte behaue þe at þe tabul; 8. Of slepinge; 9. Of obsequies and seruice; 10. Of messe; 11. Of confescion; 12. Of þi selle and of obedience; 13. Of vertuus redinge; 14. Of disciplyne to be kepte in euery place; 15. How þou shalte behaue þe amonge þi broþerin and sistris; 16. Of shamefaste maneris; 17. Of goynge; 18. Of sittynge; 19. of lauȝwynge; 20. Of wordis; 21. Of wordis of detraccion to be avoydid; 22. [no chapter with this number]; 23. Knowe no tidingis; 24. Of myche spekynge; 25. Of ydulle wordis; 26. Of fleynge contencion in disputacion; 27. Of maner of spekynge; 28. Of ydulnes; 29. Of vayne glory and maner of singynge; 30. Of þi siȝtte kepynge; 31. Of gode ensampul to be gevynne; 32. A compendius rehersalle of þe materis above touchid.[3]

---

3   This work has six further chapters, ending with ch. 38; those listed in this Appendix are taken from the first book of the *De... compositione.*

Appendix 3

General Table of the Compilation Incominciano certi capitoli (ch. 7)

In the first column I indicate in bold type the order of chapters in Arabic numbers written in the manuscript, with the reference to the source chapter in the *Revelations* given in the manuscript in Roman numbers, followed by the indication of the folio where the chapter begins. I have corrected a few mistakes, giving also the original manuscript reading. In the chapters taken from *Book IV*, when the numbering differs, normally by one, from the critical edition by H. Aili, I give the modern number in brackets.

In the second column I give the corresponding chapters written in Roman numbers in the printed book, standardizing final '-i'. Many mistakes in the numbering of the rubrics have created a discrepancy with the number which is correctly given (except in two cases) in the general table at the end (ff. 112v-115v). I follow the numbering of the table, putting into square brackets, when different, the corresponding number as it appears in the body of the book, except when the two coincide. The indication of the folio follows the modern numbering in pencil on the bottom left of the page.

First volume

1. I 47 *(4r)*   i *(1r)*
2. I *(7v)*   ii *(4r)*
3. I 2 *(9r)*   iii *(5r)*
4. I 6 *(10r)*   iiii *(6r)*
5. I 8 *(11r)*   v *(6v)*
6. I 9 *(11v)*   vi [v] *(7r)*
7. I 10 *(12v)*   vii *(7v)*
8. I 11 *(16v)*   viii *(10v)*
9. I 13 *(17r)*   viiii *(11r)*
10. I 14 *(18r)*   x *(11v)*
11. I 16 *(18v)*   xi *(12r)*
12. I 22 *(19v)*   xii *(13r)*

13. I 25 (*21r*)	xiii (*14r*)
14. I 26 (*21v*)	xiiii (*14v*)
15. I 34 (*24v*)	xv (*17r*)
16. I 35 (*26v*)	xvi (*18v*)
17. I 32 (*27r*)	xvii (*19r*)
18. I 56 (*28v*)	xviii (*20r*)
19. I 59 (*31r*)	xviiii (*22r*)
20. II 16 (*33v*)	xx (*24r*)
21. II 18 (*34v*)	xxi (*24v*)
22. II 20 (*36v*)	xxii (*26r*)
23. II 23 (*38r*)	xxiii (*27r*)
24. II 24 (*40r*)	xxiiii (*28v*)
25. II 30 (*40v*)	xxv [xxv + xxvi][4] (*29r*)
26. II 15 (*41v*)	xxvi [xxvii] (*30r*)
27. III 4 (*43r*)	xxvii [xxviii] (*31r*)
28. III 5 (*45r*)	xxviii [xxviiii] (*32v*)
29. III 6 (*45v*)	xxviiii [xxx] (*33r*)
30. III 10 (*47r*)	xxx[5] (*34r*)
31. III 12 (*48r*)	xxxi (*35r*)
32. III 16 (*50r*)	xxxii [xxx *sic*] (*36r*)
33. III 17 (*51r*)	xxxiii (*37r*)
34. III 18 (*53r*)	xxxiiii (*38v*)
35. III 21 (*55r*)	xxxv (*40r*)
36. III 27 (*56v*)	xxxvi (*41r*)
37. III 28 (*58v*)	xxxvii (*43r*)
38. III 29 (*60r*)	xxxviii [*om.*] (*44r*)
39. III 30 (*61v*)	xxxviiii [xxxviii] (*45r*)
40. III 14 (*63r*)	xxxx (*46r*)
41. III 19 (*64v*)	xxxxi (*47r*)

---

4   Part of *Rev.* II,30 (§ 19-23) has been taken by the editor of the book as a 'new' chapter, which he numbers xxvi. In fact the manuscript notes in the margin (f. 41v): "Nota d'uno ch'era dal popolo diputato sancto e dimostra Cristo alla sposa el come non è." This addition, with a slightly different wording, forms the title of 'capitolo xxvi' in the book. But this 'chapter' is not numbered in the general table, so that from here on there appears to be a discrepancy in the numbering of the book itself. The words of the 'Nota' do not exist in the Latin text of the *Revelations*.

5   Number xxx is repeated in the rubric within the book, so that from here on the rubric numbering coincides again with the general table.

42. IV 22 (*66v*)

43. IV 36 (Aili: 37) (*67v*)

44. IV 57 (*68r*)

45. IV 130⁶ (*68r*)

46. IV 7 § 1-55 (*69r*)

47. IV 7 § 56-75 (*72r*)

48. IV <12> *ms.* 16 (*73r*)

49. IV <23> § 22-31 *ms.* 33 (*74*)

50. IV <13> *ms.* 62 (*74v*)

51. IV 49 (*75v*)

52. IV 50 + 51 (*77v*)

53. IV 101 (Aili: 102) (*79r*)

54. IV 106 (Aili: 107) (*80v*)

55. IV 91 (Aili: 93) (*82v*)

56. IV 4 (*83v*)

57. IV 35 (*86r*)

58. IV 36 (*86v*)

59. IV 61 (*87r*)

60. IV <62> *ms.* 71 (*89r*)

61. IV 63 (*90r*)

62. <VII> *ms.* om. 21 (*92r*)

63. VII 15 (*93r*)

64. <VII 16>⁸ (*95r*)

65. VII 26 (*95v*)

66. VI 74 (*95v*)

67. VI 77 (*96r*)

68. VI <83> *ms.* 99 (*96r*)

69. VI 90 (*96r*)

70. VI 92 (*96v*)

71. VI 100 (*97r*)

72. VI 33 (*97v*)

xxxxii (*48v*)

xxxxiii (*49v*)

xxxxiiii (*50r*)

xxxxv (*50r*)

xxxxvi⁷ [xxxx *sic*] (*50v*)

xxxxvii [xxxxvi] (*53v*)

xxxxviii [xxxxvii] (*54r*)

xxxxviiii [xxxxviii] (*54v*)

l [xxxxviiii] (*55v*)

li [l] (*56r*)

lii [li] (*57v*)

liii [lii] (*58v*)

liiii [liii] (*60v*)

lv [liiii] (*61r*)

lvi [lx *sic*] (*63r*)

lvii [lvi] (*63r*)

lviii [lvii] (*63v*)

lviiii [liiii *sic*] (*65r*)

lx [lviiii] (*65v*)

lxi [lx] (*67r*)

lxii [lxi] (*68r*)

lxiii [lxii] (*69v*)

lxiiii [lxiii] (*69v*)

lxv [lxiiii] (*69v*)

lxvi [lxv] (*70r*)

lxvii [lxvi] (*70r*)

lxviii [lxvii] (*70v*)

lxviiii [lxviii] (*70v*)

lxx [lxviiii] (*71r*)

---

6   The ms. indicates it as 'capitolo ultimo', and in fact it concludes Book IV in the Alfonsian redaction: see Aili, p. 371.

7   The book treats as one single chapter the translation of *Rev.* IV,7 which in the ms. is divided in two.

8   This chapter, marked 64 in the margin, has in fact a rubric, but without any reference to the source. In the book it is amalgamated with the preceding chapter as part of it.

73. VI 44 (*98v*)
74. VI 94 (*99r*)
75. VII 7 (*100r*)
76. VII 8 (*101r*)
77. VII 10 (*101v*)
78. VII 31[9] (*102v*)
79. IV 40 (*103v*)
80. IV 45 (*104r*)
81. IV 47 (*104v*)
82. IV 53 (*105v*)
83. VII <20> *ms.* 33 (*106r*)
84. VI 34 (*107v*)
85. VI 54 (*109r*)
86. VII 30 (*110r*)
87. VI 67 (*111r*)
88. III 1 (*112r*)
89. III 2 (*114r*)
90. III 3 (*115v*)
91. III 7 (*117r*)
92. III 15 (*118r*)
93. IV 125 (Aili: 126)[11] (*118v*)
94. IV 17 (*121r*)
95. IV 8[12] (*123r*)
96. IV 9 (*123v*)
97. IV 10 (*125r*)
98. IV 1 (*126v*)
99. IV 54 (*127v*)
100. IV 28 (*128r*)
101. IV <11> *ms.* 40[13] (*128r*)

lxxi [lxx] (*71v*)
lxxii [lxxi] (*72r*)
lxxiii [lxxii] (*72v*)
lxiiii [lxxiii] (*73v*)
lxxv [lxxiiii] (*73v*)
lxxvi [lxxv] (*74v*)
lxvii [lxxvi] (*75r*)
lxxviii [lxxvii] (*75v*)
lviiii [lxxviii] (*76r*)
lxxx [lxxviiii] (*76v*)
lxxxi [lxxx] (*77r*)
lxxxi (*sic*) [lxxxi][10] (*78r*)
lxxxii (*79v*)
lxxxiii (*80r*)
lxxxiiii (*80v*)
lxxxv (*81v*)
lxxxvi (*83v*)
lxxxvii (*84r*)
lxxxviii (*85r*)
lxxxviiii (*85v*)
lxxxx (*86r*)
lxxxxi (*88r*)
lxxxxii [lxxxxiii] (*89v*)
lxxxxiii [lxxxxiiii] (*90r*)
lxxxxiiii [lxxxxv] (*91r*)
lxxxxv [lxxxxvi] (*92r*)
lxxxxvi [lxxxxvii] (*92v*)
lxxxxvii [lxxxxviiii] (*93r*)
lxxxxviii [ic] (*93r*)

---

9   Ms.: libro vii e ultimo e capitulo ultimo xxxi.
10   By repeating 'lxxxi' the general table resumes the numbering in the body of the book.
11   Only § 1-44 of IV,125 (Aili, 126) are translated, while the rest of the chapter (§ 45-137) is not. The translator adds: "L'avanzo di questo capitolo e di questa bella doctrina nel quaderno che viene inanzi a questo e in questo si contiene volgarizzato" (f. 121r).
12   The rubric reads: "Questi due capitoli che ora seguitano si continuano col capitolo vii° nel libro iiii° dinanzi volgharizzato etc.... libro iiii° ca.° viii et ix°'" (f. 123r). See chapters 45 and 46 above.

102. IV <14> *ms.* 17[14] (*129r*) lxxxxviiii [c] (*94r*)
103. IV 16 (*130r*) c [cii] (*94v*)

Second volume

104. IV 126 (Aili: 127) (*132r*) ci [cii] (*95v*)
105. IV <12> *ms.* 127 (*132r*) cii [ciii] (*95v*)
106. IV 23 § 1-21[15] (*133r*) ciii [ciiii] (*96r*)
107. IV 33 (*134v*) ciiii [cv] (*97r*)
108. IV 34 (*136v*) cv [cvi] (*98v*)
109. IV 46 (*137r*) cvi [cviiii *sic*] (*99r*)
110. IV 58 (*137v*) cviii[16] [cviii] (*99v*)
111. IV 70 (*141r*) cviiii (*102r*)
112. IV 74 (*143v*) cx (*103v*)
113. IV 71 (*146r*) cxi[17] (*108v*)
114. IV 68 (*148v*) cxii (*109r*)
115. IV 90 (Aili: 91) (*150v*) cxiii (*110v*)

---

13   The Roman numbering can explain the mistake: *xi* could be confused with *xl*.
14   Again *xiiii* could easily be taken as *xuii*.
15   *Rev.* IV,23, § 22-31, forms chapter 49 (see above).
16   By omitting ch. *cvii* the Table restores the correspondence with the numbering of chapters in the rubrics of the book.
17   The order of these two chapters is inverted in the book, so that *cxi* corresponds to 114, and *cxii* to 113.

Appendix 4

Latin Text of Marian Antiphons and Hymns (ch. 10)

1. ANTIPHONS

Alma Redemptoris Mater

Alma Redemptoris Mater,
quae pervia coeli porta manes, et stella maris,
succurre cadenti, surgere qui curat populo:
tu quae genuisti, natura mirante,
tuum sanctum Genitorem,
Virgo prius ac posterius,
Gabrielis ab ore sumens illud Ave,
peccatorum miserere.

Ave, Regina coelorum

Ave, Regina coelorum,
ave, Domina angelorum,
salve, radix, salve, porta,
ex qua mundo lux est orta.

Gaude, Virgo gloriosa,
super omnes speciosa;
vale, o valde decora,
et pro nobis Christum exora.

Regina coeli

Regina coeli laetare, alleluia,
quia quem meruisti portare, alleluia,

resurrexit, sicut dixit, alleluia:
ora pro nobis Deum, alleluia.

Salve Regina

Salve, Regina, mater misericordiae;
vita, dulcedo et spes nostra, salve.
Ad te clamamus, exsules filii Evae.
Ad te suspiramus, gementes et flentes
in hac lacrimarum valle.
Eia ergo, advocata nostra,
illos tuos misericordes oculos ad nos converte.
Et Iesum, benedictum fructum ventris tui,
nobis post hoc exsilium ostende.
O clemens, o pia, o dulcis Virgo Maria.

2. HYMNS

Ave maris stella

Ave, maris stella,
Dei mater alma,
atque semper virgo,
felix coeli porta.

Sumens illud Ave
Gabrielis ore,
funda nos in pace
mutans nomen Evae.

Solve vincla reis,
profer lumen caecis,
mala nostra pelle,
bona cuncta posce.

Monstra te esse matrem,
sumat per te precem,
qui pro nobis natus
tulit esse tuus.

Virgo singularis,
inter omnes mitis,
nos culpis solutos
mites fac et castos.

Vitam praesta puram,
iter para tutum,
ut videntes Iesum
semper collaetemur.

Sit laus Deo Patri,
summum Christo decus,
Spiritui Sancto
honor, tribus unus.

Quem terra, pontus, aethera

Quem terra, pontus, aethera
colunt, adorant, praedicant,
trinam regentem machinam
claustrum Mariae baiulat.

Cui luna, sol et omnia
deserviunt per tempora,
perfusa coeli gratia
gestant puellae viscera.

Mirantur ergo saecula,
quod angelus fert semina,
quod aure virgo concipit
et corde credens parturit.

Beata mater munere,
cuius supernus artifex
mundum pugillo continens
ventris sub arca clausus est.

Beata coeli nuntio,
fecunda Sancto Spiritu,
desideratus gentibus
cuius per alvum fusus est.

O gloriosa foemina,
excelsa super sidera,
qui te creavit provide
lactas sacrato ubere.

Quod Eva tristis abstulit,
tu reddis almo germine,
intrent ut astra flebiles,
coeli fenestra facta es.

Tu regis alti ianua
et porta lucis fulgida;
vitam datam per virginem,
gentes redemptae, plaudite.

References

Primary sources

Aelred of Rievaulx 1971, ³1995. *Treatises and Pastoral Prayer.* Kalamazoo, Michigan: Cistercian Publications.

Aelred of Rievaulx 1997. *The Life of Saint Edward King and Confessor*, translated by Jerome Bertram. Southampton: Saint Austin Press.

Aelred of Rievaulx 2005. *The Historical Works*, translated by Jane Patricia Freeland, edited with an Introduction and Annotations by Marsha L. Dutton. Kalamazoo, Michigan: Cistercian Publications.

Aelredus Rievallensis. *De Institutione Inclusarum*: see Dumont 1961, Hoste / Talbot 1971, Ayto / Barratt 1984, Pezzini 2003.

Aili, Hans (ed.) 1992. Sancta Birgitta. *Revelaciones. Book IV.* Stockholm: Almkvist & Wiksell.

Aili, Hans (ed.) 2002. Sancta Birgitta. *Revelaciones. Book VIII. Liber Celestis Imperatoris ad Reges.* Stockholm: Almkvist & Wiksell.

Allen, Hope Emily (ed.) 1931. *English Writings of Richard Rolle.* Oxford: Oxford University Press.

Ayto, John / Barratt, Alexandra (eds) 1984. *Aelred of Rievaulx's De Institutione Inclusarum: Two English Versions.* EETS OS 287. London: Oxford University Press.

Barlow, Frank 1992. *The Life of King Edward.* Oxford: Clarendon.

Bavaud, G. / Deshusses, J. / Dumas, A. (eds) 1960. Amédée de Lausanne. *Huit homélies mariales.* SCh 72. Paris: Éditions du Cerf.

Bergh, Birger (ed.) 1967. Sancta Birgitta. *Revelaciones. Book VII.* Uppsala: Almkvist & Wiksell.

Bergh, Birger (ed.) 1971. Sancta Birgitta. *Revelaciones. Book V.* Uppsala: Almkvist & Wiksell.

Bergh, Birger (ed.) 1991. Sancta Birgitta. *Revelaciones. Book VI.* Stockholm: Almkvist & Wiksell.

Birgitta of Sweden. *Revelaciones*: Lübeck: B. Ghotan 1492; modern critical edition: Book I (Undhagen 1977), Book II (Undhagen-

Bergh 2001), Book III (Jönsson 1998), Book IV (Aili 1992), Book V (Bergh 1971), Book VI (Bergh 1991), Book VII (Bergh 1967), *Revelaciones Extravagantes* (Hollman 1956), *Regula Salvatoris* (Eklund 1975), *Sermo Angelicus* (Eklund 1972).

Blake, Norman F. (ed.) 1972. *Middle English Religious Prose.* London: Arnold.

Bloch, Marc (ed.) 1923. La vie de S. Édouard le Confesseur par Osbert de Clare. *Analecta Bollandiana* 41, 5-131.

Blunt, John Henry (ed.) 1873. *The Myroure of Oure Ladye.* EETS ES 19. London: Oxford University Press.

Bolard, A. Clovis / Rigollot, Louis-Marie / Carnandet, Jean-Baptiste (eds) 1865. *Vita Jesu Christi per Ludulphum de Saxonia.* Paris, Rome: Victor Palmé (repr. 2006 in four volumes as Ludolphus the Carthusian. *Vita Christi.* Salzburg: Institut für Anglistik und Amerikanistik).

Brook, George Leslie (ed.) 1956. *The Harley Lyrics.* Manchester: Manchester University Press.

Brown, Carleton 1924, 2nd ed. revised by G. V. Smithers 1952. *Religious Lyrics of the 14th Century.* Oxford: Clarendon.

Brown, Carleton 1932. *English Lyrics of the 13th Century.* Oxford: Clarendon.

Brown, Carleton 1939. *Religious Lyrics of the 15th Century.* Oxford: Clarendon.

Cola, Silvano (ed.) 1982. Anonimo Francescano del 1300. *Meditazioni sulla vita di Cristo.* Roma: Città Nuova.

Colgrave, Bertrand (ed.) 1968. *The Earliest Life of Gregory the Great By an Anonymous Monk of Whitby.* Lawrence, Kansas: The University of Kansas Press.

Colgrave, Bertrand / Mynors, Roger Aubry Baskerville (eds) 1969. *Bede's Ecclesiastical History of the English People.* Oxford: Clarendon.

Cumming, William Patterson (ed.) 1929. *The Revelations of Saint Birgitta, edited from the Garrett MS.* EETS OS 178. London: Oxford University Press [Kraus Reprint 1989].

Daniel, Herman Adalbert 1855. *Thesaurus Hymnologicus.* Reprint 1973 Hildesheim-New York: Olms.

De Luca, Giuseppe (ed.) 1954. *Prosatori Minori del Trecento, Tomo I: Scrittori di religione.* Milano: Ricciardi.

Dreves, Guido M. / Blume, Clemens (eds) 1886-1922. *Analecta Hymnica Medii Aevi*. Leipzig: Reisland.

Dumont, Charles (ed.) 1961. Aelred de Rievaulx, *La Vie de Recluse, La Prière Pastorale*. SCh 76. Paris: Éditions du Cerf.

Dyce, Alexander (ed.) 1885. *The Poetical Works of Skelton and Donne*. Cambridge, Mass.: The Riverside Press.

Eklund, Sten (ed.) 1975. Sancta Birgitta. *Opera Minora I. Regula Salvatoris*. Stockholm: Almkvist & Wiksell.

Eklund, Sten (ed.) 1972. Sancta Birgitta. *Opera Minora II. Sermo Angelicus*. Uppsala: Almkvist & Wiksells Boktryckeri AB.

Ellis, Roger 1987. *The Liber Celestis of St Bridget of Sweden*. Volume I - Text. EETS OS 291. Oxford: Oxford University Press.

Esser, Kajetan (ed.) 1978. *Opuscula sancti patris Francisci Assisiensis*. Grottaferrata: Coll. S. Bonaventura di Quaracchi.

Gardner, Helen (ed.) 1952. John Donne. *The Divine Poems*. Oxford: Oxford University Press.

Gejrot, Claes 2000. The Fifteen Oos: Latin and Vernacular Versions. With an Edition of the Latin Text. In Morris / O'Mara (eds), 213-238.

Ghotan, Bartholomaeus (ed.) 1492. *Revelationes S. Birgitte*. Lübeck.

Godden, Michael (ed.) 1979. Aelfric. *Catholic Homilies. The second series. Text*. EETS SS 5. Oxford: Oxford University Press.

Gray, Douglas (ed.) 1985. *The Oxford Book of Late Medieval Verse and Prose*. Oxford: Clarendon Press.

Greene, Robert L. (ed.) [2]1977. *Early English Carols*. Oxford: Clarendon.

Hamer, Richard F. 1978. *Three Lives from the Gilte Legende*. Heidelberg: Winter.

Hamer, Richard F. / Russell, Vida 2000. *Supplementary Lives in Some Manuscripts of the Gilte Legende*. EETS OS 315. Oxford: Oxford University Press.

Henderson, Philip (ed.) 1959. *The Complete Poems of John Skelton*. London: Dent.

Hirsh, John C. 1974. A Middle English Metrical Version of *The Fifteen Oes* from Bodleian Library MS Add. B 66. *Neuphilologische Mitteilungen* 75: 98-114.

Hollman, Lennart (ed.) 1956. *Den Heliga Birgittas Reuelaciones Extrauagantes*. Uppsala: Almkvist & Wiksell.

Horstmann, Carl (ed.) 1895. *Yorkshire Writers*. London: Swan Sonnenschein & Co (reprint 1976, Cambridge: Brewer).

Horstmann, Carl (ed.) 1901. *Nova Legenda Anglie*. 2 Vols. Oxford: Clarendon.

Hoste, Anselme / Talbot, Charles H. (eds) 1971. *Aelredi Rievallensis Opera Omnia*, Vol. 1: Opera Ascetica. CCCM 1. Turnhout: Brepols.

Jönsson, Ann-Mari (ed.) 1998. Sancta Birgitta. *Revelaciones. Book III*. Stockholm: Almkvist & Wiksell.

Levasti, Arrigo (ed.) 1935. *Mistici del Duecento e del Trecento*. Milano: Rizzoli.

Luard, Henry Richards 1858. *Lives of Edward the Confessor*. Rolls Series 3. Her Majesty's Stationery Office, Kraus Reprint 1966.

MacCracken, Henry Noble (ed.) 1911. *The Minor Poems of John Lydgate*, Part I, *Religious Poems*. EETS ES 107. Oxford: Oxford University Press.

Mackenzie, Norman H. (ed.) 1990. *The Poetical Works of Gerard Manley Hopkins*. Oxford: Clarendon.

Maggioni, Giovanni Paolo (ed.) 1998. Iacopo da Varazze. *Legenda Aurea*. Tavarnuzze (FI): SISMEL – Edizioni del Galluzzo.

Meier-Ewert, Charity 1971. A Middle English Version of the *Fifteen Oes. Modern Philology* 68: 355-361.

Miller, Thomas (ed.) 1890 (repr. 1959). *The Old English Version of Bede's Ecclesiastical History of the English People*. Vol. I, 1. EETS OS 95. London: Oxford University Press.

Moore, Grace Edna 1942. *The Middle English Verse Life of Edward the Confessor*. Philadelphia: University of Philadelphia Press.

Mynors, Roger A.B. / Thomson, Rodney M. / Winterbottom, Michael 1998 (eds). William of Malmesbury. *Gesta regum Anglorum*. 2 Vols. Oxford: Clarendon.

Oliger, Livarius 1928. Regulae tres reclusorum et eremitarum Angliae saeculorum XIII-XIV. *Antonianum* 3, 151-190 and 299-320.

Oliger, Livarius 1934. Regula Reclusorum Angliae et Quaestiones tres de Vita Solitaria. *Antonianum* 9, 37-84.

Oliger, Livarius (ed.) 1938. Speculum Inclusorum Auctore Anonymo Anglico Saeculi XIV. *Lateranum* n.s. IV.1.

Patterson, Frank Allen 1927. Hymnal from MS. Additional 34193 British Museum. In *Studies in Memory of Gertrude Schoepperle*

Loomis. New York: Columbia University Press: 443-488 (Genève, Slatkin Reprints 1974).

Pezzini, Domenico 1986. *How resoun schal be keper of þe soule*: una traduzione del Quattrocento inglese dalle *Rivelazioni* (VII,5) di S. Brigida di Svezia. *Aevum* 60, 253-281.

Pezzini, Domenico 1988. *The twelf poyntes*: versioni di un trattato brigidino (*Rev*. II,16) nel Quattrocento inglese. *Aevum* 62, 286-301.

Pezzini, Domenico 1992. *Wordys of Christ to hys spowse*: una compilazione di testi brigidini nel MS Oxford, Bodleian Library, Rawlinson C. 41. *Aevum* 66, 345-360.

Pezzini, Domenico 1993a. 'The meditacion of oure Lordis passyon' and other Bridgettine texts in MS Lambeth 432. In Hogg (ed.), Vol. 1, 276-295.

Pezzini, Domenico 1994b. Un trattato sulla vita contemplativa e attiva dalle *Revelationes* (VI,65) di Santa Brigida: edizione di *An Informacion of Contemplatif Lyf and Actif* dal MS Oxford, Bodley 423. *Aevum* 68, 379-406.

Pezzini, Domenico (cur.) 2003. Aelredo di Rievaulx, *Regola delle Recluse*. Milano: Edizioni Paoline.

Quaracchi 1899. Fr. David ab Augusta. *De exterioris et interioris hominis compositione*. Quaracchi: Collegio S. Bonaventura.

Raby, Frederic J.E. (ed.) 1959. *The Oxford Book of Medieval Latin Verse*. Oxford: Clarendon.

Reimer, Stephen R. 1987. *The Works of William Herebert, OFM*. Toronto: Pontifical Institute of Mediaeval Studies.

Robbins, Rossell Hope 1952. *Secular Lyrics of the 14th and 15th Centuries*. Oxford: Clarendon.

Ruscone, Filippo Augusto 1848. *Squarci delle celesti rivelazioni di S. Brigida*. Milano: Ditta Boniardi-Pogliani.

Sargent, Michael G. (ed.) 2005. Nicholas Love. *The Mirror of the Blessed Life of Jesus Christ*. Exeter: University of Exeter Press.

Segre, Cesare / Marti, Mario (cur.) 1959. *La Prosa del Duecento*. Milano: Ricciardi.

Sherley-Price, Leo (trans.) 1978. Bede. *A History on the English Church and People*. Harmondsworth: Penguin.

Södergård, Östen 1948. *La vie d'Édouard le Confesseur*. Uppsala: Almqvist & Wiksell.

Spechtler, Franz Viktor (ed.) 1972. *Die geistlichen Lieder des Mönchs von Salzburg*. Berlin: Mouton de Gruyter.

Stallings-Taney, Mary (ed.) 1998. *Iohannis de Caulibus Meditaciones Vite Christi*. CCCM 153. Turnhout: Brepols.

Stevenson, George S. 1918. *Pieces from the Makculloch and the Gray MSS*. Edinburgh: Scottish Text Society.

Szövérffy, Joseph 1976. *Hymns of the Holy Cross: An Annotated Edition with Introduction*. Leyden: Classical Folia Editions.

Talbot, Charles H. (ed.) 1971, Aelredus Rievallensis, *De Institutione Inclusarum*, in *Aelredi Rievallensis Opera Omnia*. Vol. 1. CCCM 1. 635-682.

Terrin, M. Gabriella (cur.) 1992. *Pregate, pregate, pregate*. Monte San Vito: Shalom.

Thomas, Ronald S. 1979. *Selected Poems 1946-1968*. London: Granada.

Twysden, Roger / Selden, John 1652. *Historiae Anglicanae Scriptores X*. London: Cornelius Bee.

Undhagen, Carl Gustaf (ed.) 1977. Sancta Birgitta. *Revelaciones. Book I*. Stockholm: Almkvist & Wiksell.

Undhagen, Carl Gustaf / Bergh, Birger (eds) 2001. Sancta Birgitta. *Revelaciones. Book II*. Stockholm: Almkvist & Wiksell.

Voaden, Rosalynn 1993. The Middle English *Epistola Solitarii ad Reges* of Alfonso of Jaén: an Edition of the Text in British Library MS Cotton Julius F.II. In Hogg (ed.), Vol. 1, 142-179.

Wallace, Kathryn Young 1983. *La Estoire de Seint Aedward le Rei attributed to Matthew Paris*. London: Anglo-Norman Text Society.

Zupitza, Julius 1892. Die Gedichte des Franziskaners Jakob Ryman. *Archiv* 89: 167-338.

Secondary sources

ADB = *Allgemeine Deutsche Biographie*, Vierter Band. Berlin: Duncker/Humblot, 1968, reprint of the 1876 edition.

Ahldén, Tage 1952. *Nonnenspiegel und Mönchsvorschriften. Mittelniederdeutsche Lebensregeln der Danziger Birgittinerkonvente*. Göteborg: Acta Universitatis Goteburgensis.

Anonymous 1918. *Divozione delle Quindici Orazioni di Santa Brigida*. Rome.

Bandini, Angelo Maria 1778. *Catalogus codicum manuscriptorum Bibliothecae Mediceae Laurentianae*. Florentiae. (Reprint 1961. Lipsiae: Zentralantiquariat der Deutschen Demokratischen Republik).

Barratt, Alexandra 1984. Works of Religious Instruction. In Edwards (ed.), 413-432.

Baugh, Albert C. / Cable, Thomas [3]1978. *A History of the English Language*. London: Routledge & Kegan Paul.

Bergant, Dianne 1993. Prophecy. In Downey (ed.), 782-784.

Bernarello, Franco 1961. *La formazione religiosa secondo la primitiva scuola francescana*. Roma: Edizioni Francescane.

Bersano Begey, Marina / Dondi, Giuseppe 1966. *Le cinquecentine piemontesi*. Torino: Tipografia Torinese Editrice.

BHL = *Bibliotheca Hagiographica Latina Antiquae et Mediae Aetatis*. 1898-1901. Bruxelles: Société des Bollandistes.

Binski, Paul 1990. Reflections on *La estoire de Seint Aedward le rei*: hagiography and kingship in thirteenth-century England. *Journal of Medieval History* 16, 333-350.

Blake, Norman F. (ed.) 1992. *The Cambridge History of the English Language, II: 1066-1476*. Cambridge: Cambridge Univ. Press.

Blake, Norman F. 1969. *Caxton and his World*. London: Deutsch.

Blake, Norman F. 1972. Middle English Prose and its Audience. *Anglia* 90, 437-455.

Blake, Norman F. 1974. Varieties of Middle English Religious Prose. In Rowland (ed.), 348-356.

Blake, Norman F. 1977. *The English Language in Medieval Literature*. London: Dent.

Bohl, Cornelius 2000. *Geistlicher Raum. Räumliche Sprachbilder als Träger spiritueller Erfahrung, dargestellt am Werk* De compositione *des David von Augsburg*. Werl: Coelde.

Brown, Carleton / Robbins, Rossell Hope 1943. *The Index of Middle English Verse*. New York: Columbia University Press.

Brunner, Karl 1937. Kirchenlieder aus dem 15. Jahrhundert. *Anglia* 61, 138-151.

Burnley, David J. 1989. Late Medieval English Translation: Types and Reflections. In Ellis (ed.) 1989, 37-53.

Burrow, J. A. 1982. *Medieval Writers and Their Work*. Oxford: Oxford University Press.

CCCM = *Corpus Christianorum Continuatio Mediaeualis*. Turnhout: Brepols.

Cacciotti, Alvaro / Faes de Mottoni, Barbara (cur.) 1997. *Editori di Quaracchi 100 anni dopo. Bilancio e Prospettive*. Roma: PA – Edizioni Antoniane.

Chélini, Jean 2000. La mission d'Augustin de Cantorbéry dans la vision missionnaire de saint Grégoire le Grand. In de Dreuille (ed.), 41-53.

Cipolla, Adele / Nicoli, Mosé (cur.) 2006. *Testi agiografici e omiletici del medioevo germanico*. Verona: Fiorini.

Clark, James M. 1949. *The Great German Mystics: Eckhart, Tauler and Suso*. Oxford: Blackwell.

Cnattingius, Hans Jacob 1963. *Studies in the Order of St Bridget of Sweden. 1. The Crisis in the 1420s*. Stockholm: Acta Universitatis Stockholmiensis, Almqvist & Wiksells.

Colledge, Eric 1956. *Epistola solitarii ad reges*: Alphonse of Pecha as Organizer of Birgittine and Urbanist Propaganda. *Medieval Studies* 18, 19-49.

Connolly, Margaret 1994. Public Revisions or Private Responses? The Oddities of BL, Arundel MS 197, with Special Reference to *Contemplations of the Dread and Love of God*. *The British Library Journal* 20: 55-64.

Copeland, Rita 1984. The Middle English 'Candet Nudatum Pectus' and Norms of Early Vernacular Translation Practice. *Leeds Studies in English*, n.s. 15: 57-81.

Copeland, Rita 1991. *Rhetoric, Hermeneutics and Translation in the Middle Ages: Academic Traditions and Vernacular Texts*. Cambridge: Cambridge University Press.

Cré, Marleen 2007. *Vernacular Mysticism in the Charterhouse. The Medieval Translator – Traduire au Moyen Age*. Vol. 9. Turnhout: Brepols.

Crépin, André 1986. L'importance de la pensée de Grégoire le Grand dans la politique culturelle d'Alfred roi de Wessex (871-899). In Fontaine, Jacques / Gillet, Robert / Pellistrandi, Stan (eds). *Grégoire le Grand, Actes du Colloque du CNRS à Chantilly, 15-19 sept. 1982*. Paris: Éditions du CNRS, 579-587.

Criniti, Nicola (ed.) 1997. *Insula Sirmie: Società e cultura della "Cisalpina" verso l'anno Mille*. Brescia: Grafo.

Crivelli, Renzo S. / Sampietro, Luigi (cur.) 1994. *Il 'passaggiere' italiano. Saggi in onore di Sergio Rossi*. Roma: Bulzoni.

Dahood, Roger 1987. Review of Ayto / Barratt. *Speculum* 62, 232.

Dales, Douglas 2005. 'Apostle of the English': Anglo-Saxon Perceptions of St Gregory the Great. In Gargano, G. I. (ed.), 293-306.

de Dreuille, Christophe (ed.) 2000. *L'Église et la mission au VIe siècle*. Paris: Éditions du Cerf.

De Fiores, Stefano 1992. *Maria Madre di Gesù*. Bologna: Edizioni Dehoniane.

Delisle, Jean / Woodsworth, Judith (eds) 1995. *Translators through History*. Amsterdam: Benjamins – Unesco Publishing.

Downey, Michael (ed.) 1993. *The New Dictionary of Catholic Spirituality*. Collegeville, Minnesota: The Liturgical Press.

Doyle, Arthur Ian 1951. *A Survey of Later ME Theological Literature*. Cambridge: PhD Dissertation 2301-2302.

DSp = *Dictionnaire de Spiritualité*.

Dubois, Marguerite Marie 1943. *Aelfric sermonnaire, docteur et grammairien*. Paris: E. Droz.

Duffy, Eamon 1992. *The Stripping of the Altars: Traditional Religion in England c. 1400 - c.1580*. New Haven: Yale University Press.

Dutton, Marsha L. 1993. Aelred, Historian: Two Portraits in Plantagenet Myth. *Cistercian Studies Quarterly* 28, 112-143.

Easting, Robert 1991. Middle English Translations of the *Tractatus de Purgatorio Sancti Patricii*. In Ellis, Roger (ed.) 1991, 151-174.

Edwards, Anthony S.G. (ed.) 1984. *Middle English Prose: A Critical Guide to Major Authors and Genres*. New Brunswick: Rutgers University Press.

Ellis, Roger (ed.) 1989. *The Medieval Translator: The Theory and Practice of Translation in the Middle Ages*. Cambridge: Brewer.

Ellis, Roger (ed.) 1991. *The Medieval Translator II*. London: Queen Mary and Westfield College.

Ellis, Roger / Tixier, René (eds) 1996. *The Medieval Translator – Traduire au Moyen Age*. Vol. 5. Turnhout: Brepols.

Ellis, Roger / Tixier, René / Weitemeier, Bernd (eds) 1998. *The Medieval Translator – Traduire au Moyen Age*. Vol. 6. Turnhout: Brepols.

Ellis, Roger 1982a. 'Flores ad fabricandam [...] coronam': An Investigation into the Uses of the *Revelations* of St Bridget of Sweden in Fifteenth-Century England. *Medium Aevum* 51, 163-186.

Ellis, Roger 1982b. The Choices of the Translator in the Late Middle English Period. In Glasscoe, M. (ed.), *The Medieval Mystical Tradition in England.* Exeter: University of Exeter Press.

Ellis, Roger 1982c. A Note on the Spirituality of St. Bridget of Sweden. *Spiritualität heute und gestern.* Band 1. *Analecta Cartusiana* 35:1, 157-166.

Ellis, Roger 1984. Syon Abbey: *The Spirituality of the English Bridgettines. Analecta Cartusiana* 68:2. Salzburg: Institut für Anglistik und Amerikanistik.

Ellis, Roger 1986. *Patterns of Religious Narrative in the* Canterbury Tales. London: Sydney.

Ellis, Roger 1996. The Visionary and the Canon Lawyers. In Voaden, R. (ed.), *Prophets Abroad.* Cambridge: Brewer.

Feiss, Hugh 1993. The Many Lives and Languages of St Birgitta of Sweden and her Order. *Studia Monastica* 35, 313-329.

Fogelqvist, Ingvar 1993. *Apostasy and Reform in the Revelations of St Birgitta.* Stockholm: Almkvist & Wiksell.

Folena, Gianfranco 1991. *Volgarizzare e tradurre.* Torino: Einaudi.

Folz, Robert 1984. *Les saints rois du Moyen Âge en Occident (VIe – XIIIe siècles).* Bruxelles: Société des Bollandistes.

Frasso, Giuseppe 1997. Appunti bibliografici sui volgarizzamenti due-trecenteschi dei classici. In Criniti (ed.), 131-137.

Frati, Carlo 1933. *Dizionario bio-bibliografico dei bibliotecari e bibliofili italiani dal sec. XIV al XIX.* Firenze: Olschki.

Freeman, Elizabeth 2002. *Narratives of a New Order. Cistercian Historical Writing in England, 1150-1220.* Turnhout: Brepols.

Gameson, Richard G. 1995. Alfred the Great and the Destruction and Production of Christian Books. *Scriptorium* 49, 180-210.

Gameson, Richard G. 2000. Les implications culturelles de l'arrivée de saint Augustin en Angleterre. In de Dreuille (ed.), 123-139.

Gargano, Guido Innocenzo (ed.) 2005. *L'eredità spirituale di Gregorio Magno tra Occidente e Oriente.* San Pietro in Cariano (VR): Il segno dei Gabrielli.

Gilroy, Jane Hagan 2000. English Adaptations of Rev. 6.65 in Manuscript and Early Print Editions. *Birgittiana* 9, 3-16.

Glasscoe, Marion (ed.) 1982. *The Medieval Mystical Tradition in England: Dartington 1982.* Exeter: Exeter University Press.

Gneuss, Helmut 1960. William Hereberts Übersetzungen. *Anglia 78,* 169-192.

Gneuss, Helmut 1968. *Hymnar und Hymnen im Englischen Mittelalter.* Tübingen: Niemeyer.

Gray, Douglas 1972. *Themes and Images in the Medieval English Religious Lyric.* London: Routledge & Kegan Paul.

Gretsch, Mechthild 1973. *Die Regula Sancti Benedicti in England und ihre altenglische Übersetzung.* München: Fink.

Hecker, F. 1905. *Kritische Beiträge zu Davids von Augsburg Persönlichkeit u. Schriften.* Hamburg: Preilipper.

Heerinckx, Jacob 1933. Influence de *l'Epistola ad fratres de Monte Dei* sur la composition de l'homme exterieur et interieur de David d'Augsbourg. *Études franciscaines 45,* 330-347.

Heerinckx, Jacob 1933. Theologia mystica in scriptis fratris Davidis ab Augusta. *Antonianum 8,* 49-83, 161-192.

Hendrix, Guido 1989. Review of Ayto / Barratt. *Bulletin de Théologie Ancienne et Médiévale 14,* 705-706.

Hill, Betty 1965. The Fifteenth-Century Prose Legend of the Cross before Christ. *Medium Aevum 24,* 203-222.

Hines, Mary E. 1993. Mary. In Downey (ed.) 1993, 635-645.

Hogg, James (ed.) 1993. *Studies in St Birgitta and the Brigittine Order.* 2 Vols. *Analecta Cartusiana 35:19.* Salzburg: Institut für Anglistik und Amerikanistik.

Hogg, James 1981. *An Illustrated Yorkshire Carthusian Miscellany. British Library Add. MS 37049.* Vol. 3: *The Illustrations.* Salzburg: Institut für Anglistik und Amerikanistik.

Hogg, James 1990. Sunte Birgitten openbaringe. *Spiritualität heute und gestern.* Band 7. *Analecta Cartusiana 35:7,* 101-213.

Hogg, James 1993. St Birgitta's *Revelationes* Reduced to a Book of Pious Instruction. In Hogg, J. (ed.), Vol. 1, 234-262.

Holloway, Julia Bolton 1996. Saint Birgitta of Sweden, Saint Catherine of Siena: Saints, Secretaries, Scribes, Supporters. *Birgittiana 1,* 29-46.

Hoste, Anselm 1962. *Bibliotheca Aelrediana.* The Hague: Nijhoff.

Huntington, Joanna 2003. Edward the Celibate, Edward the Saint: Virginity and the Construction of Edward the Confessor. In

Bernau, Anke / Evans, Ruth / Salih, Sara (eds), *Medieval Virginities*. Cardiff: University of Wales Press, 119-139.

Hvidt, Niels Christian 2003. Prophecy and Birgitta of Vadstena. *Birgittiana* 16, 139-159.

IA = *Index Aureliensis*, Prima Pars, Tomus IV, Aureliae Aquensis 1970.

Iamartino, Giovanni (cur.) 1998. *English Diachronic Translation*. Roma: Ministero per i Beni Culturali e Ambientali.

Jackson, Peter 2005. *In translacione sancti Edwardi confessoris*. The Lost Sermon by Aelred of Rievaulx Found?. *Cistercian Studies Quarterly* 40, 45-83.

John, Eric 1979. Edward the Confessor and the Celibate Life. *Analecta Bollandiana* 97, 171-178.

Johnson, Elizabeth A. 1987. Marian Devotion in the Western Church. In Raitt, Jill (ed.), *Christian Spirituality II: High Middle Ages and Reformation*. London: Routledge & Kegan Paul, 392-414.

Johnson, Ian 1989. Prologue and Practice: Middle English Lives of Christ. In Ellis (ed.) 1989, 69-85.

Johnston, F. R. 1985. The English Cult of St Bridget of Sweden. *Analecta Bollandiana* 103, 75-93.

Jolliffe, P. S. 1974a. *A Check-List of Middle English Prose Writings of Spiritual Guidance*. Toronto: Pontifical Institute for Mediaeval Studies.

Jolliffe, P. S. 1974b. Middle English Translations of *De exterioris et interioris hominis compositione*. *Medieval Studies* 36, 259-277.

Julian, John 1957 (1907). *A Dictionary of Hymnology* (2nd rev. ed. with *New Supplement*). New York: Dover.

Jusserand, Jean-Jules 1895. Les contes à rire et la vie des récluses au XIIe siècle d'après Aelred abbé de Rievaulx. *Romania* 25, 122-128.

Jusserand, Jean-Jules 1909. *English Wayfaring Life in the Middle Ages*. London: Ernest Benn (Reprint 1950).

Ker, Neil R. 1977. *Medieval Manuscripts in British Libraries*. Vol. II: Abbotsford-Keele. Oxford: Clarendon.

Kieckhefer, Richard 1987. Major Currents in Late Medieval Devotion. In Raitt, Jill (ed.), *Christian Spirituality II: High Middle Ages and Reformation*. London: Routledge & Kegan Paul, 75-108.

Kuhn, Sherman M. 1972. The Authorship of the OE Bede Revisited. *Neuphilologische Mitteilungen* 73, 172-180.

Kurvinen, Auvo 1959. Caxton's *Golden Legend* and the Manuscripts of the *Gilte Legende*. *Neuphilologische Mitteilungen* 60, 353-375.

Lazar, Moshe 1960. La Légende de l'Arbre de Paradis ou 'bois de la croix'. *Zeitschrift für romanische Philologie* 76, 34-63.

Leclercq, Jean 1957. *L'amour des lettres et le désir de Dieu*. Paris: Éditions du Cerf. (English transl. *The Love of Learning and the Desire for God: A Study of Monastic Culture*. New York: Fordham University Press, 1961).

Lemoine, Matthias 2006. Le moine et le saint roi. *Collectanea Cisterciensia* 68, 34-47 and 218-227.

Leonardi, Claudio 2004. Il Venerabile Beda e la cultura del secolo VIII, in Leonardi, C. *Medioevo Latino: la cultura dell'Europa cristiana*. Firenze: SISMEL - Edizioni del Galluzzo, 115-154.

Lucas, Peter J. 1970. John Capgrave and the *Nova Legenda Anglie*: A Survey. *The Library*, Ser. 5, 25, 1-10.

Manning, Stephen 1962. *Wisdom and Number*. Lincoln: University of Nebraska Press.

Markus, Robert Austin 1983a. Bede and the Tradition of Ecclesiastical Historiography. In Markus, R. A. (ed.) *From Augustine to Gregory the Great: History and Christianity in Late Antiquity*. London: Variorum Reprints, III, 3-19.

Markus, Robert Austin 1983b. Gregory the Great and a Papal Missionary Strategy. In Markus, R. A. (ed.) *From Augustine to Gregory the Great: History and Christianity in Late Antiquity*. London: Variorum Reprints, XI, 31-38.

Matanić, Athanasius 1991. La *hominis compositio* tra la Scuola vittorina e la prima Scuola francescana. In Bernard, Charles André (cur.), *L'antropologia dei maestri spirituali*. Cinisello Balsamo: San Paolo, 163-177.

Mazzatinti, Giuseppe 1890-1997. *Inventari dei manoscritti delle Biblioteche d'Italia*, Vols. 1-18 (Forlì 1890-1912), Vols. 19-110 (Firenze 1912-1997).

McGinn, Bernard 1986. The Religious World of the Twelfth Century. Introduction. In McGinn, Bernard / Meyendorff, John (eds)

Christian Spirituality I: Origins to the Twelfth Century.
London: Routledge & Kegan Paul, 194-195.

Meens, Rob 1994. A Background to Augustine's Mission to Anglo-Saxon England. *Anglo-Saxon England* 23, 5-17.

Messenger, Ruth Ellis 1953. *The Medieval Latin Hymn.* Washington D.C.: Capital Press.

Meyer, Paul 1911. Notice du MS. Egerton 745, Appendice. *Romania* 40, 41-69.

Meyvaert, Paul 1977. Bede and Gregory the Great. In Meyvaert, P. (ed.) *Benedict, Gregory, Bede and Others.* London: Variorum Reprints, VIII, 1-26.

Mirra, Antonio 1947. *Gl'inni del Breviario Romano.* Napoli: D'Auria.

Montag, Ulrich 2000. The Reception of Saint Birgitta in Germany. In Morris, B. / O'Mara, V. (eds), 106-111.

Morgan, Nigel 1993. Texts and Images of Marian Devotion in Fourteenth-Century England. In Rogers, Nicholas (ed.), *England in the Fourteenth Century.* Stanford: Watkins, 34-57.

Morpurgo, Salomone 1900. *I manoscritti della R. Biblioteca Riccardiana di Firenze – Manoscritti Italiani.* Vol. I. Roma: Tip. Giachetti, Figlio e C.

Morris, Bridget / O'Mara, Veronica (eds) 2000. *The Translation of the Works of St Birgitta of Sweden into the Medieval European Vernaculars. The Medieval Translator.* Vol. 7. Turnhout: Brepols.

Morris, Bridget 1999. *St Birgitta of Sweden.* Woodbridge: Boydell.

Napier, Arthur S. 1894. *History of the Holy Rood-Tree.* London: Kegan Paul, Trench, Trubner & Co., Ltd.

Nolan, Barbara 1984. Nicholas Love. In Edwards (ed.), 83-95.

Nyberg, Tore 1996. Paradiso. *Birgittiana* 1, 9-14.

O'Connell, Patrick F. 1988. Aelred of Rievaulx and the *Lignum Vitae* of Bonaventure: A Reappraisal. *Franciscan Studies* 48, 53-80.

O'Mara, Veronica M. 1994. *A Study and Edition of Selected Middle English Sermons.* Leeds: University of Leeds.

Pantin, William A. 1955. *The English Church in the Fourteenth Century.* Cambridge: Cambridge University Press.

Pearsall, Derek 1970. *John Lydgate.* London: Routledge & Kegan Paul.

Pearsall, Derek 1977. *Old English and Middle English Poetry.* London: Routledge & Kegan Paul.

Pearsall, Derek 1992. Lydgate as Innovator. *Modern Language Quarterly* 53, 5-22.

Pezzini, Domenico 1974. "Velut gemmula carbunculi": Le versioni del francescano William Herebert. *Contributi dell'Istituto di Filologia Moderna.* Serie Inglese - I. Milano: Università Cattolica del S. Cuore, 3-38.

Pezzini, Domenico 1977. *Le glosse anglosassoni di Rushworth al vangelo di S. Luca.* In Bolognesi, Giancarlo / Sichel, Giorgio (cur.), *Studi di Filologia Germanica e di Letteratura Tedesca in onore di Nicola Accolti Gil Vitale.* Firenze: Olschki, 63-83.

Pezzini, Domenico 1991a. Brigittine Tracts of Spiritual Guidance in Fifteenth-Century England: A Study in Translation. In Ellis, Roger (ed.) 1991, 175-207.

Pezzini, Domenico 1991b. Versions of Latin Hymns in Medieval England: William Herebert and the *English Hymnal. Mediaevistik* 4, 297-315.

Pezzini, Domenico 1993b. Una "Vita della Beata Vergine" tratta dalle Rivelazioni di S. Brigida. In *Santa Brigida profeta dei tempi nuovi.* Roma: Casa Santa Brigida, 723-739.

Pezzini, Domenico 1994a. Translation as Interpretation and Commentary: John Lydgate's version of *Vexilla regis prodeunt* and *Christe qui lux es et dies.* In Crivelli, Renzo S. / Sampietro, Luigi (cur.), 73-98.

Pezzini, Domenico 1995-96. The Translation of Hymns and Other Religious Texts in the Middle Ages. *Koiné* V-VI, 185-195.

Pezzini, Domenico 1996a. Book IV of St Bridget's *Revelationes* in an Italian (MS Laurenziano 27.10) and an English Translation (MS Harley 4800) of the Fifteenth Century. *Aevum* 70, 487-506.

Pezzini, Domenico 1996b. Late Medieval Translations of Marian Hymns and Antiphons. In Ellis / Tixier (eds), 236-263.

Pezzini, Domenico 1997. La tradizione manoscritta inglese del *De exterioris et interioris hominis compositione* di Davide d'Augusta. In Cacciotti, A. / Faes de Mottoni, B. (eds), 251-259.

Pezzini, Domenico 1998a. David of Augsburg's *Formula Novitiorum* in Three English Translations. In Ellis, R. / Tixier, R. / Weitemeier, B. (eds), 321-347.

Pezzini, Domenico 1998b. Two Middle English Translations of Aelred of Rievaulx's *De Institutione Inclusarum*: An Essay on the Varieties of Medieval Translational Practices. In Iamartino, G. (cur.), 81-95.

Pezzini, Domenico 2000. The Italian Reception of Birgittine Writings. In Morris, B. / O'Mara, V. (eds), 185-212.

Pezzini, Domenico 2003. How and Why a Translation May Be Revised: the Case of British Library, Arundel MS 197. In Voaden, R. / Tixier, R. / Sanchez Roura, T. / Rytting, J.R. (eds), 113-125.

Pezzini, Domenico 2005. The Prophetic Voice in St Birgitta's *Revelations*: An Analysis of *Incominciano certi capitoli,* A Late Fifteenth-Century Italian Compilation (MS Florence, Bibl. Naz. Centrale II, II, 391). *Aevum* 79, 591-614.

Pimont, S.G. 1874. *Hymnes du bréviaire romain*. Paris: Librairie Poussielgue Frères.

PL = *Patrologia Latina.*

Plaine, B. 1893. Hymni marialis 'A.m.s.' explanatio. *Studien und Mitteilungen aus der Benediktiner Orden* 14, 244-255.

Raby, Frederic J.E. [2]1953. *A History of Christian-Latin Poetry*. Oxford: Clarendon.

Rayez, André 1957. David d'Augsbourg. *DSp* 3: cols 42-44.

Renevey, Denis 1996. Anglo-Norman and Middle English Translations and Adaptations of the Hymn *Dulcis Iesu Memoria*. In Ellis / Tixier (eds), 264-283.

Robbins, Rossell Hope / Cutler, John 1965. *Supplement to the Index of Middle English Verse*. Lexington: University of Nebraska Press.

Robbins, Rossell Hope 1954. Middle English Versions of *Christe qui lux es et dies*. *Harvard Theological Review* 47, 55-63.

Roschini, Gabriele M. 1973. *La Madonna nelle* Rivelazioni *di S. Brigida*. Roma: Edizioni Marianum.

Rossi, Sergio 1964. *Poesia cavalleresca e poesia religiosa inglese nel Quattrocento* (2a ed. riveduta e corretta). Milano: Cisalpino.

Rowland, Beryl (ed.) 1974. *Chaucer and Middle English. Studies in Honour of Rossell Hope Robbins*. London: Allen and Unwin.

Rüegg, Claudia 1989. *David von Augsburg*. Bern: Peter Lang.

Ruh, Kurt 1956. *Bonaventura deutsch*. *Ein Beitrag zur deutschen Franziskanermystik und -scholastik*. Bern: Francke.

Ruh, Kurt 1993. David von Augsburg. In *Geschichte der abendländischen Mystik*. München: Beck, II/524-537.

Sahlin, Claire L. 2001. *Birgitta of Sweden and the Voice of Prophecy*. Woodbridge: Boydell & Brewer.

Salter, Elizabeth 1974. Nicholas Love's *Myrrour of the Blessed Lyf of Jesu Christ*. *Analecta Cartusiana* 10. Salzburg: Institut für Englische Sprache und Literatur, Universität Salzburg.

Sander, Max 1969. *Le livre à figures italien depuis 1467 jusqu'à 1530*. Vol. I. Milano: U. Hoepli (Nendeln: Liechtenstein, Kraus Reprint of the 1936 edition).

Sargent, Michael G. 1984a. Minor Devotional Writings. In Edwards (ed.), 147-175.

Sargent, Michael G. 1984b. Bonaventura English: A Survey of the Middle English Prose Translation of Early Franciscan Literature. In *Spätmittelalterliche Geistliche Literatur in der Nationalsprache*. Band 2. *Analecta Cartusiana* 106:2, 145-176.

Savage, Anne 1989. Translation as Expansion: Poetic Practice in the Old English *Phoenix* and Some Other Poems. In Ellis (ed.) 1989, 123-134.

SCh = *Sources Chrétiennes*.

Schirmer, Walter F. 1961. *John Lydgate: A Study in the Culture of the 15th Century* (transl. A. E. Keep). London: Methuen.

Scholz, Bernard W. 1961. The Canonization of Edward the Confessor. *Speculum* 36, 38-60.

Seumois, André V. 1953. *La papauté et les missions au cours des six premiers siècles*. Paris-Louvain: Église Vivante.

Smedick, Lois K. 1979. Parallelism and Pointing in Rolle's Rhythmical Style. *Mediaeval Studies* 41, 404-467.

Squire, Aelred 1960. Aelred and King David. *Collectanea Cisterciensia* 22, 356-377.

Squire, Aelred 1969. *Aelred of Rievaulx. A Study*. London: S.P.C.K.; reprint Kalamazoo, Michigan: Cistercian Publications [1981].

Steer, Georg 1987. David von Augsburg und Berthold von Regensburg: Schöpfer der volkssprachigen franziskanischen Traktat- und Predigtliteratur. In Weber (Hg.), 99-110.

St-Jacques, Raymond C. 1983. 'Hwilum word be worde, hwilum andgit of andgiete': Bede's *Ecclesiastical History* and its Old English Translator. *Florilegium* 5, 85-104.

Stöckerl, Dagobert 1914. *Bruder David von Augsburg*. München: Lentner.

Stone, Robert Karl 1970. *Middle English Prose Style: Margery Kempe and Julian of Norwich*. The Hague: Mouton.

Szövérffy, Joseph 1985a. *Marianische Motivik der Hymnen. Ein Beitrag zur Geschichte der marianischen Lyrik im Mittelalter*. Turnhout: Brepols.

Szövérffy, Joseph 1985b. *A Concise History of Medieval Latin Hymnody*. Leyden: Classical Folia Editions.

Voaden, Rosalynn (ed.) 1996. *Prophets Abroad*. Cambridge: Brewer.

Voaden, R. / Tixier, R. / Sanchez Roura, T. / Rytting, J.R. (eds) 2003. *The Medieval Translator – Traduire au Moyen Age*. Vol. 8. Turnhout: Brepols

Vocabolario degli Accademici della Crusca. 5th impression. 1893. Firenze: Tipografia galileiana di M. Cellini e C.

Waite, Greg (ed.) 2000. *Annotated Bibliographies of Old and Middle English Literature*, vol. VI: *Old English Prose Translations of King Alfred's Reign*. Cambridge: Brewer.

Wallace-Hadrill, John M. 1988. *Bede's Ecclesiastical History of the English People: A Historical Commentary*. Oxford: Clarendon.

Warren, Ann K. 1985. *Anchorites and their Patrons in Medieval England*. Berkeley: University of California Press.

Weber, Albrecht (hsg.) 1987. *Handbuch der Literatur in Bayern vom Frühmittelalter bis zum Gegenwart*. Regensburg: Pustet.

Wenzel, Sigfried 1986. *Preachers, Poets, and the Early English Lyric*. Princeton: Princeton University Press.

Whitelock, Dorothy 1962. The Old English Bede. *Proceedings of the British Academy* 48, 57-90. Also in Whitelock, D., *From Bede to Alfred*. 1980 London: Variorum Reprints.

Wogan-Brown, Jocelyn 2001. *Saints' Lives and Women's Literary Culture. 1150-1300*. Oxford: Oxford University Press.

Wolpers, Theodor 1950. Geschichte der englischen Marienlyrik im Mittelalter. *Anglia* 69, 3-88.

Wood, Ian N. 1994. The Mission of Augustine of Canterbury to the English. *Speculum* 69, 1-17.

Wood, Ian N. 2000. Augustine and Aidan: Bureaucrat and Charismatic?. In de Dreuille (ed.), 148-178.

Woolf, Rosemary 1968. *The English Religious Lyric in the Middle Ages*. Oxford: Clarendon.

Workman, Samuel K. 1940. *Fifteenth Century Translation as an Influence on English Prose*. Princeton: Princeton Univ. Press.

Wright, Cyril Ernest 1972. *Fontes Harleiani*. London: The Trustees of the British Museum.

Yohe, Katherine 2003. Aelred's Recrafting of the Life of Edward the Confessor. *Cistercians Studies Quarterly* 38, 177-189.

Manuscript Index

Bodleian Library, MS 425: 257
Bodleian Library, MS Ashmole 41: 98 n. 7
Bodleian Library, MS Canon. Misc. 475: 325 n. 11
Bodleian Library, MS Digby 59: 341 n. 14
Bodleian Library, MS Digby 186: 362
Bodleian Library, MS Eng. Poet. A.l. (The Vernon MS): 83-84, 87, 89-92, 262, 245 n.
    5, 257, 262
Bodleian Library, MS Laud Misc. 215: 250
Bodleian Library, MS Laud Misc. 668: 341 n. 14
Bodleian Library, MS Rawlinson C. 41: 16, 23, 48-49, 315, 315 n. 1, 316-332
Bodleian Library, MS Rawlinson C. 72: 125 n. 10
Bodleian Library, MS Selden Supra 55: 362
Merton College, MS 248: 218, 220, 226 n. 6, 257, 280 n. 17
Trinity College, MS XI: 368

Princeton
University Library, MS Garrett 145: 22-26, 26 n. 8, 27, 30, 34 n. 12, 35, 47, 47 n. 2,
    49, 56, 65

Ravenna
Biblioteca Classense, MS 16: 161

Rome
Vatican Library, MS Reg. Lat. 489: 361, 364

Siena
Biblioteca Comunale degli Intronati, MS I.V.25/26: 143, 381

Taunton
Somerset Record Office, MS DD/SAS/C1193/68 (Taunton Horae): 23 n. 4, 43

Udine
Biblioteca Comunale V. Joppi, MS 81: 163

Uppsala
Universitetsbibliotek, MS C 15: 160
Universitetsbibliotek, MS C 802: 98 n. 9

Volterra
Biblioteca Guarnacci, MS 252: 163

Welbeck Abbey
MS ICI: 364

Yale
Beinecke Library, MS Z111 0141-2: 143, 381

Name Index

Abel 279
Abishag 356
Abraham 279, 330
Acciaiuoli de' Borgherini, Margherita 159
Acciaiuoli, Niccolò 173, 173 n. 14
Adam 115, 278, 278 n. 15
Aelfric 301, 304, 308, 308 n. 24, 312-313, 399
Aelred of Rievaulx 11, 16, 75, 77-78, 83, 85, 88-89, 91-92, 93,121-124, 124 n. 6 & n. 8, 125, 245, 317, 317 n. 5, 333-335, 337, 337 n. 7, 339-341, 341 n. 14 & n. 15, 342, 342 n. 17, 343-347, 349-350, 352-354, 354 n. 27, 355-357, 359-361, 361 n. 34, 362-366, 366 n. 42, 367, 367 n. 43 & 44, 368-372, 397, 399, 400-402
Æthelwold, St 11
Ahldén, Tage 95 n. 3, 98, 98 n. 9, 105 n. 15, 402
Aidan, St 295
Aili, Hans 21 n. 2, 52, 54, 54 n. 9, 145 n. 14, 164 n. 24, 175, 321 n. 13, 393, 393 n. 6, 394 n. 11, 395, 397-398
Alberic of Ostia 338
Alexander III, pope 340
Alfred, king 301, 301 n. 17, 349
Alfred, Edward's brother 347, 370
Allen, Hope Emily 124 n. 7, 125, 277 n. 14, 397
Alphonse of Pecha (or of Jaén) 21, 22 n. 2, 52, 149, 150, 152-153, 176 n. 16, 178, 188, 321, 402
Ambrose, St 189, 189 n. 22
Amédée de Lausanne 262 n. 24, 397
Anna, Mary's mother 322, 325
Angelico da Verona 163

Anselm, St 124, 321
Antonius 145, 153-154, 172
Augustine of Canterbury, St 294 n. 2, 296, 298-299, 299 n. 11 & 12, 300 n. 15, 311
Augustine of Hippo, St 103, 141 n. 7, 237 n. 12, 296, 301 n. 17
Ayto, John 76, 77 n. 2, 84, 84 n. 7, 89, 107 n. 19, 121 n. 2, 245 n. 5, 254 n. 19, 397, 405
Bandini, Angelo Maria 52, 52 n. 7, 403
Barlow, Frank 335, 335 n. 1 & n. 2, 336, 336 n. 3, 337, 343-346, 346 n. 23, 349-350, 350 n. 26, 353, 357-358, 397
Barratt, Alexandra 10, 12, 46 n. 23, 76, 77 n. 2, 84, 84 n. 7, 89, 107 n. 19, 121 n. 2, 245 n. 5, 254 n. 19, 397, 403, 405
Baugh, Albert 65 n. 11, 403
Bavaud, Georges 262 n. 24, 397
Becket, Thomas 365
Bede the Venerable 294, 294 n. 4, 295-297, 297 n. 8, 298-299, 299 n. 12, 300, 300 n. 14, 301, 301 n. 17, 302-306, 308, 308 n. 24, 309-313, 398, 400, 401
Benedict, St 170, 189-190, 295
Bergant, Dianne 167, 403
Bergh, Birger 145 n. 14, 146, 150, 321 n. 13, 397-398, 402
Bernard, Charles André 409
Bernard of Chartres 128
Bernard of Clairvaux 95, 97, 103, 103 n. 13, 248 n. 11, 262 n. 24, 317, 319
Bernard, archbishop of Naples 152
Bernardino da Siena 17
Bernarello, Franco 95 n. 2, 403

Bernau, Anke 408
Berruerio, Giuseppe 176
Bersano Begey, Marina 177 n. 17, 403
Berthold of Regensburg 96
Bertram, Jerome 397
Binski, Paul 366 n. 42, 367 n. 42 & n. 44, 403
Birgitta (Brigida) of Sweden 10-11, 22, 36, 36 n. 15, 42, 50, 140, 142, 143 n. 10, 144, 144 n. 14, 145-146, 149, 152-153, 153 n. 18, 154, 159-161, 163-165, 167-168, 168 n. 4, 169-170, 170 n. 6, 171 n. 7 & n. 10, 173 n. 13 & n. 14, 174-175, 176 n. 16, 177 n. 17, 182, 185-187, 190, 195, 197-198, 200-201, 214, 315, 321-323, 325, 328, 330, 332, 397, 399-403
Blake, Norman F. 15, 46 n. 24, 65 n. 11, 376 n. 2, 378, 398, 403
Bloch, Marc 337 n. 6, 338 n. 8 & n. 9, 339 n. 11, 343-345, 348, 351 n. 25, 353-354, 354 n. 27, 355, 358, 398
Blume, Clemens 219 n. 2, 258 n. 22, 264 n. 25, 269 n. 6, 281 n. 18, 293, 399
Blunt, John Henry 251 n. 14, 398
Boccaccio, Giovanni 124
Boethius 301 n. 17
Bohl, Cornelius 94 n. 2, 403
Bolard, A. Clovis 316 n. 4, 398
Bolognesi, Giancarlo 411
Bonaventure, St 95, 317, 377
Boniface IX, pope 146
Bray J. 55-56
Brihtwald, bishop of Wiltshire 354
Brook, George Leslie 250, 398
Brown, Carleton 219 n. 2, 224 n. 5, 228 n. 8, 231 n. 10, 240 n. 16, 249, 250, 250 n. 13, 251 n. 14, 253 n. 16, 254, 254 n. 19, 255 n. 20, 257, 259, 261, 261 n. 23, 264, 267 n. 2, 398, 403
Brunner, Karl 262, 403
Burnley, David J. 270 n. 7, 403

Burrow, John A. 377, 404
Cable, Thomas 65 n. 11, 403
Cacciotti, Alvaro 404, 411
Caesarius of Arles 281 n. 18
Capacci, Antonino 149
Capgrave, John 363, 363 n. 36
Carnandet, Jean-Baptiste 316 n. 4, 398
Catherine of Siena 10, 143
Cavalca, Domenico 17
Caxton, William 15, 334, 368, 371
Cecily of York 21
Chad, St 295 n. 7
Chaucer, Geoffrey 29 n. 10
Chélini, Jean 294 n. 2, 300 n. 15, 404
Christopher, St 175
Cipolla, Adele 293 n. 1, 404
Clark, James M. 95 n. 2, 404
Clemence of Barking 365
Cnattingius, Hans Jacob 141 n. 4, 404
Cnut, King of England 346
Cola, Silvano 320 n. 8, 398
Colgrave, Bertrand 294, 294 n. 4, 295 n. 6, 298 n. 9, 299 n. 10, n. 11 & n. 13, 300, 300 n. 14, 302, 305, 305 n. 22, 307 n. 23, 398
Colledge, Eric 21 n. 2, 325 n. 11, 404
Connolly, Margaret 198, 213, 404
Copeland, Rita 404
Cré, Marleen 377 n. 3, 404
Crépin, André 301 n. 17, 404
Criniti, Nicola 405-406
Cristofano di Gano Guidini 143, 143 n. 10
Crivelli, Renzo S. 267 n. 1, 405, 411
Cumming, William Patterson 22, 23-24, 25 n. 8, 47, 47 n. 2, 48-50, 54, 56-57, 65, 72-73, 139-140, 315, 398
Cuthbert, St 295 n. 7
Cutler, John 267 n. 2, 412
Dahood, Roger 77 n. 2, 405
Dales, Douglas 294 n. 3, 405
Daniel, Herman Adalbert 253 n. 17, 398

David, king of Israel 116, 205, 208, 213, 278-279, 351, 347, 356
David of Augsburg 95, 95 n. 2, 96-98, 100 n. 11, 101-102, 104-105, 108, 108 n. 20, 117, 119-120, 197, 199, 211 n. 4, 385, 401
De Allegro, Stefano 176
de Dreuille, Christophe 405, 414
De Fiores, Stefano 246 n. 6, 405
de Guibert, Joseph 95
De Luca, Giuseppe 141 n. 5, 398
Delisle, Jean 9 n. 1, 405
Deshusses, Jean 262 n. 24, 397
Domenichi, Lodovico 159, 171 n. 10
Dominic, St 170, 181-182, 189
Dondi, Giuseppe 177 n. 17, 403
Donne, John 277 n. 13, 399
Dossena, Marina 18
Downey, Michael 403, 405, 407
Doyle, Arthur Ian 77 n. 3, 405
Dreves, Guido Maria 219 n. 2, 258 n. 22, 264 n. 25, 269 n. 6, 281 n. 18, 293, 399
Dubois, Marguerite Marie 304, 308 n. 24, 405
Duffy, Eamon 161 n. 21, 405
Dumas, Antoine 262 n. 24, 397
Dumont, Charles 317 n. 5, 397, 399
Dutton, Marsha L. 342 n. 17, 397, 405
Dyce, Alexander 271 n. 8, 399
Eadburge, St 338
Easting, Robert 15, 405
Edith (Queen), Edward's wife 335, 344, 346, 350, 354, 356, 367, 370
Edith of Scotland (Queen Matilda) 348
Edmund of Abingdon, St 12
Edmund, king and martyr, St 338
Edward the Confessor 333, 335-336, 336 n. 3, 337, 337 n. 5, 338, 338 n. 9, 339, 339 n. 10, 340-342, 342 n. 18, 343-344, 344 n. 20 & n. 21, 345-351, 351 n. 25 & n. 26, 352-354, 354 n. 27, 355-359, 365-366,

366 n. 42, 368-370, 374, 397-398, 400-402
Edward the Martyr 335 n. 3
Edward IV 21
Edwards, Anthony S. G. 403, 405, 410
Eklund, Sten 176, 321 n. 11, 398-399
Eleanor of Provence 366
Eliu Buzites 117
Elizabeth, wife of Zechariah 234, 322, 327, 330
Elizabeth, St 163, 330-331
Ellis, Roger 9 n. 2, 18, 21 n. 1, 23, 29 n. 10, 37 n. 16, 42 n. 20, 44 n. 21, 47-48, 48 n. 6, 61-62, 64-66, 68-70, 72, 75, 80, 93, 95 n. 1, 106 n. 17, 110 n. 21, 167, 245 n. 1, 262, 270 n. 7, 315, 315 n. 2, 320 n. 10, 321 n. 11, 373, 378 n. 4, 399, 403, 405-406, 408, 411-413
Elziarius of Ariano 36, 36 n. 15
Esdras 280
Esser, Kajetan 238 n. 13, 399
Ethelbert, St 338
Eusebius of Cesarea 296
Eve 255, 258-259, 261
Faes de Mottoni, Barbara 404, 411
Fazio degli Uberti 230 n. 9
Feiss, Hugh 143 n. 10, 144, 144 n. 12, 145 n. 14, 406
Flete, William 36 n. 14
Fogelqvist, Ingvar 171 n. 9, 406
Folcard of St Bertin 335 n. 1
Folena, Gianfranco 73, 73 n. 13, 141 n. 6 & n. 7, 406
Folz, Robert 337, 337 n. 5, 340, 344 n. 19 & n. 21, 351, 351 n. 26, 406
Fontaine, Jacques 404
Francesco del Rosso 163
Francis of Assisi, St 170, 227, 238 n. 13, 399
Frasso, Giuseppe 141 n. 6, 406
Frati, Carlo 171 n. 10, 406
Freeland, Jane Patricia 337 n. 7, 397
Freeman, Elizabeth 342 n. 17, 406
Gabriel, archangel 242, 258-259

Linguistic Insights

Studies in Language and Communication

· · · · · · · · · · · · · · · · ·

This series aims to promote specialist language studies in the fields of linguistic theory and applied linguistics, by publishing volumes that focus on specific aspects of language use in one or several languages and provide valuable insights into language and communication research. A cross-disciplinary approach is favoured and most European languages are accepted.

The series includes two types of books:

- **Monographs** – featuring in-depth studies on special aspects of language theory, language analysis or language teaching.
- **Collected papers** – assembling papers from workshops, conferences or symposia.

Each volume of the series is subjected to a double peer-reviewing process.

Vol. 1   Maurizio Gotti & Marina Dossena (eds)
          Modality in Specialized Texts. Selected Papers of the
          1st CERLIS Conference.
          421 pages. 2001. ISBN 3-906767-10-8. US-ISBN 0-8204-5340-4

Vol. 2   Giuseppina Cortese & Philip Riley (eds)
          Domain-specific English. Textual Practices across
          Communities and Classrooms.
          420 pages. 2002. ISBN 3-906768-98-8. US-ISBN 0-8204-5884-8

Vol. 3   Maurizio Gotti, Dorothee Heller & Marina Dossena (eds)
          Conflict and Negotiation in Specialized Texts. Selected Papers of
          the 2nd CERLIS Conference.
          470 pages. 2002. ISBN 3-906769-12-7. US-ISBN 0-8204-5887-2

Editorial address:

Prof. Maurizio Gotti   Università di Bergamo, Facoltà di Lingue e Letterature Straniere,
                        Via Salvecchio 19, 24129 Bergamo, Italy
                        Fax: 0039 035 2052789, E-Mail: m.gotti@unibg.it